# THE CURRICULUM:
# RETROSPECT AND PROSPECT

# Officers of the Society
## 1970–71

(*Term of office expires March 1 of the year indicated.*)

EDGAR DALE
(1971)
*Ohio State University, Columbus, Ohio*

N. L. GAGE
(1972)
*Stanford University, Stanford, California*

JOHN I. GOODLAD
(1973)
*University of California, Los Angeles, California*

ROBERT J. HAVIGHURST
(1971)
*University of Chicago, Chicago, Illinois*

HERMAN G. RICHEY
(*Ex-officio*)
*University of Chicago, Chicago, Illinois*

HAROLD G. SHANE
(1972)
*Indiana University, Bloomington, Indiana*

RALPH W. TYLER
(1973)
*Director Emeritus, Center for Advanced Study in the Behavioral Sciences
Stanford, California*

## Secretary-Treasurer

HERMAN G. RICHEY
*5835 Kimbark Avenue, Chicago, Illinois 60637*

# THE CURRICULUM: RETROSPECT AND PROSPECT

## The Seventieth Yearbook of the
## National Society for the Study of Education

PART I

*By*

THE YEARBOOK COMMITTEE
and
ASSOCIATED CONTRIBUTORS

*Edited by*

ROBERT M. MC CLURE

*Editor for the Society*

HERMAN G. RICHEY

19  71

*Distributed by* THE UNIVERSITY OF CHICAGO PRESS • CHICAGO, ILLINOIS

The responsibilities of the Board of Directors of the National Society for the Study of Education in the case of yearbooks prepared by the Society's committees are (1) to select the subject to be investigated, (2) to appoint committees calculated in their personnel to insure consideration of all significant points of view, (3) to provide appropriate subsidies for necessary expenses, (4) to publish and distribute the committees' reports, and (5) to arrange for their discussion at the annual meeting.

The responsibility of the Society's editor is to prepare the submitted manuscripts for publication in accordance with the principles and regulations approved by the Board of Directors.

Neither the Board of Directors, nor the Society's editor, nor the Society is responsible for the conclusions reached or the opinions expressed by the Society's yearbook committees.

Library of Congress Catalog Number: 6-16938

*Published 1971 by*

THE NATIONAL SOCIETY FOR THE STUDY OF EDUCATION

*5835 Kimbark Avenue, Chicago, Illinois 60637*

© 1971, by HERMAN G. RICHEY, Secretary

*No part of this Yearbook may be reproduced in any form without written permission from the Secretary of the Society*

First Printing, 10,000 Copies

*Printed in the United States of America*

# The Society's Committee on
# The Curriculum: Retrospect and Prospect

ROBERT H. ANDERSON
*Professor of Education*
*Harvard University*
*Cambridge, Massachusetts*

ROBERT M. MCCLURE
*(Chairman)*
*Associate Director, Center for the Study of Instruction*
*National Education Association*
*Washington, D. C.*

ROBERT J. SCHAEFER
*Dean, Teachers College*
*Columbia University*
*New York, New York*

HAROLD G. SHANE
*University Professor of Education*
*Indiana University*
*Bloomington, Indiana*

RALPH W. TYLER
*Director Emeritus*
*Center for Advanced Study in the Behavioral Sciences*
*Stanford, California*

# Associated Contributors

HARRY S. BROUDY
*Professor of Philosophy and Education*
*University of Illinois*
*Urbana, Illinois*

CHARLES E. BROWN
*Division of Education and Research*
*The Ford Foundation*
*New York, New York*

RICHARD H. DE LONE
*Lecturer in Administration, School of Education*
*University of Massachusetts*
*Amherst, Massachusetts*

v

**FRANK J. ESTVAN**
*Professor of Education*
*Wayne State University*
*Detroit, Michigan*


**FRANK G. JENNINGS**
*Secretary*
*Teachers College*
*Columbia University*
*New York, New York*


**BRUCE R. JOYCE**
*Associate Professor of Education*
*Teachers College*
*Columbia University*
*New York, New York*


**JAMES B. MACDONALD**
*Professor of Education*
*University of Wisconsin*
*Milwaukee, Wisconsin*


**NORMAN A. NEWBERG**
*Director, Affective Curriculum Development Project*
*Philadelphia Board of Education*
*Philadelphia, Pennsylvania*


**OLE SAND**
*Director, Center for the Study of Instruction*
*National Education Association*
*Washington, D. C.*


**MARK R. SHEDD**
*Superintendent of Schools*
*School District of Philadelphia*
*Philadelphia, Pennsylvania*

# Editor's Preface

After a series of discussions by the Board of Directors in 1967 and 1968, it was decided to explore the possibilities of bringing out a yearbook on the curriculum to be published in 1971. Mr. Robert M. McClure was invited to present a proposal. After meetings with the board and with a committee assembled to assist in the preparation of the proposal, Mr. McClure presented a plan for the yearbook in 1968. The proposal was approved and Mr. McClure as Chairman of the Yearbook Committee with the dedicated assistance of a group of outstanding scholars completed the long and arduous task of bringing together the materials of this scholarly and timely book.

In a statement which might have been used as an introduction to the yearbook, Mr. McClure writes:

This yearbook is presented in three parts. It deals with the past, the present, and the future, with great differences of emphasis, intent, and central ideas occurring within all of these sections. These differences are interesting to note because they reflect so vividly the vigorous and rich ideas which permeate our profession in the seventies.

In the first section three authors review selected achievements, using as their principal reference the remarkable and highly influential Twenty-sixth Yearbook of this Society. In the second section, "Using Today To Look to the Future," four authors reflect on the accomplishments and omissions of the past and view certain phenomena of the present. Section III, "A Confident Walk into the Future" (a title which reflects the essential optimism of much of this book), provides the reader with an almost staggering array of options.

Differences here are balanced by certain agreements common to most, if not all, of the thirteen chapters. These ideas will not be particularly startling to today's informed teacher. What may be compelling, however, is the multifaceted approach to what appear to be commonly recognized problems:

1. The school has served America exceedingly well; it is not as effective an instrument for individual fulfillment and social change as most would like; indeed, the school as an institution is seen by most authors in this book as being in serious trouble.

2. There is clearly a charge to reform the school; the specifics of the charge are unclear at this time; there is urgency to make more exact our ideas of the kinds of schools we wish to have.

3. There are a bewildering number of options for change; many of them are effective in capturing learner interests. It is mandatory that criteria be agreed to so that proper evaluation of innovative programs can be made.

One outcome of reform seems certain to many of the authors in this yearbook: certain groups—students, teachers, parents, and other citizens—will have significantly changed roles within a renewed system. If the visions described here are realized, the school as we know it today in every important respect will be entirely different in the future.

Fundamental curricular questions are dealt with in many of the Society's yearbooks—one of the most comprehensive treatments occurring in the 1926 volume. This current contribution, too, treats basic curricular issues but in ways somewhat different than its predecessors. Lacking is an overall systematic attention to the traditional guiding conceptions of the field. Hopefully not lacking are a coherent set of assumptions about the need for reshaping curriculum and instruction and creative suggestions for achieving reform in our schools.

This yearbook fills a need in the literature on the curriculum. It should add impetus to the rethinking of the broader aims and purposes of education, to the reconsideration of new and untried methods, and to the refinement of procedures that have been developed. It should be read by all who are seeking to provide a relevant, quality education for the rapidly changing clientele of the schools.

HERMAN G. RICHEY
*Editor for the Society*

# Table of Contents

## SECTION I

## The Past

## SECTION II

### *Using Today to Look to the Future*

## SECTION III

### *A Confident Walk into the Future*

SECTION I

THE PAST

# CHAPTER I

# Retrospect and Prospect

ROBERT J. SCHAEFER

Whatever one's view of the world, 1927 has to have been a memorable year. For sports enthusiasts there was the "long count" in the Dempsey-Tunney rematch for the heavyweight boxing crown, a record production of sixty home runs by George Herman Ruth on behalf of the New York Yankees, and Bobby Jones's deft wizardry with a putter named "Calamity Jones" to win his third United States Amateur Golf championship. For those whose imaginations soared with aviation, and indeed for all the world, there was Charles A. Lindbergh's lonely flight from New York to Paris. For forerunners of the Women's Liberation, there were Gertrude Ederle's conquest of the English Channel, Ruth Elder's splashdown and subsequent rescue after an unsuccessful effort to fly the Atlantic, and a whole feminine generation demonstrating their freedom by bobbing their hair. For students of the curriculum it was the year the field attained its maturity—the year of the publication of the Twenty-sixth Yearbook of the National Society for the Study of Education, *The Foundations and Technique of Curriculum Construction.*

Each of these culminating events had a history and none could have occurred without a wealth of antecedents. Nonetheless, adequate historical explanation would be exceedingly difficult, for the roots of each of these 1927 events extend backward into ancient times and connect laterally to a wide range of human affairs. In every case, be it gladiatorial combat, the use of spheroids in competitive sports, man's aspirations for flight, relations between the sexes, or the problem of what knowledge is most worth knowing, we are dealing with broad and venerable topics. To sketch the his-

3

tory of curricular ideas which preceded the 1927 yearbook would perhaps require a whole stable of Toynbees and Müllers, since inquiry into the nature and purposes of education has pervaded Western civilization from its beginnings in Greece and has engaged the minds of philosophers, statesmen, historians, admirals, and the public at large, as well as practicing educators. It would seem feasible, rather than attempting to follow the dynamic flow of curricular thought from Plato to Dewey, to try to arrest the current arbitrarily and to examine it as a moment in time. This chapter, therefore, is neither a short history of curriculum nor a review of the particular ideas expressed in the 1927 yearbook. It is rather a more modest effort to sit on an intellectual riverbank and take samples of the ideas which flow by. Hopefully, by such a stratagem, viewpoints and practices which have long been part of the curricular stream may be captured as well as orientations and assumptions which are relatively new additions to the current.

## Curricular and Pedagogical Theory in the Twenties

First, consider elements of curricular and pedagogical theory on which there was relative consensus by the twenties. To specify such ideas is not to suggest that there was anything approaching unanimity of opinion. Neither is it to deny that individual spokesmen provided varying emphases and shades of meaning to the discussion. Least of all is it to assert that such ideas were accepted out of context or as representative of the whole truth about education. It is to recall, however, that certain basic points of view were in large degree shared by all.

*That education must take account of the developmental needs of children.* Rousseau contended that all educational reform depends upon centering attention upon the powers and weaknesses of children and that we mistakenly "devote ourselves to what a man ought to know without asking what a child is capable of learning." Or, in a more extended passage:

A man must indeed know many things which seem useless to a child. Must the child learn, can he learn, all that the man must know? Try to teach a child what is of use to him as a child, and you will find that it takes all his time. Why urge him to the studies of an age he may never reach, to the neglect of those studies which meet his present needs? But, you ask, will it not be too late to learn what he ought to know when the time comes to use it? I cannot tell. But this I know; it is impossible to teach it sooner, for our real teachers are experience and emotion, and adult man will never learn what befits *him* except under his own conditions. A child knows he must become a man; all the ideas he may have as to man's estate are so many opportunities for his instruction, but he should remain in complete ignorance of those ideas that are beyond his grasp. My whole book is one continued argument in support of this fundamental principle of education.[1]

G. Stanley Hall confirmed the advice offered in *Emile* in asserting that rather than the child being forced to fit the school, the school must fit the needs of the child. "The guardians of the young," he argued, "should strive first of all to keep out of nature's way, and to prevent harm, and should merit the proud title of defenders of the happiness and rights of children. They should feel profoundly that childhood, as it comes fresh from the hand of God, is not corrupt, but illustrates the survival of the most consummate thing in the world; they should be convinced that there is nothing else so worthy of love, reverence, and service as the body and soul of the growing child."[2] By 1895 the N.E.A.'s Committee of Fifteen observed: "Modern education emphasizes the opinion that the child, not the subject of study, is the guide to the teacher's efforts. To know the child is of paramount importance."[3]

Dewey's own writings confirm this theme repeatedly. "The child is the starting point, the center, and the end," he wrote in *The Child and the Curriculum*. "It alone furnishes the standard. To the growth of the child all studies are subservient; they are instruments valued as they serve the needs of growth. Personality, character, is more than subject matter. Not knowledge or information, but self-realization is the goal."[4]

*That learning cannot be externally imposed but must involve activity of mind of the learner.* Since pedagogical theory held that education must take account of the developmental needs of children, it closely followed that externally organized knowledge could not be merely imposed upon learners. Rousseau warned that, "The

1. Quoted in John Dewey and Evelyn Dewey, *Schools of Tomorrow* (New York: E. P. Dutton & Co., 1962), pp. 2-3.

2. G. Stanley Hall, *Forum* 32 (1901-2): 24-25.

3. National Education Association, *Addresses and Proceedings* (1895), p. 242.

4. John Dewey, *The Child and the Curriculum* (Chicago: University of Chicago Press, 1902), p. 14.

first meaningless phrase, the first thing taken for granted on the authority of another without the pupil's seeing its meaning for himself, is the beginning of the ruin of judgment." Similarly, he asked, "What would you have him [the child] think about, when you do all the thinking for him?"[5] Dewey noted in the *Child and the Curriculum* that "subject matter never can be got into the child from without. Learning is active. It involves reaching out of the mind. It involves organic assimilation starting from within."[6]

In *Schools for Tomorrow,* Dewey wrote:

One more contrast between teaching which guides natural growth and teaching which imposes adult accomplishments should be noticed. The latter method puts a premium upon accumulating information in the form of symbols. Quantity rather than quality of knowledge is emphasized; results that may be exhibited when asked for rather than personal attitudes and methods are demanded. Development emphasizes the need of intimate and extensive personal acquaintance with a small number of typical situations with a view to mastering the way of dealing with the problems of experience, not the piling up of information. . . .

. . . Textbooks and lectures give the results of other men's discoveries, thus seem to provide a shortcut to knowledge; but the outcome is just a meaningless reflecting back of symbols with no understanding of the facts themselves. . . .

If it was true in Rousseau's day that information, knowledge, as an end in itself, is an "unfathomable and shoreless oeacn," it is much more certain that the increase of science since his day has made absurd the identification of education with the mere accumulation of knowledge. The frequent criticism of existing education on the ground that it gives a smattering and superficial impression of a large and miscellaneous number of subjects, is just. But the desired remedy will not be found in a return to mechanical and meager teaching of the three R's, but rather in a surrender of our feverish desire to lay out the whole field of knowledge into various studies, in order to "cover the ground." We must substitute for this futile and harmful aim the better ideal of dealing thoroughly with a small number of typical experiences in such a way as to master the tools of learning, and present situations that make pupils hungry to acquire additional knowledge. By the conventional method of teaching, the pupil learns maps instead of the world—the symbol instead of the fact. What the pupil really needs is not exact information about topography, but how to find out for himself. . . .

5. From Rousseau's *Emile.*
6. Dewey, *Child and Curriculum,* p. 14.

*To find out how to make knowledge when it is needed* is the true end of the acquisition of information in school, not the information itself.[7]

Writing somewhat later and in a different style, Whitehead affirmed this rejection of externally imposed, inert ideas. Recall his two educational commandments, "Do not teach too many subjects," and again, "What you teach, teach thoroughly." "The result of teaching small parts of a large number of subjects," he warned, "is the passive reception of disconnected ideas, not illumined with any spark of vitality. Let the main ideas which are introduced into a child's education be few and important, and let them be thrown into every combination possible. The child should make them his own, and should understand their application here and now in the circumstances of his actual life."[8]

By 1927 the members of the National Society's Committee on Curriculum-Making could express similar views in a composite statement. Specifically, paragraph 4 reads:

In times past, and too much in the present, school practice has imposed adult forms of thought, feeling, and behavior upon children. It must indeed be recognized that the best conceivable forms of adult behavior represent goals towards which the education of the child must proceed. But, much more vigorously than has been true in the past, it must be recognized that the steps necessary in moving towards these goals are dictated by the character of the child's interests, needs, capacities for learning, and experiences, as well as by the larger demands of society.[9]

*That knowledge is gained through participation in activities of social life.* Rousseau's prescription for an ideal tutorial relationship with a single pupil could not have been so influential if his ideas had not been recast for school purposes. "Pestalozzi and Froebel," Dewey wrote, "were the two educators most zealous in reducing inspiration got from Rousseau into the details of schoolroom work. They took the vague idea of natural development and translated it into formulae which teachers could use from day to day."[10] Their

7. Dewey and Dewey, *Schools of Tomorrow,* pp. 9-10, 12-13.

8. Alfred North Whitehead, *The Aims of Education* (New York: Macmillan Co., 1929), p. 14.

9. *The Foundations of Curriculum-Making,* Twenty-sixth Yearbook of the National Society for the Study of Education, Part II (Bloomington, Ill.: Public School Publishing Co., 1927).

10. Dewey and Dewey, *Schools of Tomorrow,* p. 45.

essential contribution was in constructing curricula based upon activities of social life. In Pestalozzi's own words: "Nature educated man for social relations, and by means of social relations. Things are important in the education of man in proportion to the intimacies of social relations into which man enters. He continued:

> The direct sense of reality is formed only in narrow social circles, like those of family life. True human wisdom has for its bedrock an intimate knowledge of the immediate environment and trained capacity for dealing with it. The quality of mind thus engendered is simple and clear-sighted, formed by having to do with uncompromising realities and hence adapted to future situations. It is firm, sensitive and sure of itself.
> The opposite education is scattering and confused: it is superficial, hovering lightly over every form of knowledge, without putting any of it to use: a medley, wavering and uncertain.[11]

That Dewey was himself influenced by Pestalozzi's advocacy of the educative force of participation in social activities was clearly seen in his Chicago laboratory school. There the initial emphasis was upon involvement in occupations and associations that serve man's social needs. It was judged that learning, even in the skill subjects, could be induced naturally through activity—playing and doing—so that the child saw the need for technical capacity to enhance his pleasure in those subjects which appealed to him on their own account.[12] By the early decades of the twentieth century, school curricula were in considerable degree based upon comparable convictions. Teachers in the Francis W. Parker School held that "self-actuated work causes the greatest gain in the pupil; that training in initiative is a child's great need; that in his own interests they often find the educative spirit; . . . that one of the most effective and wholesome motives for work is the social motive."[13] The Gary Plan essentially represented an effort to apply to an urban school system Dewey's idea of education as an "embryonic community life, active with types of occupations that reflect the life of the larger society and permeated throughout with the spirit of

11. Quoted in Dewey and Dewey, *Schools of Tomorrow*, pp. 46-47.

12. See Katherine Camp Mahew and Anna Camp Edwards, *The Dewey School* (New York: Atherton Press, 1966), passim.

13. *The Social Motives in School Work*, Francis W. Parker Yearbook, Vol. 1, Chicago, Ill., 1912.

art, history, and science."[14] Each school within the Gary system was organized as a miniature community. Working closely with staff members, children in school shops handled the maintenance of the plant, those in home economics handled the work of the school cafeteria, and those in commercial science took partial responsibility for school records.

*That education must take account of the needs of society.* By the 1920s educators were well-nigh unanimous in proclaiming that the curriculum must reflect the needs of society. The problem, of course, was that societal needs could be and were interpreted in the most widely divergent fashion. Harold Rugg and the young George Counts, for example, were profoundly convinced of the fundamental changes portending in American society and sought to encourage the schools both to explain and to influence social forces. Franklin Bobbitt and Werritt W. Charters, on the other hand, adopted a more static view and sought through survey analysis of current social behaviors to shape activity curricula responsive to society's "real" needs. Ernest Horn appears to have vigorously supported the social responsibility of the school in part as an antidote to, in his view, an overly child-centered emphasis in the curriculum.

There was great variation, too, in the visions of the great society which educators assumed and occasionally articulated. The gross difference between Dewey's conception of a democratic education and the views of adherents of social efficiency doctrine will be examined at a later point in this chapter.

*That curricular decisions may be improved by the application of scientific method.* A relatively new but nonetheless volatile ingredient of the current of curricular thought by the 1920s was a faith in the efficacy of scientific method applied to educational issues. A full discussion of the influence of scientism in education will be provided in chapter ii, but no sampling of curricular currents which preceded the 1927 yearbook can wholly ignore it.

While almost everyone verbally acknowledged the efficacy of scientific method, there was great unevenness in the extent to which its 1920 tenets captured the enthusiasm and commitment of edu-

14. Lawrence A. Cremin, *The Transformation of the School: Progressivism in American Education, 1876-1957* (New York: Alfred A. Knopf, 1961), p. 155.

cators. To Bobbitt, "scientific" activity-analysis seemed to afford a rational guide to curriculum construction. The following exposition of his central theory in *The Curriculum* is illustrative:

> The central theory is simple. Human life, however varied, consists of the performance of specific activities. Education that prepares for life is one that prepares definitely and adequately for these specific activities. However numerous and diverse they may be for any social class, they can be discovered. This requires only that one go out into the world of affairs and discover the particulars of which these affairs consist. These will show the abilities, attitudes, habits, appreciations, and forms of knowledge that men need. These will be the objectives of the curriculum. They will be numerous, definite, and particularized. The curriculum will then be that series of experiences which children and youth must have by way of attaining those objectives.[15]

On the other hand, George Counts, himself trained as a social scientist and deeply committed to the uses of scientific inquiry, was not so sanguine in interpreting the uses of science in curricular decisions. He held that the larger goals of curriculum and education must be determined by philosophical and analytical conceptions of the good society. Charles Judd, himself an ardent believer in the methods of science, worried lest trivial, scattered, and unsystematized studies be pursued in the name of science by untrained and unsophisticated minds. Frederick Bonser voiced the familiar Progressive lament that measurement experts had thus far only succeeded in testing the "relatively subordinate objectives" of education. William Bagley expressed his commitment to scientific method wisely used, but warned that inadequate conceptualization of the problems to be investigated and unwarranted conclusions from inadequate data were ever present dangers.

*That the curriculum and the teacher must take account of individual differences in the learners.* The new science in education enlarged and deepened awareness of individual differences among pupils. Tests for individual I.Q., educational aptitude, and educational achievement were produced by the score and were rapidly pressed into service in the schools. There was, in Rugg's phrase, "a veritable orgy of tabulation" as school surveys studied children in local school systems, took inventories on every conceivable topic,

---

15. Franklin Bobbitt, *The Curriculum* (Boston: Houghton Mifflin Co., 1918), p. 42.

and developed batteries of devices to measure educational output. For teachers it marked the beginning of pontification that they should be aware and somehow adjust instruction to the individual variation among their pupils.

As in the contemporary period, vitriolic argument raged as to the proper uses and interpretations of tests. While the actual and potential pedagogical value of knowing more about the learner was generally recognized, there was bitter disagreement about what specific school policies and practices should follow from such knowledge. There were those who maintained that there was new indisputable proof of the ineducability of at least half of the students and others who concluded that only a fraction of the population had the intelligence and the ability to apprehend and to utilize the traditional academic disciplines.

Such interpretations of the import of the new scientific data on human differences converged with views held by many of the supporters of the activity-analysis techniques for curriculum construction. In seeking to base school learning upon an empirical tabulation of activities deemed most frequent and most useful in social and vocational life, the "cult of efficiency" invaded the realm of curriculum. In essence, the doctrine of social efficiency in curricular terms held up all school subjects against the criterion of social utility. If, as the measurement experts demonstrated, human beings differed so dramatically in ability and capacity, it seemed to follow that the activities in which they would engage as adults and, therefore, in which they should engage as children, should also vary drastically.

There was strong generative pressure, then, in the first quarter of the century for the familiar dichotomies of the curriculum field —the academic versus the practical, the college preparatory versus the general student, education for life versus education for college, and education for an elite versus education for a "democracy." The *Cardinal Principles of Secondary Education* with its emphasis upon worthy home membership, vocation, and citizenship could thus be cited, in all seriousness, as a touchstone upon which to judge the worth of merely academic learning in language, algebra, or history. Frank Spaulding could instruct his colleagues in the N.E.A. on economically efficient means of reaching curricular decisions.

"I know nothing," he stated, "about the absolute value of a recitation in Greek as compared with a recitation in French or English. I am convinced, however, by very concrete and quite local considerations, that when the obligations of the present year expire, we ought to purchase no more Greek instruction at the rate of 5.9 pupil-recitations for a dollar. The price must go down, or we shall invest in something else." [16]

*That schools of a democracy are intended to maximize the development of the individual.* To note the reinforcement of dichotomies and the hardening of narrow conceptions of utility in educational thought and practice is somewhat to question the dominance of Dewey's thought upon curriculum development. It may even lend credence to Karier's assertion that "while Dewey was being feted by young and old alike, American culture was rapidly building an educational system which in many respects was the very antithesis of what he was talking about . . ." [17] It may indeed be historically questionable to associate the origins of the curriculum field, as a professional specialty, with the educational ideas of Dewey. Certainly, Dewey's vision of an education appropriate to a democratic society bears no resemblance to the doctrines of social efficiency.

"There must not be one system for the children of parents who have more leisure and another for the children of those who are wage-earners," Dewey wrote in the concluding paragraphs of his *Schools of Tomorrow.* "The physical separation forced by such a scheme, while unfavorable to the development of a proper mutual sympathy, is the least of its evils. Worse is the fact that the over-bookish education for some and the over-'practical' education for others brings about a division of mental and moral habits, ideas, and outlook."

He continued:

"The academic education turns out future citizens with no sympathy for work done with the hands, and with absolutely no training for understanding the most serious of present-day social and political diffi-

16. Raymond E. Callahan, *Education and the Cult of Efficiency* (Chicago: University of Chicago Press, 1962), p. 73.

17. Clarence J. Karier, "Elite View on American Education," *Journal of Contemporary History* 2 (July 1967). Quoted by Herbert Kliebard in unpublished paper "The Curriculum Field in Retrospect."

culties. The trade training will turn out future workers who may have greater immediate skill than they would have had without their training, but who have no enlargement of mind, no insight into the scientific and social significance of the work they do, no education which assists them in finding their way on or in making their own adjustments. A division of the public school system into one part which pursues traditional methods, with incidental improvements, and another which deals with those who are to go into manual labor means a plan of social predestination totally foreign to the spirit of a democracy.

The democracy which proclaims equality of opportunity as its ideal requires an education in which learning and social application, ideas and practice, work and recognition of the meaning of what is done, are united from the beginning and for all. . . .[18]

Growth, Dewey wrote in *Democracy and Education,* "is constant expansion of horizons and consequent formation of new purposes and new responses."[19] Therefore, as Cremin has aptly summarized in his *Genius of American Education:*

When Dewey argues that education is a continuous process of growth, having as its aim at every stage an added capacity for growth, he is merely saying that the aim of education is to make not citizens or workers or soldiers or even scientists, but human beings who will live life to the fullest, who will never stop expanding their horizons, reformulating their purposes, and modifying their actions in light of those purposes. Given this conception of growth, a democracy can be defined simply as a society in which each individual is encouraged to continue his education throughout his lifetime.

. . . In the last analysis there is no more humane view of education than as growth in understanding, sensibility, and character, and no more noble view of democracy than as the dedication of society to the lifelong education of all its members.[20]

What has thus far been discussed are aspects of curricular and pedagogical thought, both old and new, which were clearly visible and articulated in the decades preceding the publication of the 1927 yearbook. These samples taken from the historical current of curricular thought could hardly have been missed with even the most desultory retrieval process, for in varying forms of expression they were abundantly and explicitly available. A more precarious

18. Dewey and Dewey, *Schools of Tomorrow,* p. 226.

19. John Dewey, *Democracy and Education* (New York: Macmillan Co. 1916), p. 206.

20. Lawrence A. Cremin, *Genius of American Education* (New York: Vintage Books, Random House, 1966), pp. 19, 35.

but perhaps more rewarding task might be to try to identify what Lovejoy has called the "implicit or incompletely explicit assumptions, or more or less unconscious mental habits, operating in the thought of an individual or generation."[21] What were some of the actions not taken, assumptions not made explicit, decisions made by default which, at least in retrospect, can be seen to have influenced the development of curricular thought and practice? What developments outside curriculum thought itself—in the organization of the study of education, in society at large, in the development of the university—tacitly but compellingly affected the subsequent directions of the curriculum field?

*Field of education effectively delimited to the study of schools and the preparation of practitioners for the specific institution of the school.* From Plato to Rousseau to Jefferson to the early Dewey, as Cremin points out in *The Genius of American Education,* practically everyone who wrote about education took it for granted that it is the community and the culture that educates. Plato's *Dialogues* scarcely mention schools; education is identified with all the influences that mold the mind and character of the young: music, architecture, drama, painting, poetry, laws, and athletics. While an ardent advocate of schools and of universities, Jefferson assumed that it was the press and participation in politics and community affairs which really educated the populace. And, for the great bulk of our history, Americans have felt that the teachings of the church and the learning which flowed naturally from family and community life exerted the important formative influences upon the young.

For some critics schools have been seen as the arch enemy, the basis of the miseducation which seems to prevail in every age. Rousseau warned that, "our pedantic mania for instruction is always leading us to teach children things which they would learn better of their own accord."[22] In the contemporary period, Paul Goodman, John Holt, and Edgar Friedenberg, apparently direct descendants of Rousseau, continually contrast romantically perceived successes of informal learning to the widespread failures of formal

21. Arthur Lovejoy, *The Great Chain of Being* (Cambridge: Harvard University Press, 1936), p. 7.

22. Quoted in Charles Silberman, *Crisis in the Classroom* (New York: Random House, 1970), p. 126.

schooling. Illich explains "Why We Must Abolish Schooling" and current journals are full of proposals suggesting alternatives to public education.[23]

But most men who would improve the education of youth and of adults have focused their attention upon the reform of the schools. John Amos Comenius was as harshly critical of the schools of his day—in the *Great Didactic* he referred to them as the "slaughterhouses of the mind"—as Rousseau was of those of his day, but Comenius proposed to reform rather than to abolish them. To Rousseau, Nature made formal education unnecessary; the best education was to let Nature unfold, to permit the child to follow his own instincts and desires. Comenius, on the other hand, saw Nature as providing the basis for education, but not education itself. "While the seeds of knowledge, of virtue, and of piety are naturally implanted within us," he wrote, "the actual knowledge, virtue and piety are not so given. These must be acquired." Hence, "all who are born to man's estate have need of instruction" if they are to realize their potential as men.[24] Pestalozzi, Froebel, Herbart, Mann, Dewey, all shared Comenius's perspective. They saw the school, despite its inanities and its insufficiencies, as an institution which could be reconstructed.

In the years preceding the Twenty-sixth Yearbook, almost all effort for educational reform was school-centered. Rugg was quite explicit about it. Asserting that industrialism had transformed an individualistic order into a social one requiring cooperative and interdependent modes of life, he wrote that, "the school is the only organized agency at all competent to cope with the problems of developing in our youth tolerant understanding of this complicated order. Neither the home, the church, nor the press can be expected to do it." Certainly, the home is not now equipped to handle the problem; "it is the product itself of an eighth-grade education . . . ; its attention is still centered on the struggle for physical existence. Typical American home life, dominated as it is by fatigue, seldom reflects. Conduct in it is fundamentally impulsive and, owing primarily to its eighth-grade education, unintelligent." In similar vein he despaired of the press serving an educative function and dis-

23. Ivan Illich, "Why We Must Abolish Schooling," *New York Review of Books* 15 (July 2, 1970) :9-15.

24. Silberman, *Crisis in the Classroom*, p. 122.

missed the church as "unequipped and unable," except to render occasional assistance.[25]

Of all the contributors to the yearbook only Counts made explicit reference to the educative influences of institutions other than the school. "The school," he wrote, "is but one among many educational agencies and forces in society . . . Only as the school recognizes the work of other institutions can it perform its own functions effectively." Counts's purpose, however, was only in part to suggest a division of labor among educational institutions and to urge a broader base for the analysis of curricular issues. His essential intention was to counsel that, "in so far as it is able, the school should correct the educational errors committed by other institutions. . . . Many of the influences which play upon the child in the home, on the street, and in the community can produce only harmful results. Most of the preventable ills from which men suffer can be traced to the defective or evil education supplied by society's own agencies."[26]

Further evidence of the school-centeredness of the emerging curriculum field can be found in the yearbook itself. All of the Society's Committee on Curriculum-Making as well as all its officers in 1926-27 were professors in schools of education. All of the contributors to the yearbook were professors or practitioners in actual schools. Even Dewey did not contribute directly to the yearbook's production; excerpts from his writings were merely appended to the second volume. It was apparent that by 1927 the "professional" schools of education "owned" the field of curriculum, and scholars from other divisions of the university were not interested, or at least did not participate, in a major inquiry into the question of what should be learned in childhood and adolescence.

On other national commissions and committees of the period, there was a comparable absence of members from the disciplines or other than school-oriented representatives. To a large degree preparation for work in the educational arena, at least at the lower levels, had been "professionalized" and duly relegated to the "pro-

25. Harold Rugg, "The School Curriculum and the Drama of American Life," *Curriculum-Making: Past and Present,* Twenty-sixth Yearbook of National Society for the Study of Education, Part I, (Bloomington, Ill.: Public School Publishing Co., 1926), pp. 5-6.

26. George S. Counts, "Some Notes on the Foundations of Curriculum-Making," *The Foundations of Curriculum-Making,* pp. 75-76.

fessional" normal colleges and schools of education. The insatiable needs of school systems for additional personnel created an ever-burgeoning credentials market and, in turn, reinforced the school of education's tendency to equate education with mere schooling.

In hindsight, the results are clear. Curriculum thought, still alive and vibrant for the publication of the yearbook, had progressively to suffer the deprivation of isolation. More importantly, curriculum students were condemned to operate from a needlessly narrow conceptual base and to deny themselves the refreshment and the insights which might have come from conceiving of teaching and learning apart from the constrictions of schools. As Joyce observes in a later chapter, "By far the most paralyzing effect of the assumptive world in which the curriculum specialist lived was that it tended to filter out all ideas which might have improved education but which fit awkwardly into the school pattern." The broad question of what experience and what knowledge contribute most powerfully to human development cannot logically be pursued within the restrictions of the typical classroom.

*Field of education abdicated by the university as a whole and preempted by the schools of education.* Integrally related to the process of limiting the study of education to that which transpires in schools, and equally fateful for curriculum specialists, was the rift which developed between academicians and educationists at the turn of the century. Certainly, schools and departments of education within university settings were not originally conceived or established as lower-caste adjuncts assigned to carry out tasks ill-suited to nobler minds. When Nicholas Murray Butler and Frederick A. P. Barnard envisaged a training college which would eventually be brought into Columbia's orbit, for example, they were interested not simply in the vocational preparation of teachers, but in encouraging studies as broad and as deep as culture itself. The study of education to which Butler was attracted was conceived as a branch of philosophy and implied an essentially theoretical approach which offered the possibility of creating a unified perception of the world of education. He assumed that the new Teachers College would not only prepare teachers but would serve to stimulate the university to give high priority to the systematic study of the purposes and processes of education at all levels.

As the later record makes abundantly clear, however, Butler's vision of the uses of a school of education did not prevail, at Columbia or elsewhere. What happened, in part, was that the newly created university departments and schools of education were overwhelmed by the unexpected need to train huge numbers of practitioners, as the extension of free public schooling to the secondary school produced an explosive rise in school populations. Thus, the implementation of the ideal of universal education, certainly at the elementary and secondary school levels, achieved its greatest gains in the first decades of the twentieth century—during the very period in which patterns of university–college of education relations were established. To many academicians and educationists, concern with the common learnings associated with the lower schools seemed of a different order from the problem of popularizing the higher culture. The traditional arts and science faculties, it was agreed, were not suited to prepare teachers committed to popular schooling. The skills and knowledge demanded of a teacher in the lower schools, it was asserted, needed to be "professionalized"—organized in ways foreign to mere academicians. The university was accused of harboring an elitist conception of education, and the educationist was assumed to be anti-intellectual. Education in schools and colleges was perceived not as closely interwoven parts of the same tapestry, but as alien fabrics of wholly different texture and color.

The projected role of the school of education as a center for fostering the systematic study of education and the development of new knowledge about it has rarely been recognized by the university. And its presumed, and often real, vocational preoccupation has seemed antithetical to the university spirit. Rather than encouraging wide attention to educational studies, the existence of a school of education within the university has frequently legitimated university indifference towards problems of education in the lower schools. The defects of the school could be piously lamented while responsibility for their correction was duly delegated to a lower-status faculty.

But the failure of the original vision of the school of education to materialize was not only due to the indifference of the university. As the new century wore on, it was frequently asserted in schools

at least from the perspective of hindsight, is the experience of conversion and a feeling of enthusiasm for what individuals almost intuitively knew to be right. Even the accounts of Dewey's Chicago school primarily provide a careful historical record of a school's efforts to use materials and methods based upon broad, philosophical principles; they do not reveal systematic, cumulative, laboratory-based analyses of aspects of the teaching-learning process or of the individual child's interactions with materials. While it is necessary, of course, to view the methods of experimentalism in their historical context and not to impose contemporary frames of reference, one still searches hard for excitement born of disciplined inquiry rather than of unrestrained conviction.

Observers during the period were by no means unaware of the deficiencies and omissions of even the most feted schools. In summarizing the work of the schools which he and Shumaker had investigated as sources for *The Child-Centered School,* Rugg criticized the lack of continuity in program development and the subsequent inability to conduct studies based upon accumulated knowledge. "This is in part," he wrote, "because the teachers have not become students—either of society, of child needs, or of curriculum construction. They do not recognize the technological character of their task. There is insufficient critical discussion. There is great need for hard intellectual study. Theories and practices must be called in question to compel clear thinking, if for no other reason." [28]

Acknowledging that the basic weakness of experimental education was the meager knowledge upon which school practices might be based, Dewey warned that, "if progressive schools become complaisant with existing accomplishments, unaware of the slight foundation of knowledge upon which they rest, and careless regarding the amount of study of the laws of growth that remains to be done, a reaction against them is sure to take place." [29] In comparable mood, there were numerous statements in the 1927 yearbook itself urging greater reliance upon sustained investigations. Judd prophetically opined that, "the day is not far distant when

28. Harold Rugg and Ann Shumaker, *The Child-Centered School,* Yonkers-on-Hudson, N.Y.: World Book Co., 1928), p. 315.

29. John Dewey, "How Much Freedom in New Schools," *The New Republic* July 9, 1930.

the educators of this country will find that it is essential to the
successful accomplishment of their task to organize a National Educational Research Council, which can coordinate in a large way
the scattered efforts which are being made to reconstruct the curriculum."[30] Perhaps the most critical appraisal of the work of the
laboratory schools was provided in a summary chapter in the yearbook by Counts and Rugg. They state:

"Finally, in retrospect, after thirty years of curriculum-making in
laboratory schools, one of the most regrettable wastes lies in the lack
of definite scientific information concerning the results of these fine
dynamic types of education. After a quarter century of work there are
almost no measured records of the output of these schools. In only rare
instances have these laboratory schools set up machinery for obtaining
eye-witness accounts and measured records of innovations in the content and organization of the curriculum. Although teaching and the
critical study of child learning are two fairly distinct sets of processes,
the laboratory schools have assumed that the teacher could carry on
both at the same time. The result has been that such accounts as we
have of learning and teaching processes in these schools are casual and
retrospective—not systematic and objective. Most of them are stimulating accounts of what teachers *think* they had produced in growing
children; indeed, of what they *hoped* they had produced. That these
suggestive accounts of a rich educational environment, casual though
they may be, are valuable goes without saying. But to be of real service
in curriculum-making they must be based upon definite and systematic
measurement, controlled experimentation, records of eye-witness observations by persons of real insight into child learning and masters of
psychological and experimental techniques. The truth is that there are
almost no *controlled* experimental studies now underway in the laboratory schools of America. In view of the unusual progress that has been
made in the past decades in the development of the necessary techniques, and the large sums of money which have been made available
for the development of experimentation, this neglect of the use of scientific methods of appraisal is to a marked degree indefensible."[31]

*Relative lack of interest in the workaday world of teachers.*
Whatever excitement and fervor the experimental schools of the
period generated, it is clear, in retrospect, that they did not become
ongoing centers of inquiry. Whatever institutional restructuring may
have been required for a continuing commitment and capacity for

30. *Foundations of Curriculum-Making,* p. 117.

31. Harold Rugg and George S. Counts, "A Critical Appraisal of Current
Methods of Curriculum-Making," *Curriculum-Making: Past and Present,* pp.
438-39.

investigations, it is clear that the necessary organizational steps were not undertaken. On the contrary, the literature of the period is remarkably devoid of analysis as to how curriculum revision and serious pedagogical study could be expected to flourish for long in schools. While Dewey had frequently noted that in the school as in the university, "the spirit of inquiry can be got only through and with the attitude of inquiry,"[32] no one wondered how the university traditions of research and scholarship could be appropriately expressed and internalized in the schools. The realities of the school environment and of the workaday world of the teacher were simply ignored.

Yet the currents of curricular thought which converged in the early decades of the century placed almost unendurable responsibilities upon the backs and consciences of teachers. As Cremin has pointed out, the teacher was expected to be "an artist of consummate skill, properly knowledgeable in his field, meticulously trained in the science of pedagogy, and thoroughly imbued with a burning zeal for social improvement."[33] Furthermore, he was expected to teach all day, work with parents and the community, collaborate with central staff personnel in thoroughgoing and continuing revisions of the curriculum, attend university classes in the evenings and during the summers, translate the general pronouncements of educational theoreticians into usable here-and-now procedures, and in many increasingly bureaucratic school systems cooperate with mindless directives emanating from higher echelons in the system. What was worse was that whenever he failed in any particular, he alone was to bear the psychological burden of his guilt.

While most of the new responsibilities thrust upon teachers were bestowed in the name of freedom and democracy, they were none the less burdensome. At the same time, educators in the university failed to develop a supportive technology for the teacher's use. Neither did preparatory programs provide the technical and analytical skills sufficient to allow, in anything approaching the professional freedom the ideology of teacher education assumed, actual diagnoses of individual learning difficulties, for example, or more reasoned decisions about what should be taught and how it should

32. John Dewey, *The School and Society* (Chicago: University of Chicago Press, 1899), p. 93.

33. Cremin, *Transformation of the School*, p. 168.

be taught. Neither did the university exert its efforts to assure the schools and the teachers the continuing intellectual sustenance and refreshment which truly professional activity requires. Thus, there was an ever widening gap between the freedom verbally bestowed and the capacity to utilize such freedom in an honest, workmanlike fashion.

Furthermore, precisely as curriculum theorists were urging teachers to assume greater responsibility, the schools themselves were fast becoming more and more standardized. Typical school procedures became in large part based upon the assumption that teachers cannot function as free scholars but must be carefully standardized and controlled. Rather than encouraging individual professional decisions, conditions in the schools dictated following detailed rules and filing prefabricated forms. The school as an institution became primarily concerned with the efficiency, as opposed to the effectiveness, of its operation. It had to rely on a given existing supply of teachers regardless of the transiency or the impermanency of many persons on the staff and irrespective of the gross differences in ability and motivation among instructors. As schools were operated more and more on a mass basis, everything was done to standardize procedures and, hopefully, to insure that the children learned something, whatever the intellectual power of the particular teacher. Increasingly, teachers became mere functionaries—replaceable cogs—in school bureaucracies.[34]

A noticeable failing, then, in the curriculum literature of the period is the lack of an appropriate concern for the educative effects of life in the schools upon teachers. The program of reform which was envisaged made the teacher's role central; it could have little hope of fruition unless, in Dewey's phrase, teachers became "students of teaching." And teachers cannot be pedagogical inquirers unless the institutions in which they work are deliberately organized to support their continuing scholarship.

## Concluding Statement

What, then, has our heritage provided? In my judgment, a still persuasive vision of what education might become which has not

34. The workaday life of the teacher has been discussed in greater detail in Robert Schaefer, *The School as a Center of Inquiry* (New York: Harper & Row, 1967).

yet been realized. The hopes and aspirations of the period—indeed, the basic principles and tenets on which education can and should be built—remain viable. The best hope for the future still seems, in Cremin's phrase, "a new, tough-minded progressivism that is at the same time consonant with the best in our tradition and appropriate to contemporary needs." [35]

35. Cremin, *Genius of American Education,* p. i.

# CHAPTER II

# Curriculum Development
## in the Twenties and Thirties

RALPH W. TYLER

Director Emeritus, Center for Advanced Study
in the Behavioral Sciences

## Scientific Curriculum Building

The American leaders of curriculum development after World War I sought to base their guiding principles upon the results of scientific studies of education. Thorndike's investigations of transfer of training had destroyed the earlier confidence in the educational value of school subjects as such. Formal discipline could no longer be invoked to justify the inclusion of such fields as Latin and geometry in high school programs. The relevance of the content of the curriculum to the problems and activities of contemporary life had to be considered. Furthermore, scientific studies of memorization showed that children forget material in a short time unless they have frequent occasions to recall what they have memorized. These findings suggested that curriculum content must be selected which children will have early and frequent occasions to use.

The curriculum leaders of that period were also influenced by the training programs utilized in 1917-18 for war-related occupations. With the greatly increased demand for skilled workers created by the war, apprentice training took too long to provide the numbers required. To solve this problem, the jobs actually performed by skilled workers were analyzed to identify the knowledge and skills involved. In most cases, the knowledge to be learned and the skills to be developed could be acquired by an average young adult in a few weeks of training. This suggested to educators the possibility of analyzing the activities which modern men carry on in order to identify the knowledge, skills, and habits involved. The results of this analysis, they could see, would furnish essential content for the school curriculum.

Dewey's Laboratory School of the University of Chicago, as well as his writings, was also influential in the thinking of students of the curriculum in the interwar years. Dewey's work was interpreted in different ways that led to vigorous debate. Although all of the contenders accepted the importance of students being actively involved in school learning, the controversy arose from differing views about the policy and practice of basing curriculum content and classroom procedures upon children's interests. To some, phrases such as, education is life itself, not preparation for life; the school is society in microcosm; content consists of the ideas which emerge from and are utilized in the attack which students make on problems, suggested a school without structure or predetermined objectives and content, while to others the phrases represented criteria to be kept in mind both in the process of curriculum building and in teaching.

By 1924, these new foundations for curriculum building were being utilized in whole or in part by a score of educational leaders, in some cases for programs involving all subjects throughout the school, but more commonly in one subject or for one course. As experience was being obtained and debates were developing, the Board of Directors of the National Society for the Study of Education approved what was up to that time "in several respects among the most ambitious undertakings of the Society."

## Curriculum-Making—The Twenty-sixth Yearbook

In the editor's preface to this yearbook, Whipple states, "It was felt that the National Society for the Study of Education could perform a real service to the movement for curriculum-revision by directing its contribution to this preliminary problem of method, and particularly by making a special effort to bring together, and as far as possible to unify or to reconcile, the varying and often seemingly divergent or even antagonistic philosophies of the curriculum that were being espoused by leading authorities or by their adherents in this country."[1] Harold Rugg, the chairman of the Society's Committee on Curriculum-Making, explains in the foreword:

> The chief purpose of this yearbook is the inventory and appraisal of curriculum-making in American schools—past and present. From time to time, in a dynamic society it is imperative that we stand aside from the movement of affairs to review trends, to assay products, to map out new paths. . . . It is most important that those who are constructing our school curriculum shall maintain an overview of the total situation; lacking that, their orientation will be biased, their emphases misplaced. There is grave danger that they will continue to commit themselves uncritically to plans and movements—to take up the current modes, only to discard them as unthinkingly as they adopted them. Much of the machinery of American education has indeed developed in the past fifty years by just this method.
> Synthesis is needed especially because of the gap between school and society, and between curriculum and child growth. . . . To bring this about, the curriculum must be fashioned out of the very materials of child activity and of American life."[2]

Rugg goes on to say, "Because of the complexity of American life, it has become increasingly clear that a sound orientation will be produced only by the cooperative endeavor of many minds. The tasks of curriculum-making are manifold, highly technical, and they demand special professional training and experience. . . ."[3]

"Lacking the resources to organize the wider company, these two volumes have been prepared, therefore, by a group representing a partial range of specialized equipments, but a pronounced interest in the *general public school situation*. The members of the Committee are all professional students of the curriculum and have sought constantly to maintain a broad perspective of American life and of growing childhood."[4] The committee membership, in addition to Rugg, included Bagley, Bobbitt, Bonser, Charters, Counts, Courtis, Horn, Judd, Kelly, Kilpatrick, and Works—pioneering leaders in curriculum development from various universities.

1. *The Foundations and Technique of Curriculum-Making,* Twenty-sixth Yearbook of the National Society for the Study of Education, 2 parts (Bloomington, Ill.; Public School Publishing Co., 1927). Part I. *Curriculum-Making: Past and Present,* p. ix; Part II. *The Foundations of Curriculum-Making,* p. 6.

2. *Curriculum-Making: Past and Present,* p. x.

3. Ibid., pp. xi-xii.

4. Ibid., p. xii.

## The Kind of Curriculum To Be Made

The Committee recognized the need for curriculum reform because much of the then current program of studies was narrow in scope, did not deal with important matters of the emerging nation, and did not deeply involve the pupils in the work of the school. Against this indictment of the situation, the yearbook projected characteristics of the ideal curriculum:

A curriculum which deals in a rich, vivid manner with the modes of living of people all over the earth; which is full of throbbing anecdotes of human life. A curriculum which will set forth the crucial facts about the community in which the pupils live; one which will interpret for them the chief features of the basic resources and industries upon which their lives depend in a fragile, interdependent civilization; one which will introduce them to the modes of living of other peoples. A curriculum which will enable pupils to visualize the problems set up by human migration; one which will provide them with an opportunity to study and think critically about the form of democratic government under which they are living and to compare it with the forms of government of other peoples. A curriculum which will not only inform, but will constantly have as its ideal the development of an attitude of sympathetic tolerance and of critical open-mindedness. A curriculum which is built around a core of pupils' activities—studies of their home community, special readings and original investigation, a constantly growing stream of opportunities for participation in open-forum, discussion, debate, and exchange of ideas. A curriculum which deals courageously and intelligently with the issues of modern life and which utilizes in their study the cultural and industrial as well as the political history of their development. A curriculum which is constructed on a problem-solving organization providing continuous practice in choosing between alternatives, in making decisions, in drawing generalizatons. A curriculum consisting of a carefully graded organization of problems and exercises, one which recognizes the need for providing definite and systematic practice upon socially valuable skills. Finally, a curriculum which so makes use of dramatic episodic materials illustrating great humanitarian themes that by constant contact with it children grow in wise insights and attitudes and, constructively but critically, will be influenced to put their ideas sanely into action.

Such a proposed curriculum may sound visionary to many workers in our schools. Nevertheless, close contact with curriculum-construction convinces one that the characteristics described can be produced. Their attainment will require the deepest vision and the clearest thinking our American educational scheme can bring forth. Hard intellectual work will be demanded of many persons. Most important of all, at the present juncture, will be the necessity for the creation of a more truly experimental attitude than is now common.[5]

Thus wrote Rugg forty-five years ago. His description of the ideal curriculum is not deeply at variance with one that might be produced today by the present Yearbook Committee on the Curriculum. The problems we still recognize as critical in the development of the curriculum and the instructional program are chiefly those identified by the earlier committee. But the intervening years have demonstrated that the solution to these problems carried into actual learning in the schools is more difficult and more complicated than was foreseen in 1926.

## The Work of Earlier Committees

Part I of the Twenty-sixth Yearbook is entitled *Curriculum-Making: Past and Present*. Its third chapter reviews the work of national committees, and the criticisms made then are almost equally applicable today. Referring to the work of the Committee of Ten (1892-93), the following comments are made:

It is significant that the committee conceived of the curriculum as a mosaic of school subjects. Accordingly, the reorganization of the secondary school meant to them the revamping of the separate subjects of study, mathematics, classics, history, English, etc., as well as the better articulation of elementary, secondary, and collegiate instruction. From that day to this, curriculum-making by committees has been piecemeal—subject by subject—no committee has ever brought itself to view in close juxtaposition the total American scene and the whole school curriculum. . . .[6]

According to this first national committee, therefore, the curriculum was to be determined by the need of flexibility in school administration, not by the peculiar learning and growth needs of young people.[7]

## The Tasks of Curriculum-Making

In this volume, Rugg presents his view:

There are three definite jobs involved in the task.

First: The determination of fundamental objectives, the great purposes of the curriculum as a whole and of its several departments.

5. Ibid., pp. 7-8.
6. Ibid., p. 39.
7. Ibid., p. 41.

Second: The selection of activities and other materials of instruction, choice of content, readings, exercises, excursions, topics for open-forum discussions, manual activities, health and recreational programs.

Third: The discovery of the most effective organizations of materials and their experimental placement in the grades of the public schools.

All three tasks are of vital importance to the proper construction of the curriculum. Consciously or implicitly, the curriculum-maker is always guided by his objectives in the selection of activities or other materials of instruction, and in their organization and grade-placement.[8]

This outline is similar to the one developed in 1936 for the work of the Eight-Year Study, but the latter study developed specifications for formulating objectives that provided a clear transition from objectives to learning experiences. Furthermore, a fourth task was recognized, namely, the evaluation of the curriculum being developed, using the results of evaluations as a basis for continuing revisions to effect continuing curriculum improvement.

Rugg also presented a proposed program for national committees which could well have been considered in the work of national committees that were formed after Sputnik. He stated, "A committee should act in three capacities if it wishes to improve school practice generally. First, it should act as a deliberative body, stating ultimate and immediate aims and criteria; second, it should organize important investigations of social and psychological needs which underlie the curriculum; third, it should act as a national clearinghouse and forum for controversial discussion."[9]

Each of these three functions is analyzed in some detail in his proposal. A careful reading of this section impresses one with the complexities involved in making large-scale improvements in the curriculum and instructional programs of the schools. Since that time, failure to recognize these complexities in advance of the launching of projects has resulted in much wasted effort and disappointing results.

## The Use of Empirical Investigations

The unique contributions of the Twenty-sixth Yearbook are the formulation of this comprehensive outline for curriculum-making and the emphasis upon the use of objective studies rather than

8. Ibid., p. 51.
9. Ibid., p. 53.

armchair reflection to furnish the data on which plans are built and decisions are made. Rugg wrote:

"With two decades of careful curriculum-study behind us, therefore, we can begin to get a perspective of the efficacy of our various procedures. The story of armchair *vs.* educational laboratory sets out boldly one fundamental question: To what extent can the selection of curricular materials be made objective?

From time out of mind, laymen and school people have discussed the question "What knowledge is of most worth?" Only in our own generation have we systematically attempted to find bases other than that of the personal opinion of the text writer, theorist, professors of collegiate subjects, committee members, what not. In the past it has been very difficult, if not impossible, for even the greater minds to maintain clear perspectives.

It is exactly that tendency of individual human judgment to lose its bearings and fail to "see the woods for the trees" that has led the more scientifically-minded students of education to take the basis of curriculum-making out of the realm of individual judgment. They have been experimenting of late with the criterion of social utility and especially with objective bases of selection. It was natural in the first rush of the movement, with the initial impulse to play with the new idea, that its disciples should have been carried to extremes. It cannot be doubted that many of our workers to-day are dominated by the belief that only those facts, principles, and motives shall be taught in the school which can be utilized immediately and generally by a considerable proportion of our people. If perpetuated, this will result in a mechanistic curriculum of the rankest sort. This view is already serving to make uncritical workers over-emphasize the skills and the factual knowledge of the curriculum.

We can orient our discussion by pointing out a partial distinction between the determination of the purposes of education and the subject matter. The purposes of education . . . are discovered by thought and feeling. . . . The setting up of goals, therefore, is a matter of judgments —of the best judgments we can find. It is a matter of judgment, however, framed by minds confronted by a particular social order. . . .

Now, it is of great importance for the curriculum-maker to see that the determination of goals for a given social order will be most soundly made only when he has at hand adequate knowledge and a deep and broad perspective of that social order. *The task of stating the goals of education, therefore, is not to be consummated by an analysis of social activities alone. It will be aided by the latter but must not be dominated by it.*[10]

10. Ibid., pp. 80-82.

## Widespread Curriculum Revisions in the 1920s

The Yearbook Committee sent a questionnaire to the superintendents of selected American cities to ascertain their involvement in curriculum revision. Rugg and Counts present in one chapter a critical appraisal of the methods of curriculum-making current at that time. They state:

A nation-wide movement for the study and revision of the school curriculum is under way. In the elementary school, in the secondary school, and even in the college, there is growing dissatisfaction with the existing program. As never before in our educational history, the problem of the selection and organization of pupil activities and the materials of instruction is engaging the thought of schoolmen. The reasons for this movement are many. The growth of American civilization, fundamental changes in the social order, the extension of the period of compulsory education, and the unprecedented expansion of secondary and higher education have all made necessary the reshaping of school programs. At the same time the development of a scientific attitude and technique in education has made schoolmen increasingly critical of conventional practices. . . .

The strength of this movement has been indicated in the preceding chapters. That more than one thousand school systems in the United States are continuously engaged in the task of curriculum-revision is a conservative estimate. . . . Furthermore, scores of suggestive innovations, based increasingly on thorough-going experimentation, are being introduced into both private and public schools. At least a dozen laboratory schools, several with a quarter century of history behind them, are devoting themselves wholeheartedly to the discovery of new materials, the investigation of the abilities and interests of children, the extension to progressive teachers of opportunities to experiment along unfamiliar lines. . . .

Definite evidence of the existence of a gap between the school curriculum and American life, on the one hand, and between the curriculum and the capacities, interests, and development of the child, on the other, is presented in the earlier chapters of this volume. . . . Does the activity for curriculum-revision . . . provide the technique for the fundamental reconstruction of the school curriculum in terms of child growth and the social order? To both of these questions we must give a negative answer.

Partial, superficial, and timorous "revision" rather than general, fundamental, and courageous reconstruction characterizes curriculum-making in the public school. For the most part, the job is being conceived too narrowly and attacked by inadequate methods. The responsibility for curriculum-making is commonly borne by committees composed of teachers and administrators who are already over-burdened with work. As a consequence, the existing program is always taken as the point of departure, and attention is centered on the addition of new materials or the subtraction of old materials from the established school subjects. . . . There is little, indeed almost no movement, under way in public schools to initiate curriculum-making from the starting point either of child learning or of the institutions and problems of American life.[11]

Forty-four years have passed since the examination of the current practices of that time led to the negative conclusions stated. Although some improvements have been made since that time, particularly in the quality and diversity of instructional materials, so far as public school curriculum revision is concerned, most of these criticisms of 1926 are still appropriate today. The experiences in the thirties with the Eight-Year Study, the Southern Association Study, and several state curriculum programs throw some light on the problems and suggest some of the conditions for more effective programs of curriculum-building.

## Proposals for Fundamental Curriculum Work

In the Twenty-sixth Yearbook, Rugg and Counts outlined an organizational procedure which appeared to them to have promise for the future. They state:

Up to this point in the discussion the appraisal of methods of curriculum-making has given small grounds for optimism. Is the contemporary situation necessarily as hopeless as the routine procedure of the rank and file of schools would lead one to conclude?

We are convinced that it is not. The character of curriculum-making in progressive cities has changed markedly in the past half dozen years. . . . The leadership of Denver, Detroit, Los Angeles, Springfield, St. Louis, and a few other of the larger cities, together with the creative work of Winnetka (Illinois), Burlington (Iowa), and a handful of compact school systems, gives great promise for the future. This experience suggests that a practical program can be organized which will markedly improve the curriculum of our urban schools. . . .

. . . On the basis of these experiences a tentative practical program of administrative procedure can be outlined in a series of steps. . . .

The fundamental desideratum, the first step in any sound program of curriculum-revision, is the development of a research attitude toward the problem on the part of those in responsible charge. The superintendent, the supervisory staff, the board of education, the teachers,

11. Ibid., pp. 425-27.

must come to recognize that the task of curriculum-making is technical, professional, complicated, and difficult in the extreme. . . . Once this attitude is established, the board of education will be in a mood to make possible the second step.

This second step is the provision of adequate funds for the *continuous and comprehensive* prosecution of curriculum-construction. This involves the creation of a separate and autonomous Department of Curriculum-Construction. . . .

The third step . . . is the employment of trained and experienced specialists in curriculum-making and the organization of these workers under the direction of an executive officer. . . .

The fourth requisite is that the specialist in charge of curriculum-making must be given adequate facilities for the development of his work. . . .

The fifth step involves the organization of committees of workers under the coordinating direction of the special department of curriculum-construction. Practical curriculum-making is an enterprise of almost endless detail. . . . In an ideal situation (not actually to be found . . . in the United States) the task would be done by a technically trained research staff. . . . Practically, in the present undeveloped state of curriculum-making, it is impossible to finance such a program of specialists even in the larger cities. Actually, therefore, most of the work of preparing courses of study, syllabi, or outlines of study will be done by groups of teachers. . . .

*Apropos* of the use of teachers . . . one conclusion comes directly from the recent experience. . . . adequate funds must be appropriated to release from all classroom duties those who are doing the detailed work of preparing courses of study. . . . Furthermore, teachers who are released from the classroom must be selected in terms of intelligence, technical training in curriculum-making, understanding of child learning, and general research attitude. . . .

This brings us to a . . . sixth need. As the work proceeds through the assembling of materials, the broadening of the characteristic outlines of the entire curriculum, and the arrangement of the order of activities and topics, technical advice will be needed. The experience of Denver and other cities points very clearly to the need of utilizing outside specialists. . . . for frequent checking up by those removed from the details of the task and free from entangling alliances with the existing program.

Seventh and finally, this need . . . for seeing the curriculum as a whole . . . points very clearly to the conclusion that the number of committees working on the problem of the curriculum should be small. In the first place, there should be a general coordinating and correlating committee composed of the director of curriculum-making and others who are equipped to view the problem in its entirety and qualified to adjust the conflicting interests of the groups of specialists. In the second place, the separate and specific subjects of study should be merged to form larger groups of related subjects. . . . In the third place, the inherent weakness in recent committee procedure consists in the organization of committees in terms of grades and the various levels of the school system. To guarantee continuity and real development there should be one committee on social studies, one committee on science, one committee on reading, English, and related subjects. Each of these committees should then consider the entire school program from the first grade through the twelfth. . . . individuals responsible for visualizing the whole scheme must constantly be integrating the work of these smaller groups. By no other method can we secure the unification of related activities and materials and the continuity and development which our current school system so sadly lacks.[12]

This outline represented a tremendous advance in proposed procedure over the typical practices of that day. However, the comprehensive curriculum projects of the thirties revealed three weaknesses in the Rugg-Counts proposal. They failed to take into account the crucial role played by the individual classroom teacher in interpreting a curriculum plan, putting it into operation, and improving it on the basis of experience. Unless each teacher finds out and believes that the present curriculum and instructional program is seriously inadequate in one or more respects, he does not take the time and energy to become an effective operator of a new program. Unless he can clearly formulate his own role and see himself successfully playing it, he hesitates to invest himself in developing the competence required. Unless he has the tools for evaluation or can construct them, he has no valid way of benefiting from the lessons that could be learned as he carries out his new role. The Eight-Year Study and other projects of the thirties learned these lessons and developed some procedures for dealing with them.

## The Roles of Local and of National Groups

Rugg and Counts also identified the problem of conflict between locally produced courses of study and adopted textbooks. They wrote:

. . . What shall the committees of administrators, supervisors, teachers, and others do? . . . For example, should a course of study be prepared in each of the subjects of study, including even the skill subjects of arithmetic, spelling, handwriting, etc.? . . .

12. Ibid., pp. 439-43.

Hitherto, the question has been answered for nearly all school systems in the affirmative. As a consequence, a curious and anomalous situation has developed. The curriculum of American schools has been organized essentially around school textbooks; in the order and treatment of topics, in the choice of ilustrative activities and exercises, the teacher has followed the textbook. . . . The book itself serves as an outline and guide, indeed, as a veritable course of study. The demand of the administrative staff, therefore, that each department produce a printed course of study which may serve as an outline to guide the work of the classroom creates a curious *impasse*. On the one hand, the system has adopted a textbook in a given subject, which is in reality a course of study. It then creates committees of principals and teachers to write another course of study. . . . Now, if the adopted textbooks and syllabi have been made by careful experimental methods, they represent an organization, gradation, and integration which it would be impossible to excel or even to equal by the *a priori* methods of committee procedure. A number of illustrative instances are known to the writers which reveal the disconcerting effects of this practice. Courses of study evolved by careful experimentation through years of close application have been ruthlessly and unintelligently destroyed by school officials who have felt called upon to publish under the name of the local system a course of study which did not slavishly follow the adopted books and outlines. . . .

. . . We have . . . arrived at a certain conviction regarding the matter. . . . thoroughly subject to modification as knowledge is advanced by discussion and experimentation. . . .

For the skill subjects in which careful scientific experimentation has been conducted over a number of years, a school system can do no better than adopt the best textbooks available. . . . The first and foremost task of the committees working within a local system, therefore, is to assemble the results of these scientific studies of the various skills and factual processes and to make them available to the teaching staff of the system in the most serviceable and intelligible form. . . . They should see to the adoption of books, tests, and practice devices and should either assemble or prepare adequate manuals of teaching method.

The great task of the school, however, is *not* the development of skills and the narrower habit processes. Rather it is that of guaranteeing the growth of understanding, tolerant attitudes, powers of generalization and reflective thought, critical judgment and appreciation, and meaningful backgrounds of experience for social interpretation. Now, if the curricular developments of the past quarter century reveal anything at all, they throw into sharp relief the opportunity and obligation of persons engaged in curriculum-making in local systems to show teachers how to vitalize and make significant the activities of pupil work. At this point there is certainly no conflict between the opportunities, indeed the chief tasks, of curriculum-workers in local systems and those of the specialists who are working in laboratory centers. . . .

In the collection and organization of materials, curriculum-workers in local systems, therefore, are confronted by problems of staggering proportions. Even though they adopt textbooks in the fundamental school subjects, the genuine vitalizing of the curriculum requires that teachers be given systematic outlines of proposed or possible activities.

In other words, the task of curriculum-making in a local bureau is essentially that of the selection, organization, and integration of a tremendous wealth of available materials. If this task is to be compassed even crudely, it can be done only through the cooperation of many persons trained and experienced in the separate technical tasks involved.[13]

This resolution of the conflicts between adopted textbooks and local courses of study and between national centers of experimentation and local curriculum committees was worked out more fully in the major studies of the thirties through the development of workshops, of resource units, and pupil-teacher planning. The limitations of the scheme outlined above by Rugg and Counts arise from the failure to recognize that preparing lists of activities and materials is only a part of the larger task which also includes developing interest in using them on the part of teachers and overcoming the passive attitudes of pupils toward school work. The Eight-Year Study evolved some devices useful in dealing with these problems.

## The 1926 Consensus on Curriculum-Making

One of the chief contributions of the Society's Committee on Curriculum-Making was to formulate major issues of the day regarding the school curriculum and to achieve an unexpectedly large degree of consensus among curriculum leaders regarding acceptable positions on these issues. Part II of the Twenty-sixth Yearbook[14] states the issues and the consensus reached. It also includes statements of elaboration or qualification from each of the participants in the discussions. Space does not permit the reproduction here of the full statement, but a recounting of the positions taken on a few of the issues should furnish a bit of the flavor of the whole.

13. Ibid., pp. 443-47.
14. *Foundations of Curriculum-Making*, pp. 12-14.

One important question both of that day and this relates to the period of life that the school primarily contemplates as its end— adult life or the present life of the learner. The committee statement reads, in part, "It must, indeed, be recognized that the best conceivable forms of adult behavior represent goals toward which the education of the child must proceed. But, much more vigorously than has been true in the past, it must be recognized that the steps necessary in moving toward these goals are dictated by the character of the child's interests, needs, capacities for learning, and experiences, as well as by the larger demands of society. . . .

"We would stress the principle that in the selection and validation of curriculum materials expert analysis must be made both of the activities of adults and of the activities and interests of children."[15]

The committee also dealt with the question of educating for individual and for social ends. "It is necessary to emphasize the social nature of the individual. The individual becomes an individual in the best sense only through participation in society. He grows as an individual by appropriating the modes of behavior developed in society. It is of parmount importance, therefore, that the individual participate effectively in social life. . . . The curriculum can prepare for effective participation in social life by providing a present life of experiences which increasingly identifies the child with the aims and activities derived from analysis of social life as a whole."[16]

With regard to changing conceptions of learning and of subject matter, the committee states:

In times past, and too largely in present school practice, the curriculum has been conceived primarily as formal subject matter (facts, processes, principles) set-out-to-be-learned without adequate relation to life. . . . "Learning" was thought of as the ability to give back upon demand certain phrases and formulas which had been acquired without adequate understanding of their meaning and content.

In recent years, however, we have come to recognize that there are many different forms of memorizing and learning. Some of these are permanently davantageous; others are fruitless for the development of the child. The forms of learning which should be encouraged are those which lead on the intellectual side to generalization, on the habit side to the cultivation of useful skills, and on the side of attitudes and ap-

15. Ibid., pp. 12-13.
16. Ibid., p. 14.

preciation to the recognition of those relations which are most permanently satisfying. Advantageous learning affects favorably the individual's behavior. Meaning grows only through reaction. The term
"true learning" therefore, is applied to any change in the control of
conduct which permanently modifies the individual's mode of reacting
upon his environment. Advantageous learning is never guaranteed by
mere formulation of subject matter which is used in instruction. . . .
The essential element in "subject matter" is probably now best conceived as "ways of responding," or of reacting. From one point of view,
subject matter will be conceived as the best mode of behavior that the
race has discovered; from another point of view, the actual ways of
responding that the learner is building into his own character.[17]

With regard to curriculum planning in advance, the committee
states:

In this process of curriculum-making, it is necessary that a teacher
have at hand at any stage of his teaching an outline of the general
attitudes, the finer appreciations, the important concepts and meanings,
and the generalizations which he wishes to secure as part of the outcomes of instruction. . . .
That part of the curriculum should be planned in advance which
includes (1) a statement of objectives, (2) a sequence of experiences
shown by analysis to be reasonably uniform in value in achieving the
objectives, (3) subject matter found to be reasonably uniform as the
best means of engaging in the experiences, and (4) statements of immediate outcomes of achievements to be derived from the experiences.
That part of the curriculum from which selection of supplementary
experiences are to be used as conditions locally suggest, should be
planned partly in advance and should be made partly as new materials
become available. That part of the curriculum which represents the
daily life-situations and interests from which the immediate specific
needs of students arise should be—can only be—made from day to day.[18]

The committee also dealt with the problem of testing:

One of the most potent forms of curriculum-control is measurement
by means of uniform examinations and standardized tests. Teachers
and pupils will inevitably work for the elements represented in the
instruments by which their success is measured; therefore, it is of the
utmost importance that changes in goals and methods be accompanied
by the development and use of new tests and examinations corresponding in type to the advances made in the curriculum. To serve a useful
purpose, tests must be fitted to the requirements of the curriculum and

17. Ibid., pp. 17-18.
18. Ibid., pp. 20-21.

to the requirements of method. They must be determined by the purposes set up in the curriculum for the group of children being tested.[19]

These few illustrations of the issues with which the committee dealt and the statement of consensus reached should suggest the monumental achievement which the Twenty-sixth Yearbook represented not only in furnishing a critical review of current practices and outlining steps for the future, but also in clarifying the problems which pioneer curriculum workers were encountering in codifying the conclusions they were reaching regarding the proper perspectives, approaches, and assumptions likely to be helpful in dealing with these problems. Throughout the next two decades that yearbook was a guiding factor in the development of curricula in the United States and several foreign countries. Rereading these volumes today, one is impressed with the extent to which the proposals made are consistent with contemporary experience.

## Secondary School Curriculum Building in the Thirties

During the twenties, the reconstruction of the elementary school curriculum received major attention. Massive programs in the cities such as Denver, St. Louis, and Winnetka were underway as well as several comprehensive state programs, as in Virginia. The secondary school curriculum was largely untouched. But, by 1932, two different problems were coming sharply in focus in the American high schools. Students in progressive independent and in suburban schools were becoming outspoken in their criticism of the lack of relevance of many high school subjects and of the lock-step succession of topics that took no account of individual differences in student learning. Also, they were becoming outspoken about the isolation they felt in being segregated behind school walls with little active and responsible contact with the "real world." For many other schools, mostly public high schools, the Great Depression had brought a large influx of students who came to the high school because they were unable to find jobs in the depressed economy. The typical high school curriculum had not been designed for these students who found their courses largely meaningless, not worth putting forth the effort to learn.

19. Ibid., p. 25.

High school principals and teachers hesitated to suggest changes in the curriculum which they felt was largely dominated by the stated admission requirements of prestige colleges. The Progressive Education Association responded to suggestions from influential members to establish the Commission on the Relation of School and College, appointing Wilford M. Aikin, Headmaster of the John Burroughs School in St. Louis, as its chairman. This commission held a series of conferences with leaders from secondary schools and colleges, out of which grew the plan for what was later called "The Eight-Year Study."

Essentially, it was an agreement with a majority of the leading colleges providing that a number of secondary schools would be chosen by a joint school and college committee to engage in curriculum reconstruction. During a period of eight years, these schools would have complete freedom from college entrance requirements to follow new curricula designed to meet the needs of their students. Eventually, thirty school systems were chosen, half were publicly controlled and half were private independent schools. There were two provisos in the agreement. One was that for every student the high school presented to a college for admission there would be a record of his educational development that would enable the college to make an intelligent judgment whether or not to admit him. Second, an independent body would be established to evaluate the developments in the thirty schools and to report the progress made.

The Eight-Year Study began in 1933. Later, the Southern Association established a similar study among the schools and colleges in its jurisdiction. At about the same time, several states established high school "studies." Michigan was the first. Both the Southern Association and the states drew upon the experience, the materials, and the personnel developed in the Eight-Year Study.

These projects furnished an excellent opportunity to build upon the ideas presented in the Twenty-sixth Yearbook and to make some further developments. The Eight-Year Study established a curriculum commission chaired by Vivian I. Thayer, Educational Director of the Ethical Culture Schools, the functions of which were largely those outlined by Rugg and Counts for a coordinating committee. With support from the Rockefeller General Education

Board, a series of studies of adolescents was undertaken under Carolyn Zachry's direction to provide helpful information about the interests, needs, activities, and learning characteristics of youth. Under the leadership of Harold Alberty, subject matter committees were formed to draw upon these studies and others and to publish volumes that would furnish statements of overall objectives, subject matter, and learning activities for these subjects.

It quickly became apparent that the products of these committees were not effectively utilized in the schools until teachers and pupils were more deeply involved in developing, or modifying, or trying out ideas and materials. Examining and reviewing them were not enough. The Eight-Year Study developed summer workshops in which teachers themselves with guidance from trained staff members drew upon the materials developed by the commission and studies on adolescence to construct resource units. After having built several resource units, most teachers were then able to adapt and to use units built by others.

In the workshops, high school students were also present to afford opportunities for teachers to become familiar with pupil-teacher planning as a means of developing and selecting projects and learning activities consonant with the purposes and interests of the students which at the same time furnished learning experiences appropriate for the larger educational objectives.

Finally, the Eight-Year Study demonstrated the importance of evaluation as an essential part of curriculum-making. As new courses were being formed and resource units developed, the evaluation staff of the Eight-Year Study was helping teachers and specialists to clarify their objectives, to define them in terms of behavior, and to identify situations in which students' behavior could be appraised. This inclusion of evaluation in the curriculum process helped to clarify curriculum objectives and thus to furnish a clearer guide for selection of content and learning experiences. Furthermore, the use of the evaluation devices developed in the study provided feedback to the teachers as to the effectiveness of units and courses. Then, in the next summer workshops, revisions were made in the light of the evaluation results.

## Summary

The period between the two great world wars was one in which systematic curriculum-building emerged as a major part of educational theory and practice. The results of scientific studies of learning, the success of psychological tests, and the effectiveness of vocational curricula built to meet the manpower needs of World War I had great influence upon schools of education and the public schools. Into the void left by the collapse in the faith of formal discipline came activity analyses, job analyses, social projections, studies of children and youth, and techniques for investigating learning. By 1924 the variety of curriculum endeavors underway and the partial nature of many of them led to a demand for codification of the principles and practices of curriculum construction. The Twenty-sixth Yearbook of the National Society for the Study of Education met this need brilliantly. It served as an intellectual guide for nearly two decades and is still basic to much curriculum work. The secondary school curriculum studies of the thirties provided comprehensive tests of the yearbook proposals and developed necessary extensions to that earlier design.

# CHAPTER III

# The Reforms of the Fifties and Sixties: A Historical Look at the Near Past

ROBERT M. MC CLURE

*1890! The frontier obliterated, a continent conquered! The crude physical pattern of the new nationality sketched in. The world's greatest experiment in democracy under way, based on the premise of universal education at public expense.*

*The American Zeitgeist already reflected, at the end of the century, a trusting faith in the efficacy of education. The public school was to provide the panaceas for all political, economic, and social ills.*

*What then, has a century of curriculum-making produced?*

HAROLD RUGG (1926)

1970! The frontiers of space obliterated, man soars to the moon, man-made satellites ring the earth. The new communication technology makes the world a "global village." And in America the world's greatest experiment in mass education has survived the competitive strains of the cold war to face unprecedented internal challenge: educators and institutions struggle to learn new responses to increasingly activist student bodies.

The American public, in mid-century, was no longer so willing to trust the efficacy of public education. By the mid-sixties, determined that the schools must remedy the nation's increasingly visible social ills, the federal government had become an active partner in the educational enterprise.

What curricular changes were taking place in these decades? Rather than chronicling projects or examining in detail the curricular "Alphabet Soup," this chapter will instead identify the influences, the influencers, and the results of the curricular reform movement of the fifties and the sixties. It will discuss the atmosphere—rather than the specifics—of change; it will deal with the new players and new roles in curriculum development; and, lastly, it will examine in some detail two new curricula that typify contrasting theories of contemporary instructional philosophy.[1]

This was a period of enormous activity and major achievement. The events and ideas selected for inclusion in this chapter are necessarily only representative of those of the period; many are yet to reach fruition. References and footnotes in this chapter direct the interested reader to more detailed explanations of the period. Especially recommended is Cremin's investigations of the progressive forces at work in these decades and earlier.[2] Also, two other resources are important to those interested in greater depth: the reviews of curriculum planning and development published by the American Educational Research Association[3] and the two editions of the *Encyclopedia of Educational Research* published in these two decades.[4]

## A Society in Transition

As the fifties opened, construction, rather than curriculum, was uppermost in the minds of education's managers. The staggering task of accommodating a 33 percent increase in students, of training, recruiting, and employing 50 percent more staff, and of designing and managing a building and equipment program that multiplied by six in twelve years was draining the intellectual energies of most school people.

Nevertheless, there were sporadic efforts to improve school quality. Attempts to increase understanding of other nations, to raise the

1. The writer acknowledges with appreciation the contributions made to this chapter by Frances Quinto and Caryl Conner.

2. Lawrence A. Cremin, *Progressivism in American Education: 1867-1957* (New York: Alfred A. Knopf, 1961).

3. *Review of Educational Research* (Washington: American Educational Research Association). Published triannually.

4. *Encyclopedia of Educational Research: A Project of the American Educational Research Association* (3d ed.), ed. Chester W. Harris (New York: Macmillan Co., 1960). *Encyclopedia of Educational Research: A Project of the American Educational Research Association* (4th ed.), ed. Robert L. Ebel (Toronto, Canada: Macmillan Co., Collier-Macmillan Canada, 1969).

literacy level, to improve education for the gifted, to increase community involvement in school affairs, to expand the use of audio-visual material, to help students develop a continuing desire to read, and to improve the quality of school guidance programs were the predominant concerns when the problem of bulging enrollment was momentarily forgotten.

The nation that had sought relief from Truman's dynamism by putting Eisenhower in the White House found little educational solace during his administration. McCarthyism was to touch, at least indirectly, teachers everywhere, and the McCarthy influence was particularly destructive of the nation's heritage of academic freedom. Classroom controversy became taboo and anti-Communist indoctrination a commonplace. It would be more than a decade before the nation and its schools fully recovered from the malignant fears aroused in this era.

The whole society was in quiet ferment during the Eisenhower years: morality was being redefined; the nature of jobs and job preparation was changing; family life, encroached upon by the advent of that other parent, television, was under stress; the knowledge explosion was well underway, and increasing disenchantment with the "American Way of Life" was showing in rising drop-out rates. Perceptive teachers, though, were casting sidelong glances at several phenomena that foreshadowed the shape of the educational future. Four relatively low-visibility precursors of educational events to come were already on the horizon:

1. The beginning of fundamental misgivings about the purpose and content of the school program, particularly in mathematics and science.[5]
2. School desegregation, with its explosive impact on all aspects of education.[6]
3. Development of the "new technology"—the computer, teaching machines, and other devices—that would eventually revolutionize

5. See, from many publications, "The Pursuit of Excellence: Education and the Future of America," Rockefeller Brothers Fund, *Prospect for America:* The Rockefeller Panel Reports, No. 5, pp. 337-92 (Garden City, N.Y.: Doubleday & Co., 1961). This essay was originally published in 1958.

6. On May 17, 1954, the Supreme Court handed down its landmark decision, Brown v. Board of Education, 347 U.S. 483 (1954). For an excellent description of the impact of this event and several other headline-producing ones that occurred in this era, see Robert Sherrill, *Gothic Politics in the Deep South* (New York: Ballantine Publications, 1968).

man's data storage and collection procedures and radically revise
a variety of his activities, especially teaching.[7]
4. The development of new techniques in interpersonal relations, intergroup relations, and ultimately in intrapersonal relations.[8]

This chapter is primarily concerned with the effort to reshape
the public school curriculum in grades 1 to 12.

## The Movement to Reform

The code words that came to describe much of that which took
place in the fifties and sixties were the three forming the phrase
*curriculum reform movement.* In intent and effect, the reshaping
efforts did not always match a strict definition of those words. The
activities of the period often were not related to the classical questions of *curriculum,* for they sometimes had to do with the reorganization of teachers or students for purposes unrelated to what was
to be learned. The various improvements sometimes had to do
with *reform* (making better what already exists) but just as often
with revolution, and in no real sense was this a *movement* because
its separate parts were never related or coordinated. The period of
curricular innovation, that is, the decade beginning about 1957
and concluding about 1967, was occasionally misdescribed as one of
*national* effort. Though the bulk of the funding was national (federal or foundation), the reformers and their financial supporters
were careful to avoid the pitfalls of federal control.

The funding vehicles were the National Defense Education Act,
the National Science Foundation, and, to some extent, the great
private foundations. Though the initial impetus came from Sputnik,
the resulting pressure came from middle-class Americans who understood its implications and, with astonishing speed, demanded better
education for the children.

Quality education became the theme. Parents and citizens alike
realized that, if we were going to beat the Russians to the moon,
we had to learn more, faster. By 1960, whenever curricula and construction came in conflict, curricular expenditures won.

7. For a report of a conference of this period which gives an historical perspective, see John E. Coulson, *Programmed Learning and Computer-Based Instruction*
(New York: John Wiley & Sons, 1962).

8. See Alfred J. Marrow, "Events Leading to the Establishment of National
Training Laboratories," *Journal of Applied Behavioral Science* 3 (1967).

But today, in this eighth decade of the twentieth century, as American public education stumbles ahead into its fourth century, our schools still struggle to serve their diverse clientele, still struggle to bridge the gulf between the intellectual elite and the functional illiterate. Though man can now explore new worlds in space, in our earthbound classrooms the nation's two million teachers still seek the words to reach, the spark to set off, and the techniques to best entice our brilliant and our not-so-brilliant students.

Educators who lived through the appalling tragedies of the sixties with their students, who have seen students divided and polarized by the social and political currents of contemporary society, have become increasingly aware of the limitations of the conventional curriculum and, indeed, of many recent curricular reforms with their heavy overemphasis on discrete subject matter.

America's education professionals are as diverse in attitude and resources as is the plural American culture, but if they have come to any common agreement in this past decade of educational turbulence, it is in the recognition that we must nurture our common humanity in a world increasingly dehumanized by sheer size, by mass media and massive construction, by shrinking distance, and by a rambunctious explosion of the population. In this spirit, articulate and thoughtful educators at all levels of the educational spectrum—from the elementary classroom teacher to the scholar at the far horizon of his field—have joined in open-minded examination of the treasured shibboleths of their profession. Such an alliance was all but unknown before the 1950s; since then it has been for the most part a fruitful and productive collaboration.

## CONSTRUCTS FOR CURRICULUM WORKERS

A variety of people have contributed to the successful functioning of these alliances; prominent among them are John Gardner, James Conant, and John Goodlad. Goodlad, because his work has been of value to practitioners,[9] curriculum developers,[10] and theo-

9. John I. Goodlad, M. Frances Klein, and associates, *Behind the Classroom Door: The First Four Years of School* (Worthington, Ohio: Charles A. Jones Publishing Co., 1970).

10. John I. Goodlad, "The Curriculum," in *The Changing American School*, pp. 32-58, Sixty-Fifth Yearbook of the National Society for the Study of Education, Part II (Chicago: University of Chicago Press, 1966).

reticians,[11] is particularly noteworthy. His work ranged from school organization (with particular emphasis on nongraded schools) to change strategies (see chapter ix of this yearbook) to fundamental inquiries into the nature of curriculum. Other pioneers included George Beauchamp, Dwayne Huebner, Virgil Herrick, Bruce Joyce, Alice Miel, James Macdonald, Louise Tyler, Ole Sand, Arno Bellack, Paul Hanna, Hilda Taba, and the dean of the curriculum theorists, Ralph Tyler.[12]

In addition to the ideological contributions made by those mentioned above and others, two more immediately useful tools were available to curriculum workers—particularly to those in state departments of education and local school districts. The "Tyler Syllabus"[13] identified four fundamental questions: (a) What educational purposes shall the school seek to attain? (b) What educational experiences can be provided that are likely to attain these purposes? (c) How can these educational experiences be effectively organized? and (d) How can we determine whether these purposes are being attained?[14] The syllabus (originally written for Tyler's students) provides detailed procedures by which to arrive at answers to these questions. Almost every local curriculum guide or course of study produced during the period showed its influence. Further evidence of its popularity is that in 1968 it was in its twenty-eighth printing.

The "taxonomy" provided a second useful aid to curriculum workers.[15] It was developed by a committee of college and university examiners to aid teachers, administrators, specialists, and re-

11. See, in particular, John I. Goodlad with Maurice N. Richter, Jr., *The Development of a Conceptual System for Dealing with Problems of Curriculum and Instruction*, USOE Contract No. SAE 8024, Project No. 454 (Los Angeles: University of California at Los Angeles and the Institute for the Development of Educational Activities, 1966).

12. For an excellent review and analysis of theoretical developments see, Louise L. Tyler, *A Selected Guide to Curriculum Literature: An Annotated Bibliography*, Schools for the 70's—Auxiliary Series (Washington: National Education Association, 1970).

13. Ralph W. Tyler, *Basic Principles of Curriculum and Instruction* (Chicago: University of Chicago Press, 1950).

14. Ibid., pp. 1-2.

15. Benjamin S. Bloom et al., *Taxonomy of Educational Objectives: The Classification of Educational Goals, Handbook I: Cognitive Domain* (New York: David McKay Co., 1956). Also see, David R. Krathwol et al., *Taxonomy of Educational Objectives: The Classification of Educational Goals, Handbook II: Affective Domain* (New York: David McKay Co., 1964).

searchers in dealing with problems of curriculum and evaluation. It provided them with a range of outcomes in the cognitive area, helped them to discuss their problems with greater precision, and offered a framework with which to examine the balance of a planned program. Six major categories of cognitive behavior were systematically described in hierarchical order: knowledge, comprehension, application, analysis, synthesis, and evaluation. Scarcely a curriculum committee at work in a local school district can be found which does not have, at least in a "knowledge" sense, the "taxonomy" built into its curricular ideas.

Further examples of endeavors to provide rationales for those at work on the curriculum are described in other chapters of this yearbook. Some have described this period as one of hyperactivity in the history of American education, but one in which little attention has been given to the *basic* questions of providing a good program in the schools. Yet, it has been a productive era for those concerned with curriculum as a field of study. Future historians will have better perspective to evaluate the contributions made by those in what is still a maturing field.

### THE NECESSITY FOR CURRICULAR CHANGE

With depressingly few exceptions, curriculum design until the 1950s was a process of layering society's new knowledge on top of the hodgepodge accumulation of society's old knowledge and arranging for feeding it, in prescribed time units, to students who may or may not have found it relevant in their own lives.[16]

Curricular change, when it occurred in the elementary and secondary schools, was most often the product of profit-motivated

16. There were developments in higher education which brought about fundamental reexaminations of basic assumptions about curricular offerings, particularly in graduate programs to prepare professionals. One of the most notable, and certainly the most interesting in terms of the rigorous attention paid to essential curriculum questions, was the five-year curriculum research project in basic nursing education at the University of Washington School of Nursing. See the three-volume report of the study: Ole Sand, *Curriculum Study in Basic Nursing Education* (New York: G. P. Putnam's Sons, 1955); Mary S. Tschudin, Helen C. Belcher, and Leo Nedelsky, *Evaluation in Basic Nursing Education* (New York: G. P. Putnam's Sons, 1958); and Ole Sand and Helen C. Belcher, *An Experience in Basic Education* (New York: G. P. Putnam's Sons, 1958). The School Health Education Study gave sustained attention to the nature of the curriculum design, instructional materials, and evaluation. See Elena M. Sliepcevich, *Health Education: A Conceptual Approach to Curriculum Design* (St. Paul: 3M Education Press, 1967).

textbook publishers or of professionals in the schools. In neither case was it likely to incorporate scholarly concepts and advanced knowledge or to reflect current social concerns. Like the building codes of the fifties reluctantly incorporating the architectural breakthroughs of the twenties and thirties, mid-century curriculum codes in most of the fifty states still smugly reflected a relatively recent acceptance of the philosophies of John Dewey, Francis Parker, William T. Harris, and William Rainey Harper—an acceptance that by no means guaranteed theoretical comprehension. The avant-garde progressivism of the early twentieth century had only now been embraced by heartland America.

But the pace-setting educators had leaped far ahead of the rank and file. Driven by an aroused determination to provide excellent education in America's sprawling comprehensive high schools, they unfortunately found little interest in or popular support for their efforts. For these were the 1950s, and the postwar baby crop—grown now to throng the schoolhouse corridors—was forcing educational quality into unprecedented and unfortunate competition with educational quantity.

Casual perusal of the daily and weekly newspapers of the early fifties will confirm the general public preoccupation with the financial aspects of the public school system. Column after column of exhortation urged passage of local school tax measures and bond issues. Little if any journalistic space was devoted to policy or curricular considerations, to the notion of accountability, or to educational assessment and measurement.[17]

Nonetheless, the seeds of the curricular revolution were quietly being sown. In university enclaves, with private foundation dollars, the designers of the "new" math, the "new" biology, and the "new" physics were hard at work reviewing the obsolete offerings in each of these fields.

While school districts on double sessions struggled valiantly to build and man new classrooms for their rapidly multiplying charges,

17. An examination of the *Education Index* for June to December 1950 reveals that articles related to financing, planning, constructing, and cleaning the schools took up nine full pages while articles about curriculum and instruction occupied $2\frac{1}{2}$ pages!

a whole host of exploratory projects were getting underway—
projects that one day were to attempt a radical revision of practices
and procedures in these same classrooms.

### COLLABORATION: A FORCE FOR CHANGE

By 1959, when thirty-five prestigious scientists, scholars, and educators gathered at Woods Hole, Massachusetts, to discuss how science teaching (and, tangentially, all teaching) could be improved,
fundamental curricular revision in mathematics, in the biological
sciences, and in the physical sciences was nearly complete. Curricular reexamination in a variety of other disciplines was underway.

Virtually all the curriculum projects of the early fifties had representatives at Woods Hole. In addition, psychologists from Freudian
to behaviorist whose professional efforts had been directed to an
examination of the learning process, motivation, and the nature
of intelligence were present. Together they agreed that content and
the orderly arrangement of data in progressive degreees of difficulty was only a part of good curriculum design; that good teaching in the future—as, indeed, in the past—was essentially bound to
the teaching of thought processes. In effect, the conferees accepted
Alfred North Whitehead's definition of over half a century ago:
"Education," said Whitehead, "is the acquisition of the art of the
utilization of knowledge."

Stuffing the heads of the young with man's accumulated wisdom
has always been a difficult task, but it is simple stuff indeed compared to the difficulty of inculcating the capacity to think. In his
report, *The Process of Education,* Jerome Bruner, chairman of the
Woods Hole conference, stated what has become a classic premise
of the revisionists, "The foundations of any subject may be taught
to anybody at any age in some form,"[18] and he concluded that:

> Intellectual activity anywhere is the same, whether at the frontier of
> knowledge or in a third grade classroom . . . The schoolboy learning
> physics is a physicist, and it is easier for him to learn physics behaving
> like a physicist than doing something else . . . the curriculum of a sub-
> ject should be determined by the most fundamental understanding
> that can be achieved of the underlying principles that give structure
> to that subject. Teaching specific topics or skills without making clear
> their context in the broader fundamental structure of a field of knowl-

18. Jerome Bruner, *The Process of Education* (Cambridge, Mass.: Harvard
University Press, 1963).

edge is uneconomical . . . such teaching makes it exceedingly difficult for the student to generalize from what he has learned to what he will encounter later.[19]

A good curriculum, the Woods Hole conferees agreed, must be provocative, honest, and comprehensible. It must tailor fundamental knowledge to the interest and capacities of the students for whom it is designed and, in doing so, generate a pervasive and lasting excitement.

Conferees at Woods Hole dealt with—but did not limit themselves to—problems of curricular content. Four basic themes emerged from the ten-day conference: structure, readiness, intuition, and motivation. Discussions of structure were based on the premise that knowledge acquired without a comprehensive framework to tie it together is likely to be forgotten. Readiness was considered in the context of a resurrected and reemphasized interest in the work of Piaget and other developmentalists in the attempt to effect a sequential progression that would pair intellectual offerings with the developing skills of the learning child. Conferees explored the possibility of teaching intuition as a learned skill through classroom reinforcement of "good guessing" and other supportive teaching devices. Discussions on motivation included some old concerns, e.g., the nature of interest and how can teachers generate a pervasive sense of excitement that will far outlast the teaching tools that arouse it, and examined some new ones, e.g., the threat that television and the new technology will result in a generation of passive students who, overentertained at home and overexcited in the classroom, will sit back like an audience waiting for the curtain to go up.

With the advent of the Woods Hole report, the decisive power of the academic community in matters of elementary and secondary school curricula was confirmed; the nation's foremost scholars were increasingly to be involved in helping find the "middle language"— the intellectually correct but appropriately simplified articulations of the most advanced thinking in a given field. Out of Woods Hole came a fusion of nineteenth-century education emphasis (academic and solid subject matter elements) with the currents of the

19. Ibid., pp. 14, 31.

early twentieth century (Progressive education and the child-centered curriculum).

Though many existing curricular statements did indeed incorporate these principles, they did so only *implicitly* and only by fortunate accident. Now, in the Woods Hole report, these educational principles were *explicitly* identified as the goals for curriculum plans of the future.

In effect, conferees were agreeing to catch the pendulum in midswing, before new excesses could develop. Though orderly arrangements of extremely complicated scientific matter were the specific and most often enunciated concerns of the curriculum innovators, the revisionists put the child back in the sequential picture and thus avoided an excessive countercycle in the future.

Thus, Woods Hole was important not because it produced new knowledge, but rather because it legitimized the curricular examinations of the fifties (and before) and provided a theoretical basis for and a transition to the work of the sixties.

Organizationally, Woods Hole reflected the Sputnik-escalated concern for the state of scientific education in the nation. Joint sponsorship and cooperative funding[20] for this unique convergence of learning specialists with leading subject matter scholars was a precedent for the collaborative efforts by public and private agencies and associations that characterized the sixties.

There were other events with similar impact on the reform movement. The Disciplines Seminar convened by the NEA Project on Instruction in June of 1961, for example, was called to ". . . facilitate study and effective use of the disciplines by (a) focusing upon those fundamental ideas and methods of inquiry from selected fields of study which should be in the mainstream of the instructional program of the public schools, and (b) exploring frontier thinking and research in the nature of knowledge and ways of knowing."[21]

20. American Association for the Advancement of Science, National Science Foundation, the Carnegie Corporation, United States Office of Education, the Air Force, and Rand Corporation.

21. Project on Instruction, *The Scholars Look at the Schools: A Report of the Disciplines Seminar* (Washington: National Educational Association, 1962), pp. 1-2.

A second source of ideas that unified much of the thinking about reform was the 1956 ASCD Yearbook.[22] In it, many of the themes of the revisions that followed were enunciated and their implications for practice spelled out.

FRUSTRATION: A FORCE FOR CHANGE

Sputnik was a potent catalyst, but the quality of our educational system was not a new concern in the United States. The astonishingly high draftee failure rate on the Armed Forces Qualification Test—roughly one of fifth-grade equivalency—in World War II had graphically demonstrated that universal access to free public education was by no means a guarantee of universal literacy.

The increasing mobility of our population made this a matter of national rather than of provincial or local concern. The dropout from Los Angeles was likely to be a welfare statistic in New York City; the illiterate Appalachian youngster was likely to become a military reject in Detroit; bad education recognized no city limits and moved with ease across state lines. Local loyalties were diminishing; we were a nation on the move. By 1960 one out of every five families changed their residence every year. Recognition of such changes in our national patterns tended to temper the historic preoccupation with local prerogatives (a preoccupation and a tempering that were by no means restricted to school districts) and gave rise to a cooperative concern among the nation's education professionals.

By the mid-sixties, aroused parents, stirred by an increasingly attentive popular press, were demanding change, and a bewildering proliferation of innovative organizational and curricular offerings was forcing even the most conservative educator to pay lip service, if no more, to the need for change.

Education's administrative units, like other units of American political organization, were undergoing what political scientist Morton Grodzins described as an evolution from the "layer cake" to the "marble cake."[23] Along with this decrease in jurisdictional

22. Robert R. Leeper, ed., *What Shall the High Schools Teach?* 1956 Yearbook of the Association for Supervision and Curiculum Development (Washington: the Association, 1956).

23. Morton Grodzins, *The American System,* ed., Daniel Elazar (Chicago: Rand McNally & Co., 1966). p. v.

concern, there was a corresponding increase in traffic among and between local school personnel, academia, Washington, the private foundations, the corporations, and the professional associations.

Thus the curricular pioneers, advanced scholars in their discrete disciplines, found themselves spending summers in training institutes with the elementary and secondary schoolteachers who would be testing their new materials in the classroom. Thus, third-grade teachers who had graduated from state normal schools decades earlier found themselves enrolled in graduate courses on university campuses. Thus federal education officials who had not been outside Washington in ten years found themselves squeezing into chairs designed for considerably less than their bulk as they crisscrossed the nation visiting the schools that were putting to empirical test the revised and redesigned curricula and, later, the innovative federally supported Title III programs.

As the curricular experimenters reached down further and further, federal and foundation sponsors were able to observe an abundant smorgasbord of learning phenomena—three-year-olds learning to read with talking typewriters, kindergarteners learning to write music, first-graders dealing with basic economic concepts of supply and demand and marketing theory, second- and third-graders working with set theory in mathematics—and to see a whole host of curricular offerings once available only in colleges and universities becoming increasingly commonplace in the secondary schools, such as anthropology, Russian, Chinese, astronomy, and philosophy.

Curricular redesign was essentially directed at the elite among secondary school students—college-bound youngsters whose ambitious parents and teachers were most likely to be found in the resource-rich suburban communities.

But this work presaged and laid the groundwork for the curricular investigations that were to follow in the sixties. These same learning theories were to be propounded as the nation sought solutions (too many admittedly only palliative) to the belatedly recognized inadequacy of the system for a very substantial part of its clientele—the disadvantaged. As S. M. Miller pointed out, education, which once served as a means of ascendancy for the poor, was becoming a bar to the ascendancy of the new poor.[24]

### NEW EXPECTATIONS: A FORCE FOR CHANGE

In the late fifties, the Supreme Court continued to reinforce its 1954 decision outlawing segregated education. The Civil Rights movement, with increasing support from nonblacks, was having explosive impact on our national educational expectations. School boards, and in too many cases the educational establishment, found they had no place to hide. The little red schoolhouse, subject always to the currents of political change, was forced now to heed the urgent cry of our minority citizens.

The popular press, in the same fashion that it generated the post-Sputnik demand for improvements in the teaching of mathematics and science, moved in the early 1960s to a new focus on the plight of America's urban and rural poor.

The critical limelight and public dismay, in both instances, centered on the inadequacies of the schools. Educators—seen as the culprits in this national disaster—were conversely also seen as the saviors who would lead us to the educational millenium.

From a new breed of teachers came a flow of exciting and also disquieting publications about the nature of schooling.[25] The group, education's New Left, paralleled their contemporaries in other sectors of the society. Their concern was for relevance, individuality, freedom, autonomy, responsive environments, cultural pride, honesty, value clarification, meaningful communication, and ethical growth. Their books outsold all others about schools—indeed they captured an audience not accustomed to reading about education.

Thus the sixties saw the political, social, and curricular currents merge as the nation's community of scholars, school people, "new activists," and elected officials joined in a concerted effort to find the best ways to impart knowledge, skills, and a feeling of individual

24. "Credentialism and the Educational System" (Paper presented at the 44th Annual Meeting, American Orthopsychiatric Association, March 23, 1967, Washington, D.C.).

25. See, for example, Jonathan Kozol, *Death At An Early Age* (Boston: Houghton Mifflin Co., 1967); John Holt, *How Children Fail* (New York: Pitman Publishing Co., 1964); Neil Postman and Charles Weingartner, *Teaching As A Subversive Activity* (New York: Delacorte Press, 1969); and A. S. Neill, *Summerhill* (New York: Hart Publishing Co., 1960).

worth and power to all students at all socioeconomic and educational levels.

The old fears of federal control were subordinated to parent, teacher, and administrator demands for massive infusions of federal funds. Inspired by President Johnson's persuasive concern for the educational needs of the nation, and led by such progressive federal education executives as HEW Secretary John Gardner and Commissioners of Education Francis Keppel and Harold Howe II, the Congress moved with dispatch: from 1963 to 1968 the Congress enacted twenty-four major pieces of educational legislation—more, in five years, than in its entire history as a legislative body.[26] This new legislation touched every aspect of education as we know it, from preschool to postdoctoral.

Just as the National Defense Education Act and the National Science Foundation had earlier poured funds into improvements in the teaching and course content of the physical and natural sciences, so now did the Manpower Development and Training Act and the Vocational Education Act provide substantial funding for programs addressed to the problems of obsolescence of vocational skills and jobs.

In an earlier America, a strong back and a willing heart were enough to get anyone past the hiring gate; now, teachers began to recognize that today's technology required not only learned skills, but learned flexibility if the worker was to develop along with the nation's evolving technology.

In similar fashion, the Economic Opportunity Act directed itself to the educational deficiencies that result from living in poverty. Under its provisions, Head Start helped to offer culturally deprived youngsters a chance to enter school on an equal footing with the more privileged members of their age group; Upward Bound offered bright older youngsters from the same background some special assistance toward college admission. The Job Corps took dropouts—rejects and rejectors of the system—and put them into residential learning centers; VISTA, the neighborhood health cen-

26. For descriptions of this legislation see Committee on Education and Labor, United States House of Representatives, *A Compilation of Federal Education Laws* (Washington: U.S. Government Printing Office, February 1969).

ters, the community action councils, and other OEO programs brought new and necessary special knowledge into America's most deprived communities.

But the major thrust in the national effort to remedy inequality of educational opportunity came from Title I of the Elementary and Secondary Education Act. The billion-dollar program sought to correct generations of educational deficiencies with well-intended, if not necessarily well-designed, investments on behalf of the nation's most deprived youngsters. In what was essentially a political decision, Congress apportioned the Title I funds on the basis of census data showing the distribution of low-income families among counties or school districts. Money went directly to the states for distribution to school districts with the warning that funds must be spent to improve the quality of education in schools serving low-income areas and not to reduce existing levels of local or state support. The Congress did not build accountability into the legislation—again, for obvious political reasons.

Other titles of ESEA provided federal assistance to school libraries; funded innovative and experimental programs; underwrote supplementary education centers, cooperative research programs, and regional laboratories; and provided grants to strengthen state education agencies. Title III of ESEA encouraged intuitive leaps into unexplored areas of the educational frontier. "If there are no failures in the Title III program, it will itself have been a failure," said USOE Commissioner Harold Howe II. "All experiments cannot be successful or they have not truly been experiments." Howe urged the newly established regional laboratories to foster risk-taking and to cross-fertilize the efforts of researchers and research projects.

Under the Higher Education Act, the federal government invested in college construction and college libraries and began a cooperative program of assistance to less developed (usually small, black) colleges. Grants, loans, and work-study programs made it possible for an increasing number of disadvantaged students to look toward higher education with the result that in just four years, from 1964 to 1968, the nonwhite enrollment of our colleges and universities almost doubled (a statistic that should not lead to smugness; the entire college enrollment was also growing at an extremely rapid rate).

In other legislation, the federal government turned its attention to the needs of the handicapped, to the arts and humanities, to the growing need for health professionals, and to general expansion of vocational education programs. These years saw the missionary zeal of Teacher Corps volunteers put to work in urban ghettos and in impoverished backwoods districts. In the same period, thousands of adults enrolled in basic education courses throughout the nation as the United States intensified its efforts to have a fully literate society.

To achieve these goals, the federal government developed two kinds of relationships with state and local educational establishments. The first was a partnership directed primarily at eliminating those differences of educational quality that resulted from differences in community resources. The second was catalytic; the government provided grants (or seed money) to generate new thinking and to fund trial projects, and offered matching or partial grants for improvements in demonstrated areas of need (e.g., school libraries).

The federal investment was substantial in both areas: in 1955 the total federal investment in all educational enterprises (including veteran benefits and defense) was $1.4 billion. By 1965 it had nearly tripled ($3.6 billion), and in the next three years it more than doubled again—$8.8 billion in 1968.

The federal government was not alone in increasing its educational investment. The private foundations, led by Ford, Carnegie, and Kettering, also substantially increased their educational expenditures. So, too, did the states and communities. Thus the total amount spent for public elementary and secondary schools grew dramatically.

### PROFESSIONAL ASSOCIATIONS: A FORCE FOR CHANGE

Unfortunately, the anti-establishment mystique in our society has drawn greater attention to teacher militancy and the struggle between the National Education Association and the American Federation of Teachers than to the considerable impact made by the professional associations on school improvement. The less conspicuous but major efforts of the NEA and its affiliates provide an impressive list of examples: the NEA Project on the Academically Talented Student; the NEA Project on Educational Implications of Automation; the Contemporary Music Project of the Music Educators National Conference (an NEA National Affiliate); the Staff Utilization Studies of the National Association of Secondary School Principals (an NEA Associated Organization); and the NEA Project on the Instructional Program of the Public Schools (Project on Instruction).

The four-volume report of the Project on Instruction[27] had significant impact on school policy and practice. Twelve questions were considered and thirty-three recommendations made in two major decision areas: (a) what should be taught, and (b) how to plan and organize for teaching. The developers of national curriculum projects would have done well to consider the several curricular questions raised in this report. For example, issues of continuity and sequence received major attention in the Project on Instruction, stubborn questions of educational priorities were considered, and the importance of providing a comprehensive instructional program was stressed.

Many of the accomplishments discussed in earlier sections of this chapter were first mentioned in the project report. It preceded, for example, the important federal legislation of the decade. In 1963 the project became the NEA Center for the Study of Instruction (CSI)—an organization attempting to bridge the gap between theory and practice through its program of publication ("Schools for the 70's") and its direct work in instructional improvement with NEA local and state affiliates.

The influence of the professional associations on school improvement is increasing (see chapter ix of this yearbook). In the future, it is highly probable that the educational community and citizens at large will recognize the dynamic force for school improvement of the organized profession and the scholarly societies.

## OTHER FORCES FOR CHANGE

Most of the aforementioned influences were on curricular research and development, as opposed to the end product, i.e., what goes on in the classroom. Four other elements play a part in determining real, as opposed to intended, curricular outcomes: promo-

27. National Education Association, *Deciding What to Teach; Education in a Changing Society;* and *Planning and Organizing for Teaching* (Washington: the Association, 1963); and *Schools for the Sixties: A Report of the Project on Instruction* (New York: McGraw-Hill Book Co., 1963).

tion and marketing practices, state and local curriculum requirements, internal and external forms of school organization, and the
curricula of the schools of education—the teacher preparation
institutions.

Clearly, there is little value in the very best curriculum if it is
mouldering in a file cabinet or a laboratory school; it has to get out
into the world. Whatever else we ask of a successful curriculum, we
must insist that it be in use with learners. Marketing, then, is at
least as basic to a successful curriculum as it is to enzyme soaps,
longer cigarettes, or vacuum cleaners.

In the sixties, education was a growth industry and a host of
major national corporations bought or developed education sub-
sidiaries (G.E. and Time, Inc.'s General Learning Corporation;
IBM's Science Research Associates; Westinghouse's Learning Corporation; and Xerox's Education Group). Curriculum project
directors contracted with these new firms and with old-line textbook publishers to produce, promote, and sell their products. Overall, these commercial collaborations have been productive, if not
always profitable, and an increasing number should show a profit
as the researchers come to a better understanding of the nature
of the marketplace and as initial difficulties with copyrights and
royalties are resolved.

Less likely to find happy resolution is the problem of curricular
intrusion from state legislatures. Though federal control is the
bogey repeatedly warned against, state control in fact is a much
more substantial threat to the cherished national tradition of local
control. Mandated inclusions in the school day vary from state to
state and from the sensible to the ridiculous; in either event, they
reduce flexibility and take the decision-making authority away from
the local board. Some legislatures require that reading be taught
phonetically; some require that it be taught a precise number of
minutes per day. One eastern state permits over thirty youngsters
in grade 4 and beyond, but in grades K-3 thirty is the legal limit,
thus frustrating educators who otherwise might experiment with
team teaching or nongraded primary arrangements that require
flexible student groupings.

Until recently, the legislature in the western state known for its
heavy educational investment made driver-training a prerequisite
to a high school diploma and required its elementary teachers to

offer some thirty-three specific curricular topics including morals, manners and citizenship, public speaking, conservation, public safety, and accident prevention. Detailed prescription of the school day (twenty minutes for physical education daily; regular mention of the evils of "dope" and alcohol, fire prevention, and so forth) and of the school year severely limited the local board's options. Further, state law limited to three the courses a local board could add to the prescribed state requirements.

The third phenomenon to be taken into account as we look at curricular reform is the organization of the school itself: external —the moves toward centralization and decentralization; and internal—the move to more flexible learning units and staff groupings.

The former is in part an educational and in part a political phenomenon. The move toward consolidation accelerated after Conant's 1959 pronouncements that "The enrollment of many American public high schools is too small to allow a diversified curriculum except at exorbitant expense"[28] and that "In many states the number one problem is the elimination of the small high school by district reorganization."[29]

In the decade since publication of the Conant report, the number of high schools in the United States has decreased through unification from approximately twenty-five thousand to about eighteen thousand. Concurrently, the move toward decentralization of large urban districts was gathering adherents. There is nothing inherently contradictory about these twin movements toward larger and smaller units: rural areas with a relatively homogenous population and high schools that graduate fewer than one hundred students have good reason to pool their resources. At the same time, urban districts with a very diverse clientele of widely varying needs and ambitions and one that is increasingly making vocal demands for a part in the control of their neighborhood schools have good reason to decentralize. Their student population is large enough to guarantee economical high school units in substantially smaller political units than those dictated by the city limits. Thus it is by no means inconsistent to decentralize in New York City, where curricular diversity will not be affected, and to consolidate

28. James Bryant Conant, *The American High School Today: A First Report to Interested Citizens* (New York: McGraw-Hill Book Co., 1959) p. 77.

29. Ibid., p. 38.

in California's Central Valley, where curricular diversity will be increased. Both the resulting educational units will be large enough to sustain an adequate school program; neither will be too large to make parent involvement impossible.

The intraschool organizational problems were of a different order. They reflected educational philosophy rather than political or jurisdictional concerns. Elements in such reorganizations have included new uses of space, staff resources, mechanical aids, and new ways to group children. This was an era that saw many experimental school staffing patterns. Innovations that have found their way into enough schools to be considered past the experimental stage include team teaching[30] and nongraded classes,[31] language laboratories, and individualized instruction.[32] Less widely accepted are extended school days, extended school years, performance contracts with outside instructional organizations (though this may be the movement of the seventies), centralized instruction via television monitors in the classroom, consortia arrangements among nearby groups of schools, flexible scheduling, and work-study (or part-time) school enrollments.

The relationship between curricular content and the way the school is organized is becoming increasingly apparent. Instructional change, by itself, is of little value if notions of schools and teaching procedures remain rigid. Just as it is of little value to build new schools with movable partitions if we continue to apportion our youngsters in standard egg-crate units, so, too, is it of little value to develop new curricula if we deny teachers access to optimum situations in which to apply them.

The last of the curriculum-influencing factors is itself a curricular matter: teacher training institutions themselves have a very substantial impact on what finally occurs in the classroom. Schools of education create a climate of agreement among their graduates;

30. See, for example, Judson T. Shaplin and Henry F. Olds, eds., *Team Teaching* (New York: Harper & Row, 1964).

31. See what is probably the most influential publication on nongrading: John I. Goodlad and Robert H. Anderson, *The Nongraded Elementary School,* rev. ed. (New York: Harcourt, Brace & World, 1963).

32. An intriguing publication which deals with a number of innovations in school organization and describes a possible implementation of them is Bruce R. Joyce, *The Teacher and His Staff: Man, Media, and Machines* (Washington: National Education Association, 1967).

thus the curriculum of the teachers college to a very large extent determines teaching practices. There is some indication that the degree of success in any curriculum is directly related to the degree of enthusiasm of the participating teacher. A teacher who has been through a rigid training program is less likely to be comfortable working with his colleagues in a team-teaching arrangement, in flexible nongraded units with the opportunity to alternate large group lectures with small group seminars, in the opportunity to move in or out of the school building with his students. A teacher with this sort of background may be more secure in the isolation of a conventional self-contained classroom with thirty small desks and one large one.

This does not suggest that such flexible arrangements guarantee success, rather that the chance for success is materially improved when the teacher, in addition to well-designed curricular materials, also has a harmonious and congenial association with his colleagues and the support of his administration and school board. Teachers, like students, respond to stimulation and to approval. It may be that the specific curricular innovations of this period are no more important than the ferment and excitement they have generated among teachers.

As we continue to learn more and more about effective teaching techniques, as we learn to recognize the psychological impact of the school environment, as we develop increasingly flexible concepts of school organization and better ways to exploit the new technology, the visible results of the new curricula will necessarily increase. The most flawless diamond shows poorly in a zinc setting; even a zircon glitters in an elegant band of platinum. Thus we may not be able to judge how well the new curricula of the fifties and sixties do their job until we see them applied in the schools of the seventies and the eighties, hopefully in a school setting which offers maximum opportunity to exploit their advantages.

### ILLUSTRATIVE NATIONAL CURRICULUM PROJECTS

Two national curriculum projects demonstrate the similarities and differences in the "curriculum reform movement."[33] One, Sci-

33. For a listing and analysis of national curriculum projects, see John I. Goodlad, Renata Von Stoephasius, and M. Frances Klein, *The Changing School Curriculum* (New York: The Fund for the Advancement of Education, 1966); Robert W. Heath, ed., *New Curricula* (New York: Harper & Row, 1964).

ence—A Process Approach (S-APA),[34] is selected because it represents in part the evolution of a practice that began in the early part of the century: reducing content to the smallest possible discrete steps so the learner is led in a systematic way to a predetermined end which is the sum of the steps taught.[35] The other, Man: A Course of Study, hereafter referred to as "Man,"[36] illustrates a second force which found acceptance in this period. Chiefly, the ideas in it are those of Dewey, as extended, applied, and on several occasions redefined by Jerome Bruner[37] and others.

There are some important similarities between the two projects: (a) each values certain ultimate behaviors for the learner, such as the ability to hypothesize, to be a continuing inquirer in the discipline, and to be able to generalize broadly through the use of these new intellectual tools; (b) the material from both projects has been tested in live classrooms with teachers; (c) great attention has been paid to teacher preparation for use of the material; (d) both are for elementary schools but have implications for older students; (e) both reflect the post-Sputnik trend to involve university-based scholars as chief curricular architects; and (f) both projects were funded by the National Science Foundation, both have awarded their materials to commercial publishers for maximum distribution in the schools, and both have contracts with these publishers which return royalties to the U.S. Treasury.

*Science—A Process Approach.* The urgencies of World War II caused a renewal of efforts to provide sequencing, efficiency, and

34. A project conducted by the Commission on Science Education of the American Association for the Advancement of Science sponsored by a grant from the National Science Foundation.

35. See, for example, three publications which spell out in considerable detail the literally hundreds of steps and rules necessary for the student to follow as he receives training in the several content areas: *The Nation at Work on the Public School Curriculum,* Third Yearbook, Department of Superintendence (Washington: National Education Association, 1926); *Research in Constructing the Elementary School Curriculum,* Fourth Yearbook, Department of Superintendence, (1927); and *Fourth Report of the Committee on Economy on Time in Education,* Eighteenth Yearbook of the National Society for the Study of Education (Bloomington, Ill.: Public School Publishing Co., 1922).

36. A project conducted by the Educational Development Center and funded by a grant from the National Science Foundation.

37. Bruner, *The Process of Education.* See also two other books by Jerome Bruner: *On Knowing: Essays for the Left Hand* (Cambridge: Harvard University Press, Belknap Press, 1962) and *Toward a Theory of Instruction* (Cambridge, Mass.: Harvard University Press, Belknap Press, 1966).

economy in instruction. The Navy's guide for curriculum-building explains:

Every Navy training program has a mission. This mission is usually clearly and concisely stated and consists of overall purposes of the training. *But a mission is the sum of a great number of smaller objectives, each of which must be achieved before the mission of training is fulfilled* (italics added). In detailing these smaller objectives, much training falls down. With the mission in mind, but without carefully detailed objectives, the training goes on in the correct general direction, but without certainty that all training activities scheduled actually do contribute to the mission.[38]

The work of B. F. Skinner,[39] the Rand Corporation, Robert McNamara and his associates at Ford Motor Company and the Pentagon, and others went beyond these notions and those of earlier times, opening new ways of thinking for curriculum workers.

In a paper before the annual AERA meeting in 1966, Robert Gagné clearly laid out a curriculum design which shaped S—APA. In it he outlined his view of the nature of knowledge and its relationship to the purposes of schooling:

A curriculum is a sequence of content units arranged in such a way that the learning of each unit may be accomplished as a single act, provided the capabilities described by specified prior units (in the sequence) have already been mastered by the learner.[40]

An excerpt from an AAAS "Miscellaneous Publication" prepared by Gagné illustrates the impact of his direction on the project:

Descriptions . . . sequences of intellectual development serve a number of purposes in the execution of the educational program embodied in *Science—A Process Approach*. These descriptions are contained in *behavioral hierarchies*[41] (italics added).

38. U.S. Navy Department, Bureau of Naval Personnel, Training Standards and Curriculum Division, *Instructions for Preparing Curricula in Standard Navy Form,* NavPers 16012 (Washington: Bureau of Naval Personnel, 1945), pp. 1-2.

39. See, for example, B. F. Skinner, *Walden II* (New York: Macmillan Co., 1948) and Skinner's chapter, "The Science of Learning and the Art of Teaching," in A. A. Lumsdaine and Robert Glaser, eds., *Teaching Machines and Programmed Learning* (Washington: Department of Audiovisual Instruction, National Education Association, 1960). See also the list of Skinner's publications, page 715 of that publication.

40. Robert M. Gagné, "Curriculum Research and the Promotion of Learning" in *Perspectives of Curriculum Evaluation* (Chicago: Rand McNally & Co., 1967), p. 23.

40. American Association for the Advancement of Science, "Science—A Process Approach: Purpose, Accomplishments, Expectations," Miscellaneous Publication 67-112 (Washington: The Association, November 1967), pp. 9-10.

Gagné goes on to say that the hierarchies serve several functions: (a) provide a rationale for selecting and ordering the sequence of objectives; (b) tell the teacher what should have preceded the exercise, where to start, and what will come after; (c) assess student achievement; (d) provide program evaluation; and (e) indicate when "terminal" behavior has been accomplished.

The "graduate" of S—APA, then, will have acquired a *specific, predetermined concept of science as seen by the developers of the project.* Other projects have employed similar concepts of the nature of learning and knowledge. The Anthropology Curriculum Project, University of Georgia, Marion J. Rice, Director, and the University of Maryland Mathematics Project led by Gagné and staff are examples.

S—APA is based on two fundamental hypotheses: first, that the objectives of science education in the early grades should be the learning of a scientific process rather than of factual content or a body of "principles"; second, that the complex procedures of scientific inquiry can be separated into simpler elements and arranged in a hierarchical sequence within which those who master the earlier stages increase their ability to grasp later stages.

The new curriculum purports to approach science as does the scientist himself—as a method of inquiry about observable phenomena, rather than as a body of facts or principles to be memorized. The curriculum, therefore, concentrates on a sequence of development in which the child is taught, through concrete exercises he carries out himself, to use increasingly more complex versions of the basic scientific processes: observing, inferring, using space/time relationships, using numbers, measuring, classifying, communicating, and predicting, which lead into controlling variables, defining operationally, formulating hypotheses, and interpreting data, which culminate in experimenting. Instead of stressing the principle of momentum and its conservation, for example, the new curriculum emphasizes the ability to observe, measure, classify, and infer generalizable results about bodies at rest and in motion.

A specific fourth grade exercise is illustrative:

The teacher's guide suggests the procedure; the children are given a set of cylinders—solid, hollow, heavy, light, short, long— and the teacher asks, "Which of these cylinders do you think will roll down the incline in the shortest time? How can you find out?"

After the children test their ideas, the teacher's guide suggests a way of focusing attention on the variables. "When we rolled the two cylinders, what did we always keep the same? What things were not the same?" The children make two lists. The teacher labels the lists "Constant" and "Changed." She discusses with them the list "Changed" in terms of the manipulated variable. The children then work in small groups manipulating the variables on their list, observing and recording their effects on the time it takes a cylinder to roll down the incline.

After these experiences, the teacher's guide extends its suggestions to focus on the responding variable and on the variables held constant. "Was one of the variables the time it takes a cylinder to roll down an incline? What variables were held constant? What variables were not held constant?" Later the emphasis shifts to the students working with an assortment of round objects, investigating the effects of different manipulated variables on the time required for them to roll down an incline (responding variable)—"Will a quarter roll down the incline faster than a nickel?"

Precisely because S—APA is based on learning a process (in a sequentially developed structure), written curriculum materials are addressed almost solely to the teacher. Instructional guides and material kits have been painstakingly developed. From these the teacher organizes science-problem situations for the children in a sequence of exercises. Each exercise is designed to achieve a particular step in the grasp of one or more processes. Each exercise is accompanied by material spelling out for the teacher the learning objective of the particular exercise and its relationship to the preceding and succeeding exercises.

From simple process skills, the curriculum advances to progressively more complex skills. At each stage, tests are provided which measure both the child's increment in achievement and his overall grasp and ability to use the process learned.

S—APA's evaluations indicate that 90 percent of the children using the course have acquired at least 70 percent of the desired competencies in almost all of the exercises. Children from lower socioeconomic backgrounds, while completing fewer exercises than those from higher socioeconomic backgrounds, were equally as successful.

Most importantly, the evaluation tests showed that as children progressed in the S—APA process-oriented curriculum, achievement at lower levels of development significantly raised the probability of achievement of higher skills.

Emerging from the cooperation of scientists and educational psychologists, S—APA seeks to translate the intellectual processes of a scientific inquiry into a hierarchical learning process. It is an experiment whose objective is the mastery by the student of a complex set of skills in a sequence dictated not by the way in which the skills are ultimately used, but by the way in which the child learns. Considered as a whole process, for grades K-6, preliminary evaluations indicate a high order of success. But at the same time, it is a process which is not easy to alter or to break into in the middle; consequently, for the child moving from this curriculum to another—from one with to one without S—APA—the result may be a net loss in learning achievement. For a pluralistic system, therefore, the integrated process-oriented nature of S—APA constitutes both its strength and its major weakness.

*Man: A Course of Study.* This project is a product of the dreams of Jerome Bruner. If one can judge from the attention paid to this work in Bruner's writing and the direct relationship of his ideas to what actually appeared as material for the classroom, it is the best expression of his view of the "good life" in schooling.

In *On Knowing,* Bruner spends some time on the subject "After John Dewey, What?" The essay is an analysis of the "stirring and prophetic" *My Pedagogic Creed.* Bruner brings the Dewey creed up to date by placing it in the context of life after ". . . two world wars, the dark episode of Hitler and genocide, the Russian revolution, the relativistic revolution in physics and psychology. . . ."[42] He concludes with a prophecy of his own which shaped **Man: A Course of Study** and many other projects of the decade:

The Nobel poet or the ambassador to the United Nations, the brilliant cellist or the perceptive playwright, the historian making use of the past or the sociologist seeking a pattern in the present—these men, like the student, are seeking understanding and mastery over new problems. They represent excellence at the frontiers of endeavor. If a sense of progress and change toward greater excellence is to illuminate our schools, there must be a constant return of their wisdom and effort to

42. Bruner, *On Knowing,* pp. 114-15.

enliven and inform teacher and student alike. There is no difference in kind between the man at the frontier and the young student at his own frontier, each attempting to understand. Let the educational process be life itself as fully as we can make it.[43]

It is often difficult to review Bruner because he does not deal with basic curricular questions in an orderly, discernible way. By implication, though, he does discuss appropriate bases for curricular design and the nature and purpose of planned education:

In planning a curriculum, one properly distinguishes between the long-run objective one hopes to achieve and certain short-run steps that get one toward that objective. Those of a practical turn of mind are likely to say that little is served by stating long-term objectives unless one can propose short-run methods for their achievement. More idealistic critics may too readily dismiss short-run educational goals on the grounds that they cannot see where they lead. We are inclined to take a middle ground. While one benefits from clarity about the ends of education, it is often true that we may discover or rediscover new ultimate objectives in the process of trying to reach more modest goals.[44]

The intent of "Man" is to have the child re-create knowledge in his own individual way. The concern is with the child's curiosity, his drive to achieve competence, the identification he makes or modeling that he does in his formative years, and with his need to share his knowledge with others. Bruner offers five ideals in regard to the project:

1. To give our pupils respect for and confidence in the powers of their own mind;
2. To extend that respect and confidence to their power to think about the human condition, man's plight, and his social life;
3. To provide a set of workable models that make it simpler to analyze the nature of the social world in which we live and the condition in which man finds himself;
4. To impart a sense of respect for the capacities and humanity of man as a species; and
5. To leave the student with a sense of the unfinished business of man's evolution.[45]

Jerome Bruner's influence clearly shaped the development of "Man." A one-year course for upper elementary grades, this cur-

42. Ibid, p. 126.
44. Bruner, *The Process of Education*, p. 69.
45. Bruner, *Toward a Theory of Instruction*, p. 101.

riculum seeks to have the student ask and consider three "basic" questions about the human condition:

1. What is distinctively human about human beings?
2. How did humans get that way?
3. How can they become more human?

As Bruner puts it:

> The content of the course is man: his nature as a species, the forces that shaped and continue to shape his humanity. . . . We seek exercises and materials which show wherein man is distinctive in his adaptation to the world, and wherein there is a discernible continuity between man and his animal forebears.

The first three units in the course direct the student's attention to both the common elements and the differences between man and animals. The life cycle of the salmon, the behavior of herring gulls, and the group activities of baboons invite consideration of like and unlike characteristics. In the case of salmon, enough of the young survive without parental protection to insure perpetuation of the species. Why the need for parental protection among humans? The herring gull, on the other hand, has a family structure strikingly similar to humans. Again: what conditions led to this arrangement?

The next unit presents the far more complex behavior of baboons —group activities, aggression, family relationships, territorial concepts, infant rearing, food gathering, and a wide range of personal relationships.

The final unit concentrates on a remote human society, the Netsilik Eskimos of the Canadian Arctic. The choice of this remote culture was deliberate. Its very strangeness elicits interest. And that same strangeness helps the student separate, in his own mind, those differences due to culture from those that are common elements of humanity characteristic of both the Eskimo and his own society.

One of these common elements—sharing—is manifested in a unit on seal hunting. Films, maps, and a seal-hunting game precede the lesson on sharing, which is called "The Value of a Distribution System."

The lesson begins: "The seal hunting game demonstrates that a system of distribution is necessary for group survival. This is true in every society for there are always some people who are more productive than others. However, the need for such a system does not guarantee that people will, in fact, share. . . ."[46]

Working in groups of six, students devise formal systems for sharing in a role-playing exercise. Each child is given basic information about the seal hunter he represents (i.e., a middle-aged but strong man, a boy of fourteen, a first-class hunter), his relationship, if any, to others in the group, and the number of seals he has caught—from zero to thirty.

When the group reports its scheme for distribution, the teacher asks why the successful hunter did or did not share, who benefited from the sharing, and whether the benefits to each hunter were equal. Then the class analyzes and compares its proposals and concludes the unit with discussion promoted by a final question from the teacher: "Is our system of taxes a distribution system? Why? Why not?"

Course materials are wide-ranging and diverse: films, slides, brochures, games, artifacts, poems, and stories. No formal texts are used. The curriculum is demanding of teachers, in part because the course incorporates our new understandings from behavioral science research. In contrast to S—APA, the written materials are directed at the student rather than the teacher. For these reasons, a twenty-session NSF workshop is prerequisite to teaching the course. The special nature of the material and the training requirements are enabling factors which cause teachers to experiment with teaching teams or work as visiting teachers in classrooms employing the course.

Like S—APA, "Man" abandoned the traditional subject matter divisions of social science. It is concerned with man, his nature, and his behavior in all its modes. And, like S—APA, it stresses the learning of processes and thought-models rather than facts or pre-digested bodies of principles. But its differences from S—APA are probably greater than its similarities. It seeks to develop the affective equally as much as the intellectual faculties. It also reflects Bruner's strong view that learning is a process of inquiry. Its materials are addressed to the child in order to stimulate inquiry. Development of knowledge and thought processes usable beyond the specific subject matter flows from the activity of the child himself.

46. "The Netsilik Eskimos on the Sea Ice," in *Man: A Course of Study*, p. 50.

S—APA's materials, on the other hand, are primarily addressed to the teacher precisely because S—APA is a much more structured, integrated curriculum leading the child step by step through a precise sequence to a preordained set of achievement goals.

The contrasts between the two approaches reflect in part the difference in subject matter—the nature and conditions of man versus the processes of scientific inquiry. But they also reflect a significant difference in pedagogical approach.

## A Perspective

Flagellation of the schools became the intellectual parlor game of the sixties. The institutions and the professionals were attacked for unresponsiveness to contemporary society and especially to its youth.

Too often the response has been defensive, emotional, and not very useful. This chapter sketches the many positive responses that took place in our near past and suggests that the seeds of reform in the nation's most influential institution—its public schools— have germinated. There are two jobs to be done: nurturing the truly positive contributions made in the "education decade," and engaging in a massive "work-in" to bring about a revolution in the nature and conduct of schooling, with special emphasis on the creation of schools that serve uniquely human purposes.

The walls of the schools are literally and figuratively being torn down. In some cases this is happening because the school represents a repressive and immoral place to its hostile critics; in others, because the school needs fresh air, life, joy, style, and love from the outside. The efficacy of the schools is questionable in the minds of too many people for the issue to be ignored, "the school—a dying institution" too often the new *in* theme. Can we *re-create* the school? That is the question from our near past.

SECTION II

USING TODAY TO LOOK TO THE FUTURE

# CHAPTER IV

# Tomorrow's Curriculum: Future Imperfect

## FRANK G. JENNINGS

We educators talk a far better game than we play. We are adepts at role-playing and thus are amateurs in all senses of that word. We enter upon our mission out of a vague but generous love for our fellows. We pursue our ill-defined calling with a passion that precludes perfection. We conduct our practice under conditions that prevent us from acquiring specific high skills. Consequently, we are more often rueful than mindful of stewardship. And we possess an ever available reservoir of guilt towards ourselves, our colleagues, our charges, and our fellow citizens.

The gravamen of the Seventy-first Yearbook is to examine the profession's record since the publication by the Society of its last yearbooks devoted to the curriculum (Twenty-sixth, 1927; Forty-fourth, 1945). We believe that it should be possible to extract some wisdom from that record and to propose some alternative ways of working in the future that will be more salutary than those of the recent past. That is the implicit intent of our undertaking. Our implicit assumption is that the analyses, comments, and accounts it presents will be of some specifiable value to certain professionals, and that that value will be displayed in the creation of "better" curricula in some near future. Thus, we are haunted by the modern mystique of progress, by the conviction that "tomorrow will be better" and that "development" in itself is a realizable good.

We sometimes forget that formal education is not a natural institution like the family or the tribe. It emerges only in quite sophisticated and wealthy societies which have become powerful enough to tolerate the risks involved in its creation and continuance. Lind-

berg, commenting on the division of labor that must be precedent
to establishing formal education, observes:

There is a general system of education, adjusted to each stage of
development; there is need for liberty of choice and, above all, the
means and the leisure necessary for study and training in new skills.
As the development of surplus depends upon the previous development
of skills, so does the development of skills depend upon the previous
surplus. Thus the question of education comes largely to turn about
the availability of surplus, and the courage and vision to risk it wisely
in undertakings which offer no tangible or immediate return.[1]

We have used those surpluses so consistently and so widely in the
past that we sometimes lose sight of the gamble that education is.
On the cast of the curriculum will depend the shape of our near
future. And only by our willingness to spend time, energy, and
money prodigiously can we solve some of our most tearing social
problems. Today's goal is not merely equal educational opportunity;
it is equality of educational results. We want everyone to be assured
of minimal social and economic competence and we expect the
schools to do the job. When the tasks were simpler, they served us
well.

I insist that on any scale, by any measure, the achievements of
public schooling during these past forty-four years are impressive.
Most of the best of what we are today as a people is a consequence
of our mass education. Even our hurts, our anguish, our dissatis-
factions, our yearning for relevance, our fear of alienation, and
our plans for better worlds have been learned in the very schools
we deprecate.

We forget too readily the ancient wisdom that society educates
its members more profoundly and more lastingly than family,
church, or school. We forget, though we tell ourselves otherwise,
that, for good and ill, we are what we become because of where
and when we are born. We know that hunger shapes us, as does
the love and hate of our neighbors. We know that chance can
enlarge our vision or blind us to opportunities we would not know
how to seize. We are prisoners of our gene pools, and our liberation
depends upon the wit and compassion of a few teachers and the
accidents of friendship and love.

1. John Lindberg, *Foundations of Social Survival* (New York: Columbia University Press, 1953), p. 217.

The only hope for orderly freedom that we can reasonably create must have its basis in classrooms in the few thousand precious days that span our childhood and youth. How that time will be used, how it will be arranged, what occasions will intrude upon its regularities will depend upon the design and governance of the school. Only the school can give us a sense of the far horizon, can open us up to the myriad possibilities of existence, can help us learn how to discover and to use our special talents and common hungers. Only the school can arm us with the wit, can help us to invent those social strategies, by which we can try to make society more generous than we thought it could be.

But, we say, the schools are always and forever failing us, promising us magic and providing merely dull routines that lock us into lives that are intellectually and emotionally barely above the level of psychic subsistence. And so we join the critics of education, whom we have educated in these schools, and aver that those schools are mindless, dull, and drab, whether they are moldering in the urban slums or shining brightly on suburban hillsides. This is the large and shattering *half truth* about education in the eighth decade of the American Century. This marks the distance between our plans and our performances, but it is not an adequate assessment of the state of our educational affairs.

Charles E. Silberman in his book *Crisis in the Classroom,* which is his report on the Carnegie study of the education of educators, makes the point (and fully documents it) that:

> The United States has succeeded in doing what, until very recently, almost every European educator and a good many Americans insisted could *not* be done. It has managed to insure intellectual excellence and creative scholarship in a system of higher education. It has combined what the sociologist Martin Trow calls the traditional or "elite" function of the university—the transmission of high culture and the creation of new knowledge—with its "popular" functions, i.e., educating large numbers of students, particularly for the professions and vocations, and providing other services to society.[2]

Those "other services" include educating and training teachers and supporting professionals for all precollegiate education. They involve the creation of congeries of ancillary "disciplines," including

2. New York: Random House, 1970, p. 47.

one for "curriculum specialists," whose training has become a model for the rest of the world.

Perhaps the most telling measure of our success is the depth and intensity of our present discontent and the quality of our social anguish over the performance of education and all the "helping professions." We Americans are forever going about the business of making the good society. In so doing we have gone beyond the uses of rhetoric, though our time seems more given to rodomontade than even the early Christians could summon up against decadent Rome. For more than a generation now, we have been engaging in an intense, informal national assessment of our natural, civic, intellectual, and political resources, and we are variously engaged in rebuilding every essential institution for more effective, more widely available social service. And some of our successes have been considerable.

In sharp contrast to our attitude and performance, consider the comments about contemporary European education by Piaget:

> . . . the tragic fact is that the widespread educational renaissance of recent years has coincided with an increasing dearth of teachers. And, moreover, there is nothing fortuitous about this coincidence. The same reasons that have rendered our school system inadequate have also led to the inadequacy of the social and (as an indirect consequence) of the economic position of the teacher.[3]

Reading such comments, one's impulse is to observe that there is an apparent time lag of at least two decades between the European and the American teacher's economic position, but Piaget, who has rarely written formally about these matters, goes on to say:

> These reasons may be summed up by saying that our school system, as much under left-wing as under right-wing regimes, has been constructed by conservatives (from a pedagogic point of view) who were thinking much more in terms of fitting our rising generations into the molds of traditional learning than in training inventive and critical minds.[4]

In Europe, as in this country, those old molds can no longer contain or define either the student's or the society's needs. As far as the teacher is concerned, however, Piaget points out that those

3. Jean Piaget, *Science of Education and the Psychology of the Child* (New York: Orion Press, 1970), p. 123.

4. Ibid., p. 124.

. . . old educational conceptions, having made the teachers into mere transmitters of elementary, or only slightly more than elementary, general knowledge, without allowing them any opportunity for initiative and even less for research and discovery, have thereby imprisoned them in their present lowly status.[5]

Before we congratulate ourselves that this is evidence of our own measurable progress, it is sobering to remind ourselves that identical comments were made by Dewey more than half a century ago; that as recently as 1967 Robert Schaefer in his powerful little book, *The School As a Center of Inquiry,*[6] detailed not only these consequences but proposed some remedies that emerge from the logic of the situation itself; and that except for the exercise of people such as Robert Schwartz and his colleagues in the John Adams High School in Portland, Oregon, we Americans are still "telling the mournful numbers," still planning to consider new beginnings.

I suggest that we do as well as we do in spite of our "practice" and not because of our plans. This is one way to read McClure's chapter on the reforms of the past two decades. We have changed the climate by changing the atmosphere within which education is regarded. Consequently, both the critics and the defenders of the "educational establishment" have brought the problems of the schools into the center of society's focus of attention. In so doing we have unleashed the *paideia*. We have exposed our moral nerves to the assaults of social conscience. As Michael Harrington observed (it seems a century ago though it was only 1965), our youth are now taking our democratic house platitudes seriously. One of our persisting problems on college campuses and in the halls of secondary schools is that our youth are trying to act and think programmatically. Thus, they cry for *relevance,* and we lecture to them about the dangers of semantic shift. They call for engagement and we warn them about priorities. They want to talk about social contract, and we recall vaguely that a Frenchman who had pedagogical interests wrote about such matters some time before the days of Terror that led to Napoleon.

We have a foreboding sense that we are attending the onset of a new instauration in which all things are to be changed. It creeps into our diction even here. McClure's final paragraph begins with

5. Loc. cit.
6. New York: Harper & Row, 1967.

the sentence: "The walls of the school are literally and figuratively being torn down."

All of our social institutions are under searing and close examination—or so it would appear. We are suffering from some great aleatory spasm. If choice cannot help us, chance might. If we try everything, something might just turn out right. We act as if we believe that good can come out of evil, that the curse of war and our delinquent discovery of racism, the exposure of pervasive poverty behind our nationwide affluence are at long, long last forcing us to declare and act upon generous national purposes. We must re-create the school.

We know better than this. Only on paper are societies planned by old men writing books to get even with an unresponsive prince, or by young men seeking preferment and ready to settle for an early-option pension plan. Societies emerge as men do, over time and out of experience. They respond to the iron law of ecology which declares that "you can never do merely one thing." Every act we commit has consequences other than those we planned or anticipated. Every choice we make forces us to consider options that were hidden behind the decision that "logic required." But as St. Augustine observed a long time ago:

> It is often easier for people to attain the objectives for the sake of which they study a subject than to pursue the very complicated and thorny study of the rules. . . . Those who have learned the rules may take on the desire to deceive other people by plausible talk and questions; or they may give the impression that they have acquired for themselves some powerful tool with which to establish their ascendency over good and innocent people.[7]

St. Augustine was writing about teaching and learning, in school and out. He was commenting upon the difference between the world as it is experienced and life as it is perceived in the distorting mirror of the school. He was writing out of a tradition, already old in his time, which requires that the educator be somehow self-deprecating of his talents and his practice and rather nastily modest about the virtues of his calling.

Perhaps such attitudes are inevitable when formal education sets itself aside from its social and cultural contexts. And this is

7. *Augustine on Education*, ed. and trans., George Howie (Chicago: Henry Regnery, 1969), pp. 285-86.

exactly what is accomplished when educators speak of the veridical role of the school as the transmission of the high culture in a contemporary context of appropriate social and cognitive skills to produce self-sufficient citizens with enough margin of creativity to assure some measure of progress beyond their parents' estate. We need the poet's impatience and the anthropologist's honesty to free ourselves from such a heavy legacy.

Kimball, who for more than a decade has been offering such service, observed:

> Under conditions of rapid change, we can no longer assume that the knowledge or the practices that served us adequately in the past are sufficient for either the present or the future. Hence, we must rethink what we mean when we speak of education as the transmission of the cultural heritage. . . . we must consciously construct an educational system to serve a society that is in a state of continuous emergence. . . . Now we must build selective processes into educational procedure.[8]

What Kimball is saying is familiar enough. It has been part of the persuasive arguments that led to the development of "Man: A Course of Study" and "Science: a Process Approach," which McClure described and discussed in the preceding chapter. But Kimball's intent is more profound. Most of the professional and all of the amateur curriculum reformers of the past decade have conceived of the school on the Tinker-Toy model. The elements are always the same, the arrangements are infinitely variable. The school as an institution is accepted as a natural "given," like the second law of thermodynamics. We can ring changes upon the way it is employed, but it will always remain what it is and where it is. We can make it more inclusive of the population. It can be programmed to provide ever expanding services, generally of a custodial nature. It can respond to surface fads in policy, but it would never be shockingly unfamiliar to Horace Mann.

Kimball and McClellan have argued cogently that what is now required is a new philosophy of curriculum practice and, concurrently, a reorganization of elementary and secondary school administration that will provide a favorable environment for the learning process. They have argued that any honest examination of suc-

8. Solon T. Kimball, "Culture, Class, and Educational Congruency," in *Educational Requirements for the 1970's,* ed. Stanley Elam and William P. McLure (New York: Frederick A. Praeger, 1967), p. 8.

cessful contemporary organizational systems would expose the school as the most archaic of all our institutions in the matter of the structure and practice of its administration.[9]

Consider how short is the half life of any pilot project, any curriculum "innovation." Like Carl Sandburg's "Grass," the school covers all diremptions, all stirrings in the social soil. It meets all challenges to its position and its function with a "treason of the clerks," knowing from history that when the latest conqueror leaves, the civil servants will still be at their little desks, filling out the old forms, filing their reference cards, maintaining order.

Kimball and McClellan warn:

> Until the learning function actually becomes the paramount goal, and until the custodial, housekeeping and managerial functions are relegated to their proper service roles, we can expect little change in the present situation.[10]

Dewey said something like that in *School and Society*. Bertrand Russell made identical comments in *Education and the Good Life*. Piaget has been pleading this cause since 1923. Bruner has been addressing himself to the argument's substance since the publication of *A Study of Thinking*.[11] It is almost as though we have all accepted a new catechism to use in an old ritual. It is like Hamlet done in modern dress. Nothing fits, and the virtues of both old and new are wasted in the clash of styles.

We must forewarn ourselves, however, that we do not, in an orgy of *mea culpas,* go primitive or classical as we re-create the school. We know that whatever it is that the "learning function" is, it must be the school's central intent. We also know, much though we might wish it were otherwise, that the school is a place, that it exists in real time, that someone has to see that the drains work, that bookkeeping must be done for legal and financial reasons. Custodial care in itself is not a vicious undertaking. Children do have to be kept off the streets and out of the cold. And it is unreasonable to expect that every golden minute will be properly celebrated. There-

9. Solon T. Kimball and James E. McClellan, Jr., *Education and the New America* (New York: Random House, 1962).

10. Ibid., p. 9.

11. Jerome S. Bruner, Jacqueline Goodnow, and George A. Austin, *A Study of Thinking* (New York: John Wiley & Sons, 1956).

fore, though the statement has a meaching tone, school must be *kept* if real education is to flourish.

We are always potential victims of our own rhetoric. Declarations of intent might be evoked by a clearly perceived evil or ill, but rhetoric is not a dependable carrier of precise information. When we speak of "re-creating the school" or of "restructuring education," we may be moved to do so out of millennial visions, which are rather easy to come by in the final decades of the last century of the second millenium. We may be moved by a *carpe dium* impulse in this unique time of troubles to sanction violent change and call it social growth. But social institutions are not very malleable, even under revolutionary assault. They are capable of absorbing many new elements, of undergoing quite extensive structural changes, of tolerating quite massive incursions of new kinds of personnel without losing the integrity of their received function. So it is with the school.

Curriculum innovations, apprenticeship training, and certification of teachers, cost-benefit analysis, educational analogues, model building, computer-assisted instruction, design-function administrative techniques, decentralization, community control, voucher systems, business-based franchise systems, performance contracts and merit pay: none of these singly nor all of them together could eradicate the school as we know it. Some of these proposals can and a few will undoubtedly alter educational operations. Some can reduce the incidence of error in decision-making. Some can enrich the scope and quality of participation by all who are affected by educational processes. The leadership function can become lawful and fully supportive of teacher, student, supervisor, and administrator. School itself may become a process rather than a place only. But the institution will remain. It will be.

Brandwein[12] recently reported that in the preceding four years he had visited something more than 190 teachers in their classrooms. These were teachers who had attended National Science Foundation institutes or had become actively concerned with the then "new curriculum movement." He also interviewed some three hundred other teachers who had been similarly "exposed"

12. Paul F. Brandwein, *Notes Towards A General Theory of Teaching* (New York: Harcourt, Brace & World, 1966), pp. 4-5.

or "interested." From these visits and discussions Brandwein was led ". . . to suspect that *teaching through inquiry* per se has not necessarily been encouraged by the practices of these institutes; indeed, academic and summer institutes have encouraged *teaching through telling*—that is, through lecturing." How often before had those teachers listened to a lecture on the limitations of lecturing? How often had they sat, massed by the score in auditoriums, to learn about the virtues of small-group learning?

Orderly inquiry, free-ranging creativity, open-minded exploration: all of these we have warrant to believe even the youngest child brings to his encounters with the variety of experience. With whatever limitations of time, place, and condition, the child comes first to school with a lively mind and a skilled imagination. How to celebrate those possessions? How to enlarge those gifts? How to enrich those repertoires? These are the crucial questions to which the school, in the person of the teacher, must be ready to offer provisional answers.

Kubie in his unwisely neglected (by educators) little book, *Neurotic Distortion of the Creative Process,* suggests:

> . . . we do not need to be taught how to think; indeed this is something that cannot be taught. Thinking processes actually are automatic, swift, and spontaneous when allowed to proceed undisturbed by other influences. Therefore, what we need is to be educated in how not to interfere with the inherent capacity of the human mind to think. . . . Education will continue to perpetrate a fraud upon culture until it accepts the full implications of the fact that the free creative velocity of our thinking apparatus is continually being braked and driven off course by the play of unconscious forces."[13]

Kubie is not writing a defense of the "noble savage" within us. He is not reverting to some simpering romanticism that regards the child as a sacramental object. He is saying that we honor what is most humane in ourselves when we cherish and celebrate the child as a person. But again it must be warned that this is not the position of those unlamented proponents of "tender loving care," either. This is a tough-minded declaration in favor of health, of sanity. The child, any sentient child, is ready at some discernible level of awareness to participate in the grand existential adventure

---

13. Lawrence S. Kubie, *Neurotic Distortion of the Creative Process* (Lawrence, Kans.: University of Kansas Press, 1958), pp. 104-05.

that education seeks to be. Too quickly does he discover that he is caught in a shill game beside which the television set is an honest friend. And his teacher will enlist, for a stipend, in yet another curriculum workshop in search of ways to trade up his performance.

Several contributors to this yearbook offer definitions of "curriculum." None will be found to be in sharp disagreement either with his colleagues or with historical practice. Nor can any of us ignore the professional imperatives of the recent past. Curricular activities over the past quarter of a century have conferred such significance to the field that its practitioners must be forgiven if they see it as inclusive of all education. In fact, the term "pedagogy" has been disinterred and is being offered by some as the label for the supervening discipline within which all teaching and learning transactions can alone be properly considered.

It is a uniquely American practice to attempt to solve recalcitrant problems by collecting and merging disparate things. In the world of business, the conglomerate corporation is the most recent example of this impulse. It is a strange notion that simplicity, elegance, and efficiency can be achieved under the sign of the stewpot. A generalized taste never begets a sharp palate. There must be better ways to find out where we are so that we can decide where we might go.

However, it is not productive of anything but trivial commentary and superficial scholarship to enunciate curricular goals. The consequence is a collectivity of *post hoc* statements that assign meaning-by-collage to the record. It is more profitable to consider curricular consequences, though again one must be wary of assigning or imputing more logic to the production of "results" than that record will support.

In the sense that we are "exploiters of accidents" (see chapter *v*) American educators are artists, or self-deceivers. When something happens in the classroom or in a pilot program, or in some piece of "action research" that has a happy ending, or at least looks good at the moment of closure, we celebrate that event as our implicit, if unarticulated, intention. We really *did* mean to plan it that way. We got where we did because of the logic of events. We really do know where we are going.

Consider our "activist youth." We made them inadvertently what they are in the elementary and secondary classroom of the fifties and sixties. Remember "democratic problem-solving"? Remember the "group process"? Remember those human relations workshops, the get-smart-quick rat race to space superiority, and Project Talent? The teaching profession, at least in its secular aspect, eschews the teaching of values, which has never been—can never be—successful in practice. Remember the obscenities of the "McCarthy period" and California's "Year of the Oath"? Remember Owen Lattimore's *Ordeal by Slander?* Did we really believe that the children were not watching?

Every now and again, in those dark hours at convention's end, we talk of the "teacher as model." We remind ourselves that the "teacher teaches best what the teacher is." What have we been? I am not inviting an exercise in deprecation. On the contrary, the evidence is abundant that teachers practice more nobly than they preach. I am suggesting that we attend our central folk wisdom. We teach *within* our *paideia*. We teach out of our hidden curriculum. Thus, we respond, along with our students, our colleagues, and our fellow citizens, to the total culture, even as we contribute to its growth and decay. But teachers, I insist, and most especially those educators who manage the curriculum, need to be armed with a more active awareness of our cultural compulsives than most of us are.

With every "advance" of our technology, with each new evidence of environmental despoliation, with every social spasm, be it the "discovery" of racism in the polity, of poverty and malnutrition in slums and ghettos, of corruption in high office, a new distortion is introduced into our reading of our way of life. We teach that distortion far more surely than we teach quadratic equations or the fact that the Reconstruction period was not an utter disaster.

What I am suggesting is that there has been a long-growing revolution in the "hidden curriculum." Historically, the school has responded to the rest of society as though it were in fact "an outside world." In the United States, we have sought to make connections, "build bridges to the world of work," establish vocational curricula, devise programs that lead to the acquisition of marketable skills; but we have acted, as educators always have, on the belief that there is a separation between the institution of the school and all other institutions. This is true, even for the missionary schools, for street academies, for home-study programs, and for "Sesame Street."

*Revolution* is perhaps too precise a word to describe the phenomenon. It has no order, it is driven by no discernible ideology. It is not programmatic. It is commanded by no leadership. It is a kind of social tidal movement—or perhaps it can better be described as an ecological redistribution of institutional roles. If a motive force can be assigned to it, it is perhaps a growing sense that there are better ways than we now use to translate this nation's constructive social values into meliorative programs. It expresses an emerging public consciousness that our essential democratic ideals are sound and can indeed be incorporated into the workings of all our institutions so as to assure a practice that squares with those ideals.

This "revolution" surely had its origin in the early Progressive education period and in the social gospel of the late nineteenth century. It received new impetus through the social welfare legislation of the New Deal. It grew more slowly through the years of World War II. The G.I. Bill of Rights connected it at various levels with formal education. The short-lived Life Adjustment movement in the late forties and early fifties added a modest thrust. The spread of psychoanalysis and psychotherapy and their broad acceptability among larger segments of the middle class contributed to its momentum. The civil rights movement, the brief Kennedy years, the compulsive social meliorism of the Johnson administration, with its disorderly War on Poverty, added recruits from among the well-born young. And always the wars and threats of war during the past quarter of a century have kept clear the awful distinction between this nation's power for good and its differential employment.

In short, while schoolmen and their allies tinker with the curriculum, there is a rising tide of expectation that it is possible and desirable to rebuild the social order. Thus, George S. Counts's question of almost four decades ago is being answered affirmatively, with school being read as co-extensive with society itself. This "revolution" goes beyond the earlier critics of the school. Its bill of indictment is bitterly specific. Its language of complaint is maddeningly imprecise, but the burden of its demands is unequivocal.

This "revolution" is declaring that this nation has the power, the wit, the techniques, and the commitable talent to identify all social wrongs and to right them. It need only read its priorities aright. It need only acquire the courage to confess its failures and defeats. It need only regain its ancient energy to look upon this golden land of fair prospects and gently seize the fading but persistent opportunities. America, it says, can and must be good and just and beautiful. Now!

All of this is, of course, the language of high and fuzzy romance. It goes against the grain of practicality. It does not understand that the way to tomorrow is roundabout. A sense of tragedy is lacking. There is no recognition of the persistence of evil. There are old scores still to be settled. There are some ill-written contracts that must be honored. There are prudential reputations that have to be defended. This nation has been discharging its global responsibilities with some measure of honor and probity. It has successfully held the very survival of our species in trust since Hiroshima's awesome sacrifice. It did rebuild Europe. It has attended the dissolution of empires. It has nourished more than it has been forced to destroy.

But all of this is not a way to catalogue an answer. The "revolution" is saying, with many different voices, that that record is known and there is still something vital that is missing. America is both fact and symbol of all that is wrong and can be put right. In the sense that Athens was "the school of all Hellas," we have been the school for the modern world. We have taught what the best actions can be. We are deeply flawed in our own performance on our own expectations. For we are in and of the whole world now to a depth that no preceding nation ever was. Our youth are the brothers and sisters of the young in Moscow, Paris, London, Tokyo, Lagos, Cairo, and Peking, and a thousand nameable cities around the planet. They have a sense of Eden. They glimpse the City of Man. And we talk of a downturn of the gross national product, of Vietnamization, of the SALT talks, and we dump coffers full of nerve gas into our ocean's depths.

It is easy to confess guilt, and the *mea culpa* is the gentlest of all penance in its recital. But to define oneself as a nation or a man is to accept a terrifying burden. To declare, and to act upon the declaration, that we know what first things are and will put them first is to incur irrevocable duties that must be borne with an exhausting grace and must be shared by the enemy-brother that all men are.

Thus, all that we can say to the seventies is that some of us will be there, practicing far short of perfection whatever we have learned to do well. Some of us will resist, as prudential men must, the more extravagant plans, the less possible dreams of our colleagues. For none of us is ever very far from banality. We do not play very well the role of God's fool. We want some measure of ease in the rest of our time. Therefore, some of us will not participate in the rebuilding of the social order, or even of a single school. But a few will, and we will use them up without mercy.

So, let us talk of first things:

The single, most telling indictment of "mass education" is that educators allowed it to remain mass education long after its smothering wastefulness had been discovered for what it was. Its inertia is enormous. How can the mass be deflected and in what direction? How can mass education be converted to or replaced by universal education? And what should this universal education be?

We are talking about system changing and system building. We are concerned to find ways, means, time, energy, patience, and courage to re-create out of what we possess a new educational order. We must have inventories of our physical and human resources. We must build, in large part, with the materials and the manpower of the system we seek to replace, and maintain parts of the old system as we change it. We must assume the dangerously romantic obligation to change people even as we change structures, methods, and goals. We must begin by changing ourselves.

Herewith are some old provocative assertions:

1. The primary mission of education is to make sound citizens.
2. Such citizens are self-validated by the quality of the state they show themselves capable of creating. They must give evidence to each other that they are engaged in that enterprise.
3. The quality of that state is best displayed by the condition of life of the least fortunate, least endowed individual.
4. The quality of that state is enhanced to the degree that each citizen is free to follow a life-style peculiar to himself, limited, sometimes

severely, where it impinges upon or limits the life-styles of his fellow citizens.

5. Every citizen, except the severely brain-damaged, must possess a high minimum level of literacy, broadly defined as the ability to get, hold, record, transform, analyze, and transmit subjective and objective information. He should be able to deal with facts and values, know the differences and the relations between them.

6. Every citizen, through his formal education, must have learned how to learn. This is essential if he is to choose and pursue an initial career, be able to decide when to change it, and know how to go about doing so.

7. Every citizen must learn how to identify and tolerate ambiguity; he must have some ability to withstand and to learn from failure.

8. Every citizen must have the ability to understand and assume several social roles beyond that of his suffrage: son, father, follower, leader, worker, user, and critic.

9. All citizens must be capable and possess the will to perform various kinds of community and national service defined and assigned in terms of ability and competing responsibilities.

The preceding assertions are not an exhaustive list. The acquisition of amenities is assumed. So are the roles and peculiar rights of artists. The acceptance of the verities is implicit.

None of this is new. What is new is our conviction that all of this can be accepted as a collective goal for all children and youth. What is new is an awareness that mere talk about goals and priorities never leads to programs. What is new is the realization that beginnings have been made, some of them very long ago, and that we do have the resources and some considerable skill in their employment to realize increasing portions of that goal. What is required is a willingness to settle for small victories, to tolerate provisional defeats, but to persist in our search, our endless search for better roads from childhood to maturity.

# CHAPTER V

# Curriculum Development in Relation to Social and Intellectual Systems

JAMES B. MACDONALD

The development of the curriculum in the American public schools has been primarily a historical accident. Any description or statement of what the curriculum consists of is essentially a political and/or ethical document rather than a scientific or technical one. It is a statement which indicates the outcome of a very complex interaction of groups, pressures, and events which are most often sociopolitical in motivation and which result in decisions about what ought to be.

Too often, educators talk as if curriculum development were a completely rational-technical process based upon scientific and/or technical data abstracted from foundation areas (especially the behavioral sciences) and tested by educational research. This, of course, is only a statement of an ideal that some educators share. The danger in this rhetoric is that it fails to take into account that this ideal is essentially unfruitful in explaining how we got where we are or the developments taking place today.

When we say curriculum is a historical accident, it is not intended to suggest that there are no reasons for its existence. By calling it a historical accident we mean that it is the outcome of a very long and dynamically complex process of social involvement and interaction. It is not something that has been deliberately chosen and rationally developed for a specific purpose it is intended to serve.

Further, curriculum plans as political and/or ethical documents have been hammered out of a decision-making process that provides a prescription for a form of social action and not a set of principles and techniques in a scientific sense.

A notable illustration of the myth of scientific-technical curriculum development may be found in our concern for Progressive education. This myth has been fostered both by professional educators who have extolled its virtues and by those who have criticized its weaknesses. The relevance of the myth for curriculum planning is simply that both advocates and critics are somehow under the mistaken impression that a carefully engineered development of curriculum took place, is taking place, or can take place which made, is making, or will make the schools "progressive." There is really little evidence to suggest that the vast majority of American schools have ever been "progressive," nor are they moving in this direction. The danger of the myth rests in the tacit assumption that curriculum development is a result of some carefully engineered process like that which would have had to have taken place if the schools truly had become progressive.

A second illustrative misunderstanding deals with tacit assumptions about the process by which recent revisions of disciplines found their way into schools as "new" mathematics, science, and so forth. It is extremely easy to suggest that our subject matter was out of date, that we arrived at this decision by a rational consensus, that we commissioned discipline experts to rewrite materials and that we have proceeded to implement the new curricula. Unfortunately, this rational chain of simple links soon becomes so complicated that its value as explanation is highly doubtful.

It is, for example, historically reasonable to suggest that the Progressive era (in American society) began to run its course by World War II and had reached a low point by the McCarthy era in the early 1950s.[1] Also, the critics of the schools were out in full force after 1945. Further, after the launching of Sputnik the federal government began to make massive amounts of funds available to interested academicians and universities for curriculum revision. Many resulting revisions found their way into commercial hands, and the prospect of publishing a whole new series of textbooks for all subjects to sell for the use of every child in each classroom in

---

1. See, for example, Lawrence A. Cremin, *The Transformation of the Schools* (New York: Random House, Vintage Books, 1961).

each school in the land offered more than a minimal stimulus for the developmental process.

Within the schools themselves pressures were being felt. Administrators and teachers began to feel tremendous pressures to change what they were doing. Fads and competitive "developments" sprang up across the country and are continuing a gradual flow, working their way into every small crevice in each backwater school.

There is little doubt that great changes have been and are taking place. What is not often so apparent, however, is that the process of curriculum development has not been a simple rational one, but a complex political and ethical phenomena with a quality of rational-technical support.

Curriculum development, then, is a very complex and dynamic process. It is subject to historical tradition and tendencies, to diverse and sometimes contradicting cultural and social pressures, to the relation of institutional and social living in the schools, and to the personalities and characteristics of those involved in the development and implementation of curricula.

## The Goal of Curriculum Development

The process of curriculum development is oriented toward the goal of a systematic organization of available cultural beliefs, expressive symbols, and values. It includes selection from the total culture and the creation of a pattern of encounter which will maximize the authenticity of the material and the probability of its being internalized by learners.

As a system of ideas and beliefs it includes aspects of the cognitive world isolated by disciplines and/or subjects in terms of facts, information, generalizations, principles, laws, and the like. It also includes awareness of and facility in the use of expressive symbols such as art, music, and language. Further, it includes systems of value orientation(s) for action in the form of such things as modes of inquiry, seeking new knowledge, respecting the integrity and worth of individuals, being concerned for other peoples, using democratic procedures, and so forth. These have often been called goals.

The concepts of goals and/or objectives are misleading, however. There is a connotation implicit in these concepts of a transcendence of the social and personal aspects of the dynamics of living, a suggestion that goals exist prior to social and personal phenomena. This is misleading because cultural systems are substantive aspects of social and personality systems and evolve in a constant interaction shaped and influenced by the dynamics of structures and actions in all three areas (culture, society, and personality).

Thus, to consider the curriculum as outside the motivational contexts of broad social forces, including the social nexus of intellectual activity or the ongoing school social action contexts, or to consider the curriculum without reference to individual personality systems is to limit perspective to an almost meaningless extent. Cultural systems are not motivated systems. Only people as individuals or acting in consort in groups are motivated to act. If we wish to influence students in such a way that they will internalize certain aspects of the cultural system, we cannot exclude any of the three basic systems from consideration (cultural, social and personality), and we cannot consider any of the three outside of the context of the others.

## Social Influences on Curriculum Development

The major trend in curriculum development over the past decades has been directed toward the updating, revision, and replacement or development of subject matter for school programs. Generally, one might describe this trend as an effort to provide more and better structure in the disciplined learning experiences of students. This trend has been paralleled by a concern for greater efficiency and effectiveness in instructional processes illustrated by the increased use of technology in classrooms. In retrospect this development appears to be explainable as a rather reasoned revision and clarification of learning goals combined with a rational attempt to improve the effectiveness of teaching and learning. Indeed, there may be some merit in describing the outcomes in such a manner, but to attribute the actual developmental processes to such a simplistic format provides us with minimal understanding of what has been happening.

It should be clear to most knowledgeable and thoughtful observers of the American scene during the past twenty-five years, that any reforms in institutional settings, whether in education, occupations, churches, families, recreation, or whatever, are intricately related to multiple social pressures and set in the context of a general cultural ethos. Educational reform has emerged from a complex interaction of seemingly unrelated factors (in terms of linear rationality). Some of these will be noted in what follows.

Curriculum developments, for example, have been influenced by international factors. During the 1967–68 year this writer had the opportunity to work with a curriculum development group in England and visit with persons involved in a great many of the curriculum reform projects going on there, as well as to observe in many school settings. Comparing English trends with those in the United States suggests that the English school curriculum is in a process of "loosening" and becoming more varied and flexible. Curriculum development in the United States, on the other hand, involving, as it does, national projects and the developing national assessment, would more accurately be described as being in a "tightening" phase.

Examination of the historical emergence of the United States as the leader and defender of the free world, indeed in many ways as the nation which has picked up the declining British world commitment in the past twenty-five years, suggests at least that the international role or image that a nation takes on has some general influence in creating an ethos that contributes to the direction of institutional changes (in this case, curriculum development). Certainly it is not unreasonable to hypothesize from the foregoing historical data that our curriculm development projects were at least partially made possible by our role in the world and perhaps most specifically by our competition with Russia, symbolized by the American response to Sputnik.

On the national level we have witnessed the growth of violence, technologically fostered pollution, urban sprawl, racial strife, and disaffection of many of the young over the past few years. Furthermore, we have seen the federal government enter into the funding of local education in an unprecedented manner and have witnessed as well the tremendous growth of the education "industry."

Educators have been directly influenced by these broad social forces. Within colleges and universities the "experts" of knowledge have had unusual opportunities for funding and raising their salaries and for finding new prestige and promotion through participation in the curriculum development processes of the public schools. There is probably no aspect of recent curriculum reforms more unprecedented than the degree of involvement of members of academic disciplines in curriculum development.

The public school has been confronted with the appearance of a potentially serious competitor during the past few years. Private and parochial schools, of course, are still active and numerous, but the formal federal sanction of industrial concerns in such acts as letting contracts, for example, to industries for running the Job Corps is a development of far greater potential import for education. Similar occurrences in the development of national commercially run chains of nursery schools are also just beginning. What these things mean to education and specifically to the development of curriculum are presently unknown. It is not difficult to surmise, however, that should these developments continue and grow in magnitude another social influence of considerable import will be added to the list of already complex pressures on curriculum development. It is difficult to see how such developments dependent on a profit motive can contribute to anything but the general technological ethos in education.

School systems in many areas, perhaps those serving as many as 70 percent of our young, have grown into large bureaucracies. With bureaucratization has come predictable centralization, specialization, rationalization, depersonalization, and loss of participation. Reactions to this may be noted in the reemergence of local control and the community school, most notably, but not only, in black areas of cities.

The influence of bureaucratization on curriculum development cannot be easily explicated. Yet growing alienation of teachers and pupils as well as local communities from "the curriculum" is apparent in many urban schools. Thus, in an era of social centralization and national large-scale development of curricula, the cry for relevance and the alienation of participants in the instructional process seem to be emerging as concomitant developments. As to the relationship between the two phenomena, we can only guess.

It does seem clear, however, that the educational bureaucracy has often entered into reform as a way of maintaining its own stability. Thus, as pressures have grown, the adoption of new curricula, new organizational schemes, etc., have taken on almost a "fad" characteristic. This phenomenon one might reasonably presume is not clearly related to rational curriculum development processes, but primarily to bureaucratic social adjustments to broader social pressures.

Classrooms take on qualities of the bureaucracy if for no other reason than the general climate of the school and the phenomenon of record-keeping. But beyond this, the classroom as a social living unit of the school is subject to influences that may sometimes preempt the best curriculum development procedures. Consider for a moment the generally cool or negative reaction of youth to authority figures in our society. Teachers are not "pigs" but may often be "goats."

The peer group, under the pressure of a mass media and an advertising aura, concerned about sex and bathed by media nudity, initiated into drugs, and encouraged by the still prevalent anti-intellectualism embodied in many of our American attitudes, can create an awesome barrier to learning.

A clear example of how broad social forces may undercut the good intentions of teachers and curriculum workers may be inferred from a careful analysis of television advertising. Absurd and sometimes obviously misleading "pitches" abound. But more disastrously the major effect is to create a kind of impulse buying. The young are bombarded with expensive and carefully developed ads which represent an investment of far greater effort, skill, and financial resources per minute of time than we have in classrooms. One major goal of schooling, the development of thoughtful and rational human beings, is thus continually undermined by highly influential mass media procedures. This does not provide the kind of social reinforcement necessary to help teachers, and this is especially so for youngsters coming from homes where parental behavior reflects the same impulsivity and immediateness of activity.

Social influences, then, have played (and continue to play) a crucial role in curriculum development. When one enumerates just those few discussed above—the competition with Russia; the social crisis of alienation from self, others, and the environment; federal funding; opening new commercial vistas; the new career opportunities for academicians; and the social response of bureaucracies —one begins to appreciate some of the complexities of the processes.

In the end, then, curriculum development is interwoven throughout in some crazy-quilt pattern by social forces from the broader social contexts, from forces within the school setting, and by processes in local communities.

## Intellectual Influences

### TECHNOLOGICAL RATIONALITY AND CULTURAL REACTION

Intellectual influences are part of their social settings. Yet the developing culture seems at times to take on a kind of symbolic life of its own. At least some influences on curriculum development are more easily discussed in terms of culture than of society. Four kinds of intellectual influences will be discussed here: (a) the developing broad cultural ethos; (b) ideas gained from what are called foundation areas for education; (c) developments in the substantive disciplines of content; and (d) ideas generated primarily from within the task orientation of curriculum development.

The prevailing intellectual ethos of our society is that of technological rationality. America has long been noted by anthropologists as a "doing" culture.[2] This is becoming more and more clear with the upward spiral of our industrial and electronic mode of existence. The Seabees[3] of World War II, the only arm of the services to originate at that time, epitomized this ethos with their motto: Can Do.

The important point to make is that it is not just the existence of computers, television, etc., as technology that we are concerned about, but, more importantly, (a) the pervading rationality which enters into the way we perceive ourselves, others, the environment, and (b) our orientation to existence. There is no necessary one-to-one correlation between technology as artifacts and technological rationality, although the connection is obvious. Neither is it clearly demonstrable that science and the scientific method are forerunners of technology, since technical objects and operations may well have preceded what we would call science (or at least coexisted with it).

2. In contrast to what anthropologist Florence Kluckholm and others have called "being" and "becoming" cultures.

3. Naval Construction Battalions.

Nevertheless, the present "objective"[4] aura of man's social existence has emerged from a cultural ethos out of these myriad influences and has projected a prevailing intellectual approach to tasks throughout most areas of our life. This intellectual orientation is in fact so pervasive an influence encountered so early that it is taken to be almost the "natural" way of thinking about the world for many Americans and Western Europeans.

Essentially it is a process of objectifying all phenomena, abstracting from reality some bit of matter, event, or behavior and manipulating reality as if this objective part of it were all there were. At a more sophisticated level it conceives of the world as a potentially finite set of causal relations. It is essentially the creation of "closed" systems which work in terms of certain predefined goals.

Marcuse,[5] for example, has dealt critically and at length with technological rationality and has counterposed what he calls "aesthetic rationality" as an antidote for restoring the completely human process in society. However much one agrees or disagrees with Marcuse's assessment of the destructiveness of technological rationality for human values, it is surely fair to say that the ethos of this form of rationality may be observed in curriculum development processes and has greatly influenced educational change.

Broad social reaction to this ethos may be seen in what Roszak has called the "counter culture."[6] According to Roszak some of our young are beginning to create an alternative culture which restores to social living a fuller participation of human potential in relationship to self, others, and the environment. Elements of this culture may be seen variously in the emphasis upon mystical experience, the attempt to enlarge perceptual awareness, aesthetic communion, communal living, the "cop out" and dropout problems, and university unrest.

It is clearly too soon to define the dimensions of this cultural reaction or to identify the more productive and useful means for realizing it. Yet the existence of large numbers of young people, and especially those who could "make it in the system," who are

4. See, for example, Everett Knight, *The Objective Society* (New York: George Braziller, 1960).

5. Herbert Marcuse, *One Dimensional Man* (Boston: Beacon Press, 1964).

6. Theodore Roszak, *The Making of a Counter Culture* (Garden City, N.Y.: Doubleday & Co., Anchor Books, 1969).

struggling to create a life which they believe cannot be fulfilled by our technological society is some confirmation of the difficulties being created by a technocratic society.

## FOUNDATIONS OF EDUCATION

Anthropology, sociology, philosophy, history, and psychology (along with other disciplines) have long held a foundational relationship to curriculum development as intellectual influences upon educators. Indeed, even a partial list of curriculum projects during the past ten or so years clearly demonstrates an increasingly sophisticated application of ideas drawn from these disciplines.

Anthropology, for example, may be loosely credited with providing source material for dealing with curriculum developments relating to subcultural language patterns that have heavily influenced the teaching of reading, the "hidden dimensions"[7] of use of time and space, and the general influence of values upon motivation, perception, and development of social needs.

Sociological data have provided a useful awareness of the influence of poverty, social class, and ethnic and racial factors on school learning. The building of group identity through "black studies" is one example of what may loosely be labeled sociological influences upon curriculum development.

It is clear, however, that foundation-area ideas do not always come in pure discipline forms and, further, that the major discipline which has absorbed ideas and contributed them to curriculum development is that of psychology.

We might even go so far as to say that no curriculum development project is "respectable" today without some careful accounting for the ideas stimulated by and often attributed to Piaget.[8] At very least, curriculum developers seem compelled to account for the phenomena of cognitive growth in some reasonable and acceptable manner when they consider curriculum development.

Learning theory and/or research has also become a more powerful intellectual influence. This is especially noticeable in the "behaviorist" orientation found in programs which are based upon

7. See Edward T. Hall, *The Hidden Dimension* (Doubleday & Co., 1966) for a general analysis of cross-cultural use of time and space.

8. See, for example, the works of Jean Piaget, or for an overview of implications of Piaget's thought, J. H. Flavell, *The Developmental Psychology of Jean Piaget* (New York: Van Nostrand Co., 1963).

behavior modification techniques and reinforcement theory, as well as in structures in programmed learning and autotelic environments for stimulus control.

Most persons would agree that the single most influential figure in curriculum development over the past ten years has been the psychologist Jerome Bruner.[9] Bruner, operating with a sometime Deweyan philosophy, a cognitive growth orientation, and an intellectual approach to curriculum, has come closest to validating the "great man" theory of history in this area.

Child development (and psychology) has had major impact upon curriculum if for no other reason than the emergence of Head Start programs. Again, it is evident that the "time" had to be ripe for these developments and major social pressures concomitant with them, but the child development field with emphasis upon language and cognitive development in general has had a tremendous intellectual influence upon recent innovations in curriculum.

In many ways it is unfortunate that psychology has taken the lead (or was more able to contribute at this time). As Huebner, for example, has so ably noted, there are grave problems which arise when the educational process becomes thoroughly psychologized in its intellectual foundations.[10] This is probably a fair indictment of education in that the major impetus for curriculum development growing from the foundation areas seems to have found its point of entry through psychologically shaped applications.

What this reflects rather precisely in most instances is a general acceptance of the broad cultural-intellectual ethos of technological rationality in the idea-orientation of the foundations of education as they become applied through psychological concepts.

### THE SUBSTANTIVE DISCIPLINES

Academicians have been anything but quiescent during the recent spasm of curriculum development. The renewal of the academic interest in school programs has brought about a number of interestingly cogent observations on their part, and a flurry of

9. See, for example, *The Process of Education* (Cambridge: Harvard University Press, 1960) as the seminal contribution of Bruner to curriculum development.

10. Dwayne Huebner, "Implications of Psychological Thought for the Curriculum" in *Influences in Curriculum Change,* Association for Supervision and Curriculum Development (Washington: National Education Association, 1968).

activity by some of them is notable. Perhaps the three most relevant circumstances central to the activity by those in the substantive disciplines were (a) the rapid growth of knowledge, (b) the revision of concepts in the disciplines, and (c) the growing awareness of the misrepresentation in and outdatedness of discipline content in the public school curriculum. These circumstances combined with previously mentioned social factors and the psychological shift toward emphasis upon cognitive growth provided a platform for considerable substantive curriculum reform.

The knowledge "explosion" has been noted for many years as one of the phenomena of the twentieth century. The implications of this reality for curriculum development have become more and more apparent in recent years. Given the limitation of time available for schooling and a social commitment to general education, critical curriculum decisions have been forced upon the schools. If knowledge was doubling every five to ten years, then how could the schools possibly keep up with a coverage of it?

The answer lay in the revision of the disciplines in terms of identification of their basic structures, key ideas, or fundamental generalizations as focal points for curriculum development and in greater emphasis on their syntax or modes of inquiry. Revisions of content thus moved toward identifying fundamental inquiry processes, critical elements of content, and points of interrelatedness between disciplines.

In the rush to develop and market new curricula, many fundamental issues have been submerged. By and large, basic assumptions which have plagued education, such as the one which limits curriculum to cognitive content areas alone, have been unexamined. The whole trend appears primarily to share in the general technical ethos and may be phrased as "teaching more disciplined and authentic knowledge earlier, faster, and better."

### PROFESSIONAL EDUCATORS

The experts in curriculum development, though sometimes bypassed in recent years by the subject specialists, have also provided intellectual tools for curriculum developers. Perhaps the most notable contributions have been (a) the "Tyler" rationale,[11] (b)

---

11. Ralph W. Tyler, *Principles of Curriculum and Instruction* (Chicago: University of Chicago Press, 1950).

the taxonomy of educational objectives,[12] and (c) behavioral objectives.[13] These developments also reflect the general technical-intellectual ethos of our times.

The taxonomy of educational objectives has provided a grid for locating the kinds of goals within any substantive area. The Tyler rationale—(a) stating objectives, (b) selecting experiences, (c) organizing experiences, and (d) evaluating experiences—provides an intellectual phase analysis for a curriculum of the learning cycle which can carry out the fulfillment of objectives. This has been extended by many from the original statement to the specification of objectives in highly specific behavioral terms rather than in terms of the more generalized behavior in the original.

Given these tools, connected now with content revision by academicians, placed in a psychological nexus of new findings relevant to the cognitive growth of children, and stimulated by the urgency of social and political influences growing out of the urban military-industrial bureaucratic complex, one has a complete chain of curriculum development links from general to specific events.

To claim that these series of intellectual and social factors have been a highly rational planned set of events is patently ridiculous but, on the other hand, highly predictable with hindsight when one understands the cultural technical ethos within which the developments at all levels lie.

## Social and Intellectual Stirrings

The picture is not, however, all "bad" or all "good," which ever the case may be, for a general social and intellectual stirring which may be noted at all points on the line (from broad social issues to specific curriculum developments) is unquestionably afoot.

Neither society nor academicians nor curriculum developers have escaped the impact of existential movements in the general ethos, specific disciplines, or school settings. The Age of Aquarius, whether "hairy" or not, must be reckoned with. The anguished cry for quality in existence, perhaps at the sacrifice of quantity, for justice in social living, and for moral concern is present everywhere.

12. Benjamin Bloom et al., *The Taxonomy of Educational Objectives: Cognitive Domain* (New York: David McKay Co., 1956).

13. J. Popham, *The Teacher Empiricist* (Los Angeles: Aegus Press, 1965).

Curriculum developments have begun to be concerned with the affective domain and with the quality of living in school settings. Movements toward reconsideration of who makes curriculum decisions and what curricula are most relevant for what groups may be noted in many places.

The problem of "cultural pluralism and education"[14] is rapidly coming to be a key issue, at least in our urban areas. With the growth of a mass technological society, the local community has lost much of its intermediary protective function of the individual. This is reflected in the area of curriculum development in terms of the expert-developed national curriculum projects, national assessment, and the increasing activity of national-scope commercial firms in producing curriculum materials. This has meant in effect that the student (as a person or as a member of some racial or ethnic group) is becoming not only more and more subject to the direct influence of mass media and broad social forces, but also more directly subject to the cultural content of a curriculum developed outside the context or at least without the screening of intermediaries such as the community and its local school system.

The issue reflects a much deeper cultural crisis than simply increasing the efficiency, effectiveness, and authenticity of the teaching of a body of school subject matter. Subject matter is an integral part of the total culture and not a separate "objective," a free-floating set of ideas, expressive symbols, and values. The processes of curriculum development and schooling in toto participate in the general interactive dynamics of our cultural ethos.

What lies before us in curriculum development as we enter the 1970s is no less than what we are encountering in our general culture crisis, only focused on a specific problem. It is in essence a moral-value dilemma created by the growing awareness of the impact of our mass technological society upon the individual and his community.

The community school movements and their interest in the local participation in the development of curriculum have already emerged as reactions to these centralized trends. Although, as in the case of all curriculum developments, the community school

14. See E. G. Seymour and W. Itzkoff, *Cultural Pluralism and American Education* (Scranton, Pa.: International Textbook Co., 1969) for an overview of this problem.

movement has deeper and broader concerns than curriculum, it has entered curriculum development most notably through such things as "black studies." In essence, what is being said is that the cultural content of the curriculum should reflect a pluralistic cultural value position, and that local cultural variation is a relevant consideration in the selection and organization of content in the curriculum.

Movements within the profession to humanize educational processes have also been growing. Recent publications of such organizations as the Association for Supervision and Curriculum Development[15] and journals like the *National Elementary Principal*[16] reflect the discomfort many professionals feel with the major trends of our time in curriculum development and school organization. Although such professional reactions have a history which sometimes borders upon sentimentality, it would appear that the infusion of such data as those from ego and self-psychology, concerns for aesthetic qualities of existence, and growing realization of the reflection of broad moral concerns in school practices have contributed to a renewal of "harder" positions.

Academicians, by and large, have not been prone to examine the nature of the knowledge they are concerned about. Recent developments may stimulate this concern and have important influences upon future curriculum developments.

What many persons apparently thought was a rather straightforward job of organizing and presenting *what we know* is being challenged by many thoughtful persons.

Polanyi[17] has made a clear case for the personal element in knowledge. His "tacit dimension" has exciting possibilities for developing our understanding of the nature of knowledge and rather fundamental potential implications for curriculum development. According to Polanyi "we know more than we can tell" and it is what we cannot tell that is fundamental to the acquisition of new knowledge. This tacit knowledge can only be known *after* we have experienced new performances from which we may then

15. See, e.g., *Humanizing the Secondary School* (Washington: the Association, 1969).

16. The September 1969 and November 1969 issues are devoted to the theme, Humanizing the Elementary School.

17. See, for example, Michael Polanyi, *The Tacit Dimension* (Garden City, N.Y.: Doubleday & Co., Anchor Books, 1967).

infer what we must have known but that we could not tell prior to that time. The principle involved is roughly that whenever we are conscious of something (know it), it is our tacit knowing which will make sense of it in terms of our immediate experiences.

In effect, then, if Polanyi is correct the whole problem of tacit knowing introduces a rather dramatic set of questions into problems of sequence in various fields or, even more fundamental, into basic tacit knowledge underlying academic achievement.

Intellectual developments in physics, mathematics, and biology[18] also raise questions which may well produce effects upon the way we develop curriculum. Thus, for example, the principle of uncertainty which posits that "the more accurately we measure one variable, the less accurately we are able to define a related variable" provides some basis for humility for absolutists. If one considers this, together with the relativity of observers in time and space and the awareness of the disturbance of nature through the process of observing and the interaction of persons, objective "knowledge out there" becomes much more complicated than simply mastering reality.

The recognition of complimentarity of mutually exclusive explanations of phenomena (wave and particle) made possible by the work of Niels Bohr is further evidence of a movement away from the mechanistic-technical conception of reality. Thus, in some of our most advanced fields of knowledge we are now able to accept two mutually exclusive frames of reference as two sides of the same coin.

Essentially, intellectual developments in the sciences have dramatically reaffirmed the role of humanity in the creation of knowledge. In this sense, the sciences are now outdistancing technology, whose paradigm is still a mechanistic one; and it is perhaps this growing awareness more than anything else which highlights the danger of the human one-sidedness of technological rationality. How these developments will influence curriculum is not clear.

In a rather loose and tenuous way the kinds of social and intellectual stirrings indicated above have a common relationship. Each in its own way and area of concern has reawakened men to the

18. See, for example, Floyd Matson, *The Broken Image* (Garden City, N.Y.: Doubleday & Co., Anchor Books, 1964) and Jacob Bronowski, *The Common Sense of Science* (Cambridge: Harvard University Press, 1953).

subjective-objective relationship of reality and knowledge, to the partnership of the "inwardness" of the person and the outthereness" of observed phenomena. This reawakening could be the harbinger of some very dramatic and humanly eventful social stirrings and, in turn, of curriculum developments.

## The Challenge Ahead

Cultural pluralism in curriculum development is in many ways a truer reflection of the reality of how curriculum development takes place than are the broad-scale technical planning efforts. It does not fall into the acceptance of the myth of rational control of social and intellectual forces which influence development. Further, it preserves at least on the surface a community mediation and participation which touches some of our deepest democratic value commitments. Yet its potential for parochialism and narrowness is apparent and inherent in the very nature of its conception.

The challenge ahead would appear to lie in the resolution of the conflict between mass curricula and the concomitant powerlessness, alienation, and potential irrelevance to individuals and groups which accompany it, and, in the development of planning procedures which preserve the integrity of cultural growth as well as the personal and group participation which creates a specific motivational nexus for learning and living.

It would seem impossible to do this without some conception of a series of participant levels of "planned happenings." By this process curriculum developments would need to filter through levels where rational-technical planning would provide broad frameworks within which the next lower level, guided by the prior environmental structuring, could have a "planned happening" which in turn would become structured for the next level to have its "happening." It is only by some process similar to this that the entrance into curriculum development of both technological *and* aesthetic rationality could take place. Further, it is only by some process similar to this that even minimal integrity of content, persons, and groups can be maintained.

The challenge thus becomes one of taking curriculum development out of the "accidental" category and introducing some form of general rational input into planning, but maintaining the participation and integrity of the persons and groups involved.

The enlargement of the general trend toward technological rationality alone, as we have seen its emerging procedures in curriculum development, will not suffice. It will be no more than a shadow and will make a mockery of the complexity of social and intellectual influences which impinge upon the curriculum. Its logical outcome can only be a further estrangement of the school from the total culture. Yet the need to preserve curriculum development from parochial chaos while still preserving the meaningful participation of needed persons and groups will continue to be the great challenge.

# CHAPTER VI

# Democratic Values and Educational Goals

H . S . B R O U D Y

## Introduction

The theme of this chapter in the yearbook, the role of democratic values in the shaping of educational goals, subdivides
itself into two major questions: What are the democratic values,
and how are they to be construed in our time? and, How do democratic values shape the goals of education? A host of subquestions
could be raised about such terms as "values" and "educational
goals" and their relation to "democratic values." Surely no short
essay can hope to discuss these topics with any pretense of com-
pleteness or adequacy. This chapter will, therefore, concentrate
on the thesis that several and not always compatible concepts of
democracy have shaped educational goals. It will be argued that
if democratic values are to serve this function effectively today, they
must be construed so as to be appropriate to a modern technologically dominated mass society.[1]

A few preliminary distinctions may be in order. Educational goals
can refer to the aims and aspirations of the society as a whole, viz.,
its ethos, as when we speak of the "aims of the American people,"

1. This theme has been discussed voluminously. The literature on mass society
is too famiiar and too vast to cite, but much of the following discussion utilizes
views to be found in Karl Mannheim's *Man and Society in an Age of Reconstruc-
tion* (New York: Harcourt, Brace & World, 1940); C. Wright Mills's *Power Elite*
(New York: Oxford University Press, 1959); and W. O. Stanley's *Education as
Social Integration* (New York: Teachers College, Columbia University, 1953).
See also Philip Olson, ed., *America as a Mass Society* (New York: Free Press of
Glencoe, 1963); Solon T. Kimball and James E. McClellan, *Education in the
New America* (New York: Random House, 1962); Willis Rudy, *Schools in an
Age of Mass Culture* (Englewood Cliffs, N.J.: Prentice-Hall, 1965); *Social Forces
Influencing American Education,* Sixtieth Yearbook of the National Society for
the Study of Education, Part II (Chicago: University of Chicago Press, 1961).

or it can refer to outcomes of formal schooling. Although the first meaning of educational goals can scarcely be avoided, the main stress will be on the second and more restricted meaning, viz., the goals of schools. To confuse these meanings is to exacerbate the Babel into which much of the discussion of value education and education for democracy has degenerated.

It is also important to distinguish the rhetoric of democracy, i.e., the verbalized ideals of a democratic society as found in the Declaration of Independence, the Bill of Rights, the United States Constitution, in school textbooks, and in the ordinary speech of the citizenry, from the policies and practices that exemplify these ideas. It will be argued that the rhetoric of democracy, as exercised even today in the press and the classroom, is that of eighteenth-century liberal political theory. That was a rhetoric consonant with the doctrines of natural rights, with the belief that progress, prosperity, and happiness were best assured by a maximum of freedom for each individual in the commonwealth. But it was a rhetoric that also presupposed a contractual relationship between citizens and their government as well as with each other, a covenant entered into freely, in good faith and with goodwill.[2] To what extent does the social reality of our time conform to these presuppositions? I think it is fair to say that although vestiges of eighteenth- and nineteenth-century conditions can be found here and there in our society, for the most part they are no longer the salient characteristics of that society. Their presence in the rhetoric and virtual disappearance from the reality is in no small part responsible for our "problem."

Yet, the longing after the qualities of life connoted by liberal democracy is still strong. It manifests itself in many ways. We try desperately to break up the megalopolis into small face-to-face groups; we try pathetically to "relate" to each other; we try to decentralize; we try to find redemption in bizarre deviations from conformity—if not in morals, then at least in manners. We try— or at least the young, the poor, and the assorted disadvantaged ones try—to force or shame establishments of one kind or another

2. The contractual relationships involved in the concepts of capitalism and democracy, according to P. A. Sorokin, lose their basic presuppositions in the degenerate phase of a sensate culture. *The Crisis of Our Age* (New York: E. P. Dutton & Co., 1941), pp. 170 ff.

to live up to the rhetoric of democracy they profess. But if, as so many students of society aver, this rhetoric no longer presents a true image of America or democrary, then are we doing our children or the country or anyone else a service in using the schools to ritualize a myth? This inquiry, therefore, can be regarded as a search for meanings of democratic values that are not mythical and for a possibility of using them educationally, not merely ritualistically.

## What Are Democratic Values?

How is a democratic society to be distinguished from other kinds? What are the characteristics of the democratic values? These queries are of some pedagogical importance because virtually all modern societies claim to be democratic and values are called democratic for a number of reasons.

Can we distinguish, let us say, the United States's political philosophy from that of Soviet Russia or Communist China or Rhodesia by the things that their respective populations crave? I doubt it. The physiological needs are about the same; so are their needs for security, physical and emotional. Their needs and desires for self-realization, for self-determination, for some sort of self-integration are not significantly different from each other.[3] Nor do they differ in their desires for social justice. At this level of generality, it makes sense to speak of "man," "mankind," and the "humanity of man."[4]

Differentiating characteristics begin to emerge when we ask about the decision-making procedures of democratic and nondemocratic societies and the attitudes toward these procedures.

For example, the almost spontaneous response in a democratic society in a decidable situation that involves a diversity of interests

3. The same point is brought out by Matson commenting on Lasswell's democratic values: power, respect, affection, rectitude, well-being, wealth, skill, enlightenment. "The most striking thing about this workable list of democratic values is that they are in no discernible sense democratic; they are the 'preferred events' of men everywhere." Floyd W. Matson, *The Broken Image* (New York: George Braziller, 1964), p. 111.

4. I recall frequently and vividly being marooned for several days with about a score of truck drivers, a bus load of tourists, and a small contingent of automobilists on a rise of land surrounded by flood waters. In a few hours the common predicament reduced us all to our human commonalities and plunged us into mutual aid, a state that did not last more than a few minutes after we had been "rescued" and restored to "civilization."

is that all those whose interests are affected should have a voice—usually an equal voice—in influencing the decision. I am not at all sure that Soviet or Communist China citizens "feel" this way. On the contrary, they are told that only the leaders of the Party have a right to make some decisions. Much of the theoretical efforts of Lenin and Stalin were expended in convincing the Russian people and the world that the dictatorship of the proletariat was a necessary phase of the Communist revolution. This would justify denying—until the Revolution was no longer menaced by reactionaries, foreign and domestic—to all the citizens the right to participate in decisions affecting them. In many situations, to be sure, the principle of democracy was to apply, e.g., in the local soviets, but in principle as well as in practice the Party, not the people as a whole or even their elected representatives, had a superior claim in the decision-making process. One can be sure that the Russian educational apparatus would be expected to turn these principles into reliable attitudes on the parts of the citizenry.[5]

That these outcomes are attitudes and habits is of central importance. Most Americans learn them just as they learn the skills involved in baseball, football, going to the movies, and buying things in the supermarket. They are folkways, as indeed they must be if they are to be effective social forces. In this sense American education (formal and informal) must be judged successful; our citizens not only "know" but "feel" the forms of decision-making appropriate to democracy and feel guilty about not using them.

As William Graham Sumner would have it, folkways when infected with the notion of public weal take on ethical import. They are turned into mores, the violation of which subjects the offender to blame and punishment. In our culture the forms of democratic decision-making have acquired such ethical overtones, so that politicians, however cynical, dread the charge that they have violated important mores. To deny the citizen a chance to voice his opinion in debate and/or to vote is prima facie bad, even though this denial could not under any conceivable circumstances have affected the outcome. The burden of justifying the

5. Cf. George Z. Bereday and Bonnie B. Stretch, "Political Education in the U.S.A. and the U.S.S.R.", *Comparative Education Review* 6 (1963): 9-16.

denial falls on the denyer, and the reasons have to be strong and overriding to allay the general disapproval.[6]

One ingredient of these attitudes and habits is knowledge about decision-making procedures, i.e., the machinery of government. It is fashionable to downgrade the teaching of these formal democratic procedures. The argument has two prongs. One is that knowledge about the machinery is no guarantee of its use. The other is that these forms conceal the actual decision-making processes that go on in smoke-filled rooms and air-conditioned lobbies of legislative chambers. The argument is sound in stressing that the forms are of little use if the substance and spirit are ignored. It is even sounder if these forms are no longer able to articulate the spirit and the substance of democratic decision-making.

But the argument mistakenly assumes that we teach about the democratic machinery of government without a commitment to the beliefs that make up the democratic value cluster. The allegiance to voting and debate as participatory forms would not long survive if their connection with certain beliefs about the self, human good, and justice were severed completely. Just as it is difficult to imagine forms wholly devoid of content, so is it difficult to think of content without form. So far as linguistic behavior is concerned, schooling for democracy is an attempt to teach the criteria for its proper application.

The democratic attitude contains more than knowing the democratic thing to do. As well as strong pro feelings about doing the democratic thing in relevant situations, we must include the habits of thinking and acting that make up an attitude, i.e., what some psychologists call an "incipient action." A democratic society is made up of a population which, by and large, has formed these habits firmly enough so that they not only function in the appropriate situations almost semiautomatically, but also seek out situations for which they are appropriate.[7]

Finally, it is sometimes argued that one can differentiate a democratic society from others in terms of beliefs about man in general and especially about the standards of right and wrong, good and

6. See W. D. Ross, *The Right and the Good* (Oxford: Clarendon Press, 1930) on the notion of prima facie duties as fundamental to ethical theory.

7. On this dynamic nature of habit, see John Dewey, *Human Nature and Conduct* (New York: Holt, Rinehart & Winston, 1922).

evil (the moral norms), by which the democratic attitudes and procedures are justified. The conceptual strands that comprise the democratic ideology are too snarled to disentangle here; it is approximately what Gunnar Myrdal in *An American Dilemma* called the American creed. This creed, which Myrdal regarded as unique to the United States, is composed of generalizations at various levels. At the highest level they constitute the ideals of democracy. For convenience one might think of them as conceptions of liberty, equality, and fraternity, to borrow the slogans of a famous revolution. However, at the levels of legislation and personal commitment, these generalizations are interpreted differently by conservatives and liberals, the rich and the poor, the pushers of one interest as against the backers of another.

As slogans, the concepts of liberty, equality, and fraternity unite the American people; controversy and conflict are reserved for their implementation. This difference between rallying slogans and prescriptions for action operates at the international level as well. For all civilized societies—or at least all modern ones—claim that only under their particular form of government can the citizens realize the maximum of liberty, equality, and fraternity, not to speak of prosperity and glory. The slogans of democracy do not differentiate a democratic society from any other. Clearly, therefore, when education claims to aim at democracy, it cannot stop at the slogan level of the concepts involved. It has to descend or ascend, if you like, to their interpretation by the conflicting parties as applied to the social issues of the day. The temptation is to stay at the storm-free level of slogans, but a curriculum which does so invites the question as to whether it is worth bothering with at all.[8]

8. In recent years, much has been written about slogans in educational thinking. An outgrowth of the emphasis on the analysis of ordinary language in philosophy, the distinction between prescriptions and descriptions is now commonplace. Many famous educational aims, e.g., "education is growth," or "democracy," do not describe matters of fact, but rather give verbal form to wishes and aspirations. They do not describe what schools do, but rather name vague states of feeling or character or societal conditions toward which we are supposed to have positive feelings. For a sample of a fairly voluminous literature on this topic, see "The Logic of Slogans" by B. Paul Komisar and James E. McClellan in *Language and Concepts in Education,* ed. B. Othanel Smith and Robert H. Ennis (Chicago: Rand McNally & Co., 1961). Put in other words, slogans are utterances that do something as well as describe the aspirations of the speaker. Among the things they do is to exhort or persuade the listener to feel as does the speaker. For a recent discussion of this well worked over topic, see J. Vuilleman, "Expressive Statements" and "Expressives, Descriptives, Performatives" by A. I. Melden in *Philosophy and Phenomenological Research* 29 (1969): 485-505.

To go beyond the rhetoric to the changes in the interpretation of the key concepts of democracy and testing their congruence or lack of it with social reality poses difficulties for the school. For one thing, it involves the school in controversy; for another, it makes exorbitant demands on the intellectual resources of classroom teachers.

What follows will confine itself pretty largely to the interpretations of the trinity of concepts—liberty, equality, and fraternity— that characterize the democratic ethos, largely because these are the justifications for the more specific attitudes and habits by which the ethos is manifested.

## Changes in the Concept of Democracy

What have been the basic changes in the concept of democracy? What have been the basic alterations in the interpretation of liberty, equality, and fraternity? Liberty can be considered in its economic, political, moral, intellectual, and religious aspects and so can equality and fraternity. Volumes could be written on the diverse interpretations of these three key concepts in these various aspects, and obviously I have neither the space nor the competence even to sketch such a development. At best we can try to illustrate a few changes in interpretation which have influenced educational goals.

Take, for example, the notion of liberty. Economically, liberty to the Founding Fathers meant the free competition of individual workers or entrepreneurs in an open market controlled by the automatic and invisible wisdom of supply and demand; the state should intervene only to keep the rules of the competition fair.

As Adolf A. Berle put it in a recent article:

The self-interest of men levering against each other and controlling each other through competition resulted in a splendid ethical balance wheel, which was the open market. This leveled out inequalities, eliminated the inefficient, and through competition prevented an undue concentration of power.[9]

The *Encyclopedia Britannica* defines liberalism as the creed, philosophy, and movement which is committed to freedom as a method and policy in government, as an organizing principle

9. "Second Edition/Corporate Power," *Center Magazine* 2 (January 1969): 76.

in society, and as a way of life for the individual and the community.

So it was in its 17th century beginnings, 18th century revolutionary triumphs, and in its 19th century consolidation as the dominant political order of the West. But by the turn of our own century, it was clear that Adam Smith's invisible hand, which was presumed to set human affairs aright if all were guaranteed freedom of thought and economic action, had disappeared in the smoke of the urbanizing Industrial Revolution. In an increasingly complex society free men could starve, and properly endowed democrats could founder in political impotence.[10]

Politically, freedom was defined by the Bill of Rights, by the procedures for electing officials of one kind or another, and by voting on legislative proposals. It was assumed that all potential voters had about the same opportunity to know the issues and how they would be affected by the outcome of the vote. Morally, man was free in that he could make many decisions despite certain limitations of nature and nurture, in that he could determine his will by reason and knowledge, and in that he was free to try to achieve his goals.

Equality and fraternity also could be defined economically, politically, and morally in light of the assumptions about the sort of society the Founding Fathers had in mind. The small farmer, individual craftsman, and small businessman constituted such a society in the America of the nineteenth century.

But, of course, that sort of society did not last. Towns increased in size, so that the old-fashioned town meeting with every citizen free to participate gave way to representative town meetings in which only elected officials voted. At the state and national levels, American democracy was always representative; the problem has been how to make it more and more adequately representative. Size alone, however, was not the villain; size itself was the result of a qualitative change in the organization of society. This change came with the spread of large-scale mass-production techniques in industry, commerce, and government itself. As it affected the social organization, the process has been called bureaucratization.

Just as mass, large-scale, machine industry forced a complex division of labor that had to be coordinated, so the laborers, man-

10. Harry S. Ashmore, "Where Have All the Liberals Gone?" *Center Magazine* 2 (July 1969): 33-34.

agers, owners, clerks, and financiers had first to be specialized and then coordinated. I shall not dwell on what ought to be familiar by now. I merely want to stress the point that this type of production and the bureaucratization that supervenes upon it have a logic of their own. It is what Karl Mannheim referred to as "functional rationality"—the meshing of many factors to bring about a result. It is the internal necessity of the system.[11] Nor is it necessary to belabor the fact of the benefits that have flowed from this organization of economic life. It is cited merely to note that these developments ran counter to the assumptions of Jeffersonian democracy; they changed the meanings of liberty, equality, and fraternity, if not their rhetoric.

According to C. Wright Mills, bureaucratization has resulted in the real power being exercised by three power elites: the military, industrial, and political. The traditional jousting of various interests continues among middle-management, elected officials, small businessmen and their professional associates. But these parliamentary maneuvers are about secondary matters or merely ritualize the nineteenth-century rhetoric of liberal democracy. As for the masses, Mills regards them as virtually powerless.[12]

I am not as sure as was Mills about the political impotence of the masses or the merely ritualistic nature of the middle-level activity of politicians. As to the first, so long as the masses have the franchise, they can put muscle into the parliamentary process whenever they become sufficiently aroused. In the elections of 1968, for example, the masses made their feelings about crime on the streets, protest on the college campus, and integrated housing felt, and the government did respond to the pressure. Nor can one overlook the effect on President Lyndon Johnson of the mass sentiment about the Vietnam War that in the end overpowered the manipulations by which the public is supposed to be kept perpetually duped and quiescent.

11. *Man and Society in an Age of Reconstruction* (New York: Harcourt, Brace & World, 1940).

12. On bureaucratization, see Irving Louis Horowitz, ed., *Power, Politics and People: The Collected Essays of C. Wright Mills* (New York: Oxford University Press, 1963), p. 30. For a good interpretation of Mills, see Donald C. Hodges, "The Fourth Epoch: Epilogue to the Unfinished Social Philosophy of C. Wright Mills," *Philosophy and Phenomenological Research* 29 (1969): 327-50.

The power of the masses at the polls is exceeded only by their power in the marketplace. The industrial system demands that the consumer spend at a fast clip; so does every large-scale commercial enterprise, including the information media. The power elites, paradoxically, cannot maintain themselves while keeping the masses powerless; for the great bureaucracies to live and prosper the masses must be given considerable power to satisfy their own wills and whims.

As for the parliamentary machinery being ritualistic, it is a ritual that channels the power of both the elites and the masses, especially when they confront each other or when their several interests collide. The parliamentary process furnishes an arena for settling issues—at least for the time being. Because of the possibility of a parliamentary test, it pays to stir up the masses and to try to persuade them. To be sure, issues have to be sharply polarized and oversimplified, and the appeal may not always be to knowledge and reason, but it is premature to say that the whole process is a ritual relegated to secondary issues.

### DEMOCRACY AS FORMAL AND SUBSTANTIVE

Formally, liberty is a declaration of rights to be exercised, qualified by the proviso that the rights of others are not to be violated; equality, formally, is the principle of even-handed treatment before the law or equality of opportunity; fraternity is formally expressed as the brotherhood of man or as the principle of altruism. The Founding Fathers, if pressed to prove that they had provided for liberty, equality, and fraternity, could point to the documents that stated their allegiance to the principles concerned. And so long as the social reality afforded reasonably concrete referents for these abstractions, the justification was fairly convincing.

The new masses of the twentieth century were harder to convince. They realized that formal principles were of little help to the laboring man who, according to Marx, had nothing but his labor to sell and little choice but to sell it or starve. To such a worker, freedom of enterprise meant only freedom to starve or to be exploited; equality meant that only if other things were equal would his opportunity to compete be equal, but for him the other things—birth, wealth, and position—were not and would not be equal. As for fraternity, the working man was not satisfied with membership in a mystical theological brotherhood, but sought rather a collective attack on mutual misery. A labor union brotherhood was nearer to his needs. For the common man, the proper referents for liberty and equality and fraternity were not principles, but social arrangements. He wanted laws that allowed him to bargain collectively, laws that gave him a larger share of the economic pie, barriers against want that he could not erect out of his own earnings. Fraternity he reserved for those with whom he was associated in the economic and political struggle.

And so emerged the state of affairs that Gunnar Myrdal described in *An American Dilemma,* viz., the tension between the high-level generalizations about liberty, equality, and fraternity in the rhetoric of nineteenth-century liberal democracy and the lower-order proposals that tested their meaning in legislation for social reform. The masses in America did not become the exploited monstrosities predicted by Marx, nor have they staged the "revolution." Yet it would be idle to deny that few working men today think of themselves as latent, albeit delayed, individual entrepeneurs working for wages only until they can accumulate enough capital to go into business for themselves. It is not necessary to trace the analogous attrition in the ranks of the yeoman farmer and pioneer settler. True, not all farmers are tycoons of agribusiness, nor have all the little businessmen disappeared, but the prospect of their proportion increasing is slight if one reflects on the amount of capital investment needed to go into any sort of business for oneself. The hero of the one hundred fifty or more Horatio Alger sagas remains an admirable image, but his embodiment in the American society of the late twentieth century must be regarded as a sensational exception rather than the rule.[13]

And what is true of economic self-determination is no less true of moral and political freedom. While formally the individual's freedom in these domains remains on the books, the power that makes freedom effective is no longer individualizable; to count, individual power must be pooled; it must be organized and bureau-

13. By the beginning of the 1960s only 15 percent of the nation's workers were self-employed. About 85 percent were employees, and half of these worked in corporate organizations. In manufacturing, 361 corporations out of 263,000 firms employed 40 percent of the employees. E. Lloyd Warner, *The Corporation in the Emergent Society* (New York: Harper & Row, 1962), p. 26.

cratized. This is a far cry from the power structure in the minds of the Founding Fathers.

DEMOCRACY AND NATURAL RIGHTS

Underlying these changes in the conceptions of democracy (liberty, equality, and fraternity) is a change in the theoretical strategy of justifying these rights in the first place. Such a strategy revolves around a concept of human nature. If the changes of interpretation of democracy are important to the shaping of educational goals, the change in the basic view of man on which they are predicated is no less so.

The classical liberal position on the rights of man to life, liberty, property, equality before the law, and the pursuit of happiness was based on a theory of natural rights such as that espoused by John Locke. In the Declaration of Independence these were referred to as unalienable rights. Thomas Jefferson in that document stated that "We hold these truths to be self-evident, that all men are created equal, that they are endowed by their Creator with certain unalienable Rights, that among these are Life, Liberty and the Pursuit of Happiness."

I have elsewhere commented on the awkward position in which this proclamation puts the public school teacher trying to teach the Declaration.[14] The doctrine of natural or inalienable rights has been severely criticized. First, there are those who deny existence of the Creator and therefore his power to confer rights. Second, there is the difficulty of asserting inalienable rights that are not absolutely inalienable.

As to the religious problem, the teacher is hemmed in by the Scylla of attributing atheism to Jefferson and the Charybdis of incurring the scorn of the social scientists and positivistic philosophers in whose theorizing the Creator has at best an obfuscating role.

With regard to the second point, there is the fact that the Founding Fathers, and indeed almost everyone else who wrote about inalienable rights, qualified them so that they could be alienated under special conditions. Thus the right to life was not

14. "What Can the School Say about Human Rights?" *Phi Delta Kappan* 47 (1966): 467-71.

held to disqualify execution of murderers, and the right to free speech did not include the right to cry fire falsely in a theater.

Theoretically, one can get around the impasses in several ways. It has been suggested that the Founding Fathers did not mean there would be no circumstances in which it would be right to deprive the individual of inalienable rights, but rather that they could not be waived or transferred by their possessor.[15] It has also been suggested that they could be interpreted as prima facie rights which could be abrogated under certain circumstances, but that every such abrogation would require moral justification.[16]

While these latter ploys have their merit in logic, they tend to miss the main thrust of the doctrine, the authors of which, one must assume, were not ignorant of logic. The language of the Declaration is not purely descriptive specification of legal prerogatives; rather it is intended to draw attention to a conception of man. Man is the sort of creature who by nature cannot refrain from claiming the rights enumerated. Should he cease to claim these rights, he would not qualify as a "man." If man is not this sort of creature, then these rights are not inalienable. In other words, the doctrine of natural rights can be construed as the minimal context in which the term "human" is properly applied. This context places a limit on the flexibility of human nature and in this sense only can be regarded as absolute. The rejection of this limit on the modifiability of human nature, one can argue, stultifies the teaching of democracy insofar as it depends for its meaning and implementation upon human rights.

However, once it is conceded that the exercise of a right depends to any extent on circumstances, then the correctness of its exercise is determined by authorized personnel. In our country the legislature and the courts make this decision; hence the demands for the substance of rights in terms of social decisions rather than an enunciation of them. To satisfy the campus protesters, it is not enough to assure them that they have the right to protest within

15. For example, see B. A. Richards, "Inalienable Rights: Recent Criticism and Old Doctrine," *Phenomenology and Philosophical Research* 29 (1969): 391-404.

16. See W. D. Ross on prima facie rights in *The Right and the Good* (London: Oxford University Press, 1931), pp. 60-61, and W. K. Frankena, "Natural and Inalienable Rights," *Philosophical Review* 64 (1955): 212-32.

the limits set by the administration; they want the right to set the limits.

## Changing Conceptions of Democracy and Education

We find an interesting intersection between the formal principles of liberty, equality, and fraternity and their substantive implementation in the numerous and fervent reform movements that swept this country during the first half of the nineteenth century. It was the period of Concord transcendentalism, the equalitarianism of Jackson, and the communistic experiments of Robert Owen. Above all, it was the period of the fight for free schools for all the people. Indeed, the free school movement was regarded as the means par excellence of securing the real blessings of liberty, equality, and fraternity.[17]

The labor movements of the time recognized this. They wanted tax appropriations for free schools that were not restricted to children of paupers. "The original element of despotism is a Monopoly of Talent. . . . Real equality of power means equality of education. No real liberty without a wide diffusion of real intelligence."[18]

Moreover, these sentiments found their way into the state constitutions. Vassar quotes excerpts from several of them:

Wisdom and knowledge, as well as virtue, diffused generally among the body of the people, being necessary for the preservation of their rights and liberties; and as these depend on spreading the opportunities and advantages of education. . . . Constitution of Massachusetts, 1780, Chap. V, Sec. II

Knowledge and learning, generally diffused through a community, being essential to the preservation of a free government, and spreading the opportunities and advantages of education through the various parts of the country being highly conducive to this end. . . . Constitution of Indiana, 1816, Article IX, Sec. I

A general diffusion of the advantages of education being essential to the preservation of the rights and liberties of the people. . . . Constitution of Maine, 1819, Article VIII

17. *Social History of American Education*, Vol. I, ed. Rena L. Vassar (Chicago: Rand McNally & Co., 1965), p. 153. Also see Rush Welter, *Popular Education and Democratic Thought in America* (New York: Columbia University Press, 1962).

18. Quoted from a report of a committee investigating schools in Philadelphia, *Working Man's Advocate,* March 6, 1830.

After the American Revolution, the republican form of government and patriotism toward the new nation seemed to dominate the writings on education. Erastus Root in his *Introduction to Arithmetic* (1795) demonstrated his patriotism by rejecting the "British intricate mode of reckoning," which he considered "suited to the genius of their government." To him it was the policy of tyrants "to keep their accounts as intricate and perplexing a method as possible." Similar sentiments prompted Noah Webster to shape an American language that would be spoken and written by all social classes.[19]

Democracy as an ideal of government required education, according to Jefferson, for two reasons. In the first place, to guard against what he thought to be the almost inevitable loss of natural rights to tyranny, the best weapon would be:

. . . to illuminate, as far as practicable, the minds of the people at large, and more especially to give them knowledge of those facts, which history exhibiteth, that, possessed thereby of the experience of other ages and countries, they may be enabled to know ambition under all its shapes, and prompt to exert their natural powers to defeat its purpose.[20]

But in the second place:

. . . those persons, whom nature hath endowed with genius and virtue, should be rendered by liberal education worthy to receive, and able to guard the sacred deposit of the rights and liberties of their fellow citizens, and that they should be called to that charge without regard to wealth, birth or other accidental condition or circumstance. . . .[21]

Later, the full impact of the industrial revolution with its Protestant ethic shaped the values of both democracy and education. No less important was the tide of immigration which has been credited as being the chief impetus to the development of the

19. *Social History of American Education*, p. 100. However, the notion that popular education was a response to the demands of an enlightened working class is challenged by M. B. Katz, *The Irony of Early School Reform: Educational Innovation in the Mid-Nineteenth Century* (Cambridge: Harvard University Press, 1968).

20. "Bill for the More General Diffusion of Knowledge (1779)," in *Social History of American Education I*, 109 as taken from Edgar W. Knight, *Documentary History of Education in the South Before 1860*, Vol. II (Chapel Hill: University of North Carolina Press, 1949).

21. Ibid., p. 109.

free public common school. Yet the domestication of the immigrant was itself guided by a conception of democracy.[22]

## Dewey's Conception of Democracy

For education the most significant challenge to the interpretation of democracy we have been discussing was the view of John Dewey. The challenge consisted in not regarding liberty, equality, fraternity, and the assorted rights that went with them as absolute principles or as rules for economic and political competition. Rather they were to be means toward a collective reconstruction of experience and criteria of success in achieving it. Instead of using the school to sharpen the individual's weapons in the struggle for achievement, eminence, and privilege, Dewey proposed that it be an ideal community in which pupils developed the dispositions and skills needed for collective inquiry and cooperative action.

The key notion in Dewey's theory of democracy is sharing. The criterion for the good society is the degree to which sharing is made possible among its members. If Dewey can be said to have an absolute—an attribution from which all of his disciples zealously defend him—it is the continuity of experience. Dichotomies, ruptures, discontinuities of any kind, he regarded as challenges to restore continuity. Hence the importance he attached to community and communication, both of which entailed shareability. But even more important theoretically is the fact that communication necessitated the formalizing of experience so that it could be made an object of thought, discourse, foresight, imagination, planning, and verification. In this way Dewey established a virtual synonymity among the terms "human," "inquiry," and "community."

In the good society community is constantly deepened and perfected by the sharing of pooled resources. In a progressive society these resources are not merely replenished from generation to generation but reconstructed by the method of intelligence. Accord-

22. For several pertinent readings on this topic see Daniel Calhoun, ed., *The Education of Americans: A Documentary History* (Boston: Houghton Mifflin Co., 1969), pp. 407-25. See also Max Weber, *The Prostestant Ethic and the Spirit of Capitalism* (New York: Charles Scribner's Sons, 1930). On the relation of schools to a free society, especially on the contributions of Horace Mann and Henry Barnard, see Merle Curti, *The Social Ideals of American Educators* (New York: Charles Scribner's Sons, 1935), chaps. 3,4.

ingly, by equating the good society with democracy and with shared intelligence Dewey created a model not only for social organization, but for teaching and learning as well. Despite certain limitations as a formula for schooling, it remains the most original and fruitful paradigm of education in modern times.[23]

Dewey's view of democracy was a move away from the economic individualism and formalism of the classical liberal position. For one thing, it aimed at concrete welfare rather than at formal principles. For another, it rejected the laissez-faire philosophy of economics and government. Despite these qualifications, Dewey did not abandon the ideal of the individual rational man; he merely took seriously the Aristotelian dictum that *all* men were by nature rational, a dictum that Aristotle himself in one important respect ignored. Unfortunately, the sort of collective problem-solving Dewey envisioned was limited to circumstances in which small groups of individuals could carry on face-to-face collective inquiry; such circumstances still exist, but they are not the circumstances in which the great societal problems of our time are dealt with. Dewey saw the need for collective deliberation, but it was not the kind of collective inquiry that was suitable for a mass society.

The attractiveness of the Dewey position owed something to a number of factors:

1. The social conditions, especially in the cities, were steadily contradicting the assumptions of classical individualism.
2. Community was breaking down and education, while homogenizing the language and customs of the immigrants, was only sharpening the inequalities among social classes and interests.
3. Scientific humanism seemed to be an answer to a Platonic elitist humanism that arrogated intelligence to a special guardian class. It was also an answer to laissez-faire doctrine that competition was the only road to well-being, and to religious creeds that put man's destiny beyond his control.
4. The picture of the school as a community in which shareability was unimpeded by the distortions in the nonschool world was an attractive one for still another reason. The school as a place for intellectual development through study of the traditional disciplines was part of the elitist philosophy of education. Hordes of immigrant and poor children fitted awkwardly into a school designed to perpetuate an elite, even if they could afford to spend eight or ten

23. John Dewey, *Democracy and Education* (New York: Macmillan Co., 1916), pp. 100 ff.

years away from the job market. By contrast, the small New England community made up of people working the soil, exchanging goods and services, practicing the crafts, helping each other, and uniting for common projects towards shared goals was a democratic "school" par excellence. Dewey saw in it a model for formal schooling. Learning by solving common problems insured community, communication, and the growth of intelligence. It is no accident that Progressive education counted among its leaders so many men whose own early background was in small communities where the only important restrictive influence was religious orthodoxy. Nor is it to be wondered at that teachers could see in the community-like school a way of teaching that would be a relief from drilling verbal materials that bore no discernible resemblance to the tasks and duties of community life.

5. The practical and productive impulses of an exuberant industrial society welcomed the emphasis on science and its practical fruits. Especially congenial was his theory of knowledge which elevated science to the status of a truly humanistic enterprise and viewed the scientific style of thinking as a paradigm of humanistic thinking. Labor was dignified theoretically by the testing, operational, doing aspects of scientific inquiry. On this view, man's reason was as eminently manifested in his intelligent transactions with the physical environment as it was in abstruse speculations about transcendent reality. It was possible to be spiritual without the benefit of religion or metaphysics.

6. Further, the Dewey concept of shareability was a vigorous endorsement of equalitarianism and socialism in both the political and economic domains. The right to share in the toils and benefits of social life were derived from the very nature of the social process itself, viz., from the communicative structure of a society. To be a viable society implied shareability, and the best society, therefore, was the one with the greatest potentiality for community, for communication, for shareability. Shareability was a prescription for education, for democracy, and for the good society all at once.

7. Education as a process of group inquiry into real difficulties of the group seemed admirably adapted to coping with a wide range of abilities in the classroom. However heterogeneous the interests and abilities of pupils, the group could take account of them in the choice of the problem to be solved. Because the predicaments of the group were concrete and immediate, the task of interesting children in the remote abstractions of the standard academic subjects could be bypassed. The formal mastery of these subjects could then become the last rather than the first phase of schooling.

And so the Dewey version of democracy and schooling changed the concept of the democratic man and the democratic school.

Instead of a man versed in languages, the classics, and other fields of traditional knowledge, the image in the mind of the eighteenth- and nineteenth-century liberals as the ideal governor or the image of free entrepeneurs competing in a free society, the image arose of socially sensitive problem-solvers cooperatively coping with their environment. Instead of the classical education suited to the classes and the vocational schooling presumably needed by the masses, we were offered the problem-solving activity curriculum needed by the new democratic man.

Consensus by discussion, rational self-examination, and imaginative forecasting of consequences were to be the outcomes of the new democratic education; study of the disciplines might serve as means to such outcomes, but they lost their autonomy and priority in the curriculum. And if there lingered any claim to superiority in the classical verbalistic studies, Dewey dispelled it by showing that what he was proposing was nothing less than the scientific method applied to the everyday problems of life. By showing that scientific thinking involves doing (testing), he democratized the scientific method, but he also aristocratized the common man; he allowed the common man to join the modern elite, the men of science.[24]

The act of thought transmuted by William H. Kilpatrick and others into school procedures exerted a powerful influence on the goals of the American public school. One cannot read the educational literature of the thirties and even the forties without sensing that it had permeated not only the language but also the thinking of school administrators and thousands upon thousands of teachers.

It did not affect the practice in the schools as much as one might have expected for several reasons. To begin with, it affected practice more than one might infer from reading the curriculum plans of the schools or from examining their programs. The unit method of instruction, the activity approach, the emphasis on problem-solving were introduced into many conventional courses of instruc-

24. For the Dewey version of the scientific method as the complete act of thought see *How We Think* (Boston: D. C. Heath, 1916) and *The Quest for Certainty,* (New York: Minton Balch & Co., 1929). For the attempt to elaborate the process of collective inquiry see R. Bruce Raup et al., *The Improvement of Practical Intelligence* (New York: Harper & Bros., 1950). See also H. G. Hullfish and Philip G. Smith, *Reflective Thinking: The Method of Education* (New York: Dodd, Mead & Co., 1961) and the writings of Ernest Bayles.

tion. A teacher of algebra having trouble with an indifferent class welcomed any approach that would stir things up a bit. Consequently, teachers of the most conservative schools often found themselves quite enthusiastic about Progressive methods of teaching. Further, the democratic notion certainly pervaded the schemes for student government, and even faculties toyed with the idea of having something to say about the conduct of schools. And within limits—usually quite narrow ones—the school superintendents and the school boards cautiously endorsed the idea.

However, the Dewey paradigm had relatively little effect on the curriculum of the public school, i.e., the study of more or less standard academic subjects for the prospective elites and a mixture of literacy and vocational training for the prospective working men. The reason for this, I take it, is that the people who counted in the community and their school representatives never did accept wholeheartedly the shareability concept of democracy that Dewey was advocating. Whatever in the theory could be reduced to a method of teaching was accepted; the insight that made sense of the method was ignored. It survived in the educational rhetoric and in the programs of a small number of schools—usually for the children of the upper middle class.

Those who foresaw the effects of industrialism and urbanization—and Dewey certainly saw them in 1916 when *Democracy and Education* was published—realized fully that a truly democratic society, i.e., one based on community and shareability, was being threatened in America.

The Progressive movement in education can be construed as an attempt to restore to American life the qualities of the American small town or village. In its heyday this had approximated quite well the Jeffersonian ideal of free men, each controlling enough property and commanding enough knowledge to make good their claims to liberty, equality, and fraternity. And Dewey was right in perceiving that in such a community shareability was the criterion of the good life for both the individual and society; that it corrected the latent elitism of Jeffersonian democracy and yet saved it from the mobocracy of the more extreme type of Jacksonian populism.

After all, where was the school supposed to lead American society in the thirties and forties? What did Rugg, Brameld, Counts, and the other Reconstructionists want the American society to become? It appears that the point was to make the benefits of a humane community, such as obtained in the small towns of America, accessible to the city dwellers and industrial workers of the postwar era. And this could be done, presumably, by instituting a social order that would be based on consensus achieved through collective use of the scientific mode of inquiry. This inquiry would counter-act the dogmatism of religion and the power of vested interests by subjecting them to the searchlight of free, naturalistic, debunking inquiry. What the muckrakers had turned up about the evils of American society would be "found out" by the pupils themselves, and thus pressure for liberal legislation would be created rationally and naturally in and by the schools. The schools would then dare to create a new social order, in answer to George Counts's chal-lenge.[25] That new order had for its model neither Russian com-munism nor Marxian communism but rather a socialistic democ-racy. It would be guided by social planning carried on by a highly intelligent and concerned electorate, and it would be implemented by no less enlightened social engineers.

This faith, I believe, was mistaken to the extent that the small town could not be transplanted into the modern city.

## Limitations of the Dewey Concept of Democracy

The developments in our society in the last half century argue against Dewey's collective deliberation as a design for democracy in a modern mass society. To bring this out it will be necessary to show that if we are to have liberty, equality, and fraternity, it will not be by means of the small group using the method of collective problem-solving. I propose, therefore, to examine the viability of the Dewey formula in the political, economic, intellectual, and moral areas of life as they exist today.

### POLITICAL DEMOCRACY

To what extent have we increased the participation of the citizenry in the political process?

Long ago representative democracy supplanted the direct partic-ipation of all the citizens in the deliberative process. The old New

25. George S. Counts, *Dare the School Build a New Social Order?* (New York: John Day Co., 1932).

England town meeting had to give way to the representative town meeting and this, in turn, to the council form of even local government. On the state and national level, the opportunity to participate in policy formation is limited to testifying at committee hearings or writing letters to legislators. Obviously only a tiny fraction of the electorate can take part. Only the most aggressive, the most directly concerned citizens, on any issue, can be expected to expend the time and energy needed to appear before committees and boards. Some expertise and courage are also required, and these are never in great supply.[26] At the national level, the situation is even more limiting for reasons that need no elaboration. Aside from eccentrics, the testimony givers at congressional hearings are there by invitation or at the behest of highly professional lobbies. There is little room for the "average citizen." In universities the open faculty meeting is a decreasingly effective forum for exploring issues that require technical data and expert interpretation of the data.

Democracy, to be sure, is exercised in the final vote of the electorate. To prepare for it, a measure has to be shaped so that a yes or no can be registered on relatively few alternatives. If the electorate is large, even voting seems like a meaningless ritual, because the value of the fraction represented by one vote is minuscule, and the chances that an election will be decided by one vote are depressingly small. It requires considerable imagination and dedication to the principle of voting to bring the individual back to the voting place time and again, especially if he has no pressing interest in the outcome. The political process, therefore, more and more is a matter of convincing the large body of voters that they do indeed have such an interest. Because the issues are increasingly technical and complex, they have to be simplified, emotionalized, and personalized before the voter is sufficiently involved to play his voting role. The pollsters are not the least important agents in this process.[27]

26. In 1962 only 13 percent of a national adult sample knew what the European Common Market was, according to Hazel G. Erskine, "The Polls: The Informed Public," *Public Opinion Quarterly* 26 (1962): 677. College seniors had more information on entertainment, sports, and brands of merchandise than about public affairs, reported Josef E. Garcia, "Information of College Students on Current Affairs," *Journal of Educational Sociology* 36 (962): 58-60.

27. For a survey of communication problems and decision-making processes in complex societies, see Alfred Kuhn, *The Study of Society: A Unified Approach* (Homewood, Ill.: Dorsey Press. 1963).

The current revolt against representative democracy is a symptom that political sharing no longer seems possible even as an ideal. The moderately interested citizen feels that his one vote does not really affect action, and if he is passionately interested, some other way of registering his interest becomes urgent. Demonstrations and violent confrontations, whatever be their merits or demerits, force officialdom to act. This is psychologically satisfactory and for the short run, at least, brings results.

In one way, the resort to direct participation by the small group is a return to the Dewey face-to-face mode of problem-solving; in another, it is about as far as one can get from it, because it abandons the collective inquiry process as a means and the maximizing of sharing as a goal. On balance, the revolts in behalf of participatory democracy are a repudiation of the Dewey solution. This does not make it a bad solution, but it does indicate that the shape of the problem has radically changed.

### EQUALITY OF ECONOMIC OPPORTUNITY

There is little doubt that for sheer volume of available economic benefits our country is second to none. In absolute terms even our most depressed people have more than their counterparts in most other countries. There is also little doubt that labor organization and welfare legislation have evened things up a bit if judged by conditions of a century ago. Two questions still remain, however. First, has the progress gone anywhere nearly far enough; is inequality rather than growing equality the most salient feature of our economic life? Second, is greater equality to be achieved by small groups of men of goodwill working patiently through the processes of representative democracy or by some other means?

No attempt will be made to set forth a detailed case in answer to the first question, but a few comments on what the issue seems to be may be in order. Nobody, so far as I know, argues for absolute, literal equality of men as regards talent, initiative, and so forth. This might be called natural inequality, and it explains the fact that once the race is underway the runners may become widely spaced. The unjust inequality appears when those who have gained a just advantage use it to gain even greater advantages by keeping less fortunate competitors from evening things up. It is as if the leaders in the race strewed glass behind them. In theory, the government is supposed to prevent such skullduggery, but, in fact, laws are the very best way of insuring one's privileges. In other words, natural or justifiable inequality inevitably turns into arbitrary and iniquitous inequality. And if we deny that the differences of ability and energy are innate, the injustice is even greater, because many of those who have been severely handicappd by unfair competition might have done better in a really free and fair race.

Put this way, the problem seems to be primarily a moral one, and the remedy suggests itself, viz., let men of goodwill bring about reform. But this assumes that individual morality will suffice to get rid of collective evils. The assumption becomes very dubious if the responsibility for the evils has to be distributed among large numbers of agents. Accordingly, if one turns from the evils of a small community to those of a very large interdependent society, one may come to the conclusion that, although the moral principle of equity must be maintained, the way to do so is by inventing or perfecting a social mechanism for that purpose and not leaving it to individual morality.

Such a mechanism is the insurance principle that has been applied so well in so many fields of life when responsibility cannot be allotted to individuals. It represents an admission that in a modern mass society the moral question cannot always be answered in terms of individual responsibility, guilt, and atonement. Efficiency may demand changes in our economic system, but morality will demand a social method of spreading the benefits and costs of such changes equitably.

Whether the gains in substantive equality have been caused by the implementation of Dewey's theory of collective deliberation about ends and means is harder to judge. To be sure, the issues have often been settled in the polling places and subsequently in the legislative halls. Nevertheless, it could be argued that the legislative confrontation was less the result of collective inquiry into the social good of the commonwealth than of the exercise of economic power. Without the use of the strike and the machinery of collective bargaining, it is doubtful that labor unions could have acquired enough political muscle to hold their own. Collective bargaining, it appears, is not the same as application of the scientific method by face-to-face groups to social problems; nor is it simply a matter of sensitivity training. It is a power struggle.

To the extent that this is a power struggle, the emerging shape of our society weakens the Dewey hypothesis that the community of the small American town can be restored to the city. Power today is not lodged in individuals but in large interest groups. These groups are politically effective because they already have economic power or can threaten the economic power of others and not vice versa, although having achieved political power the groups can improve their positions in other phases of the power struggle.

## MORALITY

The thrust of Dewey's doctrine is that moral experience does not differ essentially from any other type of practical activity. All such activity has a means-end structure. The best end is the one we would choose after assessing as many relevant alternative ends as we have the wit to conjure up. When the group deliberates about its problems, it is going through the moral experience of weighing conflicting interests in terms of their consequences. Accordingly, when a group seeks to share its valuings, its preferences, and its desires, when by the method of intelligence and imagination it arrives at what the group *really* wants, then all moral requirements are satisfied.[28]

Is the current disenchantment with the middle-class, Protestant, Puritan ethic a rejection of Dewey's moral theory? Or is it a confirmation of it? Some of both, one would guess. On the one hand, Dewey's rejection of a priori absolute standards of conduct certainly opens the door to moral experimentation. To judge the right and the good by their consequences for happiness makes moral experience amenable to prudential calculation. Nevertheless, the moral judgments at which intelligent citizens, bent on the widest degree of sharing, arrive probably approximate pretty much what is now referred to as middle-class standards. Supernatural justification for these judgments would be missing, but intelligent utilitarianism, however naturalistic, has never thought to justify violence in the streets or on the campus, sexual promiscuity, the use of drugs, withdrawal into flowery communes, and the like.

28. For the relation of morality, democracy, and scientific inquiry see John L. Childs, *The Experimentalist Educational Theory,* Bode Memorial Lecture, 1957 (Columbus: College of Education, Ohio State University Press), pp. 14-15.

The Dewey formula when used as a design for moral education had the charm of sweet reasonableness, for what more sensible and enlightened way to teach values to the young than by having them explore the consequences of their conflicting desires? And what better criterion for the success of the collective moral deliberation than achievement of uncoerced consensus? Once more it must be noted that what seemed brilliantly plausible for small groups of children sharing a fairly homogeneous cultural tradition has not worked when groups having diverse cultural traditions and diverse aspirations demanded the right to set their own moral standards, i.e., when they rejected the widest sharing as the moral criterion. For the sharing criterion, at least in principle, applies plausibly only when all those concerned in the problem participate in the sharing group. When consensus is reached by such a group, it exerts a moral demand on the members because it is a demand in which they have had a share; it is more than majority rule in which possibly 49 percent of the group do not share in the majority will.

The alternative to the one all-inclusive group seeking consensus is a diversity of groups appealing to the principle of pluralism, but pluralism and sharing are difficult to apply simultaneously as operating principles. Today pluralism seems to be the governing principle with many groups challenging others; the cement is supplied by the law and the police who as best they can enforce the will of the legislative majority. Uneasy negotiations and compromise rather than sharing is the current mode of decision-making; the right is what can be made to work with diverse groups, but I take it this is not the sort of moral education Dewey contemplated.

### INTELLECTUAL VALUES

I have tried to show how in the economic, political, and moral realms the Dewey criterion of democracy that has permeated the thinking of American educators and guided their policy has been made dysfunctional and nonfunctional by the changing shape of our society. Yet its major test must come in the intellectual realm, for it is the Dewey version of inquiry that buttresses his views of politics, economics, and morality.

This act of inquiry or the complete act of thought is familiar enough to all readers of professional educational literature. If they have not read *The Quest for Certainty*, they are at least familiar with *How We Think*, which is a prescription for how we ought to think in a democratic society. There is no need to repeat the description of Dewey's problem-solving sequence. The important point to keep in mind is that it is the essence of rational procedure for dealing with social issues, as well as the paradigm of learning, teaching, and moral integrity.[29]

Consequently, a revolt against this paradigm hits very close to the heart of the Dewey philosophy and therewith at the ideology of American public school educators. I believe this revolt has occurred and is accelerating. I shall comment on two manifestations of it.

*The revolt of the classes.* Shortly after 1957 and Sputnik, the scientific-technological elite made its bid to redirect public school goals. This was done in the name of the intellectual rigor of the academic disciplines, which, in turn, was justified by the need for scientists and technologists to regain American superiority in scientific and military affairs. This revolt was not against the intellectualism inherent in the Dewey problem-solving paradigm, for that paid more than ordinary homage to science and scientific method. The stiletto was driven into the heart of a curriculum that revolved around, or was alleged to revolve around, the activity program, the project method of teaching, and the child-centered school. Could such a school produce the scientists needed for the space effort? To the derision poured on this type of curriculum by the Council for Basic Education was now added the implied charge that the Progressive theory of education had become a danger to the safety of the republic. The combination of Professor Bestor and Admiral Rickover was too powerful for any educational theory to withstand in 1957. It became obvious that scientists believed that early and specialized study of mathematics, chemistry, physics, biology, and every other respectable academic subject was the way to revitalize the intellectual elite. So at a stroke the activity curriculum of Dewey gave way to the discipline-centered curriculum of the National Science Foundation–sponsored projects. But what is

29. This is made clear in *Democracy and Education,* and much of the power of that book and of Dewey's influence on education lay precisely in the enormous range of applicability or relevance of the formula of the complete act of thought. See also my article "Dewey's Analysis of the Act of Thought," *Bulletin of the School of Education, Indiana University* 36 (1960): 15-26.

even more significant, the leadership of educational theory was changed. Leaders were to come from the academic disciplines and not from men brought up in professional education. The leadership battle is not yet over.

Without probing too far into these changes, I think it can be said that their primary significance lay less in the precise nature of the curriculum contents or the identity of the leadership than in the priority of educational goals. For the time being, at any rate, the American public school was to give its first attention and effort to the augmenting of a scientific-technological-professional elite rather than to mere literacy or the implementation of democratic values.

*The revolt of the masses.* The resurgence of poverty and racial discrimination as important educational problems in the sixties turned the goals of the schools around 180 degrees. The difficulties encountered in teaching the disadvantaged not only disclosed an alleged class bias in the curriculum and methods of teaching used in the public schools but also in the very criteria of intelligence itself. There are three aspects of this revolt: (a) the cry for relevance on the college campus is antidisciplinary and therefore antiuniversity, the university being discipline oriented; (b) there is a demand that the disadvantaged be treated in the light of their psychological and social impairments brought on by damaging environments; and (c) middle-class values must be rejected as biased, and each group is to be its own standard—intellectually, morally, and politically. All three aspects are anti-intellectual, and all three have their counterparts in the political struggle for the control of the public schools.

The campus protesters want to wrest control of the university from administrators and their sympathizers in the faculty; the Holts, Goodmans, Kozols, and Friedenbergs want to wrest control of the schools from the middle-class schoolmen and make it human and personal and liberating; and the blacks want to run their own show with black soul. While the Dewey vision glimmers here and there in the interstices of these revolts, it really illuminates none of them, for the positive side of his vision is sharing by means of rational communication. Even the somewhat emotionalized group-dynamic variation of it portrayed in *The Improvement of Practical*

*Intelligence* did not, if my information is correct, receive the approval of Dewey himself. And small wonder—Dewey was not the prophet of revolution against bourgeoise democracy; he was the charismatic figure who proposed to save its spirit in the modern technological society. That he could not do this must be attributed to the fact that this society was not commensurate with the kind of society that Dewey was trying to save, viz., the small face-to-face community made up of self-determinable, rational individuals reconstructing their own experience and that of their society—pretty much as the members of the John Dewey Society are still trying to do in their conclaves several times a year.

Although the activity, problem-solving curriculum was proposed as an alternative to systematic study of the academic subjects in the elementary and secondary school, it may be that this is not the most fertile ground for it. Inasmuch as the method is admirably suited to interdisciplinary problem-solving, the place to put it into effect is at the upper division of the college, after the student has completed the systematic study of the academic disciplines. It is the bright college students who have mastered the disciplines who are impatient to get on to interdisciplinary study. The activity, informal approach also seems prescribed for levels of schooling where formal disciplinary teaching is ruled out by the psychological limitations of the learner, whether these be cognitive or emotional. In other words, the Dewey approach is best suited to the intellectually very able and the intellectually least able, rather than as a substitute for disciplinary study in the elementary and secondary schools.[30]

30. There are those who say that Wilford M. Aikin's *Story of the Eight-Year Study* (New York: Harper & Bros., 1942) proves that the activity program could be a substitute for the formal study of academic subjects, at least as far as success in college is concerned. I hesitate to express my doubts about this too strongly because this was a fine study, and yet I also hesitate to accept it as evidence of the point at issue here, viz., whether a logically structured subject matter can be learned as an incidental or even instrumental concomitant to solving a concrete social problem. Many activity programs do smuggle in a good deal of formal study, once the problem approach has motivated the study, and this would fudge the evidence considerably. The current diatribes against the "joyless" classrooms and the pleas that American schools imitate the British open classrooms, in the light of what was being written less than a decade ago, boggle the mind. For an example of this change of heart by the elitist critics of the public schools, see Charles E. Silverman's *Crisis in the Classroom* (New York: Random House, 1970).

The institutional reverberations of these revolts against the Dewey formula for schooling have already been touched upon. First, there is the bid for control by the academic discipline specialist, strongly backed by the elites of science, industry, politics, and academe. Second, there is the bid for control of the college curriculum by the dissident students. Third, we have the bid for control of the total conduct of black schools by the black separatists. Fourth, there is the attempt to remove teacher training from the professional schools and turn it over either to the liberal arts departments or to people who are communally engaged in such organizations as the Peace Corps, VISTA, and the like. The last development is, of course, a most serious one and deserves an extended analysis on its own account, especially because it involves the ingress of technology into the school system in the teaching-learning phase as well as in its more logistical phases.

One might summarize the failure of the notion of democracy as sharing by saying that the problems of a modern mass society involve what Karl Mannheim called correlational thinking and what systems analysts do with a large number of complex variables. And yet this does not quite get to the root of the matter. Democracy, defined as using the problem-solving approach to group problems, also involves correlational thinking; in its deliberation the variables are made explicit and discussed. But the small face-to-face group tackling a felt difficulty could carry on its deliberations with confidence that it knew what the problem was and the outcomes it desired. Occasionally an expert might have to be consulted on some technical points but, by and large, commonsense generalizations, passable intelligence, and decent intentions sufficed. This is simply no longer the case in any social problem that can be called significant. Correlational thinking today has to be not only multivariable, but it involves technical knowledge in many fields as well; no less important, it requires a high order of imagination to conceive the consequences of such phenomena as pollution, nuclear war, inflation, and so forth. There is little reason to believe that more than a tiny fraction of our citizenry—despite statistics on school attendance—can meet these requirements, and, should the American schools ever seriously undertake to supply the kind of elementary and secondary schooling that might at least get the bulk of our citizens onto this plane of thinking, the real revolution in education would come about. Very few of our educational statesmen have taken this goal seriously.

But there are other requirements of democratic problem-solving that we cannot meet. Individuals have become less free in every aspect of their lives; their individuality tends to be lost in the collectives through which they have to work, think, and act. Alienated from themselves they become more liable to herdism, to forming masses.

To be a moral, intellectual, political unit who is really significant, the American citizen has to be something fairly special as a person. If democracy is to be a reality, he as a person has to be something more significant than a vote. Otherwise, sharing smacks too much of a contrived "charity," because the needs of most individuals are out of proportion to their abilities to contribute to the general good.

Despite these shortcomings, the Dewey conception of shareability does express perhaps in the simplest, most straightforward way the most enlightened version of democracy available to us. For one thing, it is not committed to laissez-faire theories of economics or society in general. Cooperation rather than competition is the key to shareability; any new version of democracy will have to take a similar view.

Furthermore, the stress on community is not a mindless manifestation of herdism, of Sumnerian subjection to the mores and folkways or to the supremacy of the group over the individual. On the contrary, the style of collective inquiry upon which Dewey insisted saves it from such slavishness. It relies heavily on the possibility of a group growing in rationality. Not the least of its strengths is its generalizability. In one formula, the complete act of thought, we have a design for individual and group problem-solving—for democracy, for morality, for science. It fits as well in society as in the classroom. The new democracy will also need a theory that can unify our moral, civic, and intellectual life.

Finally, if the future of democracy is to be tied to the technological developments of modern large-scale machine industry, then the Dewey formula indicates some avenues for its salvation. For such a society to retain its human dimensions it needs a mechanism for its own reconstruction in accordance with human criteria.

## Democratic Values and Educational Goals

What does the foregoing discussion imply for the shaping of educational goals? The import of the discussion thus far is that the goals of education have to make their peace with the constraints of a modern mass society on the one hand, and the demands of democracy on the other. I have argued that by and large the changes in our society in certain respects have rendered the concept of democracy we inherited from the Founding Fathers (and that of Dewey) anachronistic. The problem, as I see it, is to stand fast on those values which democracy must always embody and to build them into the society in which we are destined to live. This point must not be passed over too quickly, for it is not universally agreed that the notion of democracy or any other notion does have such constant elements. Yet if it does not, then the task of the educator is confounded not so much by the fact of social change, but rather by the loss of any criteria for assessing that change.

If we think back on the conceptions of equality, freedom, and fraternity that were guiding the thoughts of the Founding Fathers, the elements that we would not want to sacrifice are summed up in the notion of the person as the locus and ultimate criterion of value. This notion is explicated in the cardinal virtues of the Greek tradition and the theological virtues of the Judeo-Christian one. I doubt that these will change in the sense of losing their meaning or their definitiveness in our judgments about what is human, inhuman, and nonhuman. The inalienable values of the person and the obligation to share the goods that persons have a right to seek are the constants on which society and education must build.[31]

I would regard Dewey's concept of democracy as shareability as an affirmation of these virtues, for, although Dewey emphasizes the collective aspect of community, it is still a collectivity of individuals functioning as persons, each with a residual value and integrity that cannot arbitrarily be dismissed however exigent the

31. Although this is fairly old doctrine to classical humanists and realists, it is encouraging to find psychologists like the late Abraham H. Maslow so confident that empirical evidence will support this view. The writings of Maslow are too numerous to list here, but especially appropos is his *The Psychology of Science: A Reconnaissance* (New York: Harper & Row, 1966) and a recent article "Toward a Humanistic Biology," *American Psychologist* 24 (1969) : 724-35.

group welfare may be. On what other grounds can every individual claim a right to community? But the behavioral forms, the life-styles that exemplify these virtues or are thought to do so, do vary. Therefore, each generation and each individual faces the task of determining what is the truly courageous act, the truly honest act, the truly democratic act.

However, it is at this juncture that the constraints of modern society press most acutely on the school. As we have noted a number of times, the kind of freedom that is now available—politically, economically, and morally—has to be searched out and redefined, and the same must be said about equality and fraternity. This seeking out and translation of the findings into educational programs is the immediate goal of education and schooling.

If these goals are to be translated into programs and procedures, what skills, attitudes, and knowledge are we to aim at? Certainly a strong reliable pro attitude toward a democratic society would rate very high in the list of such outcomes in the pupil, and there is no mystery as to how attitudes can be formed, firmly and reliably. Totalitarian societies know how to do it very well. They not only control the psychological means, but all the social mechanisms to reinforce them as well. The temptation to use the totalitarian techniques of concealed coercion—because mass media for mass persuasion are available to us also—is very great. The temptation is strengthened by the slowness of parliamentary machinery and the fact that this machinery is used by the establishment for its own preservation.

The attitude toward democracy that we shall want to foster is neither that of direct action in the name of social justice, nor simply the attitude of "go slow, postpone, discuss, let us reason together." Both attitudes, it seems to me, are inimical to democracy in a modern society. The former precludes all relevant interests from being represented in decision; the latter nullifies these decisions by interposing obstructive and sometime irrelevant maneuvers to any action that those in control of the machinery do not want to take place.

The appropriate attitudes are that (a) I have a duty to become informed on and involved in all great social issues, whether their impact on me is obvious or not. For the nature of a modern society is such that I may not be able at a glance to detect this impact on myself. Citizens no longer can pick and choose the issues in which they shall be involved; (b) I have a duty to respect the rights of others, which means that I shall automatically feel uneasy about taking action that ignores or overrides these rights.

Attitude (a) is positive and (b) is negative. The latter marks the abiding validity of the sanctity of the individual, precisely the attitude that totalitarian regimes try to stamp out. As indicated earlier in this essay, the schools have not failed in developing this attitude; the most ruthless enterpriser thinks twice before flouting the "rights" of others openly.

The positive aspect I have phrased not as a right but as a duty *to become eligible to exercise a right,* which is quite a different thing. Let me elaborate this because it is almost certain to be misconstrued. The traditional rights to free speech, to participate, to discuss, to vote have justification in the supposition that the individual has a fair chance of knowing what he is talking about and what he is doing. That he might be a crackpot was a chance one had to take, and it was wisely decided to risk some foolishness— even dangerous foolishness—to maintain the principle. I am not arguing against this view, nor against the importance of habitually jumping to the defense of these individual rights. Nor am I saying that uninformed and irresponsible talk is too dangerous to tolerate today; this is a risk that democracy must always take. But the task of being informed has become so onerous that it must be seen as a duty, and this feeling of obligation must be regarded as condition for the exercise of one's right. The exercise of the right without acknowledging the duty, therefore, makes one liable to demand for justification. One cannot by law or force deprive anyone of the right to speak, but morally one is justified in asking whether he has fulfilled his duty upon which this right properly depends.

However, if this knowledge is to be a duty, the individual can reasonably demand that the conditions for his being knowledgeable exist, and this, of course, is where education plays its most distinctive role.[32] What sorts of knowledge, then, does the citizen have a right to expect in order to exercise the rights and freedoms that we associate with democracy?

32. I say distinctive, because other components of the democratic attitude are nowhere near so exclusively in the domain of the school.

First of all is a thorough familiarity with the history of democracy itself. One must stress historicity because the context in which democracy is preached and practiced has changed and may change some more. Although there are numerous ways in which such knowledge can be curricularized, I suppose the social studies would take major responsibility for it. Whatever the particular organization and sequence these studies assume, by the time formal general education is completed the pupil should have a reasonably thorough familiarity with the development of his economic, social, and political institutions that claim to be democratic.

One source of relevant knowledge for assessing these claims are the humanities. The humanities can be construed—and I would urge that they be so construed—as exemplars of life-styles and value complexes. This is not to urge that the student quarry nuggets of social history and wisdom from the humanities—the history of institutions and ideas is a more economical source for that. The humanities provide exemplars—vivid, aesthetically appealing, perpetual challenges to rejection or emulation. They *exhibit* value schema, including the democratic ones, and not merely describe them. I am not suggesting the substitution of humanities for social science, but neither is social science an adequate substitute for the humanities.

There is still another reason for serious study of the humanities in relation to democracy. It is that in the search for a life-style, for behavioral forms appropriate to the democratic values in our time, the artist has a role as well as the scientist and technologist. For if the latter alter the possibilities of action and value, the artist is the one on whom we depend to conjure up images for their embodiment. When art is not successful in this regard, the people flounder about, following every fad and fashion in the hope of finding a satisfactory expression for their lives, or what has been referred to as a "life-style."

One of the major handicaps of the Dewey version of the democratic society is that the way of life that seems to be demanded is that of a committee member forever deliberating on good causes, but such a life-style seems to lack drama, heroism, and excitement. Confrontations with the police and street demonstrations seem to have more dramatic potency. The drama of the intellect today is staged by space exploration and breakthroughs in genetics and communication, not by the search for consensus on a new school building or even a school bond issue. Indeed, the emphasis in small groups today is toward community via physical contact, expansion of the mind through drugs, and sundry variations of the ancient mysteries and their rituals. These are occasions for feeling together rather than for reasoning together.[33]

I do not know what image of life will capture the imagination of our time. *Playboy Magazine,* the mass media as used by Madison Avenue, as well as all sorts of popular and serious artists, are casting up models for our consideration. Any life-form that sweeps our culture and gives it style will come from one of these sources or from a combination of them. Educationally, the issue for the schools is whether its resources should be used to favor one source rather than another. I can only offer my own reasoning on this matter and that is that formal schooling should concentrate on those sources of value expression that cannot be acquired by informal means. Hence I would argue that the humanities, insofar as they embody the serious arts, should be the first concern of the school. The more popular influences, one may assume, will do their work anyway; the serious arts cannot work upon us until we acquire cultivated aesthetic sensitivity and the rudiments of a cultivated aesthetic judgment.

Certain attitudes and knowledge are necessary conditions for embodying the democratic values in the lives of the citizen, but without skills in collective deliberation and in using knowledge in these deliberations, the school will not have provided the sufficient conditions for democratic education.

Developing readiness and competence for sharing in the economic, political, and moral values of the modern society entails two important skills. One is the interpretive use of the basic academic disciplines for the understanding of societal problems. For example, perceiving and thinking about the quality of the environment in terms of chemistry, physiology, economics, psychology, and sociology is not an automatic byproduct of a high school or even a college diploma.

33. I do not mean to attribute to Dewey a lack of aesthetic sensitivity. *Art as Experience* is a clear refutation of any such charge, but only in recent years have educators paid much attention to this book.

Once the basic sciences and the humanities are really made part of the interpretive framework of the individual, the problem-solving curriculum is the only sensible way of testing and using that knowledge, but the activity curriculum cannot be substituted for formal and systematic study of the basic disciplines. Such study probably never will be easy or intrinsically interesting for everyone, not even for all who are gifted. Nevertheless, this kind of generalizable study is a condition for genuine shareability in a modern technological society. As yet, this condition cannot be met and there is little evidence that the American schools will be able to meet it very soon. There are reasons for this and it is not easy to get around them. One is the belief that the academic disciplines do not really matter much in the life of the average citizen. Another is the belief in the desirability of early induction of youth into vocational or prevocational schooling—despite the evidence for a shortened work-week and work life.[34] These beliefs, to my mind, are mistaken ones. In addition to these reasons there is the fact of the apparent indifference of so many youngsters to academic learning. This situation can be countered partially by improved methods of instruction, but this is not the only task children dislike which we insist they perform. The point is whether there is good reason for being insistent.

The other skill entailed in developing competence for sharing in modern society, in addition to that of interdisciplinary thinking or the use of school learnings to interpret problems, is that of working with others in the act of collective problem-solving. This skill unites the attitudes and feelings about the "democratic thing to do" regarding the duties and rights of decision-making with the art of reasoning in the hypothetico-deductive mode. This art is partly habit and partly creative imagination. It is habitual in the use of

34. The U.S. Department of Labor has estimated that during the 1960s the number of people employed in professional and technical occupations will have increased 44 percent, the number of semiskilled workers 13 percent, and the number of unskilled workers not at all. *Mobility and Worker Adaptation to Economic Change in the United States* (Washington: U.S. Government Printing Office, 1963), p. 34. Also see Burton R. Clark, *Educating the Expert Society* (San Francisco: Chandler Publishing Co., 1962); Sigmond Nosow and William H. Form, eds., *Man, Work, and Society* (New York: Basic Books, 1962); Henry Borrow, ed., *Man in a World at Work* (Boston: Houghton Mifflin Co., 1964); Grant Venn, *Man, Education, and Work* (Washington, D.C.: American Council on Education, 1964).

the forms of thought we call logical; it is creative in the formation of hypotheses, thinking about possible testable consequences, and hitting upon generalizations that might be relevant to the situation at hand. It also involves sensitivity to the utterances and moods of others in the group and imaginative reconstruction of the experience of others. Group inquiry, therefore, as the authors of *The Improvement of Practical Intelligence* understood it, is more than a logical game; it is an interaction among persons that involves coming to understand *oneself,* or in modern jargon, to know *who one really is.*[35]

If the concept of democracy really shapes our educational goals, then it will specify these attitudes, knowledges, and skills in the program of every pupil, for these are the minima for living a democratic life in a modern mass society.

Perhaps the most disturbing reorientation demanded of us is to accept the changing perimeter of the moral domain. The Judeo-Christian tradition regards human life as a drama in which the actors are moral agents. Man is responsible for his actions and therefore subject to praise and blame. However, one of the results of modern technology is the extraordinary division of labor that makes it almost silly to try to fix responsibility for social phenomena.

In such a world, efficiency rather than morality is the relevant criterion; efficiency is bureaucracy moralized. For example, when a development in technology makes it efficient to displace thousands of workers, there is an indifference to the fact that innocent individuals are asked to bear the total burden of an event from which the rest of society may benefit. In a modern mass society the inner logic of the system will generate all sorts of consequences, and they might all be defended as efficient for the system as a whole. But because the individuals do raise the moral question, we have social problems; the search for social justice is a symptom of the discrepancy that exists between morality and efficiency.

The current protest against science and technology betokens an unwillingness to live in an amoral or demoralized world; human beings, it seems, have an incurable craving for villains and heroes,

35. See also Kenneth D. Benne, *Education in the Quest for Identity and Community* (Columbus: College of Education, Ohio State University, 1962) and Irving L. Horowitz, "Consensus, Conflict and Cooperation: A Sociological Inventory," *Social Forces* 41 (1962): 177-88.

i.e., the moral categories. And so we must search for areas of action in which morality is still relevant, where identity and responsibility still make sense. Hence the need for new behavioral forms that can exemplify the moral virtues for individuals and for society. The commitment to social justice entails a duty to search for new ways of distributing equitably both the benefits and costs of social action, but this search, I repeat, involves a high level of intellectual as well as moral development.

We have heard a good deal in recent years about the inadequacy of the Protestant ethic to assay the quality of either individual or social life. This ethic has also been called the middle-class ethic and is supposed to be the target of the revolt of protesting youth —flower youth, black and white militant youth, and others. This has confused everything. Rugged individualism in economics is to be rejected, but no individualism is too rugged for personal conduct; moral arguments, when raised by the establishment, are to be shouted down, but participatory democracy is to be justified on moral grounds; intellectuals were traditionally identified with faith in and commitment to the methods of reason; today, avant-garde intellectuals are supposed to be anti-intellectual.

What does all this confusion mean for the goals of the school? One result, as might be expected, is uncertainty and indecision. Textbooks in the social studies usually are written by the more advanced intellectuals; the teaching staff and the majority of the students in our public schools belong to the lower middle class or the conservative segments of the upper middle class, as do many school board members. The textbooks are likely to announce the relativity of all values in the preface and then proceed in the subsequent chapters to make judgments about society that are as firm as absolutes, and this is confusing to those who read with understanding.

I see no early escape from this confusion because an escape involves a radical rethinking of the values of democracy, and one doubts that the school will take leadership in this intellectual task. Yet the redefinition is going on. The diffuse but industrious efforts of the behavioral sciences, together with the natural sciences, are changing our perception of the social reality. The arts and the other humanities are groping for life patterns that will

embody the abiding values of democracy in the dress of new circumstances. In time, these will filter down into the curricula of
the schools. But in anticipation of that day educational leaders
have little choice but to achieve and maintain an awareness of
what is going on in the social reality. Otherwise, their goals will
be shaped by notions of democracy tuned to another age or perhaps by notions that are not democratic at all.[36]

36. For many valuable discussions of topics touched upon in this paper, see
V. T. Thayer and Martin Levit, *The Role of the School in American Society,*
2d ed. (New York: Dodd, Mead & Co., 1966).

# CHAPTER VII

# Yesterday's Curriculum/Today's World: Time to Reinvent the Wheel

MARK R. SHEDD

NORMAN A. NEWBERG

RICHARD H. DE LONE

To those who have studied the history of American public education it is evident that by the time it was clear that free, universal education was a national goal, it was also clear that the definition of education as something that takes place in schools was a tricky and perilous one. The early Progressives grappled in various ways with this problem, e.g., Jane Addams's attempts to link education and the settlement movement, or the Gary schools under William Wirt. They were living in and were aware of major social changes brought about by the industrial revolution. They felt that social and economic change was producing special needs for education—such as vocational training—but they also saw that education was starting to take over functions that had traditionally been family or communal functions; hence Wirt's efforts to make the school a neighborhood center. There was an effort—a noble experiment—to make education the province of a special new creature called the public school. This new creature would assume those crucial functions of village and family, institutions maimed by the industrial revolution, functions that constituted what John Dewey later called growth. The "whole child" became the concern.

Whatever else one may think of it, this was an extraordinary venture in the sociocultural history of mankind. In retrospect, it seems a shame that those pioneer pedagogues did not have a chance to really test out, think, rethink and begin anew more than once as they undertook this job, which is still the task of public education. But the times did not permit such essential luxuries. From its beginning, public education has been the servant of demands for increased quantity—more years in more kinds of programs for more children with more teachers (smaller classes). With few exceptions, neither individual schools nor school systems have had the real chance or the leisure needed to pause, think, restructure, evaluate, and seek alternative, possibly better, ways of operating which such an experiment demands.

In the transition from a society of nuclear units—family and village—to a mass society held together by concrete ribbons and electronic bands; in the drive of an oft-slighted profession to give itself status; in the face of pressure to produce, public education was literally driven to become the arrogant monolith it is today. A monolith because, in the interests of expedient production, a kind of modular social system was developed with all classrooms, schools, and school systems essentially interchangeable. Arrogant because of the disappearance somewhere along the way of the humbling realization that it was an experiment, that the equation of schooling with education was novel and untested.

It is almost as if some demiurge decreed that public education would be ruled by the law of the lowest common denominator; that some impulse would force, on a massive scale and within each mirrored microcosm of that mass, gravitation towards the simplest answers, the most expedient forms of organization, the tritest objectives. So the Progressive movement debased Dewey's complex thought into the banalities of the Life Adjustment movement or free expressionism. So today we have schooling which masquerades as education but in reality is little more than a process of training, socializing, and nationalizing in the interests of production.

It is not that these functions are a priori illegitimate. At certain times and to certain extents, in the service of certain ends, they are certainly necessary, though it is a mistake to view them as ends in themselves. In the early decades of this country, for instance, there was a legitimate need to "nationalize" the waves of immigrants coming to this land and to help them cope with this society. They wanted a country and the country needed to make them part of it. One may deplore, however, the extent to which that process was characterized by the assumptions articulated by Ellwood Cubberley of Stanford University, who declared that the coming of the immigrants had "served to dilute tremendously our national stock and to corrupt our civic life." Cubberley felt education must "implant in their children, so far as can be done, the Anglo-Saxon conception of righteousness, law and order." His ghost can be found today haunting the halls of schools attended by black, Indian, Mexican American, Puerto Rican children, and the children of the poor in general, schools which seem so often bent on breaking those children to notions of Anglo-Saxon civility.

Training is a valid function as well. There are skills, academic and vocational and social, to be learned. One questions, however, the pervasive belief that such skills can be *taught* by will or fiat of the teacher without a corresponding will on the part of the learner.

Questions of validity aside, we would assert that it is a fundamental error to think that these functions, no matter how they are structured or performed, constitute education. Education worthy of the name is growth. Growth is not simply a process of mimesis. It is not simply a matter of cognition. It involves feeling. It has its own rhythms, independent of the metronomic bells of schools: rhythms of contemplation as well as action, of dreaming as well as analysis, of rest as well as motion. It is to a certain extent the product of accident—the accident of environment. The self-contained classroom is a myth. Every child brings into the four walls of the classroom a world, and he sees from his desk, as if through crystal, a world beyond. To deny these realities mocks education and may even hinder training. Students do not riot because they are reading at a third-grade level. They riot because of the dehumanization of schools.

Education, as Dewey knew, is a set of paradoxes which can only be ultimately resolved or evaluated by the people living them and on the terms of those people: the paradoxical opposition of teaching and learning; and the paradoxes posed by individual growth in a context of communal values, by the relationship of in-school reality and out-of-school reality, by an education which prepares a student to cope with society's norms but also to change them. What educator would dispute Dewey's statement that education is "that reconstruction or reorganization of experience which adds to the meaning of experience, and which increases ability to direct the course of subsequent experience"? But what school or curriculum pays more than lip service to that goal?

In the pressure to produce, the school adopted the agency of production in the society at large, the factory. This is not a new analogy; it is a truism. The describable procedures of schools are grading, sorting, selecting, assembling, and rejecting, under the guise of quality control. Schools are hierarchal agencies with hierarchal authority structures characterized as well by specialization of labor. The only questions which must be answered and hence the only questions meaningfully asked are those answered in the marketplace: How many graduates? How many get jobs? How many go to college? How do they score on standard achievement tests? The analogy can be spun out to extraordinary lengths—and has been.

But the criticisms are familiar and these code words should suffice to convey a congerie of attitudes which constitute an evaluation of "yesterday's curriculum." John Holt, among others, has probed the extent to which that curriculum—what children really learn in school—is the unwritten agenda, the world view, conveyed by the assumptions, the climate, the implicit social function and structure of the school. The school, as an organism, that is, is the curriculum. The lesson that mathematics and English are separate disciplines and never the twain shall meet, that order is preferable to creative noise, that vocational students are dumb—these are the curricula, the true lesson plans of our schools. They remain stamped in the brain long, long after the trigonometric functions are forgotten. The victims of education confuse them with reality. The survivors learn only that schooling has little to do with life. All children are "taught" to mistrust language, to see all words as phony and to expect hypocrisy behind all eloquence, because the rhetoric of the Progressive movement remains—its sole, sad legacy—while the reality of the school denies it. We talk about educating the whole child and drill him in the multiplication tables. Is it any surprise that the vocabulary of a generation sometimes seems limited to a handful of words? "Dig it?" "Far out." "Groovy."

The gap between rhetoric and reality, which we have tried to suggest has historical causes, plus an examination of what fills that hollow, indicates one place to start looking for the meaning of "irrelevance"—the code word discovered by awakening blacks and adopted by awakening students to describe "yesterday's curriculum."

*Relevance* is a curious term when applied to education. Obviously enough, if education helps connect the experiences and needs of students with useful skills and knowledge, if it is really education, it is relevant. But that tautology is not very helpful since perceptions of need do change in time. Ten years ago students asked if their education was functional: would it prepare them for the competition of college or a job? Now the root of what they are saying seems to be that classes are boring or oppressive because the learning experience does not touch them personally. They say that certain experiences are either relevant or irrelevant to their private concerns. They seem to be asking—or demanding—that schools help them bridge the gap between their personal, private concerns and the world of public knowledge, as represented more or less adequately by school subjects (which we have commonly but erroneously called "the curriculum").

It is a disturbing and challenging fact that to that kind of question teachers can not possibly give the answer. All they can give is themselves, their experience, and access to whatever tools they have found useful in facing the same issues. They can give access to those tools—which may perfectly well include geometry or a poem—but they cannot use them for the students. Nor can they force students to use the tools, unless mimicry is mistaken for use. Robert Frost once told a group of educators that "you can't correct a person into being." But training, socializing and nationalizing, the rage for order, the insistence on certain kinds of behavior, the demand for subservience of student to teacher and teacher to system seem more often than not just such an attempt.

This definition of relevance centers around the quality of relationships which permeate and bind together the school-community environment. It raises such questions about the school process as: Who has the power? How are decisions made? How are human and physical resources treated, viewed, and used? Who selects particular values or ends and how are they taught?

When a student perceives his education as irrelevant, he is often saying: "I feel trapped in someone else's need to conquer my mind and heart; I feel incidental to someone's need to conquer or placate some other authority; I feel manipulated and controlled so that authority can maintain a status quo which has become its being. Teachers and administrators don't see me as a person. They neither allow nor assist me into being."

If this is so, and if the process of becoming "being" is essential to relevant education, then relevance depends on students, parents, teachers, and administrators sharing status, power, and decision-making. Each must have equal opportunity to be a source of educational energy. When power is diffused, leadership tends to emerge from previously unnoticed sectors. But such diffusion of power requires a high tolerance for ambiguity and a willingness to accept increased complexity in dealing with educational problems. That is both the virtue and the difficulty which follow as schools and school systems move from structures of centralized, autocratic leadership through decentralization to a more democratic process of decision-making—a point we shall return to.

We have suggested that irrelevance is the product of not will, conspiracy, or ineptness, but primarily of the pressures of production. Quantity more than quality was the effective demand, and the modular organization and hierarchal structure of schools which developed to meet it contained the seeds of irrelevance as well.

The demands are changing now, and perhaps that is because in many ways the American school has met the challenge of size. While some expansion may still be "in the works" (particularly in the early childhood years), it is almost true that the material possibilities for equal educational opportunity exist for all children. There are obvious exceptions to that statement, but we think it is true that educators increasingly should be able to find the breathing space necessary to face the qualitative issues which the times demand.

We believe that a way to begin this process, a way to develop a curriculum for today's and tomorrow's world, is to find new metaphors—new ways of organizing our thinking about education and creating correspondences between concepts and constructs. We take the notion of a metaphor seriously. Education itself is a metaphor, as the Latin roots of the word suggest. There is no objective correlative to the state a student is "in" or the one to which he is "led out." These words may suggest many ideas which seem concrete: one is led out of ignorance into knowledge, or out of self into society, or out of savagery into civilization. Yet on examination these are all metaphoric descriptions themselves of relative conceptual states—relative to a particular society or a particular individual's understanding of that society. As many an operations researcher can testify, it is almost impossible to pin down what one person means by education and probably impossible to get two people to agree on the same objectifiable meaning.

Education, then, is highly ambiguous and we should not pretend otherwise. Because it is ambiguous, it can never be constrained by an absolute definition. It must always rely for its meaning on the resonances individuals bring to it. Metaphors in turn receive their vitality from ambiguity—a queer kind of ambiguity which illumines more than it obscures because a good metaphor always suggests the tenuous, tenebrous linkages between all things. Good metaphors for education should provide linkages, too. Linkages create relevance. And they should have the vitality of ambiguity. Ambiguity permits participation and participation is itself a precondition of relevance. (A bad metaphor, like the factory, pretends to a false clarity which limits participation.)

To search for new metaphors, we will go back to the beginning; back also to the problem suggested at the opening of this chapter, the problem born of but largely ignored by the effort to establish a new area of human endeavor called schools which would take over (in a specialization of social labor) the educative functions of society.

The obvious danger of specialization is that it creates alienation. This is particularly a danger in specialization of education, which from primordial times has been inseparable from the life of family, tribe, or village. Now we see that students and others are complaining that schools have no relationship to their lives. At the same time, we hear the same complaint about work, about politics, about other institutions. There is little sense of organic unity in the lives we lead and the places we inhabit. The pollution which threatens our health seems arbitrary, no product of ours, unrelated to our lives. Indeed, for a long time, as the ecologists are now telling us, we all proceeded on the assumption that buying a paper, driving a car, or cooling by an air conditioner had no particular consequences for our future (individually or collectively) other than those apparent in the act itself.

The need to rediscover a sense of organic unity is real. It is essential both to save our lives, as the ecologists tell us, and our psyches, as the psychiatrists tell us.

Ecology, itself a science of metaphors (linkages), urges on us the need to begin again, to rethink it. This need is directly related to the kind of world we have created—the technological world which began, we can say, with the invention of the wheel. No one could foresee where the wheel would lead us, that the open road we built with it and for it would have an end. It is hard to understand how it got us here. Yet, its spinning, its centripetal force, has created disarray. As Yeats said, "Things fall apart, the center will not hold." In a "technetronic" age, education must provide a "reconstruction or reorganization of experience." We must rediscover the principles and linkages that infuse and make coterminous the individual and his community, education and life.

Education, then, must be a process of reinventing the wheel.

— o —

In a funny, ironic way, while educators have talked about "parallel structures, alternatives, and competing systems"—the argot of change—kids have gone out and created them. Communes, rock groups, drug trips, ashrams, hitchhiking, motorcycle packs, the Black Panther party, Students for a Democratic Society, combinations of the above—all are at least in part educational alternatives, just a little farther out and a little less obviously so than free schools, storefront academies, and free universities.

When they work, communes quite clearly are examples of learning communities: (a) learning specific skills as part of an effort to learn about self, (b) living with others, (c) building a community, and (d) sometimes learning or creating a religion. In a commune, the banality of the do-it-yourself fad of the early 1960s can gain the dignity of a metaphysic. All sorts of skills must be learned—farming, wiring, carpentry, plumbing, auto mechanics. A variety of crafts are frequently pursued—photography, woodworking, batik, pottery, dressmaking. Political action may be a goal. And a surprising amount of "book learning" takes place in some communes we have visited—not simply learning related to the survival tasks of the community, but also reading, discussing, and guiding each other into all sorts of intellectual areas.

Many rock groups consist of self-taught musicians who "teach" each other what they know. Most rock groups write their own songs. In any case, these groups are self-directed classes in music and creative writing. Sometimes the members also live together and constitute a kind of commune.

Behind these two contemporary phenomena lie the age-old educational models of family and/or village. So too with the Black Panther party, which is out to create (a) a new identity for a race and its members and (b) new black-controlled "communities," and which in its own orientation and educational programs is very explicitly in the education business. Black studies and social studies (a neo-Marxian historical revisionism) serve as the core of the curriculum. SDS, with its fragmented subgroups, represents a variant of this model: clans within a tribe, including Mark Rudd and the nomadic Weathermen.

The highways of the Northeast were flooded with hitchhikers following the early closing of hundreds of colleges after the Cambodian invasion of May 1970. One of the authors who picked up a number of students during this period was told by several of them that they were traveling "to find out what's happening." They were, as one put it, "just going places and rapping with people." The entire Northeast corridor, and perhaps other sections of the country as well, had become a floating seminar session.

Hitchhikers, motorcyclists, even kids "tripping out" on drugs are, like the argonauts, using another age-old educational model, the voyage, seeking to learn from experience. Travel broadens, as their parents say, and the archetype of Odesseyus stands behind that cliché.

In citing these educational alternatives of the youth culture, we are not suggesting that they provide "the answer" to the problems of public education. That would be ridiculous on the face of it. Too often, the dynamics of the educational model selected are not sufficiently understood. In his volume of poems, "At the End of the Open Road," Louis Simpson asks: "Where are you, Walt?/The Open Road leads to the used-car lot." And Whitman replies: "I

am here . . . Did I not warn you that it was Myself I advertised?"
Journeys do not lead to answers which sit around like pots of gold
at the end of the rainbow. They lead back into the self.

But we are suggesting that these phenomena are responses to
deeply felt needs, legitimate and genuine needs acted on by few
students but perceived by many. They are cues, not solutions, which
education cannot ignore. They are cues that relevance, as demonstrated by these examples, is indeed understood by youth as a
process of personal engagement, learning, discovery, or creation.
They are cues that youth really do have a deep desire for education—one that is not being met in schools. And they are also
attempts at reinventing the wheel. A commune is the most obvious
example of that. But we do not believe that most of these attempts
are adequate or based on a full understanding of what "reinventing
the wheel" means. The need to eliminate that inadequacy provides
the opportunity and sets the direction for a new "curriculum," a
new structuring of education by those who call themselves educators. In the succeeding pages of this chapter, we will attempt to
analyze first what we see as the errors—sometimes the delusions—
in many youthful efforts to "reinvent the wheel." Then we will try
to suggest what the process might mean, both in theory and in
practice. Finally, we will try to sketch what might be involved in
changing schools from neo-factories to forums for reinvention.

— o —

This is the "now" generation. The inmates of Charenton Asylum
in Peter Weiss's "Marat/Sade" give it a motto: "We want our
rights and we don't care how. We want our revolution now."

But *nowness,* for all its immediacy, is hard to define. It seems to
mean immediate gratification of all sensual desires, immediate
change of existing institutions. It means "getting out of one's head"
(anti-intellectualism) and into one's body, or else "blowing one's
mind" to achieve mystical experience. Nowness tends to deny that
anything can be learned from the collective experience of a civilization. "Haven't you heard, the past is dead!" cry the Nietzsches of
now. "All we inherit are dead traditions and decadent habits."

This denial of the past has as its corollary a refusal to examine
the future. Indeed, denial of the past does deny the future. It denies
the existence of time and so produces only scoffing when the

question is raised, "After the revolution, what?" Instead, the Abbie
Hoffmans urge "revolution for the hell of it." And in some ways,
the science of the over-thirty generation lends credence to such
attitudes. "You have no future," Dr. Ian McHarg, the famous
ecologist, said, speaking at an Earth Day gathering in Philadelphia,
April 22, 1970. That was McHarg's opening sentence and he repeated it three times to assure the audience of his sincerity.

The ominous evidence of the ecologists, coupled with the night-
mare image of the bomb, does suggest that there is precious little
future worth dreaming about. Unless, that is, there are drastic
changes in the way we perceive the consequences of our economic,
social, national, and personal practices—drastic changes in the
way we live. On a massive scale indeed, there must be reinvention
of the wheel.

The danger of nowness, the denial of time, is that it warps and
negates the process of reinvention. To carry the metaphor a step
farther, rejecting the past creates the illusion that the wheel is
being invented and not *re*invented. The distinction is one of awareness and it is crucial. For when illusion is substituted for awareness,
it can produce not only ineffectiveness but also extraordinary
hypocrisy.

Sometimes that hypocrisy is not so much vulgar as it is exalted.
The pastoral convention of Western literature provides a good
example of the latter: courtiers fleeing the corruption of the court
in search of rustic purity. In his use of that convention, however,
Shakespeare was able to illustrate the nature and the necessity of
an awareness that prevents illusion. In plays such as *As You Like
It* and *The Winter's Tale* he always makes it clear that a courtier
does not become a shepherd simply by changing clothes, carving
his lover's name into a tree, or minding sheep. Shakespeare presents
clear distinctions between Rosalind and Audrey, between Perdita
and Mopsa, between the world of the courtly swain and the real
shepherd. His point is that where you come from, what you know,
what alternatives you have the luxury of rejecting, all determine
what you are and what your new world is. To believe otherwise is
to inhabit a fragile shell of delusion. That mistake, which can be
profound, can also be crude: the youth who buys expensive hippie
clothes, lets them disintegrate and thinks he is free of material

desires; the Progressive Laborite who drops out of college, puts on a blue work shirt and thinks he is achieving solidarity with the working class; or the kid who rides out to the commune on the motorcycle his father gave him, derides "pigs" for their slavishness to affluence and thinks he is an honest revolutionary.

Sometimes the freewheeling, moving, traveling culture of the young, who are after all products of mobile America, suggests that they, like Tom in Tennessee Williams's *The Glass Menagerie,* are attempting to "find in motion what was lost in space." That is what happens if you think you are inventing the wheel but are actually just riding it.

How can an educational system be responsive to nowness—to the pessimism, optimism, folly, commitment, and chaotic energies it variously manifests? The system can, of course, respond with conventional wisdom: "Each generation sees its own crisis as the worst man has had to face. It's always darkest before dawn. Just stick to the tried and true. Solve the task at hand and avoid overwhelming globalisms." These old saws may have a modicum of truth in them, but they are unlikely to be heard. Students, particularly adolescents, have little tolerance either for piecemeal evolutionary approaches or for deferring gratification in the interest of a long-range goal.

Perhaps we must accept the notion that nowness can be a discipline, a craft, a sequence of tools. But if "reinventing the wheel" is *what* we want to do, the question remains, *how* do we go about that? This suggests to us the need for another metaphor, a metaphor for a way of teaching that acknowledges and uses "now." We would suggest that such a metaphor can be found in Aikido, a new Japanese martial art.

An Aikido master does not see his opponent as someone to beat down or overpower. Rather, he encourages his attacker to do whatever he wishes. He then finds a way to move with the attacker, to use the other's energy to protect himself. In that sense, he literally becomes one with the attacker—their energies merge. In essence, the Aikido master says, "If I allow you to be part of me, I allow each of us to survive and I don't allow you to defeat me." In Aikido, one uses *now* only to move *beyond,* for the master is tuned to more than just the now, i.e., the movements of the attacker. His skill is directly linked to his awareness both of his own center of being and its relationship with the energy of the universe—metaphysical or spiritual awareness which is physicalized in Aikido postures and movements. That awareness, Aikido adepts say, is a crucial aspect. It provides a kind of pivot on which the energies of now are turned and transformed. Surely analogous awareness— of self and of beyond—is equally essential to the teacher.

The implications of this metaphor suggest another old saw, more honored in the breach than in the observance: you have to begin where the student is. This does not simply mean beginning with an assessment of cognitive development, however. The teachers must also meet the concerns and feelings—the total situation—of the student now. Usually that does not permit requesting students to suspend gratification in the interest of long-range, abstract goals and objectives (which the student may perceive simply as rationalization for the meaningless). Frequently, students' energies available for learning seem to exist in inverse proportion to the distance of the objective. The ability to work within a framework of long-range objectives is the result of learning a process. And that means not simply learning certain skills (e.g., planning skills, which are rarely taught in school) but also developing out of experience an appreciation for the usefulness of the process.

We have talked about *what* and *how* at a very general level but we have not addressed the third member of that standard triumvirate of questions—the question most asked in schools: *why*. *Why* is no doubt a useful question, but it is also the most treacherous of the three and its value is often overinflated. When a person asks, *why*, the implication is often, "Now we'll get down to the truth." Unfortunately, that is not usually the case. Frequently, *why* is a controlling question.

*Why* is often used to attack assumptions and force the questioned into a defensive posture. There is no more dangerous question for lovers than "why do you love me?" Furthermore, the answer to a *why* question is usually "because." "Because" appears to be a solution when, in fact, it is just another assumption, as David Hume and the skeptical empiricists so carefully demonstrated.

Pete Seeger sings a song in which a son repeatedly asks his father, "Why, oh why, oh why, oh why . . ." and the father always replies, "Because, because, because, because." There's not much learning or sharing of experience in that interaction.

When someone asked Sir Edmund Hilary why he climbed Mt. Everest, he responded, "Because it was there." That answer struck a deep note and has been widely repeated. Significantly, Hilary's statement denies the validity of the *why* question by offering a *what* response: "It was there." When we ask *how* and *what* questions, we are really asking for information—concrete descriptions and specific details. *What* and *how* questions produce involvement and engagement in a dialogue, an involvement that can include all the senses ("the whole child"). *Why* questions tend to separate the person from the object or the experience. They usually mobilize only cognitive, verbal responses. When a *why* question engages more than the intellect, it is frequently because the questioner assumes the role of armchair psychiatrist and abuses the role by increasing, rather than alleviating, guilt: "Why do you feel a need to hurt me?"

The importance of the *why* is that it can help us to state intentions for our behavior. But intention is only useful if the response to our behavior is congruent with our purpose. The feedback loop in information-processing theory is designed to correct for the gap between our hoped-for response and the actual response our behavior receives. In this process, feed-back allows us to modify behavior, to transmit congruent messages with mind and body, and to stimulate responses which are congruent with our intentions. That process of modification provides an empirical way of discovering or validating some *why*s. It permits self-conscious behavior (which itself implies a sense of time). It is this self-consciousness which sometimes seems abhorrent to the disciples of "now"—abhorrent because *why* suggests a lack of spontaneity and interaction, a sense of past determining present. By extension, *why* seems to be a way of calculating and manipulating one's own behavior or the behavior of another. But when you "do your own thing," you don't ask why. The problem is created, we believe, because most *why* questions imply a fixed, a priori system of intention or value that is higher than man's private system—immutable, a prison of *why*s, of God-given standards. And of course we all know that hypocrisy is the gap between one's stated inten-

tions and his concrete behavior. To many in the student generation, elimination of *why* will enable each person to be true to himself and relieve himself of the double bind of hypocrisy. Or at the
very least, elimination of given *whys* will permit a search for new
ones, either by turning towards Zen and more esoteric religions
or to astrology, or through invention of a new religion. Such *whys*
are distinguished from the *whys* of this country's traditions or
Western religions because (a) they are different and (b) that
difference permits the feeling, whether true or not, of having discovered or invented the *why*.

We are suggesting, then, a moratorium on *why*, particularly
the kinds of *whys* that are a priori *whys*, controlling *whys*, or *whys*
answered by *because*. Instead, there should be a concentration on
the *what* of inventing the wheel and the *how* of Aikido that may
permit new or renewed *whys* to emerge.

Recently, one of the authors led a group of teachers and students who wished to make the classroom climate more open. The
session started awkwardly, and there was a long period of silence.
Finally, some teachers decided to ask the students questions about
classroom climate. They began with *why* questions. "Why don't
you like school?" The questions sounded patronizing and the students responded in kind—they had seen this film before. After a
few minutes of this line of "attack," the group leader suggested
everyone talk "out of role" for awhile, and he asked a *what*
question. "What experiences give you pleasure?"

Immediately the level of participation increased. But one girl
seemed stuck on "school-type" responses. "There's nothing I do
well in," she replied, "I just get by in school."

A spinster gymnasium teacher intervened, saying, "Carol, I
just can't believe you. Everyone has at least one thing they
excel in."

"Yeah, I know you're supposed to, but I don't," Carol said
quietly.

Then the group leader asked Carol what she did for fun. She
said she liked going out with her boyfriend, and the dialogue between the group leader and Carol proceeded like this:

"What do you do?" "Drive around, dance." "How long have
you been going with this guy?" "Three years." "That's a long

time." "Yeah." "Wonder why he keeps going with you?" "Cause we have fun." "Guess he really likes you?" (Carol smiles.) "It's no small trick to keep a boy friend interested in you for three years. Lots of adults can't do that. You must really know how to please him."

Later in the session the group leader asked participants to search out someone they knew casually and ask a question they normally would not ask of a relative stranger. They were cautioned, however, only to ask questions they would answer themselves. The gym teacher, Miss Hayes, sought out Carol. Next, the participants were asked to share what they had experienced, and the gym teacher said: "I always thought I understood teen-agers pretty well. But today, I learned things I never knew before. I also learned some things about myself."

Miss Hayes was clearly moved by what Carol had told her. It was clear Carol had taught her something about the pleasure and pain of a caring male-female relationship. Just as important, she had learned to value Carol as a person. And Carol had learned that professional teachers can listen and learn from their students.

This knowledge creates a vista of opportunities for the two of them, but the next steps in the process are very delicate ones. The teacher has an investment in Carol and Carol cares about her. Because it is her vocation, Miss Hayes now wants to help Carol learn some of the things she knows—perhaps in the area of physical education, perhaps even reading. She wants to use the new relationship to motivate Carol, probably towards achieving some standard educational goals. But if she moves in quickly and, in effect, imposes her long-range goals on Carol, the energy that permitted this relationship to grow will be smothered because the relationship is frail. Carol's interest is still in the here and now. If, however, she begins to set goals on her own and comes to trust adults on *her* terms, she may also be available for learning about past and future. This is a crucial time for Miss Hayes as well because she has to trust in her own personality to get through to Carol. For, at this time, Carol's only attraction to school—her only reason to learn—is that she perceives the emergence of an important personal connection with Miss Hayes.

To the extent that she can provide a model for Carol, Miss Hayes can teach her things of value. The trick is to be a person first and a professional second. We are not suggesting that it is either feasible or desirable for Miss Hayes to ignore the skills she knows. The Aikido master is highly skilled, and that skill is important. But rather than closing Carol in with *why,* Miss Hayes must, like all good models and teachers, resonate more than she says, imply more than she makes explicit. When a great singer hits a note at the top of his range, we are amazed not so much that he has hit it, but at the implication that he can still sing another note beyond. Schools, in the name of education, frequently explain life away and leave students with a sense of dry, precise irrelevancies which obscure the rich ambiguities of life. A Chinese sage once said that to *see* more in life is to be abstract, but to *be* more in life is to be concrete. Goethe put it another way: "Thinking brings forth only thought/But living is with feeling fraught." Students want to be more concrete; they want involvement in life. A moratorium on *why,* like the moratorium created by the intervention of the group leader in this example, permits a curriculum that emphasizes *what* and *how.* There is an analogy here to the gestalt therapy developed by the late Frederick Perls. The gestalt therapist never asks, Why are you doing that? But he does ask, What are you doing now, and how are you doing it? The therapist never interprets another person's experience for him. He assumes that only the person can make sense of his life. His job as therapist (and, we are suggesting, the teacher's job as well) is to promote awareness of the *what* and *how* of behavior. (The analogy must not be taken to mean that the teacher becomes a therapist and attempts to "treat" the psychic concerns of therapy.) In gestalt therapy, the patient's job is to integrate those parts of his experience which are alienated from himself. So, too, in education, integration of self with experience, of school with the environment(s) surrounding it, is the job of the learner. In this task, the teacher as well as student is *inevitably a learner.*

That part of learning, the integration of experience, the discovery or re-creation of wholes, is one way of reinventing the wheel. The wheel is a metaphor, that is, for unity. All radii lead to the center. In education, all experience and learning should lead to the self.

But the wheel is also a symbol of motion, of movement in time, of motion that does not result in disintegration but has a center and which maintains unity in change.

To give another example, the same group leader recently conducted a sensitivity training workshop for teachers, a workshop which employed gestalt techniques. The workshop met for eight ninety-minute sessions. At the beginning, the leader asked each teacher to attempt to state his goal for the workshop, preferably a concrete goal that could be achieved in twelve hours. One of the participants—we will call her Jenny—was a tense high school mathematics teacher who decided that her goal was "to recognize my self-worth. I don't want to always put myself down. I want to value my own experience."

At several sessions, the group had worked with Jenny on her goals but she had achieved relatively little change in her feelings or behavior. She simply talked on and on about herself, piling up neat rationalizations, stacking her identity in various piles of motive and causality. Her hands were in constant motion. Her mind often raced ahead of her ability to articulate, and she was left mouthing silent syllables, trying to find the words for a thought she had half-forgotten. She was, in short, out of touch with her own processes.

At one session, the group leader broke the tradition of opening with silence by asking if anyone wanted to work on his goals, and Jenny bolted. She started to talk, then said that as soon as she started talking her heart began to pound. She was off on a whirlwind of explanations when the group leader intervened by asking her what she was doing with her right hand. Looking down, she saw it was clutching at her heart. The leader then suggested that she let her hand and her heart have a dialogue, assuming the role of each in turn and speaking for them. Jenny did, as follows:

Hand:  I want to soothe you. I want to make you quiet and calm down.
Heart:  Let me alone. You're hurting me.
Hand:  I want to stop you.
Heart:  Don't! If you do, I'll die.

At that point, Jenny's hand came to rest on her lap. Her voice became quieter and calmer. She perceived a struggle going on in herself and stopped it—stopped giving herself orders and fighting them. She integrated those parts of her body that had been alienated from each other and hence from herself.

Shortly, however, she began again to invent reasons, *whys*, for her behavior. The leader stopped her and urged her to resume the integration she had found. Her behavior made her intentions clear. There was no need to translate them into a (preexistent) framework of *whys*.

At this point, another teacher said he thought Jenny was a lovely person—someone he had always respected and admired. Jenny bolted again and started to talk about his compliment. The leader intervened once more, asking her if she could simply experience the pleasure of being complimented. Suddenly, and with a sense of finality, Jenny smiled and became silent. Finally the experience was concrete and she did not have to interpret.

We do not mean to imply that Jenny had miraculously achieved her goal. The time, effort, and difficulty with which she temporarily reached it in the group indicate the length of the road she must travel to learn to stay in touch with what is going on inside her in the now. Rather, we cite this example as fairly representative of teachers who teach but are unaware of their need to continue to learn. A good teacher should know and use both processes.

The example also suggests the futility of *whys*—futile to Jenny in trying to come to grips with herself and equally futile had the leader simply tried to tell her why she must integrate, even though the end result, as a concept, may be the same. This suggests that process is inseparable from content; that the meaning of content is constantly modified—drained or invigorated—by the process of its determination. The same students, we suggest, who would resist reading E. H. Gombrich's *Art and Illusion* when assigned in a college fine arts course may read it avidly if they come to it through *The Whole Earth Catalogue*. The subtitle of this popular new catalogue is *Access to Tools*. It lists books, frequently of a how-to-do-it nature, by many highly respected authorities in their fields. A book read as a result of scanning *The Whole Earth Catalogue* is read because it contains *what* and *how* information. Assigned in a college course, it is more likely used in the service of *why* or as a way of talking about a subject as a piece of content, not a process. Our culture, and our educational systems, unhappily seem to value answers—preferably the "right" ones—over processes that create options for ways of solving problems, or acting.

The foregoing illustrations are drawn from the experience of one program, the Philadelphia Affective Education Project, which provides one approach to a theory and methodology for a relevant curriculum for today's world. Norman Newberg and Terry Borton, as codirectors of the project over the last three years, have worked with a team of teachers and administrators trying to develop an approach to education which speaks directly to the concerns of students *now*—which not only helps them articulate those concerns but attempts explicitly to "teach," primarily through an arrangement of experiences, processes for dealing with those concerns. The project draws on the assumption, substantiated by the so-called Coleman report, that there is a direct correlation between a student's academic achievement and his ability to control his environment, his attitudes about himself, and his relationships with other people. It also assumes that the idea that there is a specific body of knowledge students need only imbibe to be educated is obsolete. The knowledge explosion demands instead that schools adopt Jerome Bruner's theory of teaching "the structure of knowledge."

The project's basic goal is to help students learn logical and psychological *processes* with which they can gain greater conscious control over themselves, their interpersonal relations, and their environments. These are the "basic skills," the fundamentals of the program. The curriculum begins with the assumption that if these basic concerns of students are involved in it, education will be relevant to their needs. The project assumes that if teachers are in touch with these basics—if the teacher hears those concerns in himself and recognizes them in students—then meaningful learning can take place. It assumes that students are human beings first and students second. As people, they want to be seen, listened to, and understood. As students, they want meaningful information and skills to process a vast store of experience and to make a living. The first assumption reflects a humanistic approach; the second is more utilitarian. The project represents an effort to integrate the two. It believes that too often "humanistic" education has been muddleheaded and romantic, while the utilitarian approach has legitimized (or rationalized) the belief that training and socializing are education.

Bringing student concerns into the classroom is often a way of "turning kids on." But the Affective Education Project tries to move beyond the nowness of "turning on" to a stage in which students can use their energies to accomplish something tangible. To bridge these stages, it has created a "process" curriculum, in which processes or strategies for learning become curriculum content. This approach builds its theory on the information-processing loop derived from the relatively new science of cybernetics.

The first stage of the process, a response to an internal or external stimulus, is a process of *sensing*. In this stage, the question asked is *what*. What are my senses telling me? What information can I get that is useful in understanding my concern, and from what sources? As the data begins to build, the second stage—*transforming* that data into a personalized understanding of its implications— begins. The question here is really, "so what?" The transforming process may take place in many ways: it may assume a hard-driving analytic mode, for instance, or it may be a looser, free-wheeling, far-ranging, fantasizing, or contemplative mode. The theory makes no evaluative distinction between modes. The processor selects the method that he thinks is most promising.

Once the processor has developed an understanding of what he has sensed, he then begins to experiment with modes of action that will help him carry his understanding into a particular behavior, into an effective action that represents his intention. This stage of the process, *acting,* essentially asks the question, "how?"

Critical to the information-processing model, of course, is the feedback loop. Feedback tells the actor whether or not his behavior is congruent with his intentions, whether it produces the desired results. Feedback may come in "controlled" situations within the classroom. It may come outside the classroom as well. Wherever it occurs, it becomes a legitimate concern of the course.

We cannot describe the content of the Affective Education Project in depth. Space does not permit it, and furthermore we do not want to suggest that we are putting all our eggs in this basket. We have described the theory to the extent that we have in order to suggest that metaphors like "reinventing the wheel" and Aikido are not simple-minded or simple rhetorical gadgets. The job of developing them as effective educational programs demands intellectual rigor, personal involvement and risk-taking, and craft.

Nor do we wish to imply that once one has a metaphor and a theory—in this case, a theory developed, tested, modified, still changing after five years, and *working*—the rest is a neat bundle of methods. Ambiguity remains, must remain, and that means doubts and difficulties as well as moments of elation. For instance, there is a legitimate concern that process education might produce a class of new sophists, since a process, like words or technology, can be manipuated for good or ill. The project, however, does not try either to deny that, or to impose certain values. It does try to keep the question of values a vital part of the agenda. But in the final analysis it must place trust in the idea that morality is itself a process, the result of social encounters over the generations of man which have suggested the usefulness of certain standards. It seeks, by simulating such encounters in the school, to build an appreciation of that process, of the actuality of moral values, and to permit students to re-create or rediscover values.

So, too, grammar is nothing but conventions that developed because people found them useful in communicating. A comma that does not communicate has no use, no reason to exist. Grammar does not exist because certain rules say so. It exists because it is a useful tool, for some people at any rate, in communicating.

So, too, Paulo Friere, the Brazilian philosopher, radical, and teacher, discovered (much as Sylvia Ashton Warner discovered) that illiterate, impoverished Brazilians learned to read in no time if and only if the words they were learning were *charged* words, that is, words that embodied their concerns, words which received their power because the students had *first* learned that through being able to read and write such words they could gain a crucial tool for changing their own condition, for throwing off the political bondage which was preserved by an isolation their illiteracy reinforced. (For his successes, Friere was banned from his country.)

Process education, that is to say, is a way of reinventing the wheel. It does so by going back to prime causes, basic assumptions, and primal concerns which are at the root of systems of learning, which give those systems their meaning, and which, as they are recapitulated, become relevant. It makes connections not only between individual and environment but between past and future. It does so by including, not excluding: it includes private concerns of students as well as traditional pedagogic and educational concerns; it includes out-of-school experience; it includes—indeed, tries to eliminate distinctions between—cognitive and affective development. It may have a place of meeting, Room 215, but its classroom is ubiquitous.

It is a kind of education which is constrained and hampered by the various kinds of limiting modules the factory model of education imposes: by four walls of a classroom which are used to screen out and divide; by blocks of time and bells which ring, not because they have any relation to learning or growth but because they simplify and routinize production; by a priori definitions of right and wrong thought or behavior; by arbitrary distinctions between teacher and learner, and so on. Nor does the final examination suggest what the student or the teacher has accomplished. The process does not stop in June, does not take a summer vacation.

All this is to say that it will take major restructuring of schools and school systems to permit the reinventing of the wheel, the kind of restructuring which is also suggested by a number of other examples of schools or approaches which we think also provide illustrations of the metaphor:

1. The Leicestershire Plan and similar "discovery"-based programs.

2. The best of the free schools sprouting up across the country.

3. The new Adams High School in Portland, Oregon. Charles Silberman has suggested this may be the country's most important experimental high school because its central activity is the conscious exploring and redefining of what education is. That's reinventing the wheel.

4. Philadelphia's Parkway Program, a student-centered high school which finds a new physical setting in its effort to break through intellectual, programmatic, and temporal limitations and divisions of curriculum by literally making the city the school.

Or, turning back in time a half century or more, there were Dewey's Laboratory School, the Quincy school system under Colonel Francis Parker, and Marietta P. Johnson's Organic School.

These educational ventures are well known. Data about them are easily accessible. Many more models exist: schools which take their cue from students; schools where the teacher must (and does) develop skills as both colearner and guide; schools which reinvent the wheel and work.

We anticipate that at this point readers may be saying, "Fine, those are nice ideals, but they're so general. Can't you be more specific?" Our response is that *you* have to provide the specificity. In the 1920s, on the insistence of Superintendent Jesse Newlon, the Denver public school system institutionalized the idea that for curriculum to mean something to teachers, it must be the product of their own sweat and blood. A system of rotating committees and assignments was installed to give teachers a chance to interact with their colleagues (a rarity in most schools), develop curriculum, test it out in the classroom, and recycle through the sequence to refine and modify it. The system worked. It drew national attention. Soon there was demand for Denver curriculum packages. Of course, when the curriculum was packaged and exported and placed in the hands of teachers who were told to use it, it turned out to be no more effective than any other curriculum package. In Denver, they were reinventing the wheel. Everywhere else they were just standing in the assembly line.

That is not to say that it is impossible to learn from the experience of others, to get detailed information about the Leicestershire plan or the Philadelphia Affective Education Project, or the Parkway Program. It is possible. But the act of getting it, of selecting from it, of modifying it or improvising with it, is what makes it come alive. There is no such thing as teacher-proof material, for any material that is teacher-proof is also student-proof. By a mysterious alchemy that resides in the mystery of learning, any *what* or *how* that is accepted as "the answer" becomes its own stultifying *why*. For that reason, most curriculum guides or curriculum packages, no matter what the date on the cover, qualify only as yesterday's curriculum, which is no curriculum at all.

Other readers may be saying that there is nothing new in all that. But we do not wish to claim any particular originality of concept. At most, we may have rephrased some old ideas and ideals. The important question is, however, and it is especially critical because the ideas are not new, why have these ideas been so rarely realized?

One possible answer, of course, is to say that realization of them is impossible. Schools should not try to bite off more than they can chew. The task of education should be narrowly defined and other institutions will have to take up the slack. The family as a unit will have to regain its prominence. Or, churches will have to become more relevant. Or something—it's not the school's problem. That *might* of course be true. It sounds like good common sense, horse sense, sound business advice. Tough-minded. But it is probably as impossible as the idea of going back to an agrarian society, which would also solve a lot of problems. Furthermore, it implies that education should stick to various forms of skills training, maybe using computers to be more efficient and thus substituting the model of the aerospace industry for the worn-out metaphor of the old New England mill. But that begs the question of under what conditions (and on whose say-so) skills training becomes relevant or effective—an especially critical question, given compulsory education. It might even have been sound advice—simply to decrease frustration—when education did not really have time to worry about anything more complex than questions of quantity. But that time is passing, as we have suggested, both because the quantitative goals are within reach and because neither students nor taxpayers are much given to tolerating the old answers.

The "common sense" reply, we would point out, is a way of answering a *why* question (albeit a *why* with *how* implications) with "because." It may be more profitable to look at the *what* and *how* of the way school systems are organized. The crucial issue, that is, is not the idea—ideas are relatively cheap—but the implementation of the idea.

It is curious in this respect that while a great deal of attention has been focused over the years on teacher behavior, classroom style and management, and the relationship between teacher and student as they affect learning, much less attention has been given to the question of how various management systems—how administrative structure, style, and relationships—affect instruction. Following the factory model again, we have tended to treat administration and teaching as separate and specialized entities, as management and labor are so viewed in the industrial world. Only recently, for instance, has the battle for decentralization and/or community control being waged in some big cities begun to raise issues (deeper than superficialities about bureaucratic ineptness) concerning the relationship of learning to the political-fiscal-organizational structure of school systems. Yet, if "the school is the curriculum," it is equally true that the organization or system is the curriculum. As John Bremer, first director of the Parkway Program, once put it: "Modes of instruction tend to echo modes of social organization."

That apothegm has some profound implications. It is obvious enough, for instance, that "process" education demands changes in the training teachers receive. Preservice or in-service, that training should contain experiences like Jenny's which permit teachers to get in touch with their internal processes and the processes by which they relate to others, including students. It is equally obvious that prescriptive curriculum packages which limit rather than promote teacher improvisation have little or no use. But it is less obvious perhaps that (if modes of instruction echo modes of social organization) the benefits of more relevant teacher training or of curriculum which invites involvement will be dissipated unless the organization itself is changed. It's not that relevant teaching is impossible in existing school systems. It's just that it is harder, and most water tends to flow downhill. Most education tends to gravitate towards the lowest common denominator because it is easier and more convenient to fit one's activities into the mechanized routines of the factory school in the factory system. The notion that the teacher has the "right" answers echoes the notion that the principal has power and authority, more than the teacher but not as much as the superintendent, and so on. If one is reinventing the wheel, power is not legitimized by role because it is impossible to determine in advance who is the inventor.

To create an organization which encourages reinvention, an institution which resists institutionalization (John Gardner's phrase is "self-renewing"), an institution with different echoes and new resonance, decentralization is essential. We are not talking simply about administrative decentralization of big, unwieldy city school systems. Rather, because administration and instruction are really inseparable (really "the curriculum"), we are talking about decentralization of learning, the abolition of the effort to "correct into being," of which administrative decentralization is only a part. Every wheel must be a big wheel. A decentralized system, for instance, might retain a curriculum office, but that office would exist only to circulate ideas, to provide another source of energy in a learning situation where students, teachers, and parents would be the prime sources of energy, power, and leadership.

It is obvious that to design such a system one must start thinking from the bottom up, from the individual student, teacher, or group of learners. That is a difficult conceptual exercise, no doubt, but not impossible if some other conditions are met. We would simply suggest a few conditions and principles.

First, current practices in school finance must be changed. Centralized budget-making power follows from the need for systems to constantly scramble for funds. This is the source of education's vulnerability as a social system, and it operates to keep systems centralized since the delicate politics of school finance cannot be successfully engineered by diffuse power. This is the tail which wags the dog. On a large scale, the curriculum will not be changed, therefore, until the dynamics of funding education are changed. Voucher plans or formulas for "equal opportunity" funding which can be and have been devised at state and national levels provide starting places for working on this change. At the same time (and even harder, perhaps, to accomplish), the idea that "he who pays the piper calls the tune" must be reversed if the payer is a centralized state or federal agency, since that principle tends toward greater centralization. We must remove education from the politics of finance so it can become engaged in the politics of living.

Secondly, we are reinventing the wheel, not inventing it. That is, we do have existing school systems. Much as one might wish to start from scratch (the commune ideal), it is impossible. Change is involved, and that means change agents. Change agents, like teachers, need a metaphor for their jobs, and, like teachers, might well look for it in Aikido. No one rams home a change in education without denying what he is doing. Force may, in the short run, give the illusion of change. But in the long run, the medium remains the message and the message is one of power.

It follows that those whom the change must affect—students, teachers, even the adherents of the status quo—must provide the energy and give shape to the change. The best a change agent can do, be he administrator, board member, teacher, or politician, is create artful vacuums.

In the past, curriculum content has mirrored the form (the metaphor) of the school organization. In the future, the form of the school organization must mirror the curriculum. Teachers who do what they are told cannot teach students to think for themselves. Schools which run by the metronome cannot teach the rhythms of growth—collective or individual.

We will not attempt to develop these principles into a manual—in part, because it would take too long. But more important, it is because another marriage manual is not what is needed. Instead, the need is for educators who, after contemplation and reflection, find a new metaphor and follow Jerry Rubin's caveat to "do it."

SECTION III

A CONFIDENT WALK INTO THE FUTURE

# CHAPTER VIII

# Future-*Planning as a Means of Shaping Educational Change*

HAROLD G. SHANE

## Introduction

For many years, educators have been interested in and concerned with the future. They have made projections of possible developments and have argued persuasively about the alternative schools for tomorrow which their values have led them to support. As far back as 1936, Zirbes[1] had projected curriculum trends reflected in the literature of the era and described the type of programs which seemed to be emerging. Two decades later, in 1956, a conference at Syracuse University "explored" education for the year 2000 and produced a summary of the learned speculations of a number of scholars who participated.[2]

The late 1960s saw a substantial increase in publications dealing with probable educational developments. Eurich and others,[3] for example, produced *Campus 1980* which pictured both imaginative changes and persistent problems in higher education. Undoubtedly, the most extensive of the educational ventures in designing educa-

1. Laura Zirbes, *Curriculum Trends* (Washington: Association for Childhood Education, 1935), pp. 16-17.

2. C. W. Hunnicutt, ed., *Education 2000 A.D.* (Syracuse: Syracuse University Press, 1956).

3. Alvin C. Eurich, ed., *Campus 1980* (New York: Delacorte Press, 1968). Also see his more recent book, *Reforming American Education* (1969) in the chapter bibliography.

tion for the future was an eight-state project directed by Morphet which produced seven publications between 1966 and 1969.[4]

A representative selection of future-oriented publications may be found in the chapter bibliography.

In view of the diverse sponsorship of publications dealing with the future, it is evident that many groups and agencies in addition to the schools have become keenly interested in developments likely to occur during the next ten to forty years. Among them are business and industry, the military, and such groups as RAND Incorporated, the Hudson Institute, and the Institute for the Future established in Connecticut back in 1968. Not only have they been interested in probable tomorrows, they have sometimes sought to develop techniques for deploying money, effort, and time in such ways as were deemed likely to serve future corporate or national interests.

Section III of this yearbook, chapters viii through xiii, which this chapter introduces, is concerned with ways in which curriculum planners and developers can move into the future with renewed confidence in their policies and practices. It is the purpose of this particular chapter to present and to explore the idea that it is both possible and desirable to create a methodology for educational change and improvement. In other words, it is hypothesized that the present status of curriculum development can be made appreciably more significant through *future*-planning.

The term "*future*-planning" as used hereafter refers to a reasoned approach to the study of the many possible alternate educational futures which could lie ahead, subsequent selection of those which seem most promising, and then engaging in a deliberate attempt to create those particular educational tomorrows which are deemed most likely to serve learners of all ages. It is planning *of* the future, not traditional planning *for* the future. The *future*-planning con-

4. As noted in the text, Edgar J. Morphet was the director of the eight-state venture, Designing Education for the Future. David L. Jesser was associate director. The seven-volume report they edited and to which many distinguished educators contributed is available through the Citation Press, Scholastic Magazines, Inc., New York. The titles are: (a) *Prospective Changes in Society by 1980* (1966), (b) *Implications for Education of Prospective Changes in Society* (1967), (c) *Planning and Effecting Needed Changes in Education* (1967), (d) *Cooperative Planning for Education in 1980* (1968), (e) *Emerging Designs for Education* (1968), (f) *Planning for Effective Utilization of Technology in Education* (1968), and (g) *Preparing Educators To Meet Emerging Needs* (1969).

cept requires considerable explanation and elaboration because it brings to mind many questions such as: "Who would do the planning?" "Where does authority reside?" "What controls would protect education's traditional commitment to democratic processes?" and "Where would the planner find sound and authentic guidelines?" Many persons undoubtedly will find such queries threatening—and quite properly so—unless genuine reassurances in the form of social controls are an integral part of any *future*-planning.

*Passive curriculum planning.* When presenting the idea of creating improved educational futures, it is first necessary to establish the point that much present conventional curriculum planning is open to criticism in at least one important respect. It is based on the assumption that the future is *linear*. That is to say, contemporary planning usually assumes that there is *a single future,* an inescapable future to which we must conform and in which we succeed to the extent that we prepare for it correctly and prudently.

This assumed linear future, as many educators now see it, stretches out ribbon-like in a fashion similar to a straight, uninterrupted highway going across a wide stretch of western prairie. On such a road one can plan his journey by deciding where he will stop for fuel, food, and sleep—but he has only one pathway to follow to his destination.

In all forms of planning, including educational planning, the assumption of linearity which leads to the passive, conformist policy of adapting to an inferred series of coming future developments is an erroneous one. The future, because it has yet to come about, can bring with it any one of an infinite number of possible tomorrows—including none at all in a world grown capable of massive self-destruction.

Actually, the future may be construed to be a fan-shaped array of possibilities—of *alternate* futures, which can be powerfully influenced or "created" by man. *If this seems far-fetched, remember that man has created his past, and that his past was once his future!*

A proclivity to overbreed, various forms of environmental pollution, the prospect of smothering in garbage and refuse, and a medieval resistance to outlawing war are a part of the past and present. They are also representative of the possible futures among which mankind made yesterday's choices—and from among which he also must select his tomorrow's.

*Mediation and the selection of tomorrow.* If the present reflects past educational decisions and policies with which there is widespread discontent (and this seems to be an understatement), then a more prescient and methodical approach to planned curriculum change seems important to consider. More than that, if it is possible to envision possible educational futures by such procedures as analyzing and projecting trends—and many writers[5] evidently have done so—there is a growing obligation on the part of curriculum developers to choose among the trends and to intervene tendentiously whenever possible to bring about improved educational opportunities and procedures.

It is with certain reasoned conjectures as to how educators can begin to identify and to choose among possible futures and attempt to mediate or influence what is yet to happen to the curriculum that chapter viii is concerned. First, attention is directed toward the impact of change and the increasing pressure or stress under which this has placed twentieth-century man. Second, note is taken of the educationally important psychological impact of history on humans in the last thirty years. Following an examination of man's need to develop better means of preserving his deteriorating environment, the development and use of *future*-planning techniques for curriculum improvement is examined. The chapter concludes with some speculations as to what educational futures might conceivably emerge between A.D. 1975 and 2000 if *future*-planning is used to accelerate desirable changes in our schools.

## *Accelerating Change and Increasing Pressure*

As we know him today, "man" began to exist about fifty thousand years ago. That is, he crossed a great watershed as "knowing" began and as man started to think of himself as *man*. During most of the centuries that have since elapsed, the rate of change in the life of humans was glacial. For instance, forty thousand years or more passed between the origin of "man" as one who recognized him-

5. Cf. Harold G. Shane and June Grant Shane, "Forecast for the '70's," *Today's Education* 58 (January 1969): 29-32. This article was based on a review of over 400 publications containing projections and conjectures about possible futures with a bearing on education.

self as a sentient being and the next major watershed he crossed in his long trek through time. He passed this second great dividing line when he began to move from hunting to an agrarian life. This occurred in certain parts of Asia and Africa perhaps eight thousand years ago as methodical cultivation of grain foods was first devised and brought with it new basic life-styles and far-reaching social and cultural changes.

A third watershed was reached and passed in the fifth and sixth centuries B.C. We might think of this as a revolutionary religious turning point. Here, animistic and appeasement types of spirit or object worship began to be replaced by more sophisticated concepts. After the crucifixion, religious belief reached a point at which Judeo-Christian values begn to tincture virtually all aspects of life in the Western world. Roughly parallel transmigrations in ways of life occurred in the Middle East and Asia. While certain details of the emergent patterns of belief and conduct differed, the fact that ethical and often monistic religious concepts "created themselves" provided a comparable development in East and West.

The tempo of life continued slowly to accelerate. Some nineteen or twenty centuries later, in the 1300s and the 1400s, Western man climbed over the next major watershed, his fourth. This was at the time of the Renaissance, a period of man's quickening intellectual and aesthetic life. Twentieth-century humanism is rooted in this era and so is the germ of an inquiry approach to life's problems.

The fifth great change came about almost hastily when viewed in the perspective of history. This was the "production revolution" of the seventeenth and eighteenth centuries, which laid a foundation for increasing the world's goods and—temporarily—for allaying Malthusian pessimism. Industrial production on a mass basis also was a harbinger of the exploitation of the planet's resources which had become highly critical by 1970. After their beginnings in England, production techniques were soon to threaten and then significantly change long-established European ways of life, and also to create the first of many generations of both worried Luddites who mistrusted technology and persons who would look back nostalgically to a world that had changed too rapidly for their liking.

By the early 1800s a sixth era in man's history had arrived. This was the point at which, as Walter Lippmann wrote over forty years ago, man made his most important technological advance since the wheel: his system of inventing inventions or of discovering discoveries.[6] From the early golden guesses of Louis Pasteur to the hunches of Thomas Edison, man first groped and then methodically made his way to an increasingly greater power over his evironment. Discovery techniques in science and technology, after 1920, improved so exponentially that the U.S. reached a point where a president in the late 1940s could *decide* to make the H-bomb and another, in the early 1960s, *decide* to land men on the moon.

The present high point of rapid change—what Bell called a transition into a "postindustrial" society—has been reached so recently and passed so rapidly that in the 1970s man is still adjusting to his new perspectives. This current high spot is the seventh watershed, the electronic or electric era—a period of the extension of man through his development of the computer and the application of cybernetics or machine-control systems.

From the time when man first began to "know" and continuing up to the present age of the computer and other refined forms of technology, each watershed has changed his life with an irreversible alchemy. Each era extended the rim of man's vision, but also left him with a deep-seated uneasiness because of the uncertainties of the new route that awaited his exploratory footsteps. After crossing each divide the inevitable question remained: "Which of many paths into the future should he choose as each major change extended his intellectual sensors?"[7]

Especially in the twenty-five years that have elapsed since the close of World War II, developments have been extraordinary in their scope, in their rapidity, and in their consequences. It is not an exaggeration to state that in less than half a lifetime our *techno*-futures, our *bio*futures, our *socio*futures, and our inner or *psycho*-futures have been altered beyond recognition.

So rapidly and dramatically have yesterday's marvels become prosaic that it occasionally becomes necessary to jog memories made forgetful by the repeated stimuli of the unbelievable which sometimes

6. Walter Lippman, *A Preface to Morals* (New York: Macmillan Co., 1929).

7. Recent books and articles have clearly suggested how the pace of change has complicated life for man. In the chapter bibliography see Chase, Michaels, Kahn and Weiner, Davidson, H. G. Shane, J. G. Shane, Black, etc.

give innovation almost an air of tedium. In no more than a quarter of a century:

Human vision was extended a billion light years.

The molecule was made visible.

Low, virus-like forms of life were created in the laboratory.

Men landed on the moon's surface.

The number of people on the earth more than doubled.

Atomic and hydrogen bombs were exploded.

It became possible through cloning to make genetic copies of plants and animals.

Major organ transplants were made in human subjects.

Satellites internationalized the televiewing habits of people on every continent.

Ironically, during this twenty-five-year period of "marvels," problems of hunger increased, the pollution of the environment became a threat to life, and the depletion of the world's resources further impaired man's relationships with his environment.

In short, it became more and more apparent that the nature of man's environment was no longer the product of chance happenings or accidents of nature. Instead, the environment—depending on circumstances—was being threatened, or remade, or even *created* by human design. As Platt[8] has pointed out, in the fifty thousand years since man made his first great stride toward becoming a thinking animal, he has moved cumulatively from problem-solving by survival, through problem-solving by learning, to problem-solving by science.

*The premature arrival of tomorrow.* The pressure of increasing knowledge and a growing awareness on the part of the thoughtful human that he must assume personal responsibility for the futures that are being created can be a severe strain on the individual's mental and emotional health. But perhaps an even more unsettling problem which deserves study is what the rate of change in our lives today is doing to people—especially in industrially advanced areas such as the U.S. where many new techno-, bio-, psycho-, and sociofutures are rapidly taking shape.

Let us look with care at the significance of change—at the same time keeping in mind its manifold possibilities and problems for the curriculum developer.

8. John R. Platt, "Life Where Science Flows," *Environment and Change*, ed. W. R. Ewald (Bloomington: Indiana University Press, 1969), see esp. p. 69 ff.

Suppose that one of our remote ancestors lived fifty thousand years ago in the Yangtze River valleys, or in the once fertile Lake Chad area, or in a Swiss lake-village cluster, or in the Dordogne Valley caves of France. If his offspring, and their children through the centuries, had lived to be sixty to sixty-five years old they would represent an unbroken genetic chain of 799 forebears, a chain in which a man who is sixty years old today would be the eight-hundredth living link.

*In the last three decades of the eight-hundredth man's life, more changes have taken place than occurred during the previous 779½ lifetimes!*

Julius Caesar probably would have been able to understand rather quickly the lives and artifacts as they existed in the 799th man's world of 1910. However, Caesar and the 799th man both would be at a loss to understand computers, the uses of atomic power, or the sophisticated technologies that are involved when man travels in space.

From a historical point of view, it seems reasonable to say that for the first time in the history of the human race man has been propelled from yesterday into tomorrow with no familiar "today" during which to become acclimated to change. We have encountered the future so rapidly and with such violent changes in the ordered and familiar patterns of our way of life that we are suffering from what Toffler aptly called ". . . the dizzying disorientation brought on by the premature arrival of the future."[9]

The fact that half of the biotechnical changes of the last fifty thousand years have come about in the past thirty is especially important because of what this transition has done to people. Many of the changes have rendered useless the "maps" of the cultural terrain with which most persons over thirty years of age were provided by their upbringing prior to 1950.

Just as many people from the U.S. are upset when residing overseas by the absence of familiar cultural clues and suffer *culture* shock, many Americans are beginning to suffer from *future* shock. *Future* shock, like culture shock, is a condition [which may be] marked by a decline in

9. Alvin Toffler, "The Future As a Way of Life," *Horizons 10* (Summer 1965) : 109.

cognitive powers, misinterpretation of reality, and loss of the ability to communicate ideas with one's usual skill.[10]

To help explain the concept of future shock, it may be useful to point out that each human being is a member of a given subculture. As an initiation into his subculture, each individual for generations past was imprinted with an "invisible map" to guide his behavior. The "map" was tattooed on his nervous system. It was carefully drawn to guide his ways of behaving so that they were "proper" or appropriate to his subculture in every familiar situation that could be anticipated in the "human landscape" through which he was likely to travel on the route from early childhood to old age. The maps provided for young learners thirty or more years ago, however, no longer serve as reliable guides. They were imprinted for an assumed world—not the real world of the 1970s—and with little if any adequate anticipation of the "premature arrival of tomorrow" and the effect of our psychological collisions with a future for which virtually no one had been prepared. To put it in another way, the impact of future shock has been worsened for today's adults because the cultural maps they were equipped with now offer little guidance in the face of many contemporary problems and sometimes even motivate the individual to wrong (i.e., obsolete) kinds of survival behavior.

*The promise of our new cultural terrain.* However traumatic it may be for man to be thrust into the terrain of an unfamiliar tomorrow with an unreliable map, the experience also is one of great potential promise. There is promise both for society as a whole and for educators who are interested in changing the topography of traditional education which has been preserved in conventional curriculum guides and maintained by the curriculum directors, administrators, and teachers who have implemented them with varying degrees of enthusiasm.

The promise of the present resides, at least in considerable part, in the very rapidity of the changes that have unsettled the slower, evolutionary pace of less dynamic centuries.

10. Harold G. Shane, *"Future-Shock and the Curriculum," Phi Delta Kappan* 49 (1967): 67-70. Also see Toffler's 1970 article, "Future Shock," and his book of the same title in the bibliography.

The speed with which our lives are being altered suggests that *more can be accomplished now in less time than ever before in history.* Change has loosened the firm hold which established and frequently unexamined customs and traditions—often more binding than law—have had on the ordering of our lives. Exponential changes have made people more willing to accept or to begin the task of making adjustments to new ways of thinking and behaving. Changes that are unprecedented in rate, extent, and importance also have increased man's belief in what he can do—although it may have shaken his confidence in the judgment he is able to exercise in using his powers.

In short, the possibilities for successful pioneering in new terrain are good (a) because the social changes and improvements that once took centuries now can be made in years, (b) because men have been forced to think with more open minds, and (c) because man has the *evidence* of what he and his fellows can do in moving from natural selection to participation in his own evolution and to human selection of the environmental characteristics of his biosphere.

There remains, of course, the matter of man's wisdom in making his choices and his courage in planning the world we need. What knowledge *is* of greatest worth? How do we *apply* it in order to create the sociofutures, technofutures, biofutures and psychofutures that our children will find to be a useful, a humane, and a happy inheritance?

## Planning the World We Need

Since human beings created the present in the *past,* a point which has already been noted, how can we create desirable educational tomorrows in the *present?*

In the first place, *future*-planning of the curriculum must have cooperatively developed and acceptable guidelines, not the arbitrary direction of autocrats. That is to say, the shaping of educational change needs to find leadership in the merit of interacting ideas developed by people who see that the *process* of planning change—because of its involvement of many individuals—is also a goal. It is a goal in the sense that suitable, democratic involvement itself is a goal to be sought through planning. Recognizing

that a few pages hence careful heed will be given to finding direction
through *future*-planning and the meaningful interpersonal transactions it involves, let us now suggest a general direction for change.

*The restoration of significance.* Although their educational values
may suggest different routes to the goal, most adult citizens, whether
they be twenty-two or sixty-two, would probably accept the statement that greater significance or relevance is needed at nearly all
levels of U.S. education. What can be done to bring greater meaning to education?

William H. Kilpatrick,[11] writing in the 1920s, was one of the
first educational philosophers to direct attention to the way in which
teaching and learning were threatened by loss of relevance. In
general, it was his point that much education in a younger America,
ca. 1840, occurred *outside* the school. Boys, for instance, learned
farming or a trade from their fathers, and girls learned the homemaking arts from their mothers. This was at a time when virtually
all frontier artifacts, except for the large iron kettle and a few tools
and weapons, were made in the home.[12]

Under such conditions "real" education for survival in the frontier battle with an uncompromising and often hostile environment
was distinctly different from formal "schooling." The child of pre–
Civil War days, if he went to school at all, attended for as little
as six weeks in a year and was judged to be well "edjicatid" if
he could cope with McGuffey's *Readers*, spell words like *kerosene*
and *kimono,* and do a bit of ciphering. School was for the most
part an adjunct to the learning experiences one needed in order
to keep alive. Even fifty years ago, as Kilpatrick presciently sensed,
technology had begun to destroy the onetime preeminence of home
and community in imprinting children with the invisible maps that
were needed to guide them through their cultural terrain.

The school, an adjunct to life in 1840, had by 1940 become accepted as the locus of learning, if not the *locus classicus,* for what
was hopefully assumed to be the "real" education of children. Only,

11. William H. Kilpatrick, *Education for a Changing Civilization* (New York:
Macmillan Co., 1926). Three lectures delivered under Luther Laflin Kellogg
Foundation, auspices Rutgers University.

12. J. C. Furnas, *The Americans: A Social History of the United States, 1587-
1914* (New York: G. P. Putnam's Sons, 1969). See pages 260 ff for a vivid por-
trayal of 1840 frontier life.

alas, it frequently lacked the conspicuously meaningful contribution of blacksmith shop and barn, of kitchen and root cellar. As children lost significance as part of the interdependent family or community team of breadwinners, their "real" education lost the deep meaning for which schools of a later era could neither compensate nor fully restore.

In the 1970s, however, there seems to be a new opportunity for relevance. One hundred and fifty years ago Americans needed to learn to survive on a thinly settled frontier in the face of an often threatening natural environment. Today there is a need to educate children to survive in a world made increasingly dangerous for man *by* man. From an education for survival of a century and a half ago we have come full cycle to a literal need once again to protect ourselves from threats to existence such as the four mentioned earlier in the chapter: overpopulation, accumulating refuse,[13] chemical and nuclear environmental pollution, and highly destructive weapons. So severe did he deem the problem that Fischer proposed that:

> Any successful reform of American education . . . will have to be far more revolutionary than anything yet attempted. At a minimum it should be: (1) Founded on a single guiding concept—an idea capable of knotting together all strands of study, thus giving them both coherence and visible purpose. (2) Capable of equipping young people to do something about . . . the things which bother them most, including war, injustice, racial conflict, and the quality of life.[14]

He goes on to urge that fields such as biology imprint learners with clear concepts of "biological morality," i.e., that no one has the right to poison the environment and that it is wrong for anyone to have more than two children. As for fledgling engineers, they should be helped to see that ecological *moral* judgments should determine where in the interest of the general welfare we should or should not build jet runways, dams, highways, or skyscrapers.[15]

Here, perhaps, in education for survival, we may find some of the motivation that is needed to bring to education a revitalized,

13. By 1970 the U.S. was accumulating more than 350 million tons of refuse per year, and 500 million tons were forecast for 1980. The cost of disposal is approaching $5 billion annually. *Life* 67 (November 7, 1969): 32-36.

14. John Fischer, "Survival U: Prospectus for a Really Relevant University," *Harper's Magazine* 239 (September 1969): 12-22.

15. Ibid., p. 12.

appealing, and significant teaching and learning that will help in the restoration of what is now a minacious environment. As we begin to feel seriously threatened, then we may begin to be impelled to *future*-plan for the world we need. Such planning seems more than reasonable in order to avoid the danger of irreversible catastrophes or—at best—a depleted and befouled world in which, by the time today's children are middle-aged, there could be a distinct drop in standards of living that existed in the 1970s. And we must remember that a "relevant" education is not merely one that deals with what the sixteen- or twenty-year-old deems suited to his problems and interest. *A truly relevant education is one that inducts the young learner into participation in adult living:* the satisfactions, the responsibilities, the participation and the mature acceptance of Harry Stack Sullivan's insight that ". . . the satisfaction and security of another person [must become] as significant to one as one's own security. . . ."

*A "survival kit" for curriculum planners.* The need for all types of future-planning to "create" tomorrow in education should be evident to all but the most perversely misological of U.S. citizens. After all, between the early 1970s and A.D. 2000—even with a reduced birthrate—we face the task of duplicating all extant material things in the fifty states.[16]

What kind of a survival kit can we design to help educators, particularly curriculum developers, in this increasingly dynamic period to retain their sanity and even a few shreds of good humor? The remainder of chapter viii is devoted to the idea stated at the outset: that we can methodically develop the educational future from a study of possible alternative futures and make the "best"— the one most congruent with carefully reasoned values—become reality.

The conception of *future*-planning was virtually unknown prior to the middle sixties except among a small group of enthusiastic speculative thinkers whose activities go back twenty years or more

16. Cf. National Committee on Urban Growth Policy, *The New City,* ed. Donald Canty (New York: Praeger Publishing Co., 1969). This volume recommends 10 totally new cities of 1 million and 100 communities of 100,000 each to provide homes and jobs for 20,000,000 people. As of 1969, by the way, 14 "new cities" had been opened or begun in Great Britain. Fourteen more were in the works in 1970 because the first ones were successful both economically and socially. Reports from Holland, Sweden, and Finland are also encouraging.

to the late 1940s and early 1950s. It will probably be helpful, under these circumstances, briefly to review the substantial backgrounds of the movement before examining possible ways of bringing about desirable changes in the curriculum through methodic attempts to mediate or to intervene in the shaping of change.

*Backgrounds of* future-*planning.* The future is important to us for a number of reasons, the most compelling of which, as Charles Kettering once remarked, being the fact that we are going to spend the rest of our lives there. Numerous current books and articles have an air of suppressed excitement about them as their authors help the reader envision the next several decades. As far back as the 1950s, to choose an early example, Sir George Thompson was making exciting projections of what were then contemporary developments and speculating about the coming events to which they pointed.[17]

Eight or nine years ago, Alexander was able to describe ways in which U.S. corporations were investing millions of dollars to encourage the exploration of ideas which might relate to or even control future developments.[18] Furthermore, according to Kopkind, the federal government had by 1967 developed in the Washington heartland a corps of political technicians (he called them "technopols") who had the responsibility for forecasting probable futures in economics, military developments, or international crises.[19] It was about this time that the term *scenario* began to come into general use as a term for projecting and analyzing possible future trends.[20]

Other examples of descriptive and conjectural writing about the future began to be abundant after 1964. Boulding's *The Meaning of the Twentieth Century*[21] was an imaginative and often bril-

17. Sir George Thompson, *The Foreseeable Future* (Cambridge, England: Syndics of the Cambridge University Press, 1960).

18. Tom Alexander, "The Wild Birds Find a Corporate Roost," *Fortune,* August 1964, pp. 129-134; 164, 168.

19. Alexander Kopkind, "The Future-Planners," *The New Republic,* February 25, 1967, pp. 19-23.

20. Kahn and Wiener were, a few months later (1967), to describe scenarios as " . . . hypothetical sequences of events constructed for purposes of focusing attention on causal processes and decision-points. They answer two kinds of questions: (1) Precisely how might some hypothetical situation come about, step by step? and (2) What alternatives exist, for each actor, at each step, for preventing, diverting, or facilitating the process?" See *The Year 2000* (bibliography), p. 6.

21. Kenneth Boulding, *The Meaning of the Twentieth Century* (New York: Harper & Row, 1964).

liant analysis which was widely read. "The Report of the Commission on the Next 33 Years" published in *Daedalus* during the summer of 1967 also was highly influential—partly because of its sponsorship (at the original suggestion of Lawrence K. Frank) by the highly respected American Academy of Arts and Sciences. Stuart Chase's *The Most Probable World* and Donald N. Michael's *The Unprepared Society* are further examples (see chapter viii bibliography) of the spate of excellent publications that have continued to appear. So respectable had the study of the future become, even five years ago, that the United States Office of Education invested what would eventually total approximately $1 million in centers at the University of Syracuse and at Stanford University to encourage study of the implication of possible futures for education.[22]

All of these ventures—and many others—undoubtedly were beginning seriously to capture the attention of educators, if not actually to influence their thinking, by 1970. After all, as Logan Wilson pointed out,[23] the mere discussion of future educational policy eventually leads to decisions which ". . . *shape* as well as *anticipate* tomorrow's world."

Despite the endemic interest in future trends and in *future*-planning as of the early 1970s, virtually all reports in professional education, such as Van Til's excellent, thoughtful speculations on emerging changes in teacher preparation,[24] were conjectures, or forecasts, or projections. The focus of most writing and discussion was on what might be or what ought to be. Very little was done to examine tactics or strategies and then to attempt actually to bring about humane educational developments and to impede or to eliminate those that seemed malignant to society. Nor was there any appreciable awareness on the part of educationists that the ability to project educational futures (as in Morphet's massive study)

22. In addition to the works cited, there is an imposing mass of little-known writings (many in mimeograph and other fugitive forms). See chapter references to such exemplars as Massé, Lessing, and Haydon.

23. In Eurich, ed., *Campus 1980*, p. 33.

24. William Van Til, "The Year 2000: Teacher Education" (Department of Education and Psychology, Indiana State University, Terre Haute, 1968). (ED 028972).

created a professional responsibility to strive for the more promising of possible choices.

Three categories into which writing about the future could be
sorted as of the early 1970s were:

1.  Statements regarding broad, current problems (e.g., pollution) and
    presumably promising practices (e.g., ocean farming or the "new
    city" concept) intimately related to possible world futures
2.  Forecasts and conjectures as to likely happenings, assuming a sur-
    prise-free future, in the realms of science, the arts, domestic politics,
    international relations, biochemistry, morals, and so on
3.  The actual techniques and procedures of future scanning and *future*-
    planning: variations of the Delphi technique, applications of PERT-
    ing and systems analysis, scenario writing and game theory, and so
    forth

As of the early seventies, however, publications in the first two
categories were by far the more commonplace—a generalization
which the chapter bibliography conspicuously supports. Relatively
little had been published in the third category, although there were
exceptions, to be sure.[25]

Space limitations preclude a further résumé of the backgrounds
of *future*-planning. Attention turns to a hypothesis for developing
*future*-control tactics which promise first to retard and then to re-
verse education's losses to such "enemies" as race prejudice, faulty
instruction, deterioration of the environment, poor patterns of educational support and expenditure, obsolete or obsolescent curriculum
content, and organizational practices that no longer serve the purposes for which they once were intended.

*Future-control tactics in education.* It is hypothesiezd here that
the curriculum should be shaped by certain *future*-control tactics
and that these involve *future*-planning techniques. Let us first consider tactics.

It seems logical to use *future*-control tactics to shape education
despite the faint feeling of uneasiness that the term *control* may at
first awaken in curriculum workers. The discomfort should pass as
it becomes clear (a) that *control* as used here resides in democratic
processes and (b) that the absence of control tactics can lead to in-

25. Among writers dealing directly with possible future-control tactics prior
to 1969 were Bertrand de Jouvenel, Kahn and Wiener, Helmer and Rescher, and
the Shanes. See bibliography.

effectual, low-impact attacks on the "enemies" of education identified two paragraphs earlier—or even eventually contribute to social
chaos.

*Future*-control of curriculum planning resides in ORPHIC procedures[26]—in the assumption that it is feasible to develop ". . . a
cluster of procedures based on the systematic use of coordinated
expert opinion in education and in related disciplines for purposes
of (1) exploring numerous possible educational futures, (2) selecting
the best possible futures among them, and (3) development of models
for helping achieve desired educational goals."[27]

The term "ORPHIC" is an acronym derived from *OR*ganized
*P*rojected *H*ypotheses for *I*nnovations in *C*urriculum. It also has the
lexical meaning *oracular,* which is here construed to mean that the
procedures are concerned with forthcoming developments based on
educational conjectures. Readers familiar with the literature of futurism will recognize that ORPHIC procedures—our hypothecated
approach to developing *future*-control tactics—are in part somewhat
reminiscent of the Delphi technique used by RAND, Inc., for pioneering work which led to the publication of the widely known *RAND
Long-Range Forecast*[28] of the 1960s. However, as will become apparent, ORPHIC procedures make use of an adaptation of the
Delphi technique only in the first of the five phases through which
educational *future*-planning moves.

Future-*planning strategies.* The long-range strategies which conceivably may be developed as a basis for *future*-control tactics are
of particular merit because of their process values. In other words,
ORPHIC procedures do not involve a step toward an Orwellian
world of elitist direction and mind control. They are intended to
strengthen group processes in two ways: (a) to help educators avoid
blunders that can be bypassed if they make the effort needed to look
ahead intelligently and systematically, and (b) to enable planners
to foresee possible dangers and problems far enough beforehand to
allow for the study of alternatives, to avoid lost time, to identify

26. Harold G. Shane and June G. Shane, *"Future*-Planning and the Curriculum," *Phi Delta Kappan* 49 (1968): 372-77.

27. Ibid., p .375.

28. For excerpts from a long-range forecast, see Herman Kahn and Anthony J.
Wiener, "The Next Thirty-three Years: A Framework for Speculation," *Daedalus*
96 (1967): 711-16.

possible faulty approaches to learning, and to minimize possible problems of many kinds.

Before describing a hypothesized approach to cultivating methodically the more desirable of alternative educational futures, it should be pointed out that *future*-planning of the curriculum as a process for encouraging and guiding desirable innovations has several important values involving cooperation. *Future*-planning, as it is used to promote better ways of shaping educational change, should create an interplay among participants, ideas, procedures, and choices as selections are made to encourage or to inhibit possible forthcoming changes. These interactions do not violate democratic processes—they strengthen them. Some of the potential "process outcomes" that may be derived from an interplay of men and ideas are presented below:

1.  Careful consideration can be given to the identification of a wide range of possible educational developments. This brings planning into sharper focus as alternative futures are suggested and explored.

2.  When a spectrum of possible outcomes in education has been determined, appropriate criteria can be used to assess the means to be employed in obtaining particular ends.

3.  Progress may be assessed continually through such devices as PERT-ing[29] which serve to keep persons working with curriculum models from getting too far out of synchronization. Continuing evaluation also permits in-process changes (i.e., flexibility) in moving toward established ends when mitigating needs become evident.

4.  *Future*-planning suggests that curriculum workers employ intellectually demanding but rewarding procedures as carefully derived information and referents are fed into the framework for speculation. The input of specialized knowledge or data based on expertise constantly validates the sequential decisions that are made in developing a model for curriculum change. The input also serves to reaffirm or to modify educational ends.

5.  *Authoritarian* direction can be made subordinate to *authoritative* leadership through the use of (a) information input, (b) the persuasive merit of a given idea, and (c) the continuing use of research relevant to (or generated by) the processes of *future*-planning.

29. PERT (Program Evaluation and Review Techniques) has been "credited with a major contribution to making the Polaris missile operational two years ahead of schedule." See *New Uses and Management Implications of PERT* (New York: Booz, Allen, and Hamilton, 1964) p. 1.

6. The processes of *future*-planning encourage synergistic[30] outcomes. In other words, prediction, research, process, and interaction taken together produce an outcome greater than the sum of the input. Also, through *future*-planning it should be possible to increase the potential ability to predict outcomes when several lines of thought modify one another and thus increase overall accuracy.[31]

7. In education, as in the social sciences, the techniques of *future*-planning (operations research and expert judgment) offer considerable promise for developing an "interdisciplinary systems approach" to the study of curriculum problems.[32] In effect, we should be able to adopt and reconstruct some of the operational processes and methods from the realm of physical technology to the domain of social and educational technology.[33]

Now that the humanizing or "human-centric" nature of educational *future*-planning process has been stressed, more can be made clear with respect to possible specific *future*-planning strategies. Let us turn to the hypothesized ORPHIC process, including an explanation of the sequence of steps that might be taken deliberately to shape change.

## *Educational* Future-*Planning:*
## *Possible Procedures in the Shaping of Change*

The next several paragraphs present a general overview of possible procedures which might be studied and modified by professional educators seeking to create the best of numerous possible futures for children and youth in their particular districts.[34] The

30. Webster defines "synergism" as the simultaneous action of separate agencies which, together, have a greater total effect than the sum of their individual effects.

31. Points such as those given here have been carefully assessed by certain social scientists. See Kahn and Wiener, *The Year 2000* (bibliography). Synergistic interrelationships are discussed on pp. 67, 71.

32. Cf. chapter bibliography: Lessing, pp. 157, 215.

33. The foregoing list is adopted from Shane and Shane, "*Future*-Planning," pp. 374-75. The seventh point in the list was suggested by Olaf Helmer's "Prospects of Technological Progress," RAND, Inc., typescript of a speech given in Tokyo and dated August 1967, pp. 9-10.

34. The portion of chapter viii which follows is abridged from a mimeographed document prepared by the Shanes in the early spring of 1968: "ORPHIC Procedures for *Future*-Planning in Education." A number of distinguished educators read this document. Among persons who, in 1968 or 1969, wrote annotations and analyses, or who at least briefly discussed the concepts with the writers, are Robert Anderson, William Alexander, Harry Broudy, Henry Brickel, David Boynton, Kenneth Barker, David Clark, Robert Curry, William Ellena, Stanley Elam, Nicholas Fattu, Egon Guba, Robert Havighurst, James Jacobs, Edgar Morphet, Ross

*future*-planning and ORPHIC procedures presented also may have a bearing on the ensuing five chapters. That is, *future*-planning may in the long run help to provide a workable means of implementing some of the ideas of these yearbook authors and of others whose views on curriculum development long have been of appreciable influence.

*Possible phases in* future-*planning*. There are five steps which suggest themselves as a possible means of shaping educational change: [35]

1. Careful speculation engaged in by qualified persons as to possible developments, and the probability that they will occur in fields or disciplines with a bearing on future curriculum planning: an *interdisciplinary trend census*.

2. Arriving at reasoned judgments, based on trend-census data, as to the positive or negative values of possible future social, technological, or biological developments and their potential importance to education: i.e., *a social consequence projection of trends*.

3. Making carefully weighed judgments as to the probable occurrence of a given change that is forecast and as to the difficulty either of bringing it about or of impeding it: a *probability-difficulty analysis* to provide a carefully examined basis for the future deployment of time, energy, and money to accelerate or to oppose possible developments or changes in U.S. education.

4. Exploring hypothetical sequences or events through *scenario writing*[36] in order to examine and to evaluate possible curriculum changes with respect to (a) the learner and (b) substantive content.

5. Arriving at a *milestone appraisal and report* designed to summarize and to assess at a given time the tentative, emergent decisions supported by the first four steps which promise to improve education in the U.S.

The merit of deliberately planning a future or futures toward which to work also has been recognized by writers outside of education as noted earlier. Among them, for example, is Simon Ramo,

35. Originally proposed (1968) by Shane and Shane, *"Future*-Planning," pp. 375-76.

36. See the Kahn and Wiener definition of "scenario" given in footnote 20 of this chapter.

---

Mooney, Robert McClure, Gordon Mackenzie, J. Galen Saylor, B. Othanel Smith, Ralph Tyler, Ronald Welch, and William Van Til. Messrs. Broudy, Elam, and Guba were especially generous with their time in preparing detailed reactions and offering editorial advice.

whose suggestions below are generally comparable to the five steps listed above. Ramo, writing late in 1969, noted the enormous spectrum of future events potentially involved in shaping change, but contended that such events in many instances were predictable for all practical purposes.[37] He went on to suggest, on the basis of over twenty years as a science and technology consultant to the government, that various steps can be taken to give us an orderly anticipatory approach to likely social and technological advances:

*First,* we can ask outstanding specialists in various fields to list their guesses as to major anticipated change possibilities for the future;
*Second,* we can order those lists of events as to importance to the society, probability of occurrence, and estimated period of occurrence;
*Third,* for those events having strong combinations of estimated importance and high probability, we then seek to describe the potential social impact;
*Fourth,* we separate these possible consequences into good and bad;
*Fifth,* we set out to maximize the benefits and minimize the negatives.[38]

Statements such as this one had become quite common by 1970 in business, military, and technological literature. While the idea of *future*-planning in education remains virtually untested,[39] educators such as William Van Til, William Engbretsen, and Harry S. Broudy also are becoming seriously interested in what it might accomplish. Broudy stated as far back as 1968:

As to futurism, I am in entire agreement with the necessity for crystal ball gazing, and I would go so far as to say that all educational thinking and action should be divided into (a) what must be done next year in terms of fixing the machine that can't be stopped while it is in motion, so to speak, and (b) into what might be done from now on to meet the estimated needs of the culture by 1980, 2000, etc.[40]

It is in this warming climate of interest in *future*-planning, then, that attention turns to a somewhat more detailed description of ORganized Projections of Hypotheses for Innovations in Curriculum, the acronym of which, as has been stated, is ORPHIC.

37. Simon Ramo, "Wanted: Professional Futurists," *Science News,* October 11, 1969, p. 321.

38. Loc. cit.

39. The writers used a form of trend census in 1968 while preparing "Forecast for the 70's" (see bibliography) which, in part, involved taped interview material obtained from Robert H. Anderson, Frank Estvan, Edward T. Hall, Robert J. Havighurst, Sidney P. Marland, Jr., and Herbert A. Thelen.

40. From a letter addressed to the writer and dated May 6, 1968.

*ORPHIC procedures: the trend census.* The first step that educators might take[41] in an initial venture in *future*-planning presumably would be the trend census. This is an educationally oriented adaptation of the Delphi technique mentioned earlier; a technique pioneered in the 1950s and associated with Helmer[42] and others who worked on such projects as the RAND Long-Range Forecast.[43] The Delphic technique also has been applied in education, both in theory and in actual practice.[44]

Essentially, the *interdisciplinary trend census* is a proposed means of enlisting the help of specialists in fields or disciplines related to education (and a smaller number of participating professional educators) in three endeavors:

*First,* to assess the research, the opinion, and the expertise in education and in disciplines which have a bearing on possible futures that could become realities in the next quarter century. (Anthropology, biochemistry, mathematics, urban sociology, and pediatrics might prove to be among appropriate related disciplines.)

*Second,* to list possible developments in these disciplines and their likely educational implications.

*Third,* to indicate—doubtless on some type of scale—how *probable* a particular event might be, how *difficult* (in terms of time, energy, and money) it might be to bring it about, and an estimated earliest *effective* date (under favorable circumstance) at which the event might occur.

If it can be assumed that a trend census is plausible and that one can be made, probably a reasonable assumption in view of the increasingly wide use of Delphi-type forecasts,[45] such a census might

41. Obviously, individual educators cannot utilize the procedures of *future*-planning. They need to be members of organized cooperative planning groups. That is, effective approaches probably could only be made, say, in a school district of some size, by a professional association, or through funded research as proposed at Syracuse and Stanford universities when seeking the USOE support which they received in the late sixties.

42. Olaf Helmer, "Prospects of Technological Progress." RAND, Inc., typescript of speech given in Tokyo, dated August 1967. Pp. 8-9 passim present a succinct statement of his views.

43. Cf. T. J. Gordon and Olaf Helmer, "Report on a Long-Range Forecasting Study." Typescript from the files of RAND, Inc., September 1964.

44. In 1969-70, for example, William Engbretsen, president of the Governors State University in Park Forest, Illinois, used a Delphi-type questionnaire to obtain informed opinion regarding future trends and developments of relevance as they related to creating a recently authorized teacher education institution and to inventing a program based on anticipated major socioeducational changes.

45. For an illustration of a Delphi-technique approach to medicine, see bibliographic reference to *Futurist* article, ca. October 1969.

well provide curriculum workers with perhaps thirty to eighty probable or possible innovations with a potential for a direct or an indirect impact on education. Such developments, of course, are based
on what Kahn and Wiener[46] call a "surprise-free" future. Future
events, obviously, fall roughly into two sets, the expected and the
unexpected.[47] Allowance can, however, be made for the unexpected
when alternative futures are explored through scenarios.

   In the original RAND Long-Range Forecast, based upon the
systematic solicitation of expert opinions through the Delphi technique,[48] opinions were obtained as to the "World of 1984" and the
"World of the Year 2000." (A "Conceivable World of 2100" also
was projected in broad but provocative terms!) Despite the passing
years, they remain of great interest. Possible developments of twelve
and twenty-eight years hence which might influence education still
may be extracted from this original RAND forecast as discussed
by Gordon and Helmer.[49] However, a more readily available list
is the "100 likely innovations" prepared at the Hudson Institute
and originally printed in *Daedalus*.[50]

   While it does not follow that an interdisciplinary educational
trend census made in the 1970s would closely resemble the excerpts
below (which, in any case, are mostly limited to technical and biochemical innovations), the developments foreseen by means of reasoned speculation in 1967 continue to provide a provocative pre-
view of potentials for change in the next three decades. Some items
of possible educational relevance that are taken from the Kahn and
Wiener list are:

13. Major reduction of hereditary and congenital defects
14. Extensive use of cyborg techniques (mechanical aids or substitutes
    for human organs, senses, limbs)
24. Three-dimensional photography, illustrations, movies, and tele-
    vision
34. Practical use of direct electronic communication with and stimu-
    lation of the brain

   46. Kahn and Wiener, *The Year 2000.*
   47. Cf. Gordon and Helmer, "Long-Range Forecasting Study," p. 2.
   48. Cf. N. Dalkey and Olaf Helmer, "An Experimental Application of the
Delphi Method to the Use of Experts," *Management Science* 9 (1963).
   49. Gordon and Helmer, "Long-Range Forecasting Study," pp. 39-45.
   50. Herman Kahn and Anthony J. Wiener, "The Next Thirty-Three Years:
A Framework for Speculation," *Daedalus* (1967): 705-32.

39. New, more varied, and more reliable drugs for control of fatigue, relaxation, alertness, mood, personality, perceptions and fantasies

42. Genetic control or influence over the "basic constitution" of an individual

44. General and substantial increase in life expectancy, postponement of aging, and limited rejuvenation

49. Simple techniques for extensive and "permanent" cosmetological changes (features, "figures," perhaps complexion, skin color, even physique)

58. Chemical methods for improved memory and learning

66. New techniques for keeping physically fit or acquiring physical skills

76. Widespread use of computers for intellectual and professional assistance (translation, teaching, literary research, medical diagnosis, traffic control, crime detection, computation, design analysis and, to some degree, as an intellectual collaborator)

86. Home education via video, and computerized and programmed learning

95. New methods of teaching languages rapidly.

In education, during the 1970s, a trend census reinforced by estimates of the probability and difficulty of accelerating or impeding "good" and "bad" educational developments could be most useful. But how might this be done? For one thing, a form (Table 1) such as is shown below—and accompanied by careful instructions to expert consultants—might be devised to help each expert prepare a preliminary resume of possible futures in his discipline (e.g., sociology, anthropology, biochemistry) which he thinks might have a bearing on alternate educational futures. The imaginary points below, in other words, might have come from a biochemist, an instructional systems man, a sociologist, and so on.

Any type of trend census would pose a variety of problems, yet none of them appears to be insoluble. What makes an expert qualified?[51] How does one cope with the inevitable existence of a time-

51. Space precludes a discussion of the question of "When is an expert really competent?" Futurists have promising remedies (See Gordon and Helmer, "Long-Range Forecasting Study," p. 58) including a "personal probability" formula presented and explained by Olaf Helmer and Nicholas Rescher, "On the Epistemology of the Inexact Sciences," *Management Science* 6 (1959): 25-52. (See especially pp. 34-36 in which a formula for establishing expertise $[dc(H,E) = m/n]$ is interpreted.)

lapse when a Delphi approach is used?[52] How shall we avoid communications problems such as ambiguity in questions or instructions,

TABLE 1

CENSUS OF INTERDISCIPLINARY TRENDS DEEMED RELEVANT TO EDUCATION

| TREND INVENTORY: OUTCOMES SUGGESTED BY CURRENT TRENDS | PROBABILITY-DIFFICULTY WEIGHTINGS* | | INDEX FIGURE:† PROBABILITY × DIFFICULTY | ESTIMATED EFFECTIVE DATE IF MASSIVE EFFORT IS MADE |
| | Probability before Intervention | Difficulty before Intervention | | |
|---|---|---|---|---|
| (1) Perfection of memory-improving drugs | 2 | 3 | 6 | 1980 |
| (2) Highly effective computer-based instruction | 1 | 2 | 3 | 1982 |
| (3) Kibbutzim-type "boarding homes" for the disadvantaged | 5 | 1 | 5 | 1978 |
| (4) Educational programs for 3- and 4-year-olds financed at federal expense | 5 | | | |
| of schools | 6 | 1 | 6 | 1988 |

*Probability-difficulty weightings are multiplied to increase spread. 1=very high, 2=high, 3= 50/50, 4=low, 5=very low.
†The index figure presumably would be needed for Step 3 (Probability-Difficulty Analysis). See under paragraph heading, "The Probability-Difficulty Analysis" which follows.

as well as the self-fulfilling (or self-defeating!) prophecy phenomenon? Can the possibility of "bandwagon" and "underdog" effects be anticipated or otherwise taken into account?[53]

Whatever the pitfalls to be avoided, there seems no reason to conclude that their presence would outweigh the potential value of various agencies or groups participating in the careful contemplation of future developments which are likely to have a positive or negative effect on curriculum change.

*The social consequence projection.* Were *future*-planning to be explored as a potentially useful educational tool, the *social conse-*

52. The Delphi technique inherently involves time-lapse since the experts engaged in speculations and predictions are subsequently exposed to one another's opinions and then have an opportunity to modify their original views in a final trend census statement.

53. Herbert Simon, "Bandwagon and Underdog Effects and the Possibility of Election Predictions," *Public Opinion Quarterly* 18 (1954): 245-53.

*quence projection* would be one possible way of making reasoned decisions regarding what was desirable or undesirable in future developments foreshadowed by a study of trends. While it had not been tried as a phase of *future*-planning as of 1970, methodical social consequence projection probably could acquire reasonable process validity if undertaken by a group composed of professional educators and a comparable number of scholars from related disciplines.

Unlike the trend census, which doubtless could be made through the distribution of several rounds of questionnaire-inventory type instruments, a consequence analysis doubtless should be based on an interactive approach in which participants met to interact with one another. Here, in an "arena for conjecture," twenty or more competent persons might assess the implications of possible developments resulting from a trend census. The random selection of conjectures below is presented for illustrative purposes to suggest what might be forecast as a result of such census:

1.  Mandatory foster or boarding homes for children who have been removed from environments that are demonstrably harmful to their physical or mental welfare
2.  The perfection of biochemically induced therapy for producing safe, desirable, and educationally practical changes in mood, memory, concentration, and so on
3.  Environmental mediation designed to "create" whatever it is that we measure and label as intelligence
4.  A continuous school year from which young learners—and their teachers—can take "time out" for intervals of various lengths and unpatterned frequencies
5.  Educational and psychological prerequisites for candidates seeking public office
6.  Increasing U.S. dependence on a growing number of regularly employed, affluent, and influential female wage earners
7.  Average life expectancies of from ninety to one hundred years.
8.  A twenty- to thirty-hour workweek in many fields, and an eight-month working year.
9.  A "knowledge society," as Peter Drucker has called it, in which the highly prepared specialist becomes of unprecedented influence in mediating social decisions pertaining to such matters as population control, pollution, or international political policy
10. Development of a forty-five-letter English alphabet consisting of thirty consonants and fifteen vowels, and so on

Quite possibly, comparable results of a real trend census if placed in the hands of a second group of specialists, would permit these specialists tentatively to decide (on the basis of emergent professional judgments) which of the trends promised to have desirable or humanizing social consequences and which would have undesirable or dehumanizing qualities. Their personal premeeting conclusions would accompany them to the group meeting concerned with interactive discussions of the consequences of potential changes.

Once again some type of score sheet would be needed to give structure to a group examination of the social consequences of possible long-range developments with a bearing on the curriculum. The following form is suggestive of what might be prepared for participants to check prior to their confrontation to discuss possible consequences.

When using the form shown in Table 2, the participants presumably would make professional judgments as to the projected social consequences of a given development and provide a brief statement in the "Summary" as to why they rated it as they did in the range from "Very Desirable: 4" to "Very Undesirable: 1." Although these ratings, patently, would be no more than subjective judgments of the group, they should nonetheless be the expression of carefully examined opinions on which a consensus had been reached. Such opinions (based on experience and a knowledge of the implications of research in education and related disciplines) should have appreciably greater merit than opinions arrived at without the benefit of the trend census and without the synergistic and serendipitous outcomes of interaction among qualified persons assembled to evaluate the social consequences of each hypothetical development.[54]

Hopefully, both agreements and reasoned compromises as to the probable social consequences of anticipated future developments

54. In certain ways, *future*-planning through ORPHIC procedures might be similar in function to the work of the now disbanded Educational Policies Commission, which was sponsored by the National Educational Association and by the American Association of School Administrators. However, if an educational *future*-planning group were convened, it presumably would have the benefit of methodically prepared expert opinion (through the "trend census") and of a systematic process (through the "social consequence projection") when deliberating choices among possible alternate futures that might be attained through wise deployment of time, energy, and money.

TABLE 2

HYPOTHETICAL SOCIAL CONSEQUENCE PROJECTION FORM

| FUTURE POSSIBLE DEVELOPMENTS TAKEN FROM TREND CENSUS FORM: ILLUSTRATIVE EXAMPLES | EVALUATION OF SOCIAL CONSEQUENCES* (MADE BY THE GROUP PARTICIPANTS) | | | |
|---|---|---|---|---|
| | ++ Very Desirable (4) | + Desirable (3) | − Undesirable (2) | −− Very Undesirable (1) |
| | (Place One Number in a Box Below) | | | |

(1) Mandatory foster or boarding homes will be established for children who have been removed from environments that are demonstrably harmful to their physical or mental welfare . . .

Summary of main reasons for the evaluation made of the [illustrative] trend in the column to the left:

_____

_____

_____

(2) The perfection of biochemically induced therapy for producing safe, desirable, and educationally practical changes in mood, memory, concentration, and so on . . .

_____

Summary: _____

_____

(10) Development of a 45-letter English alphabet consisting of 30 consonants and 15 vowels

_____

Summary: _____

*As Table 2 implies, the four-point scale ranges from "Very Desirable," a "+ +" or "4" rating, to "Very Undesirable," which is rated "− −" or "1." Obviously, the higher the score the better the SCP score given a Possible Development.

likely to influence education could be reached by participants with such final conclusions preserved on a master summary sheet which would be used during the *probability-difficulty analysis* described below.

*The probability-difficulty analysis.* Once the assumed social consequences of a group of interdisciplinary trends have been established and rated, it should become theoretically possible to contemplate the question of how society might best invest its time, energy, and money to facilitate, divert, or prevent certain probable educational futures which could range from "highly desirable" to "very undesirable." To paraphrase Marshall McLuhan, attention would be directed toward the question of how educators can prevent schools of the 1970s from lavishing vast and increasing amounts of time, energy, and money preparing students for a world that either will no longer exist or should no longer exist?[55]

Given a roster of probable educational futures from the trend census and expert opinion as to their possible social consequences, a team of, say, twenty educators might be assembled to make recommendations as to how schools in the U.S. might best invest their resources to support "good" possible futures and resist "bad" ones. This third group doubtless would be most effective with a substantial plurality of consultant-observers carried over from the trend census and the social consequences groups.

TABLE 3

HYPOTHETICAL PROBABILITY-DIFFICULTY ANALYSIS FORM

| Possible Future Development and Estimated Effective Date *if Given Priority* | Preintervention Probability and Difficulty Index Score* | Social Consequence Score | Priority† (in Order of Importance) | Priority (in Order of Expenditure) |
|---|---|---|---|---|
| (1) Public education is extended downward to serve all children beginning at age 2 (1980) | Difficulty: 1 Probability: 1 *Score*: 1 (1 × 1 = 1) | + + (4) (i.e., very desirable) | 1 (very high) | 5 (very low) |
| (2) Shoulder carrels‡ which are analagous to a diver's mask and which can be worn in any school or home setting and set for personalized programming are available (1978) | Difficulty: 2 Probability: 3 *Score*: 6 (2 × 3 = 6) | + (3) (desirable) | 2 (high) | 2 (high) |
| (15) A linguistically acceptable 45-letter English alphabet consisting of 30 consonants and 15 vowels has been devised and reduces book-size by ⅓ (1985) | Difficulty: 2 Probability: 1 *Score*: 2 (1 × 2 = 2) | + (3) (desirable) | 4 (low) | 3 (50/50) |

*For source of index scores see Table 1. 1=very high, 5=very low.
‡Actually designed (ca. 1969) by architect Charles Colbert. Rice University, School of Architecture, *New Schools for New Towns* (sponsored by the Educational Facilities Laboratories, Inc., n.d.), p. 14.
†Priorities could be either positive or negative; i.e., a "negative priority" is associated with an undesirable trend, one in which energy is invested for opposition purposes.

55. Many readers may be asking at this point (or perhaps earlier) if ORPHIC procedures inadvertently or deliberately ignore parents, appropriate representatives of subcultures, etc. Since this is a theoretic discussion, we have deliberately avoided the question of *who* participates in order to discuss the approaches and procedures as fully as possible in the space available.

For the participants in the probability-difficulty group, some form of gaming approach (see Table 3) might be feasible and, if so, could be explored as a means of carrying out phase 3 of *future*-planning. Under an educational gaming approach, the probability-difficulty analysis team could be asked to determine how it proposed to deploy the equivalent of, say, $1 billion represented by one hundred "TEM units" in *T*ime, *E*nergy, and *M*oney in order to encourage desirable changes in U.S. schools and to reduce or to eliminate potentially undesirable ones. To serve this purpose, the team of participants would need to be supplied with a master list of trends from the census and with concomitant expert opinion as to (a) their *probability,* and (b) their *difficulty,* with (c) the earliest effective estimated date at which an innovation such as downward extension of well-planned and funded public education to serve all two- and three-year-olds could be put into effect. *Such input would be made available from the last four columns in the census form shown on Table 1.* The team also would need to have the social consequence evaluations from Table 2. It would then become the team members' task to weigh the preintervention probability-difficulty data and reach a decision as to a recommended rank order of priorities for investing the one hundred "TEM units" representing a large sum dedicated to educational change.

Decision-making might prove less simple than it sounds! For example, in contemplating the future, the probability-difficulty analysis team could decide to invest very little time-energy-money in a highly desirable future educational development if—because of its high probability—they assume that it will come about *anyway.*

A form which conceivably might be refined and used for probability-difficulty analyses is suggested in Table 3.

While it often has been reiterated that all three aspects of ORPHIC are hypothetical, they would appear to provide methodical approaches to the organization of group *future*-planning. Also, if it is conceded that in studying future educational goals *the process of effective planning is in itself a goal,* then some adaptations of the ORPHIC concept should have more than passing merit. While only a well-qualified group of experts in the arts, sciences, social sciences, and humanities seem likely to be able to develop an interdisciplinary trend census with educational significance, the sharing and discussion of "educated opinions" obtained from the census should be useful anywhere that a group of local educators, parents, or students might wish to study (a) emerging trends and their social consequences, along with (b) the priorities suggested by the processes of a local probability-difficulty analysis.

*Scenario writing: exploring hypothetical sequences of events.* Once educators have reached decisions regarding educational priorities based on phase 3 analyses, *future*-planning could be carried over into the exploration of how the schools, through curriculum change, can most effectively mediate or influence likely future events. For example, two scenario-writing groups might simultaneously develop specific curricular descriptions of (a) desirable educational changes related to students' experience (learner-centric scenarios), and (b) changes related to the content of instruction (substantive-centric scenarios). While the learner and the content of his learning experiences are inseparable, it may prove to be easier arbitrarily to separate the child as a learner from the discussion of the scope and sequence of desirable content in environment scenarios concerned with, say, the projection of a three-year plan to develop a linguistically oriented language arts program in the primary and middle schools.

As an integral aspect of *future*-planning, at some early point the two interrelated scenarios making proposals for improving the learner's school environment and the content of instruction would need to be coordinated so as to fuse them into a single body of conclusions. This would occur in the final phase of a given segment of the ongoing ORPHIC procedures: the *milestone appraisal.*

*Milestone appraisals of proposed educational change processes.* To help insure the coherence of ORPHIC procedures and to evaluate their emerging orientation, the first four educational change-tactics in the procedures need continually to be appraised to insure that they reflect sound *future*-planning strategies. Such appraisals prepared at the conclusion of the trend census, social consequence projection, and probability-difficulty analysis might be labeled *milestone reports.*

A milestone appraisal probably should review the overall developments and judgments made after scenarios have been written. If successful, such a terminal milestone appraisal would help to make sure that there were no "collision courses" resulting from hypothesized developments of the trend census, their assumed social consequences, the priorities of sought changes, or the values reflected by the learner-centric and content-centric scenarios designed to describe the "most desirable educational futures" that could be conceived.

The form and nature of the milestone report cannot be more fully described since it would be the interactively created outcome of the first four phases of the planning process.

## Reasoned Conjectures: Tools for Shaping Educational Change

*The teacher's probable world:* A.D. *1975-2000.* Whatever the teacher's "most probable world" may be in the coming decades, one thing seems certain if the future proves to be a "surprise-free" one. *More is likely to occur more rapidly between 1975 and 1990 than in the fifteen crowded years between 1960 and 1975.*

Educational *policies* seem certain to change even more rapidly and bring with them continuing *organizational* innovations. Instructional *practices* are likely to differ sharply as new *technologies* come to the fore, and the assignment or *deployment of faculty* will become more varied and imaginative. Finally, although its potentialities are only beginning to be known, *chemistry* and *biochemistry* promise both to extend and to influence our understanding of the learning process and of the mind of man.

*"Participatory evolution" and the curriculum.* Davidson[56] has noted that man is no longer the offspring of nature. "Science," he writes, "has provided him with the technology to become his own maker . . ." In a literal, physiological sense man has achieved the capacity *to share in his own evolution.*

In an intellectual, interactive sense man can likewise engage in the act of deliberately shaping educational change. In the face of the exciting, promising possibility of "participatory curriculum change," the future rightfully may deem educators of the 1970s irresponsible if they content themselves with static pedagogical discourses in the Mandarin dialect of bureaucrats and ignore the verbal

56. R. Michael Davidson, "Man's Participatory Evolution," *Current* 105 (March 1969): 4-10.

tools of reasoned conjecture and the *future*-planning through which they can help us move.

ORPHIC procedures, as described here, obviously are proposed neither as a panacea nor as a definite, prefabricated plan. They are intended to give a vigorous stir to the mental cooking fires over which our educational ideas simmer. Perhaps the idea of ORPHICs will encourage us actually to give more methodical thought to its concepts, to consequent reconstruction of the curriculum, and to the evolution of education as it *can be* tomorrow!

### BIBLIOGRAPHY

1. Ayres, Robert. *Technological Forecasting and Long-Range Planning.* New York: McGraw-Hill Book Co., 1969.
2. Baier, Kurt and Rescher, Nicholas. *Values and the Future.* New York: Free Press, 1969.
3. Beckwith, Burnhum P. *The Next 500 Years.* New York: Exposition Press, 1967.
4. Black, C. E. *The Dynamics of Modernization.* New York: Harper & Row, 1966.
5. Chase, Stuart. *The Most Probable World.* New York: Harper & Row, 1966.
6. Drucker, Peter. *The Age of Discontinuity.* New York: Harper & Row, 1969.
7. Eurich, Alvin C. *Reforming American Education: The Innovative Approach to Improving Our Schools and Colleges.* New York: Harper & Row, 1969.
8. Fabun, Don. *The Dynamics of Change.* Englewood Cliffs, N.J.: Prentice-Hall, 1968.
9. Ferkiss, Victor C. *Technological Man: The Myth and the Reality.* New York: George Braziller, 1969.
10. Glass, Bentley. "Evolution in Human Hands." *Phi Delta Kappan* 50 (1969): 506-10.
11. Gross, Bertram M., ed. *A Great Society?* New York: Basic Books, 1968.
12. Helmer, Olaf. *Social Technology.* New York: Basic Books, 1966.
13. Kahn, Herman and Wiener, Anthony J. *The Year 2000: A Framework for Speculation on the Next Thirty-Three Years.* New York: Macmillan Co., 1967.
14. Kean, Richard, ed. *Dialogue on Education.* Indianapolis: Bobbs-Merrill Co., 1967.

15. Kilpatrick, William H. *Education for a Changing Civilization*. New York: Macmillan Co., 1926.

16. Kostelanetz, Richard and Morrow, William, eds. *Beyond Left and Right: Radical Thought for Our Times*. New York: William Morrow & Co., 1968.

17. McHale, John. *The Future of the Future*. New York: George Braziller, 1969.

18. Michael, Donald N. *The Unprepared Society: Planning for a Precarious Future*. New York: Basic Books, 1968.

19. Resove, Perry E. "A Conjecture about the Teacher's Future Role." *Educational Technology* 10 (February 1970) : 13-20.

20. Sauvy, Alfred. *Mythologie de Notre Temps*. Lausanne, Switzerland: Payot et Cie., 1965.

21. Shane, Harold G. "A Curriculum Continuum: Possible Trends in the 70's." *Phi Delta Kappan* 51 (1970) : 389-92.

22. Shane, June Grant and Shane, Harold G. "Cultural Change and the Curriculum: 1970-2000 A.D." *Educational Technology* 10 (April 1970) : 13-18.

23. Shane, June Grant, et al. *Guiding Human Development*. Worthington, Ohio: Charles A. Jones Publishing Co., 1971.

24. Theobald, Robert. *An Alternative Future for America*. Chicago: Swallow Press, 1968.

25. Toffler, Alvin. "Future Shock." *Horizons* 12 (Spring 1970) : 2.

26. ———. *Future Shock*. New York: Doubleday & Co., 1970.

27. Vizinczey, Stephen. *The Rules of Chaos: or Why Tomorrow Doesn't Work*. New York: McCall Publishing Co., 1970.

28. Warshofsky, Fred. *The 21st Century: The New Age of Exploration*. New York: Viking Press, 1969.

29. Wilson, Ian H. *Our Future Business Environment*. A Re-evaluation Report of the Business Environment of the General Electric Company. General Electric Company, New York, N.Y.

30. Young, Michael, ed. *Forecasting and the Social Sciences*. London: Heinemann Educational Books, 1968.

# CHAPTER IX

# Curriculum Change

OLE SAND

This chapter has three purposes: (a) to analyze selected forces that support and those that restrain curriculum change, (b) to propose strategies for accomplishing change, (c) to describe the changes that appear to be on the horizon of the next decade.

In discussing each of these, a clear distinction among four kinds of curricular decisions is essential. These decisions are made at three levels of remoteness from the student. Close to the student, teachers make daily *instructional* decisions. These are intended for an individual student or a group of students assigned to a teacher or a team of teachers, with a time span ranging from one instructional period to a year or two. At a more remote level teachers and administrators make *institutional* decisions. These are intended for one school and the time span covered by its total program. At a still more remote level school board members, state legislators, and federal officials make *societal* or legal decisions. These are designed for groups of schools within a local or state school system—or may have even nationwide applicability—and may span all the years of schooling.[1] A fourth category of decisions is *ideological*. These decisions can influence those of the other three categories if the ideas are powerful. John Dewey's writings provide an obvious example. Curriculum change demands that the most relevant knowledge be brought to bear as precisely as possible at each decision-making point.

1. *Schools for the Sixties.* A Report of the Project on Instruction, National Education Association (New York: McGraw-Hill Book Co., 1963), p. 13. Also based on letter to the writer from Jimmy E. Nations, April 21, 1969.

## Forces That Support and Forces That Restrain
## Curriculum Change

In the Sixty-fifth Yearbook of the NSSE, Goodlad stresses the fact that in relatively stable times change is likely to be evolutionary and modest in character and come from within. But in periods of unusual political, social, or economic stress "curriculum change is likely to be more countercyclical in relation to the past, to occur rapidly, and to be led by persons not identified with earlier curriculum change or, for that matter, with the schools—in effect, to be somewhat revolutionary in character."[2] The forces that seem to have influenced the curriculum reform movement, as listed by Goodlad, go back to World War II and its immediate aftermath, which revealed extensive and sometimes shocking mathematical and scientific illiteracy among high school graduates. The cold war, the crippling economic depression that did not materialize, shifting American values, and the knowledge explosion are among the societal pressures which have affected the force, direction, and nature of the curriculum reform movement of the past decade.[3]

When one studies "the curriculum then and now," five eras can be identified—at least as reflected by the literature in curriculum. In each era one data source was primary. In the thirties, during the heyday of Progressive education, the *child* was the primary focus. In the forties, when we were engaged in a world war, the curriculum was primarily *society*-centered. In the fifties and sixties the scholars have been in the foreground, and the curriculum has been primarily subject- or *discipline*-centered.[4] The point of view of this writer is that sound curriculum change requires consideration of all three data sources—learner, society, and the disciplines.

Phase one of the reform movement of the past decade is over. It focused on academic scholarship, on the structure of separate disciplines, on comprehensive packages of instructional materials, and on in-service training of teachers. In phase two there must be peda-

2. John I. Goodlad, "The Curriculum," *The Changing American School,* Sixty-fifth Yearbook of the National Society for the Study of Education, Part II (Chicago: University of Chicago Press, 1966), p. 32.

3. Ibid, pp. 35-38.

4. For more extensive discussion, see Ralph W. Tyler, "The Curriculum—Then and Now," *Elementary School Journal* 57 (1957): 364-74, as well as Section I of this yearbook.

gogical scholarship comparable to the academic scholarship of phase one—without, of course, losing the latter. If such pedagogical scholarship prevails, then in phase two a theoretical framework will precede everything else. The curriculum will be viewed as a whole rather than as bits and pieces. Finally, up-to-date curricula will be designed that make no compromise with truth and yet prove attractive and *relevant* to all students.

One of the most discernible trends in American life today is toward greater inclusion of more nearly representative groups of people in the political process. More general participation in curricular decisions has been one of the most significant movements in education. In this blood-soaked and violent age, we are facing many conflicts—poverty versus affluence, young versus old, law and order versus permissiveness, improving life at home versus improving life abroad, the new morality versus the old dogma. Arguments about the who and how of decision-making, the dimension and design of relevant instructional programs, and the unique role of the school have frequently pitted student against teacher, black against white, parent against parent, teacher against administrator. Any discussion of forces influencing curriculum change must deal with the challenges that await solution during the seventies—the revolt of the students, racial unrest in the schools, the rise of parent and teacher power. Each of these can be a restraining force to rational curriculum change if "pure" power is the goal. Each can be a supporting force if it results in leadership and cooperative governance.

### STUDENT POWER

As every headline reader knows, student unrest reached fever pitch in the late sixties. Students protested—often violently—against the kind of curriculum that, from their point of view, was remote from life in the latter third of the twentieth century. Significantly, before they marched, staged a sit-in, or took over the public address system, they pinned on buttons reading, "I am a human being; do not fold, spindle, or mutilate." They were telling their elders rudely and at the tops of their voices that they were rejecting the role of captive audience. They were fed up with being consumers without choice or voice in schools supposedly designed for them.

College students were the first dissenters, but dissension quickly spread to the lower levels of education. A survey made recently by the National Association of Secondary School Principals revealed that 59 percent of the respondents had already experienced some form of student protest and 56 percent of the junior highs polled had seen students on the march.[5] Dissatisfaction with the school program, including teachers, curriculum, scheduling, homework, grading, and testing, accounted for student unrest in 45 percent of the schools responding. Students seemed to be asking for learning based on their own living—for a curriculum that confronted the facts of war, racism, riots, and urban decay and helped them to find remedies for these societal ills as well as answers to the urgent perennial questions, Who am I? Where am I going?

Black students took the protest route, too, to demonstrate that they no longer intended to remain without pride and ignorant of their own identity and culture. The justice of their complaints hit home in many schools during the sixties. Courses in soul music and Swahili, black history, and black culture began to multiply. Textbook publishers rushed to the presses with new books designed to make amends for years of neglect of the contributions of black people to American history. It is obvious that student power cannot be ignored, laughed out of existence, or swept under the rug. In many instances, student power has been a restraining force to change when it led to violence.[6] However, student power, along with community and teacher power, is potentially among the strongest supporting forces for really making change happen. An example of constructive student power is the Experiment in Free-Form Education (EFFE) in Montgomery County, Maryland.

### COMMUNITY POWER

Parent power has been burgeoning, too, in the late sixties, and from an unexpected quarter—the ghetto. Poverty-area and minority-group parents were hotly protesting the dismal statistical truth

5. J. Lloyd Trump and Jane Hunt, "The Nature and Extent of Student Activism," *Secondary Education in an Environment of Change* (Bulletin of the National Association of Secondary School Principals, No. 337, May 1969), pp. 150-58.

6. Joseph J. Schwab, *College Curriculum and Student Protest* (Chicago: University of Chicago Press, 1969).

that the longer their children stayed in school, the further behind they fell. These parents began seeking the same control over their children's education that they believed suburban parents exercised. Decentralization and community control became their rallying cries.

Urban parents demanded—and in some instances got—control of their schools. In some cases, community control became a bitterly contested end in itself. But in others it was a step toward a cooperative restructuring that involved all segments of the school community. Experiments in widespread community participation in schools have not always been successful, as we have seen in Brooklyn's Ocean Hill–Brownsville District. The Morgan Community School and the Anacostia Community Demonstration District, both in Washington, D.C., have, on the other hand, been able to make headway in involving the community in the schools. Each has a community board to determine school policy. Boston and Chicago have also begun to experiment with citizen participation and the utilization of external resources.

Fantini notes:

... the participants who lead reform in the 70's will be those closest to the action—teachers, parents and students. Participation of these three publics in the governance of urban schools carries the potential for triggering change in substance and personnel. If all that were to happen under this new participatory movement should be a shift in control, so that a new group controlled the schools as an end in itself, the educational institution would remain outdated. The hope, however, is that those seeking control will use their political energy to set in motion the search for institutional renewal at the local school level where it counts.[7]

### TEACHER POWER

Teachers have begun to use political power. Teacher strikes, almost unheard of before the early sixties, have become commonplace. Teachers have gained visibility and bargaining power. As a result of this newly found muscle, salaries have risen and working conditions have improved. The power of teachers in negotiation, however, has hardly touched several important areas. For example, the potential of the organized teaching profession to improve the curriculum

7. Drawn from the unpublished manuscript by Mario D. Fantini, which resulted in his *The Reform of Urban Schools* (Washington: National Education Association, 1970).

remains unexploited. One possibility for negotiation in curriculum is the formation and utilization of active and responsive instructional improvement centers at the level of the local education association—at the level of the teacher himself. To use an example, in Michigan the Lansing Schools Education Association and the Lansing Board of Education have already contracted for a process for instructional change through the establishment of an instructional council. The council, made up of twelve administrators, twelve teachers selected by the association, and six parents, acts as a decision-making body for curricular development and instructional improvement. In negotiation, the teaching profession will of course avoid the danger of engraving too much in stone—the danger of negotiating away their freedom to experiment, their freedom to make mistakes, their freedom to change their minds. The power of negotiation is a positive force that will be used to make essential reforms and will not be used to foster obsolescence.

The NEA, through its Professional Development and Instructional Services Area, has worked with a number of pilot locals to help them take the lead in instructional improvement. In a forthcoming volume in the CSI (Center for the Study of Instruction), "Schools for the 70's, Preliminary Series," by Robert McClure,[8] the CSI Field Studies Program is described and analyzed. This program helps increasing numbers of local education associations meet the growing demand of teachers to be significantly involved in the planning of the curriculum, in the development of strategies to make schooling more responsive to the needs of students and society.

In addition to the teacher having taken leadership as a member of his professional association, he also has worked as a member of his school faculty to confront and take important steps toward institutional renewal. Storefront schools sprang up in Harlem, and education became something very real for young men and women whose world was the ghetto streets and alleys.

## POWER VS. LEADERSHIP

If the reader accepts the thesis that student power, community power, and teacher power are potentially supporting rather than re-

8. Robert M. McClure, *Field Studies in Curriculum Development* (Washington: National Education Association, 1971).

straining forces for change, a series of questions needs attention at each level of decision-making—societal, institutional, and instructional. These questions will be central if leadership is the goal. They usually will be ignored if only stark power is used in the decision-making process. Can change be anything but part of a long-range, conceptual program? What part must initial assessment of existing plans and programs play in change processes? What criteria must be developed for deciding just what to change? How does one influence a social system to change? What are the consequences of change strategies which do not deal with the person before they deal with program? What necessary evaluative measures must be designed to assess the effectiveness (and effect) of change? How does a school system maintain consistency in its decisions relating to change and stability? What, briefly, are some of the already developed strategies and research findings dealing with the substantive necessities of the change process? Can a case be made for stability of such educational institutions as the family, the church, industry, and various youth-serving agencies?

Although we in the United States may take justifiable pride in the accomplishments of our decentralized school system and should not flagellate ourselves, we must look with great concern at the gap between *what could be* and *what is*. Again, to move from what is to what might be, questions like the following require thought and action. Can we make a convincing case for the teacher as an agent of change rather than the victim of change? Rather than wait for something to happen, how can we make it happen? What are the assumptions underlying change as a process? What necessary decisions must be made about people, about schools, about the good life, about the substance of change, and about leadership and role definition? What are the necessary philosophic underpinnings of curricular change? What questions *must* be answered when change decisions are considered?

Unfortunately, in too many instances, the reforms of the past have been blunted at the classroom door. Probably one restraining force derives from the fact that most of the leadership in the curriculum reform movement of the late fifties and sixties came from outside the educational establishment. When the newly discovered powers of the teaching profession are focused on problems of central concern to the planning of a good program, our hypothesis is that change will actually take place in the classrooms. The role of the organized teaching profession in curricular change can be central in the decade ahead.[9]

Even though the teacher will probably be the prime agent of change, federal government and foundation programs as well as new liaison between industry and schools will continue to be important. In addition, student power, black power, and community power will join with teacher power in genuine cooperative governance. Teacher power now gives the teacher opportunity to perform truly professional leadership functions.

Leadership is a function—not a position or person. Leadership is concerned with how people can be brought to work together for common ends effectively and happily. Leadership is the ability to contribute to the achievement of those ends either through ideas or through ways of working to accomplish them. Leadership, unfortunately, is often confused with command—as demonstrated in the contest between the Japanese commander and the British colonel in *The Bridge over the River Kwai.* Command, however, is always concerned with power over people, while leadership is concerned with power over problems.

Mary P. Follett expresses these ideas well:

When you and I decide on a course of action together and do that thing, you have no power over me nor I over you, but we have power over ourselves together. We have, however, no authority over John Smith. We could try to get "power" over him in a number of ways . . . but the only legitimate power we could have in connection with John Smith is what you and John Smith and I could develop together over our three selves . . . Genuine power is power-with; pseudo power, power-over.[10]

There is no need to spell out further the implications of Follett's statement. Enough to say again that leadership is a function—not a position or person.

9. For example, see: *The Professional Association Looks at Its Role in Instruction* (Washington: National Education Association, Professional Development and Instructional Services, 1970); Arthur F. Corey, *The Responsibility of the Organized Profession for the Improvement of Instruction* (Washington: Center for the Study of Instruction, National Education Association, 1966).

10. Mary P. Follett, *Creative Experience* (New York: Longmans, Green & Co., 1928), p. 199.

## Strategies for Accomplishing Change

Federal government and foundation programs have created several strategies for curriculum change. While we recognize the necessity for local school systems and individual schools to retain their unique ways of changing their own situations, there are broad societal issues to consider in which the federal government and foundations are taking the lead.

### FEDERAL GOVERNMENT AND FOUNDATIONS

Gallagher identifies the nature of the educational system itself as the most outstanding educational issue in the next decade. His conclusion is that there is no such thing as an educational system. Rather, there are isolated units which were and still remain encapsulated entities. Gallagher asks: "How does one transform a scattered and largely unrelated collection of service entities in over 20,000 school districts throughout the country into an organized system that is compatible with the complex technological society it is supposed to serve?"[11]

Among the linkages Gallagher suggests are: (a) research and development; (b) developmental efforts and demonstration and modeling efforts in the schools; (c) a full-scale system of dissemination of new development activities; (d) developmental efforts and the training programs for new teachers; (e) translation of demonstration efforts into actual ongoing service programs; (f) new designs of educational research responsive to the problems of service programs; (g) relationships between societal goals and values and manpower needs; and (h) relevant roles to be played by the local, regional, state, and national efforts.

One USOE (U.S. Office of Education) strategy that shows promise in building the linkages to which Gallagher refers is the new National Center for Educational Communication, formerly the Office of Information Dissemination. In addition to the more typical literature on decision-making and practice made easily available through the Educational Resources Information Center (ERIC), the Educational Reference Center, and the Educational

11. James J. Gallagher, "Major Educational Issues: The Nonexistent American School System," unpublished paper (Washington: U.S. Dept. of Health, Education, and Welfare, Office of Education, May 23, 1969).

Materials Center, the new Division of Practice Improvement purports to develop communication linkages. The purposes are to accelerate the spread of validated exemplary practices; enhance local
accessibility of tested instructional products, systems, and practices
from large-scale development efforts; develop and verify communications systems and foster articulation of dissemination resources;
and to develop models and strategies for dissemination and application. How to develop the linkages by providing technical assistance
information, retrieval services, and pharmacies of tested educational
alternatives are among the major initiatives for this new National
Center for Educational Communication.[12]

In discussing any strategy for accomplishing change, a significant
societal question is: How can the successes and failures of founda-
tion- and government-supported projects be communicated to the
groups that do not get the money? For example, the Ford Founda-
tion-supported School Improvement Program involved thirty-five
million dollars for twenty-five school systems. How are the other
twenty thousand school systems to learn from the successes and
failures of the projects in the program? Among the recommendations
made by this writer in a report for the Ford Foundation are the
following: Clearly identify the audiences. There are subaudiences
within a project as well as in other schools in the same school district in which the project is located and, of course, in school systems
across the country. They include project directors, project staff
specialists, classroom teachers, paraprofessional persons, school
boards, other lay citizens, college and university personnel.

Certain questions that need to be answered include: What do
project directors want to know? Where do the various subgroups
go for their information? What do classroom teachers want to know?
The Silberman[13] and Goodlad[14] studies actually try to get behind
the classroom door. Classroom teachers want to know about practice. All of them do not really want to know about the research that

12. Lee G. Burchinal, "NCEC at a Glance," unpublished paper (Washington:
U.S. Department of Health, Education, and Welfare, Office of Education, July
1970).

13. Charles E. Silberman, *Crisis in the Classroom* (New York: Random House,
1970).

14. John I. Goodlad, M. Frances Klein, and Associates, *Behind the Classroom
Door* (Worthington, Ohio: Charles A. Jones Publishing Co., 1970).

supports the practice. In reporting change results, four categories represented by the following activities are essential: (a) describe specifically and concretely; (b) account for or explain—interpret; (c) evaluate or judge; (d) generalize.

COMMUNICATION PROBLEMS

In addition, the following questions should be considered: What are common components in innovative projects? What components are relevant but peculiar to a region or locale and why? For whom should reports be prepared? How should they be communicated— the printed word, multimedia, interpersonal communication? What are the strengths of our present communication system and its weaknesses? What immediate and long-range steps should be taken to improve communication?

Wayne Howell of the Charles F. Kettering Foundation is engaged in planning a major national effort to improve educational communications to all sectors of society. His plan assumes that effective educational reform, the leadership for which lies with the professional teacher, depends upon the development of intensive discussion and feedback among the faculty, the students, and the community. The critical issues of education must be agreed upon and must become the basis for a nationwide system of local dialogues. To increase the impact of this dialogue upon the quality of education and the growth of the profession, a system for development, production, and dissemination must be designed which will strive to become self-supporting through membership and subscription, and will remain free from financial and political pressure. The responsibility for maintaining channels of communication about the schools has up to now been left to an elite group generally far removed from the classroom.

Inherent to the value of this system of communication is the development of a communications package designed to stimulate discussion at the national and local levels. This package would, through the presentation of options, be a major tool to update the nation's thinking about education. It would become a national program not only for in-service training, but also for an approach to total citizen involvement.

Two thoughts on how the system would work according to Howell are:

1. Development of between 60 to 90 multimedia communication packages over a period of 10 years—one each month, 6-9 months per year; each package unit designed to communicate about a single educational issue. Various media would be designed to be useful to particular audiences. The total impact of a package on society would be cumulative. Each unit provides a role for the teachers to take professional leadership.

2. Distribute each package at a pre-arranged time via private and public television; motion picture film as one part of an in-service package shipped to local teacher leadership groups and teacher education centers; release pre-developed supportive material coordinated with *Today's Education,* one or more major mass subscription journals, and with the national organization of newspaper educational writers.[15]

### DELIVERY SYSTEMS

Another strategy is to find an incentive system in the delivery system. While every analogy has its faults (particularly the medical and engineering analogies), this writer's experience in rural America leads him to cite the agricultural model. Too frequently in education we send bulletins to the teachers, call them to a meeting, and this is the end of it. The Department of Agriculture not only sends bulletins to the farmers and calls them to meetings, but it also plants the hybrid corn and demonstrates methods and values to the farmers. As Wilbur Schramm says, "They [personnel of the department] observe three communication principles—campaign, involvement, demonstration." An interesting example is cited by Silberman.[16] His study for Carnegie reveals that one of the most interesting change programs is taking place in North Dakota. In trying to upgrade the teachers of that state, the decision-makers determined that there would be little value in sending experienced teachers back to college unless they would become better teachers as a result of the experience. The question to which the program in this state is revealing interesting answers is, How can a college program change— really change—the way people teach?

15. Letter to Mrs. Helen Bain (President, NEA) from Wayne Howell, June 19, 1970.
16. Silberman, *Crisis in the Classroom,* chap. vii.

Another point is that development is the "name of the game" now. Development is defined according to Norman Boyan as "making an educational idea work under conditions that are specified." In more conventional research, one tests A, B, and C. If A works best, one forgets about B and C. In development, one has to keep working on B and C, moving them from the drawing board to the field and from the field back to the drawing board to make them all work. In plain English, development means, "See that the damn thing works!"

## SIX CHANGE STRATEGIES

Several strategies for change are actually in operation across the country. Following are brief descriptions of six of them. First, the regional educational laboratory is a well-known agent for curriculum change. It is essentially an adoption model which utilizes programs, research, and development projects from universities and other institutions. The change strategy depends in large measure upon an understanding and manipulation of environmental context, systematic procedures for planning and programming, and the application of system-selection and convergence techniques.

A second strategy is the use of an interpretive development model. The focus here is upon instructional methodologies as a handle to desired broader change in schools. An assumption in this strategy is that by dealing with the immediate concerns of teachers one can then move out of the classroom and into a better understanding and possible reorganization of the school system.

A third strategy is the utilization of change agents. This is essentially the League of Cooperating Schools' model in which principals are identified as instructional leaders, encouraged to look upon themselves as members of a new social system, given leadership training in communication skills, and rewarded according to the degree and quality of change in teacher behavior and school organization. Goodlad describes the league as follows:

In the League of Cooperating Schools, we are committed primarily to changing school settings, to creating self-renewing schools. One of the most significant things that is happening is that teachers are learning to talk together, to make decisions together, and to act together as never before. And I include "principals" under the rubric, "teachers." They not only are assuming responsibility for redesigning the school setting but also are gaining new self-insights and educational skills in the process. Clearly, the best way to grow on the job, to become self-renewing, is to attack together the problems of making schools good places for human work, good places to teach, and good places to learn.[17]

Curriculum change through representative institutional participation, with emphasis on the role of the teacher as a member of his professional society, is a fourth change strategy. An example is the NEA Center for the Study of Instruction's Field Studies Program which is designed to make significant and lasting changes in the curriculum and instructional activities of its various member sites. These changes are brought about by a study- and action-program specifically focused on problems, concerns, and issues pertinent to local schools. Leadership in the development and follow-through of this plan for making schools work is assumed largely by association members as they cooperate with state associations, the NEA, and the like in their schools. Basic to all of of the settings is the attention paid to a careful combination of theoretical and practical questions which, when answered, offer options uniquely appropriate to each of the dissimilar schools in the program.

The CSI Field Studies Program is capable of helping increasing numbers of local associations meet the growing demand of teachers to be significantly involved in the planning of the curriculum and in the development of strategies to make schooling more responsive to the needs of our society and its people.

Fantini makes a strong case for the teacher's role under this fourth strategy: "Teachers are the professional agents closest to the learner and as such they are in a better position to develop instructional policies. For teachers to develop capacity at the individual school level they must be organized to do so."[18]

A fifth change strategy—and one with great potential—is the process of negotiation. Among the issues to be resolved are:

> . . . how to differentiate between negotiation of conditions of work related to instruction and negotiation of the methods and content; how to secure the right to negotiate instruction and how to determine the appropriate method once we have the right; when to negotiate process and when to negotiate specific items; whether associations should nego-

17. John I. Goodlad, "The Jugular Vein of Educational Change," *Changing Schools* 3 (July 1969).

18. Fantini, *Reform of Urban Schools.*

tiate the kind of performance contracts being negotiated with the school boards by the commercial information and instruction "industry."[19]

A landmark conference of local, state, and national education association leaders in April 1970 discussed, among other issues, negotiation as a decision-making process in instruction. Kenneth Law raised a number of problems that need to be solved in connection with this issue. Among them were the basic schizophrenia about the many responsibilities of an association; the restraining force in the eyes of the public concerning the "establishment problem"; the appropriate wording of contract language; and the effecting of a marriage between hard-nosed collective bargaining and a different negotiating model which might serve better for curriculum change.

Law gives helpful suggestions on what might be negotiable and what might be accomplished through less rigid forms than negotiation:

There are several possibilities open to an association that becomes involved in negotiation of curriculum and instruction, no one best way. It depends upon not only the local circumstances, but what is to be negotiated. However, in general it seems that those items which relate to physical conditions under which instruction is to take place as well as general guidelines needed for effective teaching should be negotiated directly and included in the contract in specific language. Most other items, such as what should be taught and how, might best be determined by a less rigid form of negotiation; even here immediate exceptions come to mind. The important thing is that no major decision affecting any of the related items will be made without the formal participation of the association—not just teachers as teachers.[20]

A sixth strategy is Rubin's teacher-facilitation program, a major effort of the Center for Coordinated Education and one of the Ford-supported school improvement programs referred to earlier. Among Rubin's provocative conclusions are:

We can never overcome the need for a human teacher. Inservice education is unlearning as well as learning. To improve teaching it is necessary to analyze performance. A practicing teacher is the best possible trainer of teachers. Changing the behavior of a group is often easier than changing the behavior of an individual. A good method works well for most but not all teachers. The matter of incentive is

19. *The Professional Association Looks at Its Role in Instruction,* p. 75.
20. Ibid., p. 77.

234 STRATEGIES FOR CHANGE

crucial. Teachers are individuals and their styles vary. Schools have a collective staff personality. The need for a human coach is unavoidable. Technique alone does not produce great teaching. We need to find ways to exploit the individual teacher's unique strengths.[21]

Goodlad gives one of the best summaries of change strategies this writer has seen: ". . . our schools have a long, hard road ahead if they are to become stimulating places for the good work of those who reside in them. Unless schools become significantly more intense they will fall by the wayside as other institutions and media become the prime educational influence."[22]

Among the ideas cited by Goodlad are these: There is an enormous gap between what schooling is today and what it could be. Although a substantial number of principals and teachers are receptive to ideas and methods of innovation, opportunities for inservice growth have generally been minimal because of lack of models for redesigning schools.

Education presently has a less than effective structure for change. The present system too frequently stifles mobility in the sense that middle-management leaders in education often jeopardize their status when change within the system is attempted and results in failure. To shake up the system, then, a reasonable approach is a comprehensive but not overt attack on the whole. The critical problem remains; our notions about formulating the attack are not as clear as they need to be.

Goodlad proposes the following influencing notions: The key unit for change is the individual school—not the school system. The principal is the key person if change in the entire school is to take place. Any significant change calls for access to both conceptual and operating models of the changed condition and for opportunities to learn whatever new behaviors are called for.[23]

This writer agrees with Goodlad's ideas—with one reservation. One of his influencing notions seems not to take sufficiently into account the emerging power of the classroom teacher. We would

21. Louis J. Rubin, *A Study on the Continuing Education of Teachers* (Santa Barbara, Calif.: Center for Coordinated Education, University of California, 1970).

22. John I. Goodlad, "Educational Change: A Strategy for Study and Action," *National Elementary Principal* 48 (January 1969): 8-10.

23. Ibid.

rewrite that statement to read: "The teacher is the key to making change happen. He is the key as the professional agent closest to the learner. He is the key as he wears four professional hats: (a) an autonomous, competent, professional individual; (b) a member of his professional society or organization; (c) a member of a community of scholars on his school faculty; (d) a key member of a larger school system."

In a seminar on rational planning of curriculum and instruction sponsored by the NEA Center for the Study of Instruction (CSI), Clark and Guba proposed a logical structure for reexamining change roles in education. Processes related to and necessary for change in education were discussed. Research, development, diffusion, and adoption were the key ideas used to provide a rationale for engineering change. They concluded their analysis of essential change roles by providing sixteen recommendations. Of particular interest to the reader concerned with the development of new knowledge in education will be the discussion of the function of research. Clark and Guba's proposals for a new and more dynamic role for the local school in the engineering of change reflect a growing national concern.[24]

In the same volume, Brickell presented a general discussion of strategies for implementing change in instructional programs, followed by fairly elaborate descriptions of two strategies a local school system might use to invent a new program or to adopt a program invented elsewhere.[25]

In the future, this writer believes that the supporting forces will overcome those that restrain curriculum change. In the main, the teaching profession, the public, and the students expect and want their schools to change. If it is to be good, however, change has to be planned for. A student of evolution once said, "Nature never makes jumps." This is true of education, too, even though the new power groups sometimes appear to want instant change. The strat-

24. David L. Clark and Egon G. Guba, "An Examination of Potential Change Roles in Education," *Rational Planning in Curriculum and Instruction* (Washington: National Education Association, Center for the Study of Instruction, 1967), p. 111.

25. Henry M. Brickell, "Two Change Strategies for Local School Systems," *Rational Planning in Curriculum and Instruction*, pp. 134-53 (see note 24).

egies in the future probably will proceed on a broken front at different rates in different places.

## Changes That Appear To Be on the Horizon

The ideas for change have been little short of dramatic. In the seventies the unfinished business is to put the ideas of the sixties into actual practice. In this section we will attempt to discuss some of the ideas we have "going for us" and the liklihood that some of the strategies for change suggested in the preceding section will be effective.

### THE NEA PROJECT ON INSTRUCTION

In 1963, through the NEA Project on Instruction, now grown into the Center for the Study of Instruction (CSI), the NEA legitimatized most of the innovations of the past decade. Among the problems on which recommendations were made in that project were those of (a) establishing priorities for the school, (b) a balanced program, and (c) selecting and organizing content, materials, technology, and space.[26] The decade of the sixties was indeed the education decade. The end of the decade was characterized by some disillusionment which arose in part because the Congress and the Administration encouraged the idea that education is at the heart of all of our social problems and charged the schools with solving them. Because we in education accepted the notion that our major job was social engineering and forgot that education is in fact the slow process of changing human behavior, we were in some trouble.

Among the factors supporting us are new emphasis on humanizing the school, on making it in fact a place that sustains the human spirit and gives meaning to life, on early childhood education, and on making the school *the* center of teacher education. Developments that look as though they are here to stay include individualized instruction, the new technology, independent study, relevance, and student involvement. Other topics that are in the mainstream are flexible scheduling, microteaching, computer-assisted instruction, and the like.

26. *Schools for the Sixties, see note 1.*

## DIRECTIONS IN CURRICULUM REFORM

We seem to be moving in the following directions in curriculum reform:

| FROM | TO |
|---|---|
| Primary emphasis on academic scholarship | Pedagogical and academic scholarship |
| Involvement of only academic scholars and teachers | Involvement of all levels of decision-makers in the schools, including parents, students, and scholars, but with special emphasis on the participation of teachers |
| Child, society, or discipline-centered curriculum | The total curriculum, the humanistic curriculum |
| Selling prepackaged programs | Truly experimental programs; pharmacies of tested educational alternatives |
| Tinkering with the means of education | Focus on ends, aims, objectives (the philosopher returns to the center of the stage) |
| Trying to teach everything | Establishing priorities |
| Focus on the gifted and the deprived students | Focus on all students |
| Bits and pieces, one course at a time | Comprehensive school improvement programs—nursery school through college |
| Elementary and secondary reform | Higher education and adult education reform also |
| In-service training of teachers | In-service education of teachers (continuing career development) |

## INSTITUTIONAL DIRECTIONS

If the school as an institution is to change along with the curriculum, we also need to move:

| FROM | TO |
|---|---|
| The group | The individual |
| Self-contained classroom | Community-wide school |
| School building use geared to an agrarian society, nine-month year, limited to children | School building use reflecting urban society, twelve-month year, available to all age groups |
| 2 x 4 x 6 teacher[27] | The teacher and his staff; man, media, and machines |

27. Stuck between 2 covers of a textbook, 4 walls of a classroom, 6 periods of a school day.

| FROM | TO |
|---|---|
| Teaching as telling, dispensing information | Teaching as guiding, conducting the dialogue about the meaning of it all |
| Teacher as general practitioner | Teacher as clinical specialist (member of team) |
| Memory | Inquiry |
| Spiritless climate | Zest for learning |
| Classrooms that are like kitchens | Classrooms that are like libraries and living rooms |
| Boxes and egg crates | Clusters and zones of space |
| Scheduled classes | Appointments and independent learning |
| A teaching schedule of thirty hours a week with children in class and fifteen hours for planning and correcting | Fifteen hours a week with children, and thirty hours for research, planning, and development |
| The graded school | The nongraded school |
| Supervisors | Educational demonstration agents |
| Centralized, narrow-based decision-making, conducted mainly by the "educational establishment" | Decentralized, broadly based decision-making including students, teachers, parents, and others, along with the "establishment" |

All of these changes—from curriculum to school buildings, to teacher preparation, and to new overall concepts—are important. But two principles, both of them given life by the death of the old institutions, are especially noteworthy. The first is that the teacher is not the source, but the catalyst. The other is that school is a concept, not a place; that education can happen anywhere—in a classroom, in a park, in a factory. Hopefully, these changes will produce a curriculum and a style of teaching that will make no compromise with truth or significance and still prove attractive to the "bright" youngster. Hopefully, these changes will give every student a zest for learning.

A basic assumption in this chapter is that the school is only one educational institution. Dewey's disciples sometimes confuse his sound advice about schooling the whole child with nonsense about the school taking responsibility for the child's whole education.[28]

28. Drawn from Lawrence A. Cremin, *The Genius of American Education* (Pittsburgh: University of Pittsburgh Press, 1965), p. 8.

The National Committee for the NEA Project on Instruction asked "the right questions" about this issue—questions as significant for 1980 as for today. To determine the school's responsibilities, answers to these questions must be found:

1. What knowledge, values, and skills do children and youth in our culture need to learn?
2. Which of these goals can best be achieved by the school?
3. What knowledge, skills, and values can best be taught by the home, the church, and other social institutions?
4. Which learnings require the joint efforts of the school and other agencies?
5. What, then, should be included in the school program? What should be excluded from it?

After raising these questions, the committee then made the following recommendation:

Priorities for the school are the teaching of skills in reading, composition, listening, speaking (both native and foreign languages), and computation . . . ways of creative and disciplined thinking, including methods of inquiry and application of knowledge . . . competence in self-instruction and independent learning . . . fundamental understanding of the humanities and the arts, the social sciences and natural sciences, and mathematics . . . appreciation of and discriminating taste in literature, music, and the visual arts . . . instruction in health education and physical education.

The responsibilities best met by joint efforts of the school and other social agencies include: development of values and ideals . . . social and civic competence . . . vocational preparation. The decision to include or exclude particular school subjects or outside-of-class activities should be based on: (a) the priorities assigned to the school and to other agencies; (b) data about learners and society, and developments in the academic disciplines; (c) the human and material resources available in the school and community.[29]

There are no easy answers to the question of what should be included and what should be excluded from the school program. There never will be. A complex, purposeful, human enterprise like teaching does not lend itself to easy, final answers. Each school must deal with the questions listed above and base its answers on self-study and careful thought. Our plea is to avoid at all costs the creeping curriculum through which never have so many learned so little

29. *Schools for the Sixties,* p. 32.

about so much. Of one thing we are certain—there is an inverse relationship between the thickness of the catalog and the excellence of the program.

A word about the definition of curriculum! We are defining curriculum and instruction as two parts of a single entity. We are not making the fine distinction that curriculum is the message or the content and that instruction is the communication network or the method. Essentially, we are saying that curriculum and instruction deal with five substantive elements—educational objectives, selection of learning opportunities, organization, evaluation, and change processes.

If the projections in this chapter are to become a reality, rational curriculum planning is essential—with emphasis on evaluation as a base for change. Rational leadership is required with artistic application of *principles* rather than rule-of-thumb procedures.

### DIRECTIONS IN EVALUATION

Space permits only a quick summary of directions as far as evaluative aspects of rational planning are concerned. National assessment is a particularly controversial issue. While the hazards are well known, national educational indices may well be as essential to the educator as economic indices are to the businessman. It seems inconceivable that we would rather operate our schools on the basis of ignorance than on the basis of information. Some seem to fear that the more we know, the worse we will behave. We submit that the opposite should be true.

Without perspective regarding the progress we have made and the difficult tasks we face, our citizens have an inadequate basis for making judgments. As a result, decisions are frequently made on hearsay or widely publicized assertions rather than on a reasonably clear picture of the educational situation.[30]

The only place we can stand on this issue with professional comfort is on the side of all the knowledge and all the public support we can get.

The following table summarizes the directions apparent in the field of evaluation:

30. Drawn from *National Assessment of Educational Progress—Some Questions and Comments* (Washington: Department of Elementary School Principals in cooperation with the NEA Center for the Study of Instruction, 1967).

| FROM | TO |
|------|-----|
| 1. Tests as punishment | Evaluation as a stimulant, a humane guide to continued growth and learning |
| 2. Measurement by paper-and-pencil tests | A variety of evaluation techniques with emphasis on observation |
| 3. Memory of the facts | Focus on creativity and inquiry |
| 4. Exams at the end of course | Cooperative and continuous evaluation |
| 5. Narrow range of behaviors measured | Evaluation of cognitive, affective, and psychomotor behaviors |
| 6. Evaluation only by the teacher | Self-evaluation |
| 7. Colleges setting "standards" for admission | Colleges cleaning up their sterile programs and working with schools to develop valid evaluation techniques |

### A HUMANE CURRICULUM—THE PRIORITY DIRECTION

To place emphasis upon the curriculum change most needed, our final words will enlarge on the need for a *humane* program. Ask one of your students about the sun. What will he tell you? It is 93,000,000 miles from the earth, approximately 866,500 miles in diameter, with a surface rotation of about twenty-five days at the equator. If he is to live in the shadow of bigger and better bombs, perhaps he must be taught all these facts. Yet, it will always be the larger purpose of education to lead him to appreciate the radiance of a sunset.

Science is not the panacea of life's problems. We must keep our debt to it in clear perspective. Its Nembutal helps us sleep; its wrinkle-resistant, wash-and-wear fabrics clothe us; its steel beams support the great theaters. But the test tube has yet to come up with a "shake'n bake" formula for increasing man's ability to think, to feel, to appreciate, to understand, to love. It is the task of the humanities to help us understand ourselves so we can understand our fellowmen and to help us live in this "valley of the dolls" that science has fashioned for us.

The teacher who teaches with zest, who speaks and listens well, who helps his students interact with more than boredom or rebellion, is a humanist, an artist working with humanity, and his art is the one thing in this pep-pill world of ours most likely to beget in his students a thirst, a passion for the fullness of life. Is there anything in our philosophy of education that requires the teacher be a poor listener or speaker, alien to the sheer delight of being, fearful of his bright young students, and replete with fitful mannerisms? Is it a blessing that too many articles in educational journals are completely devoid of style? Is Plato less for writing well? If Socrates had spoken badly, if he had not charmed his young listeners to a view of the world and a delight in his own unique being no matter what he was discussing at the moment, would we be richer? When a concept has reached such definition that it can be adequately expressed in jargon, it can then be taught much more efficiently by a machine.

The only reason that a teacher should be a person, alive to the things that are, is that he must encourage speculation and lead it. To help a student learn about an unknown and vastly different country requires a medium, a metaphor in which the known and the unknown can meet, each taking meaning from the other. Such a medium is the essence of music, of poetry, of art. Students taught by a real humanist will become real humanists, readers, listeners, men of intellectual and emotional delight, ready for a kind of intimacy with the world which will breed not contempt but freedom of mind. These students will have a way out of the slavery of mere conformism to society.

However, there are many barriers to a humane environment in our schools. One is the school building itself, if it is the old-style egg-crate and box design. Gores revisited an elementary and middle school of modern open design and reported these observations by the school's principal:

> I don't know whether the kids test better or not, but I do observe that absenteeism of both staff and student body is less; that there is less tension, fewer tantrums, less vomiting, fewer confrontations. It's easier to get paraprofessionals and volunteers. They feel more comfortable joining a team in a large space than working in a square box about the size of a prize-fight ring, and already occupied by one professional. The open space provides room for withdrawal. In effect, both teachers and children can withdraw to the back country to cool off rather than slug it out in the ring.

Education is a soft science and we'll have to await the hard data about achievement. I think it will be better, but I can't prove it now. But we're picking up human and humane benefits and economies which make it all worthwhile.[31]

Learners in a humane environment are helped: to develop self-actualizing behaviors through opportunities provided for decision-making regarding their own learning; to understand that the principles of discipline, order, and control are largely self-regulatory and rooted in rational comment to self and to one's group; to evaluate their own learning behavior in consultation with teachers; to value the diversity that exists in and between groups of people; to understand and resolve value conflicts; to relate positively to the school, the community, and the greater society; to make decisions about their own temporal destinies; and to consider the school as a vital component of the community.

Teachers in a humane learning environment promote variance and flexibility in grouping schemes for learners; value the learner as a central decision-maker in schools; provide multiple options for learning opportunities; value divergent behavior of learners and colleagues; understand and utilize community resources as educational experiences for learners; promote one-to-one relationships with learners; behave toward colleagues with trust and honesty; help learners become what they *can* become and then maintain and sustain that condition; promote true two-way communication between school and community; and utilize technology as an adjunct to, not a substitute for, human contact.

If one recalls the 1926 yearbook and other books written since then, with their predictions of amazing changes ahead, and then looks at life in classrooms today, a funny thing happened on the way to the future. A useful cautionary exercise for the reader of this chapter is to remember the way teaching is as we look into the future. Silberman makes the point well:

"What we call necessary institutions," Alexis de Tocqueville wrote, "are often no more than institutions to which we have grown accustomed." The "necessity" that makes American schooling so uniform over time and across cultures is simply the "necessity" that stems from

31. Harold B. Gores, "The Case of the Relevant Schoolhouse," *What's Right with American Education* (Bulletin of the National Association of Secondary School Principals, No. 346, May 1970), pp. 137-38.

unexamined assumptions and unquestioned behavior. The preoccupation with order and control, the slavish adherence to the timetable and lesson plan, the obsession with routine qua routine, the absence of noise and movement, the joylessness and repression, the universality of the formal lecture or teacher-dominated "discussion," in which the teacher instructs an entire class as a unit, the emphasis on the verbal and de-emphasis of the concrete, the inability of students to work on their own, the dichotomy between work and play—none of these is necessary, all can be eliminated.

Schools can be humane and still educate well. They can be genuinely concerned with gaiety and joy and individual growth and fulfillment without sacrificing concern for intellectual discipline and development. They can be simultaneously child-centered and subject- or knowledge-centered. They can stress aesthetic and moral education without weakening the three R's. They can do all these things if—but only if—their structure, content, and objectives are transformed.[32]

## Summary

In this chapter we have analyzed selected forces that support and forces that restrain curriculum change, proposed change strategies, and described certain developments that appear to be on the horizon. It is obvious that there are no magic solutions, no easy answers. It is clear that haphazard, chaotic, and frenzied change processes are not effective. While thought without action is futile, action without thought is fatal. If the ideas in this chapter are in fact to be helpful to the practitioner, they require dialogue, study, and action. When the next NSSE yearbook on curriculum is written, the changes noted in the concluding section of this chapter should be a reality.

If this is to happen, the changes must take place on all three decision-making fronts as indicated at the beginning of this chapter —societal, institutional, and instructional. Throughout, the illustrations have been drawn from each of these levels. The ideological component discussed in the preceding section will make a difference only if societal and institutional changes find their way to where the action is—in the classroom.[33]

32. Silberman, *Crisis in the Classroom,* pp. 207-8.

33. Several of the ideas in this chapter are also discussed in Ole Sand, *On Staying Awake: Talks with Teachers* (Washington: National Education Association, 1970).

# CHAPTER X

# Emerging Priorities for the Young

FRANK J. ESTVAN

Every curriculum is based on three major sources: *the disciplines* from which subject matter is drawn, the *society* in which schooling takes place, and the *individual* who is growing and learning. Generally speaking, ideas stemming from the disciplines have dominated education in this country, but there have been periods when those relating to society or the learner have taken on added significance. As a consequence of the Great Depression, for example, more extensive curricular provisions were made for social problems. Today, certain needs of the young are emerging which must receive higher priority in the curriculum.

That there are such needs is evident in the so-called generation gap, our most widespread and vexing problem. Some degree of misunderstanding among generations is not unusual nor to be deplored. What is new is the intensity of youth's protest. Significant numbers are in open revolt, seeking either to overthrow the established order or to withdraw from it. New, also, is the extent of youth's disaffection. Among the restless can be counted those from affluent as well as deprived homes, from the majority as well as minority groups. This spirit of rebellion, moreover, has moved from the college to the high school, and is now penetrating into the junior high.[1]

Many reasons are being advanced to explain youth's overreaction. Perhaps the young see more clearly and are more idealistic than adults who have lived through world wars and our worst depression. The severity of their criticism, on the other hand, may reflect ex-

1. Helen B. Shaffer, "Discipline in Public Schools," *Editorial Research Reports* 11 (1969), 635-52.

treme pressures that have built up as society has made greater demands on them. We may be witnessing the frustration of the protected and pampered or their opposite, the neglected and deprived,
as both fail in attempts to achieve instant success. There are psychological interpretations resting on child-parent relationships, authority
symbols, guilt feelings, and so forth. All these explanations, and undoubtedly others, are different facets of the same underlying phenomenon: today's youth are preoccupied with much the same thing
as youth of the past—they want desperately "to become somebody,"
but because of the rapid, vast, fundamental, and continuing social
change they are finding it more difficult.

As one of society's basic socializing institutions, the school is increasingly being called upon to help the young cope with a changing
world. The effective discharge of this responsibility rests upon an
awareness of the nature of the changes taking place in society and
their impact on children and youth. Through this awareness it is
possible to identify the kinds of learning experiences which, presumably, will help young people attain unfulfilled physical, psychological, and social needs. Lastly, consideration must be given to the
design of the curriculum to determine how these high-priority learning experiences are to be organized and made available to students.

One promising approach to these tasks is through analysis of the
kinds of questions being asked by young people. On the whole, they
reveal a concern and searching for answers with respect to establishing identity, developing a sense of reality, determining purposes,
and becoming socially effective.

## "Who Am I?"

The world is becoming more impersonal. Rapid urbanization of a
growing population is bringing people closer together physically, but
not in their personal relationships. As government, industry, and
other institutions grow in size and function, regulatory systems come
into being which limit areas of individual decision-making. There
is, consequently, a loss in sense of self as "the system" threatens to
engulf the individual and reduce him to the level of a computer
card. In such a world, children and youth find it difficult to satisfy
their basic need for autonomy or independence. Lacking control
over their own destinies, neither can they satisfy the corollary need

for self-respect. Problematic as this may be for persons who are in the mainstream of life, the task is immeasurably greater for those who are culturally different or deprived. To give vent to his gnawing self-doubts, a young person may act in unconventional ways as if to say, "Pay attention to me; I'm important."

The school can help young people in their search for identity by placing greater priority on the study of self. One focus of such study is self-knowledge. To "know thyself" is not a disguised form of egocentrism or narcissism, but an attempt to discover one's own unique qualities and come to terms with them. It is a never ending quest that begins as soon as the infant can differentiate between himself and others. The young child can be introduced to the study of man: how he is like and yet differs from other living things; how individuals resemble each other but no two are identical. As he grows older, he can be made aware of the parts that heredity and environment play in shaping the individual and of the dynamics of human behavior which explain why he and others around him act as they do. With greater maturity, people can be studied not merely for their place in history, but as examples of "life-styles" having different beginnings, developing under different influences, and responding in different ways to the challenges of their times.

Another focus in the study of self is the building of positive self-concepts. Knowledge of self does not automatically insure self-esteem, for, if based on a limited sampling of personal qualities and a single arbitrary set of standards, such information can be detrimental to one's sense of self. What is required is the experiencing of success in a variety of undertakings as determined by the individual's own level of development. A positive concept of self is also fostered through identification with other people so that in time the learner sees himself as a person whose roots go back to a culture that has made significant contributions to our way of life and who is a member of a certain classroom or other school group, resident of a particular neighborhood or community, citizen of the United States, member of the world community, and part of the human race, here and now.

A third focus for study is the mounting concern for ways of changing the self—witness the enormous sums being spent on efforts to enhance personal appearance. A candid appraisal of the possibilities and limitations of such an approach may help youth to realize that there is more to creating a personality than simply relying on cosmetics, extreme fashion, and status symbols, or rejecting good grooming and manners because they are associated with adult expectations. The current situation with respect to drugs, likewise, demands that youth be knowledgeable about the use and abuse of chemically induced means of changing themselves—to distinguish between the legitimate use of drugs prescribed under medical supervision and the indiscriminate use of sleeping pills and "pep" pills, alcohol and tobacco, "soft" and "hard" drugs to alter physical and mental states or to escape from deeper personality problems. In the final analysis, youth must view education and training as the fundamental means of changing the self. In the process, they should make realistic appraisals of the nature of the commitments required by various career choices, including the intermediate steps which must be met along the way.

The self, of course, cannot be understood without taking human sexuality into account. This encompasses far more than knowing where babies come from and the techniques of family planning. Differences between living and nonliving things can be introduced at an early age, followed by the development of such basic concepts as: "life comes from life," "to create a new life there must be both a male and female," "most forms of animal life must be protected before they are born and for some time after." For older pupils, emphasis may be placed on the physical, psychological, and sociological differences between the sexes as well as the changes in sex roles taking place today. In view of the alarming increase of problems that youth are experiencing in their handling of sex, the school appears obligated to provide them with opportunities to critically examine responsibilities and consequences in such matters as dating, "the pill," and the general area of sex freedom.

Schools having strong convictions about the cultivation of self are examining their curricular structures for ways of accommodating the types of experiences noted above. In their attempts to personalize the curriculum as a counter to mass education, they touch on every aspect of the curriculum. Goals are being expanded in the hope that by according respect to many different kinds of achievement the individual is more likely to discover and accept his uniqueness than would be the case if only a few things, such as athletics and academics, were all that really counted. New content bearing on such matters as Afro-American history, drugs, and sex is being incorporated into existing units of study, developed as separate units within the present course structure or offered as electives in the secondary school. Teaching is being individualized, proceeding from careful diagnosis and providing opportunities for independent study instead of relying on the "best" method for instructing a "class." As a further assurance of success experiences for the student, the rate of his learning is kept flexible rather than being specified by grades. Evaluation efforts, as a result, are being based on developmental standards in which the adequacy of an individual's performance is determined in relation to his potential and past progress rather than solely in comparison with an external norm.

The part played by cocurricular activities in the development of self is also being reexamined. These activities provide avenues whereby the individual can acquire insights about a host of personal characteristics that are not usually brought to light in a strictly academic program. Far from being a "frill" or a needless expense, the significance of extracurricular experiences is directly related to the stress placed on subject matter learnings, which generally increases through the grades.

Greater priority on the self can be brought about through fundamental changes in curricular design. In a disciplines-oriented curriculum, one strand or organizing element can be devoted to the self, and the scope and sequence of such experiences carefully planned in advance from nursery school through secondary education. There are other forms of curricular design which may offer greater opportunities for dealing with the self. A society-oriented curriculum focuses on the social problems of the learner; an individual-oriented curriculum is based on his interests and needs. The flexibility inherent in both designs makes it possible to focus on the self when and as questions relating to such problems are raised by the learner.[2]

2. These three approaches to curricular design are described in Frank J. Estvan, *Social Studies in a Changing World: Curriculum and Instruction* (New York: Harcourt, Brace & World, 1968), chap. 6.

## "What Is Real?"

The world is becoming more complex. People are constantly being bombarded by stimuli emanating from all points of the globe, and now from outer space. These impressions, unfortunately, are fragmented and bear little if any relationship to one another. Those which register on the individual's consciousness go through a screening process reflecting his sex, social status, and other factors which influence perception. As a result, many persons live singularly insular lives; the suburban child may seldom break through the bounds of his middle-class culture just as the ghetto child may have limited experiences with ways of living other than his own. Regardless of circumstances, therefore, the young have an urgent need to know what is real. For in order to deal effectively with this world, each person must make sense out of it. He must distinguish between fact and fantasy, between the goals of society and practices which fall short of these ideals. He must piece together the myriad of stimuli into some kind of meaningful pattern. Thus, he places great store in "telling it like it is."

The school can help children and youth in their search for reality by giving greater priority to the relevance of learning experiences. The single most important criterion of relevance, from the standpoint of the learner, is the extent to which he is able to pursue an interest or problem that is significant to him. Many of his concerns tend to be controversial, reflecting the current unrest in society. In coming to grips with these issues, the learner can acquire a realistic notion of what it means to live in a pluralistic world: that each person plays many different roles as family member, churchgoer, worker, citizen; that in each of these roles he is identified with a different subgroup; and that, as a consequence, each person has a different perception of the nature of a problem or social situation. As this insight develops, the learner will look to the school less for ready-made answers to his questions and more for opportunities to examine points of view which bear upon crucial issues.

The student's sense of reality is more likely to be heightened when no sharp line is drawn between his experiences in school and life outside. Field trips, school-sponsored travel, student-exchange programs, and community-action projects are concrete and "real."

Work-study programs coordinate practical and academic experiences, provide opportunities for exploring vocational choices, and are a means of supplementing income. Even greater realism can be achieved when school experiences are one component of a broad educational plan that has been designed to meet the needs of all the people living in a particular area—the young, adults, and retired.

Of all the realities of this world, change is the most pervasive. Accordingly, the school must deal with change as a constant and in so doing demonstrate that change and continuity have gone hand in hand through the ages and that the quality of this partnership is the best prediction of what will occur in the future. For the young learner, so strongly oriented to the here and now, the realities of change can be developed in each unit of study by beginning with the present situation and then turning to the past and tracing its development. Equally if not more important, the unit must look to the future, for this is the world with which youth will soon have to cope. If, in addition to the study of trends, an examination of various proposals for change is included, the learner may acquire confidence in man's ability to exercise some measure of control over his destiny. The dynamics of change, in short, is two-directional, moving from the learner's point in time to include the past as well as future perspectives. Such a long look at the problems of today should make society's imperfections appear to the younger generation as frontiers which remain to be conquered—not a cause for alienation.

In order for young people to deal more effectively with the unsettling conditions of a changing world, they must have greater control of the basic elements of the various disciplines. One of these elements is a system of key concepts and generalizations which, having broad powers of application, is useful in dealing with novel situations. Another is the skills developed by scholars for conducting inquiry, many of which young people can use in finding answers for themselves. Underlying both of these elements is the spirit of scholarship itself—creative, dedicated, and courageous—which the young might emulate as they face change. Teaching the structure of a discipline does not imply, however, that each domain of knowledge is to remain a separate entity. If youth are to find reality, they must view contemporary situations from a more encompassing vantage point than is afforded by any one discipline. The greatest emphasis, therefore, must be placed on those learning experiences which bring the various domains of knowledge together in either a multidisciplinary or an interdisciplinary fashion.

The requirement of relevance in education has many implications for curriculum and instruction. Schools are redoubling their efforts to make clear their goals and the significance of what is being studied in all their procedures—"motivation," "application," "special projects," and others. Content is being scrutinized for its currency, validity in terms of changing conditions, and interest to young people. More use is being made of discovery methods which approximate those used by the scholars. The greatest activity, perhaps, is taking place in the production of resources, as evidenced in the increasing availability of concrete materials and primary sources in printed form.

A greater sense of reality may be realized through fundamental changes in curricular design. In a disciplines-oriented curriculum, the organizing center or topic to be studied can be defined as a problem or issue. In contrast to the study of "Atmosphere," for example, in which references are made to the problem of air pollution, the student searches for answers to the question, "What can we do about air pollution?"—in the course of which he develops basic concepts about the properties of air. Greater relevance is possible when the selection of what to study is not predetermined but is the outcome of ongoing teacher-pupil planning. Thus, in a society-oriented curriculum, the learner works on the solution of his own problems to which added significance is attached as they are related to the basic social functions of all peoples. An individual-oriented curriculum permits even broader choice and, hence, possibilities for relevance because the selection of what to study is based on the learner's interests, curiosities, and needs which must be satisfied *now* in order that he live more intelligently and richly.

## "What Should I Do?"

The world is becoming more confused. Thousands of voices are telling the individual what to do and how to do it. Some speak for the traditional values and old moralities while others advance proposals that are diametrically opposed to established ways. Equally subtle and powerful voices press for conformity to the "in" thing, be it a passing fad or an all-embracing style of life. Impressive arguments, if not always evidence, support various causes, compounding the difficulty of making choices. Hence, one of the imperative needs for the new generation is to build a system of values or goals, for without guideposts no one can make intelligent choices from among the growing number of alternatives available to him. Decisions based on whim or trial and error run a high risk, and the consequent disappointments may lead to resignation and aimless drifting— a case of "I don't know where I've been or where I'm going."

The school can aid young people in their search for direction by placing greater emphasis on the study of values. There are, of course, many sources to which the individual may turn for guidance in setting up goals and making choices. The special province of the school is the cultivation of democratic values basic to our way of life. Understanding of these values goes beyond the simplistic notion that democracy is freedom and rights to an awareness of a constellation of values which cluster around three major foci: respect for the individual, concern for the general welfare, and faith in rational decision-making processes. By tracing the notable progress that has been made in the realization of these values, democracy is perceived as dynamic and open-ended rather than static and closed, as ideals to be striven for rather than actual accomplishments. Such insight into the nature of democracy and appreciation for past gains hopefully will encourage youth to join forces in the improvement of our democratic way of life.

Each generation must learn how to use democratic values as guides to conduct and thinking. This is especially critical in our time of unprecedented change because social relations have become so complex that in many cases it is extremely difficult to determine the point at which concern for the individual comes into conflict with concern for the common good. When analyzing a particular course of action, therefore, it is necessary to determine its contribution to the self-realization of the individual or group concerned and its consequences for all others affected. Rules, regulations, and laws, studied from this point of view, appear as formally agreed-upon procedures which take into account the best interests of both individual and public rather than as arbitrary and capricious decisions made by those in power. In the treatment of controversial issues, likewise, more is required than a description of the parties concerned and their stated positions. The values involved should be identified and the rationality of the respective positions examined in terms of the evidence and logic on which they are based.

The meaning of democracy can be extended through the study of other forms of social organization. This will help confirm the essential relationship between structure and function in human arrangements and, perhaps more important, show how particular emphases and kinds of implementation are expressions of underlying goals or values. While it is necessary to understand various cultural forms on their own terms, as examples of the different ways people organize themselves for carrying out basic social processes, it is also instructive to note how they account for the values we hold. Units of work on primitive cultures, early civilzations, and modern societies should include, at some point, an analysis of the value placed on the individual, the importance attached to group welfare, and the extent to which shared intelligence is brought into decision-making. This is especially important when studying the so-called competing ideologies, such as socialism and communism, in order that the young may learn how to deal with them on an intellectual level rather than be swayed by blind emotion. Using a democratic yardstick for comparing and contrasting, the learner will not only distill the essence of democracy but, at the same time, become more aware of what is not democratic.

Young people must also be helped to build a maturing system of values in keeping with democratic ideals. In this effort, it is necessary to distinguish the different levels of goals. Personal enhancement, group welfare, and rational living are ultimate goals to which other values bear a supportive or contributory function. Thus, competition and cooperation, materialism and service, work and play, popularity and achievement are not prized solely for themselves, but as possible means for attaining the more encompassing goals of democratic living. It is these intermediate, rather than ultimate, values that are subject to modification with changes in circumstances, time, and place. Each young person, therefore, must study the ramifications of change on a whole network of values as he attempts to create a consistent set of standards to live by.

The decision to provide the young with many experiences for the development of values has certain implications for the curriculum. Regardless of the particular type of curricular design employed, it is necessary to explicate the affective domain of behavior to at least the same degree that is common for cognitive and psychomotor aspects of learning.[3] To begin with, goals must be defined in specific behavioral terms rather than as vague generalities so that they will be useful in giving direction to both instruction and evaluation. Defined for the total span of public education, nursery school through the junior college, such goals will reflect the developmental sequence of valuing, which begins with a mere awareness of a value, grows into a personal preference, and finally is established as a way of life.

Both indirect and direct approaches to instruction are important in the development of the student's values. Conceivably, many objectives might be "caught" as a result of the quality of human relationships fostered by the school or developed as a by-product of teaching aimed primarily at the acquisition of concepts and skills. To help young people examine and develop purposes of their own, however, requires direct instruction utilizing a variety of techniques. Some of these highlight feeling tones and encourage the expression of values as in role-playing; others stress the rational analysis of values as in the study of controversial issues and decision-making.

Because of the nature of its goals and instructional processes, evaluation of the effectiveness of a particular program of experiences for the development of values is exceedingly crucial. One of the most exciting frontiers in education is the search for more sophisticated means of making such appraisals, for, when democratic values are involved, the school cannot take easy refuge in the thought that values are hard to teach and even more difficult to evaluate.

## "How Can I Become Involved?"

The world is becoming more turbulent. Divisions among people are sharper and polarization of extreme positions on critical issues is more common. The increasing use of protest, confrontation, and

3. David R. Krathwohl, Benjamin S. Bloom, and Bertram B. Masia, *Taxonomy of Educational Objectives, Handbook II: Affective Domain* (New York: David McKay Co., 1964).

demands as a means of settling differences is being justified on one hand as a democratic right and, on the other, as the only way left for bringing about true democracy. Although the role of young people in society is highly ambiguous and entrance into adulthood is delayed even more than in the past, a growing number are seeking to satisfy certain needs through social action. In this way the individual can achieve a sense of affiliation or belongingness, for no longer does he stand alone and misunderstood. At the same time, he acquires status as collectively he is transformed into a force to be reckoned with. Such action also affords him an outlet for his idealism and boundless enthusiasm. Hence the clamor for "a piece of the action."

To help the learner in his search for involvement, the school must place greater priority on social interaction experiences. It is essential to provide him with many opportunities for joining others in the pursuit of a variety of goals—educational, recreational, charitable, governing—which are personally meaningful and have broad social ramifications. As the size and composition of groups vary, it will be possible for him to experience many levels of participation typified in classroom, school, interschool, and school-community projects. In the course of developing such activities, he can work with peers, children older and younger than he, the opposite sex, members of various ethnic and racial groups, teachers, and other adults of the community to the end that he feels comfortable with and conducts himself effectively in the multifaceted groups which characterize modern society.

As the student engages in these many forms of social interaction, the part played by goals, roles, and norms in furthering group work should become more apparent. He will see that certain individual goals are best achieved through group membership and that, consequently, the adequacy of group goals depends on the degree to which they reflect those of each person constituting the group. These members, he will find, cannot be classified simply as leaders or followers, for each person can play many different roles depending on the purposes of the group and the talents he can bring to their accomplishment. In order for individuals to work together effectively, furthermore, each must be aware of and act within the range of norms or standards of behavior acceptable to the group.

In addition to person-group interaction, the more complex group-group relationships bear investigation. Every group works in a physical and social setting that is influenced by other groups, and as projects become more ambitious their successful completion usually depends on the coordinated efforts of many groups. Because of a variety of factors, groups often differ greatly in their perceptions of what constitutes desirable ends and the best means of attaining them. Considerable skill is required to identify the exact nature of such variances and to determine commonalities which might serve as beginning points for action. Even more competence is required to propose a compromise representing a midpoint between two widely divergent views, which might be acceptable to both parties.

As a result of his social interaction experiences, the learner may acquire a deep conviction that democracy is dependent on and characterized by carefully built-in provisions for bringing about orderly change. One of these is freedom of communication, which makes it possible for all sides involved in a decision to be heard. Another pertains to organizational forms, as in the selection of representatives and the conduct of elections, which attempt to insure decisions reflecting majority wishes. Third are the safeguards for those holding a minority opinion to continue in their cause provided that they do not resort to lawlessness, violence, or the overthrow of government.

To develop the kinds of social interaction skills indicated above, the school must find ways of extending the learner's involvement in his education. He should have opportunities to participate broadly, in accordance with his level of maturity, in planning, carrying out, and evaluating learning experiences. The cocurricular program, traditionally an area of considerable freedom for students, offers many such possibilities. It may be that the quality of such social interaction experiences can be heightened for children and youth by deemphasizing certain elements as winning or putting on a show for public consumption. Also, new groups can be formed or new projects initiated which make it possible for young people to engage constructively in social action that is significant to them and to the broader community.

A more crucial area for learner involvement is the curriculum for, presumably, this is the heart of the educational enterprise. All curricula have points where the learner can be involved in decision-making. Although the typical disciplines-oriented curriculum is tightly structured regarding *what* to teach, there is room for teacher-learner planning with respect to some of the details as to *how* this might be done. Many more opportunities for involvement are present in both society-oriented and individual-oriented curricula for they depend on the learner's participation in arriving at decisions about what to learn, how to go about learning it, and the extent to which learning actually took place.

One overriding condition, if interaction experiences are to be extended in both the curricular and cocurricular fields, is that the school be organized and function as a democratic institution. Every learner should have opportunities to directly engage in or have his views represented at all levels of deliberation—classroom, student-faculty council, school-community coordinating council, and the board of education or school trustees.

## Summary

Growing up is more complicated in times of rapid social change. As our culture becomes more impersonal, complex, confused, and turbulent, the young find it increasingly difficult to gain autonomy and self-respect, develop a sense of reality, build a system of goals or values, and satisfy their desire for affiliation and involvement. These needs are so basic and the threat to them so great that youth are rebelling on a scale of intensity never before seen.

While the school cannot solve all these problems, it can give higher priority to the kinds of content, values, and skills which enable young people to cope more effectively with this changing world. One crucial area is the study of self through which the learner acquires self-knowledge, a positive self-concept, constructive ways of changing the self, and a wholesome approach to human sexuality. Another important consideration is the relevance of learning experiences as perceived by the learner—those which deal with his concerns, bear some relationship to life outside the school, emphasize change, and concentrate on the key ideas and methods of the disciplines. The study of values is a third imperative if the younger generation is to grow in understanding and commitment to democracy, use democratic values as criteria for action and appraisal of social organizations, and build a consistent value system. Young people, fourthly, require many meaningful types of social interaction experiences in order to develop effective techniques for managing goals, roles, and norms in both intergroup and intragroup participation and for facilitating orderly change through democratic processes.

These priorities can be accommodated to some degree in any type of program. In the various forms of disciplines-oriented curricula, which predominate in this country, some of the suggested learning experiences can be incorporated into existing courses and, where this appears impractical, new offerings can be devised. In addition, more ways can be explored for individualizing goals, instruction, and evaluation as well as involving the learner in decisions affecting the curriculum, cocurricular programs, and school living in general. There are limits to what can be done in a disciplines-oriented curriculum, however, because of its preplanned, highly structured nature. For greater flexibility and, hence, greater possibilities for meeting the needs of young people as they arise, a different type of curricular design would be required. Two alternatives presently available are a society-oriented approach, which is based on the learner's problems, and an individual-oriented approach, which centers on his interests and needs.

Paying attention to the emerging needs of the young is not soft, sentimental, or sloppy education. Democracy gives first consideration to the individual, and it is during the early years that the groundwork for self-realization is laid. The questions of youth, moreover, are not inconsequential or antithetical to democratic ideals but do, in fact, reflect their essence. Democracy depends on people who sense "who they are" and, thus, can relate sensitively to others. Democracy depends on people who perceive "what this world is really like" and face it realistically instead of trying to escape. Democracy depends on people who determine "what they should do" on the basis of a consistent framework of democratic values rather than by following the crowd or listening to the loudest voice of the moment. Democracy depends on people who "take effective social action" for the accomplishment of group goals instead of depending on edict or resorting to violence. In a very real sense, therefore, the survival of our democratic way of life depends on the priority that the school gives to the emerging needs of children and youth.

# CHAPTER XI

# Emerging Priorities for Continuing Education

CHARLES E. BROWN

There are a number of points of view from which one can look at the matter of continuing education and the question of the priorities we should set for it. Indeed, the needs for education are so numerous and various in today's world that it is difficult to know where to begin in either listing them or attaching priorities to them.

Many obvious problems come to mind, most of which have been analyzed and discussed by others in publications too numerous to mention. There is the matter of a rapidly changing world of work and the related need for a highly developed system of training and retraining for men and women whose jobs will change periodically during their working life. What is particularly needed, it seems, is a pattern of education that will give the worker a kind of technological knowledge base from which a variety of particular skills can be developed as the demand arises. There is the matter of women in our society and the multitude of educational opportunities that should be made available to them if they are to achieve the occupational goals toward which many of them are striving. There is the matter of shorter work hours for many and the resultant increase in the need to fill leisure hours in some useful way. Surely we can do better than we seem to be doing in filling this void: the seemingly endless increase in televised football games and the invention of the skimobile are hardly adequate responses, and a whole host of possibilities remain to be explored. Chief among these in my judgment is the development of a higher capacity to enjoy and create beauty. I really do not know how important it is that we know something of beauty, or that we are something more than passive observers of someone else's sense of what is aesthetically appealing, or that we be discriminating, not only in our intellectual tastes but in our artistic and cultural tastes as well. What I do know is that while the degree to which we can meet these challenges in our society may not determine our survival as a civilization, it will certainly do much to determine the quality of our civilization. There is the related issue of prolonged lives for many, coupled with a tendency toward earlier retirement. Again, relatively sterile retirement villages in Florida and "golden age" clubs can go only so far in meeting the needs of this group, and the development of what could be a whole new system of education for the elderly to enable them to either work at a new job or to find personal fulfillment in some other way is a matter of high priority for the future. In a similar vein, we will have to make it possible for middle-aged people to change careers more often than is now the case, and this will require a wide variety of educational opportunities that do not now exist. On a totally different plane, there is the urgent need to develop the means of providing initial and continuing education for those millions of men and women in our society who have been bypassed by our entire present system: migrant workers, Appalachian families, urban poor, and others. While the conditions under which these people are forced to live and work are influenced in a significant way by social, political, and economic issues which need also to be addressed, there can be no denying the need for vastly improved educational opportunities for them if they are to be afforded the chance to share in some of the things that the rest of us take for granted.

All of the issues identified above, plus others that could easily be brought to mind, are relatively discrete and subject to some sort of institutionalized response. Indeed, in a number of instances, they are being faced already, although in all cases much more needs to be done, and in some, such as the education of migrant workers, we really have not done very much at all. But a fair amount of organized continuing education already is taking place in our country, ranging from extensive training programs run by industrial concerns to manpower development programs to a growing number of adult education courses offered by the fastest growing segment of our educational system, the community college. In addition, people are learning about computers in newly developed computer institutes, about cooking from Julia Child on television, about new careers from some correspondence school, about the rudiments of space travel from the extensive coverage on television of the Apollo moon landings, and about a whole new musical culture from their children and their ever present transistor radios.

Beyond these more or less organized efforts, however, lies what in my judgment is a much more important system of continuing education. I have reference to our vast system of communications, particularly television. Every day of our lives most of us are influenced in one way or another by this system, whether it is in regard to the brand of toothpaste we choose, how we react to the vice president's latest speech, how we vote in a particular election, how we feel about college students, or whether we decide it is time to buy a new car. Writing in a recent issue of *Saturday Review,* Federal Communications Commissioner Nicholas Johnson said: "Television is more than just another great public resource—like air and water—ruined by private greed and public inattention. It is the greatest communications mechanism ever designed and operated by man. It pumps into the human brain an unending stream of information, opinion, moral values, and esthetic taste. It cannot be a neutral influence. Every minute of television programming—commercials, entertainment, news—teaches us something." And it is a powerful teacher—which is precisely the point. Man has always tried to communicate with other men, but never before have we had the means to do it in such a pervasive and intensive way. And what are the consequences? Let me list just a few that come to mind. Largely as a result of our systems of communication we have developed production and consumption patterns that threaten both our economy and our environment. What we think about government and politics in general as well as of particular political candidates is almost exclusively influenced by television. As has been pointed out by many others, the candidates believe this: witness the $58 million spent on political advertising during the elections in 1968. We are currently a nation divided along many lines, and again this is due in no small part to the vivid images on television of campus radicals, political rhetoricians, and urban riots. And finally, foreign policy decisions are made or at least influenced in our day by the public reaction to personal appeal over television by the administration or its "loyal opposition."

So, as the saying goes, it's a whole new ball game, and thus it seems to me that the first priority for our continuing education must be to increase our ability to use these tremendous resources we have developed to better the human condition rather than to make it worse. And it may get worse before it gets better, in view of the emerging possibilities of cable television. If we have been influenced by the existing commercial and educational stations, imagine the possibilities inherent in a system that can in the very near future provide an additional twenty to forty channels in a particular metropolitan area and with the development of laser technology within perhaps ten years will be capable of modulating a thousand channels. One has to wonder what kind of monstrous Frankenstein we are building—it all rather boggles the mind.

On the other hand, it may be that some of the problems we face as a human group are such that they can be dealt with only if we can learn to communicate with and thus educate vast numbers of people to begin to think about themselves and their world in a totally different way. To put it another way, if our communications network has created problems for us—and I am convinced it has—then it might also be used to help us solve them as well. And that there are major problems that need to be solved cannot be denied—no one should need to be reminded of the various crises we face, seemingly at every turn. To quote Peter Drucker from *The Age of Discontinuity*, "No one needs to be told that our age is an age of infinite peril. No one needs to be told that the central question we face with respect to man's future is not what it shall be, but whether it shall be."

Given this point of view, which I share, what we need to do is to use our vast resources to identify those crises that threaten man's future, and to begin the difficult task of educating and reeducating ourselves about the changes we have to make in our attitudes, values, and life-styles if we are to survive. This task, as difficult as it is for us to face, must be the matter of highest priority in any system of continuing education we contemplate for the future. H. G. Wells's words of fifty years ago ring more clearly true every day: "Human history becomes more and more a race between education and catastrophe," and much evidence can be garnered to indicate that as we enter the last thirty years of this decade we are losing this race.

And that our survival is a matter of education must be made clear. To be sure, many other forces will be operating on us in one way or another, including the matter of sheer luck, but in the final analysis, we will be saved only if we can learn to look at things in a rather totally new way. Let me give some examples.

The first is in relation to our environmental crisis and, because he says it so well, I should like to draw heavily on an article by Scott Paradise entitled "The Vandal Ideology," which appeared in the December 29, 1969 issue of *The Nation*. Paradise begins his article with these words:

Some call it an ecological crisis; others admit only to a variety of serious environmental problems ranging from pollution to ugliness. In any case, the bombardment of articles, books and television programs in the past few years have made us aware that something is wrong. Exploding populations, advancing technology and economic development have joined to face us with a triple threat. *But except for a few voices, the depth of the difficulty eludes expression* [emphasis mine]. We assume, rightly, that more science and technology, better planning, or more adequate political arrangements are needed; but we assume, wrongly, that a combination of these will save us. The argument runs, if we lack as yet the political will to solve the problems, a few local catastrophes will surely bring us to our senses and force us in due course to achieve general solutions. While admitting that stricter regulation of polluters and developers will be necessary, we talk as though the American industrial system could survive without really radical modification. The contrary is true. Not only must our industrial system be changed; *the system of beliefs about man's relationship with the natural world which underlies it must be corrected if we are to escape the jaws of the coming crisis* [emphasis added].

The truth of Paradise's statement must be apparent to any thoughtful man, and it must be equally apparent that what he is talking about is a problem of continuing education. In his article, he illustrates this point by setting forth seven propositions that describe the current American ideology of man and nature and contrasts these with seven others that must hold true if we are to live with our environment. The seven current propositions are as follows:

1. Man is the source of all value.
2. The universe exists only for man's use.

3. Man's primary purpose is to produce and consume.
4. Production and consumption must increase endlessly.
5. Material resources are unlimited.
6. Man need not adapt himself to the natural environment since he can remake it to suit his own needs.
7. A major function of the state is to make it easy for individuals and corporations to exploit the environment to increase wealth and power.

Paradise recognizes that most Americans would not subscribe to these propositions when stated this boldly, but then goes on to observe—rightly, I believe—that our policies, both public and private, operate as if these were indeed not only our beliefs but, increasingly, beliefs held by other societies all over the world.

Contrast these, then, with the points of view that he feels we must come to hold in the future:

1. Man is to be valued more highly than other creatures.
2. Man has become the guardian of the earth.
3. Man is far more than a producer and a consumer.
4. Improvement in the quality of life takes precedence over increasing the quantity of material production.
5. Material resources are to be used carefully and cherished.
6. Man is to relate himself to the natural environment, remaking it according to its nature as well as for the sake of his short-term economic advantage.
7. A major function of the state is to supervise a planning process that will prevent the impairment of the quality of the environment.

Obviously, more needs to be said about both sets of propositions (Paradise does this in his article), and there are some who might disagree with certain of them, or indeed, all of them. But for me the whole thrust of Paradise's argument is upon the educational aspects of the entire environmental issue, and it gives us some indication of the scope of the task ahead of us. Take any one of his propositions—the one regarding production and consumption, for instance. I am neither an economist nor an ecologist, but it seems obvious to me that we must make radical changes in both our production of goods and our consumer habits. As Wayne Davis of the University of Kentucky has said: "Neither the numbers of cars, the economy, nor anything else can expand indefinitely at an exponential rate in a finite world. We must face this fact *now.*" But are we ready to face it? I don't know. The thought of Americans being willing to forego that new car every three years (or to have no car at all) or being cheered by a *reduction* in our gross national product is difficult for me to consider realistic, but if men such as Professor Davis, Barry Commoner, and Paul Erlich are right, this is what we must learn to do, and learning to make these adjustments must be regarded as a matter of highest priority for the continuing education of all peoples. All of the above is not meant to suggest that we can turn our backs on our technological, industrialized culture, for if we did, surely a large proportion of the world's population would starve. Rather, what we must do is learn how to live with it in a fashion that does not sacrifice human sympathy and compassion.

A second matter of urgent priority is to develop in our people a habit of mind that enables us to look at things in a way that goes beyond nationalistic concerns. Norman Cousins, in a recent editorial in *Saturday Review,* put it this way: "There is a need today . . . for the unifying and universalizing ideas. It is the world, and not just a nation, that is now the arena which needs to be shaped and protected." And some years ago, in his book *Old Myths and New Realities,* William Fulbright stated:

Of all the myths that have troubled the lives of modern nations, the most pervading have been those associated with the nation itself. Nationalism, which is preeminently a state of mind rather than a state of nature, has become a universal force at precisely the time in history when technology has made the world a single unit in a physical sense— interdependent for economic, political and cultural purposes and profoundly interdependent for survival in a nuclear age.

He went on to state:

The nation has now become a barrier to the historical process by which men have associated themselves in ever larger political and economic communities. In the face of compelling need for broader associations, nationalism sets both great and small nations against one another, to their vast peril and at an enormous price in the welfare and happiness of their people.

It is in this context that nationalism must be placed, for as Fulbright suggests it is only after we have removed the constraints of our traditional nationalistic ideology that we can expect to live as a community of nations, free to develop fully the freedom and dignity of the individual in a civilized society. And as we broaden the frontiers of human loyalty we do not lessen our love for or pride in our own nation, but rather we widen the focus for this loyalty and recognize that it is the human individual, more than the state or any other community, in whom ultimate sovereignty is invested. As Cousins says: "Patriotism, to be truly American, begins with the human allegiance."

No one needs to remind me that this will not be an easy task. Americans are a particularly patriotic and nationalistically inclined people, and it seems to me that we have often been arrogantly and narrow-mindedly so. At least I was taught as a youngster, either directly or indirectly, that we could do no wrong in our foreign policies, that we were always on the side of right, reason, and democracy, and that our primary interest in all foreign conflicts was to protect the rights of men who wanted to be free. As I have grown older, and observed and thought about our ventures in various parts of Latin America and in Southeast Asia, and as I have come to see more clearly the dominant role that American business interests play in our foreign policy decisions, I have become much more cynical. Perhaps others have, too, but, judging from the words and actions of much of what we have come to call "Middle America" these days, there is still a great deal of blind patriotism abroad in our land, and any efforts to broaden our perspectives about our place as a nation in the lives of other nations and other peoples are surely going to be resisted in many quarters. Nonetheless, the time has come, it seems to me, to ask what it is that we stand for as a nation. Is the American dream "for real," or is it some hazy mixture of the Fourth of July, apple pie, and the good life as extolled by our friends on Madison Avenue? How wide are the differences between what we say we are and what we really are, and who is willing to examine these differences? How realistic is our apparent assumption that the American brand of democracy can be exported just as we export an American car? I cannot presume to answer these questions, but I can say that it is imperative that they be examined. One is reminded of Thomas Huxley's words of a century ago: "I cannot say that I am impressed by your bigness, or your material resources, as such. Size is not grandeur and territory does not make a nation. The great issue, about which hangs the terror of overhanging fate, is what are you going to do with all these things?" What, indeed? We have it within our power either to be a leading influence in making the world a place of peace and dignity for all men, or to destroy it, and I am not yet sure that we know in which direction we intend to move. Clearly, however, education will play a decisive role in determining our direction.

Some might say that our role in international circles will be determined in large measure by our ability to survive the conflict and turmoil that we are facing within our own country, and this is a possibility to consider. Thus I would list this problem of human understanding and compassion among Americans as my third and final matter of priority for our continuing education. Again, no one needs to be told that the problem exists. Increasingly we are becoming a nation divided: white against black, poor against rich, young against old, hawk against dove, conservative against liberal, Right against Left, minority against majority, establishment against radical, even woman against man. Everyone, it seems, must be typed or "labeled"—by style of dress, political persuasion, color, or sex—and we too often find it difficult to look at each other in basic human terms. And, of course, we must. Ronald Laing, in his book *The Politics of Experience* makes this observation:

> We cannot be deceived. Men can and do destroy the humanity of other men, and the condition of this possibility is that we are interdependent. We are not self-contained nomads producing no effects on each other except our reflections. We are both acted upon, changed for good or ill, by other men; and we are agents who act upon others to affect them in different ways. Each of us is the other to the others. . . . It is quite clear that unless we can regulate our behavior much more satisfactorily than at present, then we are going to exterminate ourselves.

A sobering thought, and given the centrifugal-like forces operating in our society, one wonders where we can begin to move in the direction Laing suggests as necessary to our survival.

Perhaps one place for Americans to begin is to reexamine the collective American conscience in respect to our record as a nation committed to the integrity and dignity of other men, "regardless of race, creed or color." While such an examination would undoubtedly uncover some things in our past of which we can be proud, an honest appraisal of our history would, at the same time, show much of what one writer has called "the dark side of the

American conscience." After all, it was we who virtually destroyed an entire American Indian civilization. It was we who created the social, economic, and moral framework that kept the black man "in his place" for three hundred years. It was we who said to the rest of the world "give me your tired and your poor" and yet forced those who came, through various social and economic constraints, to live in ghettos of one kind or another in our major cities. It is we, even now, who refuse to lift racial barriers for the black or Puerto Rican or Mexican-American; it is we who allow hundreds of thousands of American migrant workers to go hungry and sick and ignored and spurned, it is we who can lead a sensitive man such as Robert Coles to say, "God save them, these children; and for allowing such a state of affairs to continue, God save us, too."

It will not be easy for a proud nation to take such a painful look at itself, but I see no other way to move us as a people to the point where we can really begin to care for each other. And what matters today is that we care—man's inhumanity to man is real, and we must develop the sense of humility that enables us to deal with each other with a feeling of brotherhood, respect, understanding, and love. Robert Oppenheimer once spoke to this point with these words:

We have, I think, in dealing with this world, a double duty; a duty on the one hand to be constant and firm and faithful to what we really know, to what is close to us, to our art, our knowledge, our own community, our tradition, in the sense in which tradition has been the story of man's glory, where we live fully as men. To all the other traditions, to all the rest of the world with its wonders that we do not know very well, we need a sense of hospitality and openness, a willingness to make room for the strange, for the thing that does not fit. This is a hard double duty.

He goes on to say that if it is at all possible to meet this obligation, it will be because of the moderation of those things which are not purely intellectual—"by the friendship and the regard and love we bear one another."

And we have so much to learn in this regard—as Ronald Laing says, "what we love is so much less than what there is." One of our troubles is that we are so self-conscious about this matter of love— we tend to deal with it in a very superficial way, and we are wary of those who dare to speak of the need for it. And yet it is so absolutely fundamental to any life worth living, and deal with it in something more than superficial terms we must. It will not be easy, I know, but nonetheless I offer this concern for our ability to live with each other in empathy, compassion, and love as my final and most important priority for our continued education as a civilization worthy of being called human.

In closing, I should say that I recognize the fact that some who read this will be frustrated by my failure to deal with the things that one normally thinks about in relation to continuing education: dropouts, institutional forms, traditional patterns of adult education, and the like. To these people, I would simply say that I recognize that these are matters to be concerned about, but given the human condition as I see it, the usual analysis of the needs for continuing education somehow pales in significance in the face of the concerns I have tried to discuss, albeit briefly. I fully believe that unless we can come to grips in intelligent, educative ways with such problems as our system of communications, our relationship to our environment, our sense of allegiance to human beings everywhere, and our capacity to love, then we either have no future or have none worth thinking about. Any civilization that has developed the capacity to destroy itself—and we have—might do just that. My hope is that the choice between destruction and liberation is still ours to make, and my conviction is that education will play an important part in determining what that choice will be.

CHAPTER XII

# The School as an Organic Teaching Aid

ROBERT H. ANDERSON

## The Settings for Learning

Although other factors undoubtedly play more important roles than does the school's physical environment in the amount and quality of a child's school learning, no discussion of curriculum would be complete without reference to the school plant and its furnishings. Man is a multisensory animal, and as a student his daily experience both within and outside the school is significantly influenced by the space within which it occurs. Many curriculum objectives are difficult and perhaps even impossible to attain unless the physical setting enables certain things to happen. On the other hand, the environment can cause or facilitate certain learnings that may not have been intended. Sensitivity to the ways that environment can influence human behavior is therefore a part of the equipment that curriculum planners should bring to their work.

Another reason for examining the physical setting in a curriculum volume is that there is currently an unusual amount of interest in school plant planning and renovation and in alternative ways of furnishing and equipping schools. Rapid population growth, shifts of population, deterioration of existing facilities, and new demands posed by educational innovation and reform have confronted educators and taxpayers almost everywhere with the problem of expanding and renovating the school plant. Furthermore, expenditures for instructional materials and equipment have recently been estimated at $2.5 billion per annum in the United States. It is extremely important, therefore, that architectural and administrative planning for American schools should be geared as closely as possible to curriculum considerations.

For at least fifteen years, education in the United States and most other countries has been developing and testing new approaches to the individualization of instruction, to the grouping and classification of pupils, to the training and utilization of staff, to the reorganization and redefinition of school units (elementary, middle school, and secondary), to the use of instructional resources of many types, to the involvement of more persons and groups in school-based programs, and to the provision of appropriate settings for learning. The literature has abounded in criticisms of the predominant patterns of schooling, much of the criticism being focused on the irrelevance and unsuitability of the typical curriculum and the modes of instruction that prevail. Prompted to a great extent by the emergence of cooperative teaching and differentiated staffing patterns, and stimulated by ascendant interest in media-centered instruction, new approaches to the layout and design of schools have become an integral and important aspect of the educational reform movement. Unfortunately, progress on this front has been distressingly slow, the conventional school building with its box-like classrooms being so firmly entrenched in custom and in political-administrative procedures that changes have been difficult to achieve. Many corners have been turned, however, and there is now a great deal of momentum established. Perhaps this yearbook will prove to be another of the forces for change that are now in motion.

The physical environment of the school, including materials and equipment, has been a topic of much interest to scholars and practicing schoolmen over the years. The National Society for the Study of Education has reflected this interest in its yearbooks, which, in addition to frequent references to building and instructional resources and spaces, has included a yearbook (Thirty-third, Part I, 1934) on the planning and construction of school buildings, several yearbooks (Nineteenth, Part I, 1920; Twentieth, Part I, 1921; Forty-eighth, Part I, 1949) on materials, and a more recent yearbook (Sixty-fifth, Part II, 1966) entitled *The Changing American School,* within which Harold B. Gores in a most useful chapter discusses the "schoolhouse in transition." The *Review of Educational Research,* similarly, has frequently focused on either facility planning (e.g., chapter vi in volume 34, October 1964) or instructional materials (e.g., volume 38, April 1968). In a more recent *Review* report summarizing research and experience, Nystrand and Berto-laet[1] acknowledged a trend toward recognizing the interrelationship of pupil needs, staffing patterns, and housing arrangements and expressed the hope that the many ambiguities in our present under-standing of these relationships can soon be clarified. In a sense the present chapter represents an effort in that direction.

Although much progress has been made in recent years with respect to understanding of the school and its equipment as organic teaching aids, and despite the developments reported in this chapter and elsewhere in a growing literature, it is regrettably true that most school environments reflect little awareness about human space requirements. Sommer, in a valuable commentary,[2] criticizes planners and others for wasting money on unsuitable buildings and equipment. He and others emphasize that proper use of both existing buildings and of newer facilities depends ultimately upon improved teacher education and in-service training.

Usually, discussions of school planning have focused on technical and procedural matters, and even the so-called educational speci-fications transmitted by school officials to architects have generally said little or nothing about educational values and aspirations, or about the ways in which the physical environment is expected to contribute to certain instructional outcomes. As a result, familiar and conventional designs have, at least until very recently, tended to predominate. Even "innovative" schools tend to be copied and the number of educationally imaginative school buildings in this country is still a very small percentage of those that have been built since World War II.

The quality of school planning is, nevertheless, on the rise and this is due in no small measure to the contributions of Educational Facilities Laboratories, Inc., a nonprofit corporation established in the late 1950s by the Ford Foundation. Its publications (e.g., *Edu-cational Change and Architectural Consequences; The Schoolhouse in the City; Schools Without Walls; Acoustical Environment of School Buildings*) have had an enormous impact and its grant

1. Raphael O. Nystrand and Frederick Bertolaet, "Housing Educational Pro-grams," *Review of Educational Research* 37 (1967): 457-63.

2. Robert Sommer, *Personal Space: The Behavioral Basis of Design* (Engle-wood Cliffs, N.J.: Prentice-Hall, 1969).

program has made possible a great deal of research and experimentation with respect to planning, the design and construction of school elements, and the tools of education. Though its contribution to program has been largely indirect, EFL has had through its work a profound influence upon the developing curriculum in America.

Another influential group is the Council of Educational Facility Planners, formerly the National Council on Schoolhouse Construction, whose *Guide for Planning Educational Facilities* is probably the most widely consulted sourcebook on the topic.

The reciprocal implications of educational and architectural concerns are only occasionally discussed directly in the literature, and then mostly with respect only to specific dimensions. Usually the focus is a specific question such as, "How can school space be made more comfortable?" or, "What facilities are needed for team teaching?" or, "In what ways does the physical environment inform and shape and liberate the human spirit?" The latter relatively ambitious question was explored with moderate success in one collection of essays,[3] but remains as a challenge to future commentators.

It is easier to argue that the physical environment represented in the great majority of schools is capable of major improvement. For one thing, the environment has the wrong functional priorities. For example, concepts of fully individualized instruction, such as those expressly associated with nongraded schools, are very difficult to implement within the limited physical environment of many conventional schools. In the Melbourne High School in Florida, for instance, B. Frank Brown and his colleagues pioneering in the development of nongraded secondary education found it necessary to have a greater variety of more accessible spaces (e.g., science laboratory areas) and especially an expanded library. "The conventional library was no longer appropriate. It became necessary for us to construct a new library which . . . had to be 'as large as the gymnasium'."[4] The difficulties of implementing team-teaching plans

3. "Architecture and Education," *Harvard Educational Review* 39 (1969): 1-147.

4. B. Frank Brown, "An Answer to Dropouts: The Nongraded High School," *Atlantic* 214 (November 1964): 86-90.

in conventional schools provide another example of conflict in functional priorities.

Perhaps more fundamental are objections to the psychological impact of the typical school environment. Many would probably agree with the statement of architectural designer W. E. Schroeder, Jr.:

> Lecture rooms, classrooms, seminar rooms have little in common with the spaces we inhabit of our own free will. If we unlock our senses for a moment in these rooms, we encounter a thousand objectionable, irritating sensations. Each of us should consider whether these sensations are shut off with little sacrifice, or whether, in shutting down part of our mental processes, we cripple the remainder.[5]

That many young people, in fact, have been offended or at least depressed by the atmosphere of schools seems a reasonable though discouraging observation and serves to inspire the active search for better and more educationally supportive environments.

## Historical Perspective

Castaldi[6] traced the development of architecture in relation to school buildings in the Hellenistic era (500 B.C.–200 B.C.), in early American history, and in twentieth-century America. In ancient times, schooling was almost totally focused on the teacher himself, who worked with very little equipment and often taught in the open air or under shelter of a public building or a shed. In seventeenth-century America, schoolhouses were very primitive one-room structures with such cheerless and uncomfortable features as rude benches and long tables, a whipping post, an unattractive site, and very poor lighting and ventilation. A raised podium for the teacher symbolized his relationship to the pupils.

In early American architecture, there were virtually no examples of schools distinctively designed for educational purposes. Almost never was a trained architect employed, since only a simple structure of wood and/or brick was considered necessary. As cities grew and larger numbers of pupils were enrolled, the basic theme of the one-teacher classroom was repeated in larger buildings which still

5. W. E. Schroeder, Jr., "Environments for Learning," *Harvard Graduate School of Education Bulletin 13* (Summer 1969): 1.

6. Basil Castaldi, *Creative Planning of Educational Facilities* (Chicago: Rand McNally & Co., 1969).

lacked educationally distinctive features (except perhaps an assembly hall) and perpetuated the tradition of cheerless simplicity. Not until the end of the nineteenth century, when laymen were no longer able to plan the more complex buildings needed in large cities, did architects finally become involved in school planning.

In the absence of more sophisticated pedagogical advice, which did not begin to influence school planning until the mid-twentieth century, the new breed of school architects continued to specify standard cubicle classrooms and little else. Furthermore, they created what in their time seemed like works of art (in Gothic, Renaissance, Baroque, or a combination of styles) with massive entrances and corridors, and ornate decorations, most of which had little if any educational usefulness even if one grants their aesthetic impact. One is tempted to wonder what might have been the effect if all the public funds spent on cupolas and entrance archways had been spent instead on expanded school libraries, arts-and-crafts rooms for activity-oriented instruction, or even on more adequate toilet arrangements in these garish buildings.

One positive aspect of classical school design, however, was that for the first time Americans saw fit to glorify the concept of public education by proud display. In many a community, citizens took pride in the elegant appearance and design of their public school in much the same way that individual families took pride in ostentatious homes. As times and tastes changed, and particularly as higher values were placed on scientific management and cost-efficiency, buildings became more austere and more attention was paid to simplifying the custodian's tasks of cleaning and maintenance than to the emotional and instructional needs of children. The cold, hard floors and walls in these antiseptic schools were scarcely conducive to comfort or learning, and probably caused teachers to be more strict about noise (which reverberated harshly) than they might otherwise have been.

With the upswing of interest in individual differences and in keeping with growing demands for flexibility, schools in the mid-1950s and early 1960s became increasingly open. By the 1970s, at least on the growing edge of education, open-plan schools (schools without walls) had become almost standard and there was a concomitant trend toward the provision of amenities (such as carpeting, airconditioning, comfortable and multifunctional furnishings, and appealing decorations) consistent with the philosophy that school should be pleasant, "warm," and homelike.

Another related trend is the linkage of educational programs to the greater community. Field trips and excursions, outdoor education and school camping, extensive use of specialized resources such as public libraries and museums, and the exposure of pupils to training and other experiences in commercial and industrial settings exemplify the use of the community as an educational environment. In a sense, this trend marks a deliberate return to earlier history when schools provided a far smaller fraction of the total "education" received by the young.

Historically, the school building has influenced not only what might be learned but also what might not be learned. The primitive resources and limited size of schoolhouses placed definite restrictions on other than sedentary activities, and hampered the development of curriculum offerings in the creative and expressive arts, in physical education, in vocational education, and in other areas having specialized space needs. In recent times, despite a growing clamor for kindergarten and other preprimary services, many states have moved slowly in providing such services because of the high cost of providing the space such programs require. Thus both quantitatively and qualitatively the physical environment has over time exercised a peculiar power, often repressive, in the educator's world.

## The Environment and the Curriculum: Theoretical Commentary

Educators behave in accordance with various theories and suppositions, whether held consciously or otherwise, about the nature of human growth and learning and about the role that schooling should play in a given society. Probably most of the things that educators believe and do have little if any relationship to the physical environment per se, but many connections do in fact exist. A belief that physical activity stimulates learning, for example, leads to one kind of decision about space and equipment (and also inspires different policies with reference to freedom, noise, use and expenditure of materials, and the like). A belief in orderliness and in a child's need to have control over experiences (as in the Montessori approach) leads to other decisions about space, equipment, and policy. Placing a high value on a particular form of submissive discipline leads to screwed-down furniture, row-style study halls, and certain arrangements of toilet and corridor facilities. And so on: examples of the relationship between educational values and the physical setting are legion.

It is almost axiomatic that the physical environment of a school is important as a factor in each child's learning; but solid proof or support of the proposition, especially in terms of assessing the amount of difference the environment makes, is almost nonexistent. The literature of sociology is mottled with references to the importance of the physical environment in human development and behavior, and psychologists and educators commonly assert that there are subtle and profound relations between children and the "things" (including buildings) they encounter in daily living. Harold Gores, who more than any other American educator has studied these "things" as educational components, estimates that the quality of environment makes about a 15 percent difference in what the child learns. Comments on the specific educational influence of buildings and materials are often included in publications of various child-focused organizations such as the Association for Childhood Education International and the Association for Supervision and Curriculum Development. In the ASCD 1970 yearbook, for example, William C. Miller[7] discusses the role played by equipment, materials, and facilities in the development of humane capabilities in children, indicating that these can either inhibit such development through excessive mechanization or inflexibility or facilitate it by insuring variety and abundance of appropriate resources.

The contributions that environment makes to the personal and social, as well as educational, development of individuals and groups are also acknowledged by most scholars to be of some significance. Certainly it is intended that certain contributions should be made, for example, in promoting social interaction (in student lounges, in lobbies and entrances, and in lunchrooms or similar spaces) and in nourishing a sense of group identity. The need that youngsters

7. William C. Miller, "Using Equipment, Materials, and Facilities to Develop Humane Capabilities," in *To Nurture Humaneness*, pp. 154-72 (prepared by the ASCD 1970 Yearbook Committee [Washington: Association for Supervision and Curriculum Development, NEA, 1970]).

have for "belonging" has its physical dimension as well as a psychological one, and often the architect's decisions regarding space relationships, walls or barriers, and even landscaping, are related to the meeting of these needs.

Sometimes the objective is to separate a group of children, e.g., the kindergarten class, from a broader range of age groups, or a handicapped group from an entire class or school population. Increasingly, the educator now seeks also to *prevent* the isolation of groups from others. In view of the trend toward multiage grouping and instruction, the physical environment is supposed to *facilitate* interaction between pupils of different ages and minimize the artificial barriers that were once deliberately created between first grade and second grade, between primary and intermediate, between the gifted learners and typical learners, and so on. At the staff level it should enable teachers and other adults to interact across roles and interests as well.

The building, at least, can also contribute to the effectiveness and even the integrity of the educational program through providing the settings that are needed for many types of learning. At best, it also helps the total program to fit together in some sensible way. It should, for example, facilitate the potential operative interrelationships of specific school "subjects" or disciplines. Particularly in secondary schools, where departments have often been tightly insulated from each other, there is need for natural linkages to occur and for new groupings of subjects (such as communications; humanities; life skills) to take form. This emphasizes the need for space which can be reshaped or rearranged as new affinities develop and as old habits give way to new requirements.

Certainly the educational program should determine the layout, design, and equipment of a building rather than vice versa. Invariably this principle is expressed in the literature of both architecture and education wherever there is reference to relationships, and yet all too often that principle is violated in actual practice. In various subtle ways, therefore, the building sometimes symbolizes the wrong values (or at least understates the right values!) and there is transmitted to students in tangible form a sense of wrong educational priorities dominating the educational program. On the other hand, properly planned buildings can and do symbolize higher values and transmit a sense of legitimate priorities to those who inhabit them.

The building and its equipment also influence, either by supporting or frustrating, the use and development of various pedagogical approaches. Programs with a very high technological orientation, for example, obviously require much audiovisual equipment and certain acoustical and illumination provisions. Programs based largely on teachers' lectures need podia and audience-seating arrangements; programs such as Individually Prescribed Instruction need extensive storage space and special cabinets or shelves for materials, and so on.

One simple but powerful idea, namely, that the school is not so much a place in which adults teach but rather a place in which children learn, has recently gained in acceptance. In turn, planners have taken a new look at what the building itself should therefore represent. Thus the podium is not only obsolescent but anachronistic, and teacher-centered space has given way to pupil-centered arrangements. Openness, particularly conducive to such arrangements, has become desirable:

> Opening up of the classroom box signifies more than a shift in geometry for it offers the promise of a new era in learning—in a style which acknowledges that the individual child has no peer.[8]

Furthermore, the rapid acceptance by school systems of the open-area school has led to a new awareness of the contribution (positive and negative) that equipment, furnishings, and other ephemeral components of the overall environment can make to individual-oriented instruction. Teachers have discovered, for example, that children can be both comfortable and productive in various postures involving other than standard desks and chairs. Dozens of ways have been found to provide "privacy" for pupils without necessarily enclosing them in a separate room or cubicle. Conversely, dozens of ways of enabling children to work and study together have evolved, some of these made possible by arranging pieces of furniture and/or vertical space separators, and others based on different patterns of instructional management. Though the emerging arrangements are not invariably successful or even tolerable to some

8. EFL, *Transformation of the Schoolhouse,* 1969 Annual Report (New York: Educational Facilities Laboratories), p. 4.

of the people involved, they have stirred great interest in further exploration of alternatives and spurred both curriculum theorists and administrative planners to reconsider some of the inhibitions under which both have operated for the greater part of the twentieth century.

### Educational and Psychological Impact of the Physical Environment

In countless ways the school environment provides experiences which inform and influence the child. Objects in that environment have color, dimension, texture, and function. They are seen, heard, touched, smelled, and manipulated. They are either pleasant or unpleasant, relevant or irrelevant, useful or useless, monotonous or varied, stimulating or unstimulating, ordinary or extraordinary. In sum, at any given moment, they tend to play either a positive or a negative role in the morale and the learning set of individuals who inhabit the environment. Not nearly enough is yet known about such matters, but school planners are increasingly persuaded that favorable environments can be created when certain principles are honored.

Schroeder, for example, defines four desirable characteristics for a classroom environment: (a) the classroom should be nonuniform, eventful, full of contrast and variety; (b) it should be manipulable; (c) it should be engaging; and (d) it should be informative.[9] That some schools fail rather dramatically to satisfy these criteria—and even more obvious criteria relating to physical safety and comfort— is seen by many observers as undermining the educational program and damaging both the minds and spirits of children.

The extent of such damage or, oppositely, the extent of benefit when the environment is excellent is of course difficult to calculate. Furthermore, the school is only one of the environments in which children live. When the school fails to offer relief from other environmental tensions, this fact is deplorable, even dangerous.

Various psychosomatic disorders, such as gastric and duodenal ulcers or ulcerative colitis, are being reported more and more in children in association with the stress resulting from environmental

9. W. E. Schroeder, Jr., "Environment: Classrooms Set Up for Learning/A Better Use of the World Beyond," *Grade Teacher* 87 (January 1970): 109-10.

factors at home and in school. The study of these diseases and their causes is pursued in part through studies of animals. Recently these have included swine, whose anatomy and physiology resemble those of the human being more closely than do those of any other domestic animal. In an unpublished paper by T. Kowalczyk, Professor of Veterinary Science in the University of Wisconsin, it was reported that swine developed gastric ulcers when swine producers changed from open, outdoor raising to more intense, indoor-production practices which confined the animals to a more crowded and less comfortable environment.[10]

Professor R. P. Hanson, also of Wisconsin, notes that humans and animals are both structured with biological rhythms that vary from individual to individual and that can be altered by deprivation and stimulation. He recommends that methods and instruments that have been used on animals and astronauts, such as the sensing and other devices used to record body conditions and functioning (blood pressure, rate of respiration, body temperature, heart rhythms, hormonal levels), could be used to measure a man's (or a child's) responses to varying environmental conditions so that the consequences of those conditions could be better understood.[11] Extending Hanson's idea to the school environment, for example, it would be possible to monitor certain pupils under varying conditions of light, temperature, sound, odor, shape and size of surrounding space, physical presence of others, time of day, and so forth. Especially if such research could also be geared to narrative description of the psychoeducational experiences through which the child is passing at monitored moments (e.g., during a test; during story hour; while making a salt map), it would seem that a great deal could be learned about the actual impact of those experiences and of the environment within which they occur.

Quite a lot is already known about lighting, ventilation, heat control, and acoustics, at least with respect to optima. American children, for example, are said to work best at a temperature of 72° Fahrenheit: When the temperature is higher, the learning rate declines; when it is lower, discomfort interferes with concentration. In conjunction with the temperature, humidity levels between 40

10. Personal communication to the author, October 6, 1969.
11. Personal communication to the author, October 6, 1969.

and 60 percent are considered optimal. The effects of stale, stuffy, or unpleasant air are also known to be deleterious.

Illumination needs and conditions vary with the activity, and this topic is so much discussed in the literature that educators can offer no excuses when lighting conditions are poor or even injurious to the eyes. Quality of light is more important than quantity, and it is important to control glare (e.g., by holding brightness levels in the visual field to approximately thirty-seven-foot lamberts). Brightness contrasts should not exceed a ratio of ten to one, and three to one is preferable. Flat lighting is undesirable; "visual noise" or bright spots should be avoided. Colors, it is known, have various psychological loadings for people, some being much more sensitive to color stimulation than others.

Studies of the effects of noise on pupil performance are at this stage inconclusive, some showing little or no effect and others showing significant decrement in performance under noisy conditions. Factors such as motivation, concentration, nature of the task, and nature of the noise are all involved, and it seems certain that some individuals are much more likely to be disturbed by noise than others. A safe guess is that children can tolerate higher noise levels and more distracting sounds than can teachers, which probably causes teachers to conclude that noise (which to them is bothersome) is in fact disturbing the pupils.

Some researchers are, nonetheless, concerned about the possible damage, in today's world especially, to children's ears and also to their neurological systems, of extremely high levels of sound. Such levels are rare in school buildings, but unacceptable and irritating sounds certainly do exist in many schools. Sometimes this results from very poor acoustical conditions, as in gymnasiums or in some cafeterias; other times it is due to the type of activity being permitted or to excessive excitement that has been created. Teachers sometimes do fail to protect children from such disturbances.

But classrooms and other school spaces need not be absolutely quiet. Background noise, sometimes referred to as "acoustical perfume," may be very beneficial or at least tolerable so long as it does not exceed levels consistent with good speech communication.

Carpeting, which is recommended for a variety of reasons including its acoustical properties, has proved to be a major resource in coping with noise within schools, both elementary and secondary. There is some evidence to suggest that younger children, especially in the primary years, benefit more substantially from carpeting and other acoustical amenities than do older children. Of interest is John Reedy's observation that junior high school pupils, whose physiological and psychological needs are ill-served by the restrictive environment and policies of most junior highs, should have more rather than less noise in their daily school experience. Noting that there are four possible types of noise (purposeful, overt, disruptive noise; inattentive noise; pressure-release noise, or "happiness" noise; and learning noise), Reedy asks educators to appreciate and encourage the controlled, purposeful, happiness noise which reflects an exuberant and creative classroom.[12] Acceptance of learning noise, he claims, will provide a more liberal framework for teaching and also provide the students with an approved way of expending energy.

Whatever the level of sound to be desired, controls of some sort must be built into each school. Where extensive sound control is required, various provisions may be made in combination. Some of these, it may be noted, also render the environment more varied and interesting, thus more provocative of feelings and ideas. Soft and uneven textures in walls and ceilings, vertical surfaces (e.g., on portable tackboards) facing in various directions, baffles, soft furnishing (e.g., upholstered seats) and other absorbents may be used. Of interest is that, since the center of the ceiling is often needed for light reflection and walls are usually used for hangings, it makes sense to use acoustical materials at the top of walls and the edges of the ceilings.

The choice of location, size, shape, height, and total area of windows is one of the most difficult decisions for school architects these days. Windowless spaces, i.e., classrooms or other rooms which do not have windows permitting direct visual contact with the outdoors, have sometimes been specified for schools for a variety of reasons including the avoidance of external distractions. When buildings have air conditioning, it is more efficient to cut down on windows and other openings; and sometimes the shape or location of a building requires the use of inner spaces for which it is im-

12. John Reedy, "Noise is for Learning," *The Clearing House* 43 (1968): 154-57.

possible to provide windows to the outside. Some planners prefer to reduce or eliminate window area in order to avoid glare or light invasion (as in auditoriums), or to provide a greater interior wall surface, or even to reduce the temptations of a visually stimulating outside world.

Whether or not windowless spaces are beneficial or detrimental to the educational well-being and physical-emotional comfort of the occupants is a difficult question to answer, although some evidence[13] is accumulating, and on the whole there is less objection than acceptance. Apparently the absence of windows is of little concern to most children, and adults whose roles require them to remain in one windowless location for long periods of time are less comfortable than those who have occasional opportunity to peer at the outside world. Among some primary teachers there tends to be somewhat less enthusiasm for windowless classrooms because such teachers often make references to changes in weather and to visible manifestations of the seasons as part of the educational program. It is also possible that much more effort should be made to provide for inner-city children some cheerful vistas—for example, windows overlooking a planted inner courtyard.

One of the chief purposes of the school architect is to place the child in a setting which offers a healthy combination of basic security, on the one hand, and productive stimulation on the other. Probably most of the stimulation received at school by children is independent of the physical environment per se, but increasingly it is believed that the two are intertwined.

Psychologist David Krech and others have examined the relation between environmental stimulation in laboratory animals and have reported that rats placed in an "intellectually enriched" environment (freedom to roam around in one large, object-filled space) develop larger and superior brain systems than rats raised in a "deprived" environment (isolated, barren cages). After factoring out the several ingredients of the Berkeley experiments, Krech states that species-specific enrichment experiences (such as the solving of continuous and varied maze problems, which for a rat is of particular survival value) are maximally efficient in developing the brain. For each

13. C. Theodore Larson, *The Effect of Windowless Classrooms on Elementary School Children* (Ann Arbor: University of Michigan, 1965).

species, then, there are environmental enrichments which may be especially valuable, whereas other environmental conditions though perhaps stimulating may not be of special value. Krech then suggests that language, probably "the clearest instance of a pure species-specific behavior" for humans, is a particularly promising area within which to plan enrichments for the human child.[14]

Krech points to biochemical intervention as a probability, although he is conscious of the numerous problems posed as men acquire the capability to alter the intellect. For the moment, it is difficult to assess what effect the educational use of drugs may have upon the planning of physical school environments, although it seems likely that the total sensory environment will have to be more carefully planned.

There is, for example, the possibility that school environments have sometimes provided too much sensory and/or psychological stimulation for at least some of the children who come to school. Often, in fact, children assumed to be "deprived" have been shown to have an abundance of stimuli (though not necessarily of the sort that helps them to cope with conventional schooling) in their home and neighborhood environment. When such children encounter yet another barrage of stimuli, and especially if there is a poor fit between home stimuli and school stimuli, the results can be unsatisfactory or even disastrous. Educators must therefore strive to achieve for each child the right sort of environment, given what is known about his total life experience. Easier said than done!

The situation is complicated by the heterogeneity that characterizes the school population. Cultural backgrounds, ethnic memberships, family idiosyncrasies, physical handicaps—these and other factors cause child A to bring a different set of responses and expectations to the school environment than does child B or child C. Anthropologist Edward T. Hall, for example, discusses the ways that children from different cultures listen, and admonishes teachers to realize that how they listen to children and how they in turn communicate with children can be extremely important.[15] Presumably,

14. David Krech, "Psychoneurobiochemeducation," *Phi Delta Kappan* 50 (1969): 370-75.

15. Edward T. Hall, "Listening Behavior: Some Cultural Differences," *Phi Delta Kappan* 50 (1969): 379-80.

the same phenomenon operates with respect to the physical environment that is the school. In a sense, it "listens" to children and it "talks" to them as well. In all probability, it is deaf to some needs and it responds too loudly or in too many ways to the needs of others.

On this point there is relatively little speculation or comment within the literature that deals with school-age children, and for the most part that little deals with the correction of understimulation (i.e., the hypothesis that most children will profit from a more "enriched," colorful, multistimulant school environment) rather than suggesting simplicity as an antidote for overstimulation. Much more has been written about the appropriate environment in which to raise infants and preschool children. On the whole, this literature has stressed the intellectual (and other) values of saturating the child's sensory environment with objects, sounds, even smells (although on the whole, modern man has virtually destroyed that once essential sensory talent). Several recent trends within this literature appear to have particular meaning for older children as well.

Soviet psychologists, particularly at the Institute for Preschool Education in Moscow, have developed the idea that it is the patterning of early stimulation rather than the sum total of stimulation that is critical for maximum intellectual development. In guidebooks for parents, they suggest how the environment should be arranged, modified, and utilized in the development of various skills and senses at each stage of the child's growth.[16] Certainly much that is happening in the United States, particularly with reference to compensatory education and Head Start programs, is in sympathy with this view.

## Open-Space Facilities

As has already been indicated in several contexts, a major trend has been toward more open school buildings. This has been true even with respect to the secondary schools, though the pace has been slower. Reduced to simplest terms, this means elimination of nearly all interior walls, both physical and psychological. Usually it means a high degree of collaboration and interaction among teachers and minimal use of space partitions (these usually movable)

16. Sheila and Michael Cole, "And Now, A Theory from Russia's Child Experts," *The New York Times Magazine*, October 13, 1968, pp. 127-28, 130-31.

to indicate areas of ownership or occupation. Usually, too, it means heavy reliance on carpeting as an acoustical as well as comfortable and functional floor surface.

Within the loosely partitioned area, a great variety of space-use patterns may be attempted: small groups, large groups, independent activities; numerous furniture layouts, traffic patterns, interest centers, storage arrangements; and various ways of defining the instructional "stations" for staff members. Thus, ideas such as flexible scheduling and related patterns of school organization are easily implemented in open space.

However, the argument for open, flexible, carpeted space is supported not only by advocates of new organizational arrangements and those with essentially administrative orientations, but also by humanists and others concerned with spiritual and aesthetic development. Cogswell, for example, concluded that if educators follow humanistic procedures of system development, then they will need open areas which accommodate numerous activities and where change and flow of activity can easily occur.[17] Interestingly, architects and others also have picked up the humanistic theme by arguing that large expanses of internal space can protect children against the "claustrophobia" that sometimes seems to beset them when they are imprisoned within a conventional classroom space hour after hour, day after day. By endowing the large space with appropriate and varied textures, colors, and even shapes, planners can create an environment in which the child's eye (and often, his feet as well) can roam with pleasure, even while providing some of the boundaries within which he is learning to live.

The absence of walls between the spaces where different groups of teachers and pupils are working can be both an advantage and a disadvantage, depending on such factors as the degree of concentration required, the intensity of distracting sounds or sights created by one or another group, the uses being made of space separators (other than walls), the actual distance between groups, the number of people occupying various spaces, the effectiveness of acoustical installations, the degree of comradeship that is felt by the adults

17. John F. Cogswell, "Humanistic Approaches to the Design of Schools," in *Issues in American Education,* ed. Arthur M. Kroll (New York: Oxford University Press, 1970).

involved, and the general setting within which the school program is conducted. In conventional schools, walls serve not only to separate rooms from each other, but also to hold exhibits and materials (such as chalkboards) and to signal the location of sinks, closets, storage spaces, toilet rooms, and various other parts of the total school environment. The extent to which suitable provisions have been made for such functions will also influence the attitudes of staff toward a wall-less environment.

Both teachers and children have need for a certain amount of privacy within the rhythm of the day, and in some open-space designs it is more difficult to find privacy than in others. Where stub walls and other solid vertical surfaces permit a person or group to be shielded from others in one or more directions, the corners thus provided tend to be popular during much of the day. Temporary vertical surfaces, such as sliding partitions or portable equipment of many types, can also be useful as shields and it is not unusual for bookcases, file cabinets, and other large pieces to be placed to form the equivalent of a low wall. More common, perhaps, and somewhat flexible is the use of portable chalkboards, simple screens, and cabinets or shelves on wheels for space separation.

Privacy is a relative term, and sometimes one's need for privacy is inadequately met by the measures described above. For the total privacy that is sometimes required, both teachers and children should have recourse to small offices, conference areas, or work rooms scattered through the building. Ultimately, experience will help planners to know just how many such spaces are ordinarily needed in a given type and size of school; for the moment, it remains an interesting question.

Some schools have set up regular "havens" for children in the form of lounge-type areas with comfortable chairs and such amenities as a tape deck to which children can listen via earphone headsets. In one such school, certain children have found it a real blessing to be able to retreat now and then from the hurly-burly of the day, enjoy ten or fifteen minutes of therapeutic music of their own choice, and then return to the larger group with renewed vigor.

One of the most persistent and annoying problems in most schools, and particularly in some of the newer open-space schools, is the inadequacy and the inconvenient location of *storage space*. To be able to put a wide range and quantity of materials in a safe place and to be able to retrieve them easily and quickly when needed is one of the most important needs of both teachers and pupils. In the interest of economy, both in total square footage and in dollar outlay for construction and equipment, school planners almost always compromise on the matter of storage. The long-range effect of such economies on the instructional program is probably enormous, and many an important lesson has been either abandoned or damaged by the unavailability of a place where necessary resources could be found or where work in progress could be saved. Totally inconsistent with an activity-oriented philosophy of education is the administrative attitude that denies an abundance of space (or its equivalent in portable units) to the storage function.

Storage space, unlike other specified spaces, need not have any particular shape or contour and can be much more primitive than some planners assume. Architects should be encouraged to fit them in wherever possible, especially in the "leftover" space that results from putting a pair of toilet rooms here, or a music practice-room there, or a nonrectangular room somewhere else. The important thing is that they be provided; shape and location, so long as reasonably acceptable, are not urgent considerations.

The term "open" is currently being applied not only to schools having large space unseparated by walls, but also to various unconventional models of education in which American educators are showing a growing interest. "Open education" of the sort associated with primary schools in Leicestershire (England) allows a great deal of freedom to children in defining and pursuing their own activities both within and outside the school building, and inevitably implies a different way of looking at the physical environment. Interesting variations on the themes of openness and freedom are found in a number of new schools (mostly independent) springing up in the United States[18] and elsewhere, and in proposals by such writers as Bruce Joyce,[19] Leslie Hart,[20] and George Leonard.[21] A literature

18. Bonnie Barrett Stretch, "The Rise of the 'Free School'," *Saturday Review* 53 (June 20, 1970): 76-79, 90-93.

19. Bruce Joyce, *Alternative Models of Elementary Education* (Waltham, Mass.: Blaisdell Publishing Co., 1969).

20. Leslie Hart, *The Classroom Disaster* (New York: Teachers College Press, 1969).

pertaining especially to physically open schools is also emerging[22] and will undoubtedly grow in quantity and improve in quality over the next decade.

## Schoolhouse in the City: Some Urgent Notes

If I had to say which was telling the truth about society, a speech by a minister of housing or the actual buildings put up in his time, I should believe the buildings.

Sir Kenneth Clark

Applying Sir Kenneth's observation to American school buildings, one would necessarily come to six conclusions: (a) until very recently, American educators tended more to distrust than to trust their pupils with respect to self-discipline and voluntary involvement in the learning process; (b) uniformity and consistency have been valued much more than richness and diversity; (c) austerity and economy have been preferred to functionality, comfort, and flexibility; (d) verbal learning, within a sedentary framework, has been the most accepted procedure; (e) regimentation has been seen as a legitimate aspect of school life; and (f) the children of the poor, whether in the cities or in depressed rural areas, have been seldom valued by the educational establishment.

While these are harsh words, the blunt fact is that most school buildings in America are miserably unsuited to the needs of today's children, and in the cities, particularly, children are expected to learn in an environment that is often cheerless, frequently ugly and uncomfortable, usually obsolete by a whole range of standards, and not uncommonly dangerous. Little wonder, then, that much attention (at least in the form of rhetoric) has been given to the topic of refurbishing and replacing city schools.

The subject of at least one full volume[23] and many articles, city school planning has become of lively interest despite the serious

22. See in particular the *Open-Space Schools Project Bulletin,* No. 1, issued by the School Planning Laboratory, School of Education, Stanford University, March 1970, p. 7.

23. Alvin Toffler, ed., *The Schoolhouse in the City* (New York: Frederick A. Praeger, 1968). Published in cooperation with Educational Facilities Laboratories.

21. George Leonard, *Education and Ecstasy* (New York: Delacorte Press. 1968).

financial, geographic, and political problems that tend to be even more severe in the cities than in suburban and rural areas.

Among the ways that large cities can cope with the high cost and the practical difficulties in finding suitable sites for school construction are (a) the acceptance of the educational park plan, which calls for the concentration of many pupils (sometimes inclusive of all school ages) in one location; (b) the renovation of old buildings, not only of old schools but of other structures as well; (c) the use of temporary, relocatable structures; (d) the acceptance of the land-in-the-air plan, involving construction of facilities above something like a railroad yard, a highway, or a river; and (e) the adoption of the joint occupancy plan wherein the school is only part of the space included in a large building or complex of buildings, in which housing, office space, and other facilities may be included.

Another interesting possibility is what planners in Boston, Massachusetts, call "infill schools," temporary schools somewhat similar to those used by some suburbs in the past to cope with overcrowding. Under this plan, small, inexpensive, flexible units can be built on available lots, later to be converted to housing units (or other purposes) when the peak need has passed. When linked with a regular school and/or other facilities such as a resource center servicing a number of infill schools, such temporary units might be quite adequate.

That imaginative and unconventional proposals are needed if cities are to maintain adequate schools, even if massive financial support should come from unexpected quarters, is the theme of nearly all current literature about schooling in cities. Yet with the bureaucracies in the cities, with several layers of assistant superintendents and other plenipotentiaries through whom new ideas must pass (in either direction), it is especially difficult to put new ideas into practice. Consortia of schools, or schools with different types of resources attempting to share their facilities with each other, sometimes find it impossible to function within existing policies (e.g., those relating to pupil transportation at public expense) or across jurisdictions. Legal and other snarls prevent using the joint occupancy idea; laws or even petty officials stand in the way of putting, say, public libraries and schools under the same roof; commercial interests obstruct efforts to introduce programs with meaningful work experience; and so on. And often the school officials are so constantly preoccupied with operational crises that their energies can rarely be diverted to long-range planning.

It is especially unfortunate that the large city school systems do less than their suburban neighbors to provide principals, teachers, and others with in-service training that will enable them to make necessary improvements. When new buildings or renovations are being planned, rarely do significant numbers of staff members play any role in the process. If the new buildings are to be significantly different in some way, e.g., in having open-space areas or facilities for team teaching, usually the administration is derelict in preparing the staff to understand and to use the new environment. When the new facilities therefore fail to work out as well as they might, top officials tend to blame not themselves but the planners of the space.

Equally serious is the error still being made by most city officials of excluding the people and leaders of the community from the planning process as well as from the general management of their local schools. As a result, angry parents and community spokesmen are increasingly vocal in their demands for participation in the shaping and the control of school programs.

Apart from the political and sociological overtones of the problems that thus arise, it is increasingly obvious that city schools must change from places for children to places for people—people of many different ages and many different needs. As Gores puts it:

Adults need the schoolhouse as much as children do. . . . To put the matter in bluntest terms, the schoolhouse in the slums should be the people's college, their town hall, their cultural center, their country club, their school. . . .[24]

When this idea it taken seriously, it has many implications for the planning and layout of the building, for the day and night use of the facility over twelve calendar months, and for the distribution of financial and operational responsibilities across several official and unofficial agencies. Few cities are, at the moment, prepared to operate within the principles involved.

When buildings *are* to be utilized more extensively by involving members of the community, then both separate spaces that belong

24. Harold B. Gores, "The Demise of Magic Formulas," Toffler, ed., *The Schoolhouse in the City, p. 171* (see note 23).

exclusively to community functions and spaces shared with the schoolchildren will comprise the available on-site resources. Classrooms, offices and other workspaces, health rooms, the gymnasium, the auditorium, the music rooms, the library and media center, shops and crafts rooms, the cafeteria, the homemaking area, and social facilities will be the spaces most likely to be used by the community in "off hours." Spaces that belong permanently to the community, such as a "community room" (or suite of rooms) will be so arranged and located that they can serve day and night as headquarters and social centers. With the growing interest in day care for children, nursery-type facilities are being attached to such centers in some places, as are a variety of recreational, social, medical, and administrative spaces (e.g., "local city hall").

With such resources available, it becomes easier for the people of the community to find pleasure in meaningful activities and in each other's company; to develop talents not only with recreational value but with educational and vocational values as well; to organize their attack on local problems such as housing, health, political corruption or unresponsiveness, traffic and safety; and to become a force for aiding and strengthening other groups and programs within the city.

Not only because of cost factors, but also because cities and their needs are changing so rapidly, it is desirable for city schools (and probably their suburban counterparts as well) to break away from some of the old, familiar formulas for school planning. In addition to adopting the practices mentioned earlier in this section, it seems appropriate to become much more flexible about the size of the school, the size of the school site, the age groups to be included within a given school, and the anticipated life of the school building.[25] Without sacrificing safety and comfort, it should be possible to work out some solutions which can, without regret and with enthusiasm for the newer alternatives, be abandoned when their purpose has been well served.

If flexible and adaptable buildings are indeed essential to the development of better programs and to the utilization of emerging organizational patterns, many if not most existing schools will have to be either modified or, at worst, scrapped and replaced. With the

25. Gores, ibid., p. 175.

creative assistance of EFL, CEFP, and other facilities planners, much has been learned in recent years about remodeling and redesign. "New Life for Old Schools,"[26] the catchy title for reports and discussion of the renovation problem, has become a useful rallying cry even though often it refers to recently built schools that, though physically young, are conceptually and functionally old. Reports indicate that rehabilitation is economically feasible in the great majority of cases, and often the savings over replacement are very great.[27]

At the very least, school people can reconsider the way existing space is being utilized and how its characteristics and amenities influence the educational function. Libraries can be expanded, for example, by attaching adjacent spaces. Functions and groups can be relocated, consolidated, expanded, or eliminated in favor of new arrangements. Wasted or unused spaces such as lobbies or extra-wide corridors can be put to better purpose.

Next, minimum-cost improvements can be made. Beautiful paint (and other surfaces) need cost no more than ugly paint. Some walls and partitions can be removed with little difficulty. Floor areas can be carpeted. Casters can be mounted on bookcases and cabinets, the local carpentry shop can build space-separators and other equipment such as furniture blocks, planks, tote-tray cabinets, tabletops to rest on inflated inner tubes of truck tires, portable carrels, and lapboards. Discarded furniture can be redesigned or its components, such as solid-wood desk tops, reused. Corridor walls can be narrowed to create conference and work spaces. New and more suitable furnishings can be ordered as funds permit to replace the unsuitable and unsalvageable.

More expensive revisions, including expansion and/or replacement of a portion of the building, also may be in order. An imaginative master plan, which allows the old gymnasium to become an institutional materials center when a new and better gymnasium is added, can perhaps make the older building as desirable as totally new construction.

26. Title of a sound film produced by the Research Council of the Great Cities Program for School Improvement. Title also of the New Life for Old Schools Project, EFL, 20 North Wacker Drive, Chicago, Illinois 60606.

27. For five case studies see *SPL Reports* 4 (March 1969).

In some cities, where expansion or replacement of schools is difficult because of the scarcity and cost of land, it may make sense to include the school as part of a high-rise multipurpose structure, e.g., to locate a school on five floors of a twenty-story building which is devoted primarily to housing units or commercial purposes or both.

Sometimes, too, available structures can be converted to school purposes at reasonable cost: architect Walter Hill, for example, has proposed that Lowell, Massachusetts, utilize the vast floor space available in deserted textile mills.[28] Every city probably has buildings of one sort or another presently unused or inefficiently used which could conceivably be adapted for educational purposes given only the imagination and the will on the part of community leaders.

In one interesting trend, the school is defined not as a specific physical entity but as an idea. A dramatic example is the "school without walls" established in 1969 in Philadelphia under the guidance of John Bremer. Known as the "Parkway Program," this high school consists of a headquarters with several offices and meeting places, but most of the learning goes on in other parts of the city: in offices, museums, hospitals, theaters, auto repair shops, banks, even other schools. The school is divided into three self-governing "communities," and the educational program is not markedly different in scope and description from those of other high schools. There are remarkable differences, however, in the way the program is experienced by pupils for whom, in effect, the city of Philadelphia with its enormous resources is the locus of learning.[29] Similar programs based on the same principle are developing in other major cities, such as Chicago with its "Metropolitan High School," opened in 1970.

Whatever is done to put new life into city schools, it follows that the nature of the physical environment will be less crucial than the quality of the educational program. The two are interrelated, however, and sometimes it is a new building or a significant renovation

28. *Milling Around with Kids,* A Preliminary Feasibility Study of an Alternative for Facilitating Education in Lowell, Mass. (Cambridge, Mass.: Harvard University, Graduate School of Education, 1969), p. 19.

29. James D. Greenberg and Robert E. Roush, "A Visit to the 'School Without Walls': Two Impressions," *Phi Delta Kappan* 51 (1970): 480-84.

that spurs a community to greater interest and pride in the school's program.

When pride does exist, all sorts of benefits accrue to the people of the community. One of these, at least potentially, is a more valuing attitude toward not only the school but the neighborhood it serves. Not only in the suburbs do real estate values tend to rise when the local school is regarded as excellent.

The cost of school vandalism to public school systems, mostly in the decaying neighborhoods of cities but sometimes in suburban communities as well, is said to exceed $100 million annually. Some sociologists view school vandalism at least in part as the vindictive and calculated response of persons, usually youngsters under eighteen, who feel a grievance against the institution. The highest rates of vandalism occur in schools characterized by low morale among staff, boredom and frustration among students, and obsolete, unsuitable facilities and equipment. On the other hand, it is relatively rare to find chronic patterns of vandalism where the school is a source of community pride, and schools where there is much community involvement and the buildings are open evenings and weekends for community activities are seldom the targets of vandals.

## The Future: Glimpses of Possibilities

Although the emphasis in this chapter is on the educational impact of environment, it may nonetheless be interesting to examine some architectural, engineering, and other developments and products which promise to influence future school construction and/or renovation. These include improvements and economies in the manufacture of colorful, sturdy, easily cleaned, static-free carpeting; stronger, more versatile, lighter-weight, durable materials for both building structures and items of equipment; major improvements in the design and efficiency of sinks, lavatories, water closets, urinals, and showers; further improvements in light fixtures (e.g., in exhausting heat); better systems of heating and cooling, especially electrically heated radiant walls and heat pumps; quieter and less obtrusive ventilating units; breakage-resistant glazing; more effective security systems to help combat vandalism; more efficient hard-flooring materials and cleaning systems; portable aboveground instructional swimming pools; wireless projection systems; button systems for instant pupil response in class lecture situations; portable communications units (walkie-talkie in sophisticated versions); air filters and cleaners; solar energy as a heat source; portable, self-ventilated booths for "instant privacy"; and standardized, economical construction systems.

Notable examples of the systems approach to school building construction have been the School Construction Systems Development (SCSD), serving a group of participating school districts in California, the Study of Educational Facilities (SEF) in Toronto, Ontario, and the state-supported Schoolhouse Systems Project (SSP) in Florida. SCSD, a closed system, utilizes one set of basic building components (e.g. the structural subsystem and the heating-ventilating-air conditioning subsystem) specifically designed to integrate with one another. SEF and SSP, which are closed systems, utilize interchangeable components made by different manufacturers. In these systems the internal arrangement of space, and hence the type of educational program to be served, can vary significantly from school to school, but the basic building components (floor, structure, walls, roof, and utilities) are standardized and through volume purchasing plus efficiency in design the schools can be built at very favorable cost. Of great importance educationally is the feature that internal partitions can be relocated by the regular school maintenance crew with relatively little difficulty so that systems-built schools can easily be adapted to changing instructional requirements. They can, for that matter, be adapted to noneducational uses as community needs change. Since changing population patterns are difficult to predict, it has been suggested by Univer that some components of systems-planned schools should be capable of conversion, by expanding or dismantling, to a smaller or greater size.[30]

In the foregoing brief discussion, one recognizes that certain trends in engineering sciences have favorable implications for education. It is equally interesting to speculate further on the sorts of engineering and architectural inventions or trends that should stem from

30. Irving O. Univer, "Planners: Your Systems Schools Are Under-Achievers," *CEFP Journal* (Council of Educational Facility Planners) 8 (May-June 1970): 4-6.

the expressed needs and concerns of educators or of others who study human development.

However, few writers have succeeded in presenting convincingly the implications for school building design of recent research and experience in learning, development, and motivation. In one such attempt, Castaldi[31] included several interesting suggestions and implications: (a) it may be possible to manipulate lighting effects, sound effects, room temperature, and other environmental variables to increase the stimulus value of certain experiences; (b) selected units of the school's mechanical and electrical system and its structural system could be left exposed, automatic controlling devices could operate under clear plastic covers, and electronic devices could be enclosed in transparent boxes, all in order that pupils' motivation might be increased through observation; (c) the need for "belongingness" can be better met if small-group spaces and spaces that encourage socializing are provided; (d) mental, physical, and psychological fatigue can be lessened by careful attention to ventilation, the thermal and sonic enivronment, and good illumination; and (e) the environment deliberately filled with exhibits, displays, and other stimulants to incidental learning can be of great value.

Some of these suggestions already have been made operative on a modest scale in certain school situations, but in future planning it is obvious that greater effort should be made in the directions indicated. In addition to meeting the need for "belongingness," some educators also suggest that schools should help children cope with the problems of "bigness," i.e., maintaining individuality even when a school is large. Through the building design, in its orientation to the neighborhood, in its appointments, and in its facilities (study carrels, courts, seminar rooms, snack bars, student commons, little theaters, reading alcoves, and the like) environment can help give young people a sense of belonging, of security, and of identity with the school, despite its size.

Of even greater potential significance is the contribution that imaginative design and appropriate equipment can make to more mature and effective patterns of flexible school organization (such as nongradedness, collaborative staffing arrangements, and various schemes for individualized learning). These have existed only in

31. Castaldi, *Creative Planning,* pp. 107-35.

relatively primitive form prior to the 1970s, for a variety of reasons, including the physical and psychological restrictions imposed by the enivronment. Nearly all decisions made about classroom size and shape, auxiliary facilities, furnishings, hardware, and software have until very recently been permeated by the philosophy of gradedness and its sister philosophy in support of the self-contained classroom. Both gradedness and nongradedness, as one designer has observed, have their own aesthetics and their own technology. It may at least be hoped that architects and educators will choose to reject the severe, tidy, and inflexible traditions with which they have been saddled, in favor of the more humane, fluid, and versatile schemes that have been emerging.

Another probability is that school buildings in the future will be expected to serve not only a given student population during the official school year (which itself may expand to twelve months), but also a larger proportion of the total community—infants, very young children, employed persons seeking recreation or additional training, the elderly, and others with miscellanous needs. Not all schools can be planned to provide for all possible needs of such persons, but it seems reasonable to state that citizens will make more round-the-clock use of their schools in the future than they have in the past. The implications for the variety of spaces, for equipment and furniture, for storage, and for area zoning are obvious.

*Suggestions from children.* In the planning of schools, all too seldom are the pupils considered an integral part of the planning team. This is lamentable, not only because children deserve to be consulted but because they have many useful suggestions to offer. Architect Walter L. Hill has demonstrated this fact by eliciting and using the ideas of youngsters in the school planning process.[32] Bright colors, adjustable room shapes, ropes to climb, slides to be used as "down staircases," doors, windows, and ceilings adjusted to the scale of little people, furniture and wall panels on wheels, and provisions for animals were among the suggestions from elementary pupils. Other practical suggestions included provision of a clothes dryer and cabinets for messy paints and shoe polish.[33]

32. See "Using Students as School Design Consultants," *School Management* 12 (November 1968): 81-86.

33. Barbara Villet, "The Children Want Classrooms Alive with Chaos," *Life* 66 (April 11, 1969): 50-56.

A Colorado teacher, Marcia Lynch, asked her nine-year-old pupils what they would do to make school a better place. Here are some exact quotes from their responses:

1. Make the work easier for the children who can't do hard work and make it harder for children who can do hard work
2. Change the playground—make better equipment
3. *Bigger* rooms
4. Not have mean teachers
5. All would share all things and help each other
6. Longer recesses
7. Wear any kind of clothes we want to wear
8. Carpet the floors
9. Desks with no drawing on them and seats with a button you push to open the desk
10. A quiet pencil sharpener
11. Paint the rooms orange, purple, pink, red, and many other bright colors
12. Individual telephones to call people in class
13. Have a whole bunch of animals all over the classroom
14. Have P.E. more often
15. Have exercises before you start work
16. Children can play all day if they want to and have whatever they want to eat—have pets and games and fights in class

While it is not possible to accept and utilize all such suggestions, and while this list is merely one sampling, it is nevertheless of interest that young children make such frequent mention of the environment as a force to be enjoyed and encountered physically.

At the same time, although it is not noted in the Colorado list, children seeking a different and more peaceful type of encounter, also use the building and its equipment as a haven or refuge. For example, children in open-space schools sometimes try to find privacy by "holing up" under a table, or in a corner, or inside a big cardboard box; by observing children and how they behave within the available environment, we can learn a great deal about what that environment *should* provide.

Reduction of the setting to their own scale, one of the suggestions that Walter Hill repeatedly receives from elementary age pupils, is not so very difficult and probably ought to be attempted at least on an experimental basis in a fraction of the total space being planned. At the very least, some schools could experiment with reduced-scale arrangements by providing false ceilings, some small doors "just for pupils," and other possible arrangements.

Sommer, commenting on the ways children choose to sit, noted that, unlike adults, cooperating children prefer to sit alongside rather than opposite each other. "It is likely that a thirty-inch distance across the table was a much longer psychological distance on the children's scale than it would be for adults."[34] He also noted that when classroom chairs are arranged around a table, the chairs next to the instructor are filled last and their occupants rarely participate; those pupils located across from the instructor participate most.[35] Other studies suggest that there are correlations between seating positions in a classroom and student personality. Where a choice is possible, the zealous, intellectually interested students sit near the front; the bored, nonacademic students sit near the back; and the students with high affiliation needs sit near each other.[36] Probably there are dozens of other tendencies of this sort in pupils which, if better understood by teachers, could be extremely useful both in planning environmental arrangements and in making better assessments of pupil needs.

*Equipment.* Anyone who has recently walked through the exhibits of the annual AASA convention in Atlantic City, or even of smaller meetings of school administrators, scarcely doubts that there is available today a dazzling array of instructional resources and school furnishings. Similarly, one finds on the general market an amazing variety of textbooks, reference materials, tradebooks, educational toys and games, audiovisual gadgets, art supplies, musical instruments, and other types of merchandise of potential use to children in learning situations. In addition, of course, thrifty and creative teachers can and do make use of all types of raw materials, including not only items that can be purchased in various shops but also things easily available to the alert scavenger: used household utensils, rags, shells, dried leaves, rocks and pebbles, lumber scraps, shipping crates,

34. Sommer, *Personal Space,* p. 64.

35. Ibid., p. 114.

36. Herbert J. Walberg, "Physical and Psychological Distance in the Classroom," *School Review* 77 (1969): 64.

and flotsam ad infinitum. By comparison with the ill-supplied schools of earlier times, or even those of contemporary developing countries, most American schools are almost embarrassingly full of things.

Yet unfortunately it cannot be said that these things are always— or even usually—the most appropriate, nor are they always used to best advantage. Often there are full sets of standard textbooks, but too few copies of nontextual reference materials. Too often, paper and other supplies are used wastefully, too seldom do children make their own materials and play an active part in the creation and decoration of their environment. Only occasionally is the overall atmosphere one in which children (and teachers) are actively inter- acting with an impressive array of materials, equipment, flora and fauna in such a way that their school experience is reasonably faith- ful to the philosophy of "learning by doing," which has enjoyed so much lip service in the past seventy years. There is, in short, much room for progress in taking advantage of the incredibly rich re- sources that are presently available.

With respect to school furniture, some fascinating alternatives are already available, and it seems that the "revolution" in the fur- nishings field has barely begun. Spurred by new approaches to teaching and learning, especially the trend toward open-space areas serving pupils of different ages, designers and manufacturers have come up with many new arrangements for seating, display, indi- vidual storage, group storage, space separation, work surfaces, and utilization of the floor. Imaginative ways of using truck-tire inner tubes, tabletops, drop-leaf work surfaces, boxes of different shapes, planks, cardboard, and other inexpensive materials have been de- veloped.[37] It is impossible here to review in detail what seems to be happening with respect to equipment, or even all of the problems yet to be solved, but it can be said with certainty that the field is in a state of healthy and creative turmoil.

*Media centers.* With media becoming an even more important aspect of the child's educational experience, both the range and quantity of "library" materials to be used and the optimum location of these materials become important matters in planning. Helpful

37. *SPL Reports* 4 (December 1969) is an excellent review of new develop- ments in school furnishings (School Planning Laboratory, School of Education, Stanford University).

to educators are the standards for school media programs[38] promulgated by the American Library Association and the National Education Association. Widespread adoption of these standards could lead to significant improvements in the quality of programs and make individualized learning experiences possible for far more children.

Although in larger schools supplementary spaces may be needed, the tendency is to place media centers in one central and convenient location. Within this center are provided a reading area, a learning laboratory, independent study areas, conference spaces, work areas for the center staff, storage spaces, a maintenance and production area for electronic and other equipment, television studio and viewing area, and other specialized facilities. Frequently, provisions are made for both concurrent and after-hours use of the center, or portions thereof, by community groups.

*Electronic resources.* One of the greatest needs in education is to reexamine the effects of radically changing educational technologies upon the concept of a "school" or a "school building." It is at least possible that either or both of two things might happen well before the turn of the century: (a) communications systems will make it possible to connect an individual learner, possibly seated at a console in his own home, with an almost infinite number and variety of educational resources and with another person or group of persons in one or more other locations; (b) education will have outgrown the concept of retaining (some say, incarcerating) pupils within the physical boundaries of a school building for $x$ hours per day, $y$ days per year.

Schools have scarcely begun to take full advantage of the electronic and other resources that are already available to permit home-to-school, teacher-to-pupil, pupil-to-pupil, and pupil-to-program communication. Homebound children sometimes are connected to school activities by telephone, or in a few cases by radio, but imaginative and extensive use of such hookups is uncommon despite the obvious advantages, especially in sparsely populated regions. As videotelephone units, microwave cordless telephones, and similar

38. *Standards for School Media Programs* (Chicago, Ill., Washington, D.C.: American Library Association and National Education Association, 1969).

devices become more common on the American scene, their use as educational equipment will almost certainly increase.

*Sign-off: flexibility remains the key.* George S. Counts recently pointed out that "if we want to avoid imposing anything on our children, we should alter the architectural style of the building every day."[39] Unfortunately, this Olympian figure left it for others to figure out just how that trick is to be accomplished. However, his message has special significance for planners who seek to create the best possible setting for the learners of today and tomorrow. While it may be many decades before building materials and construction techniques permit the frequent rearrangement of the actual school edifice, it is already within our power to make *some* changes in the environment that the structure provides and encloses, virtually at will. Especially where we have dared to omit fixed walls and to equip the school with evocative and multifunctional "props," it has been relatively easy for us to respond to the ever-changing needs and interests of the children who inhabit school space. Further, it has been *possible* for a greater range of psychological and social benefits to be enjoyed by the adults and children within the school setting. "Possible," we stress, rather than "guaranteed," because (a) all that we know has not yet found its way into practice, and (b) what we know remains only a small fraction of what we may hope to learn in the years to come about the optimal environment for school learning.

Unless the society collapses or there are unimaginable reverses in the flow of new materials and technologies, schools will have a growing number of alternatives from which they may choose in providing educationally desirable experiences for all the different kinds of children and adults who will come to them. Whether or not they will make the best possible choices will depend on many factors, some beyond the educator's control but others clearly within his power. That progress in creating truly appropriate school environments has been painfully slow up to this point suggests that the educator has not always acted wisely. One of his worst errors, it would seem, has been to commit himself to patterns (such as gradedness or self-containment) from which retreat is difficult. Therefore

39. George S. Counts, "Should the Teacher Always Be Neutral?" *Phi Delta Kappan* 51 (1969) : 188.

he would be prudent, in a period of rapid change, to keep himself open to as many options as possible. In this chapter various ways of providing for these options, such as open-area designs, have been indicated. It is greatly to be hoped that through the use of flexible approaches school planners can make it easier, in the years to come, for curriculum improvements to occur.

CHAPTER XIII

# The Curriculum Worker of the Future

BRUCE R. JOYCE

## Overture

We view curriculum workers as technologists who cannot, as some technologists do, work without a moral purpose and corresponding ethical constraints on their behavior. The technology of the curriculum worker is the technology of education planning, for curriculum planning lies at the heart of educational planning, dealing as it does with the definition of educational ends and the engineering of means for achieving them. The moral responsibility of the curriculum worker derives from the humanistic opportunities which reside in education. Education can humanize or dehumanize, spread love or cooperate with terror, be filled with joyful vigor or awful drudgery, make a better social world or permit the old one to run on.

In the past, educational planners have been technically weak (unable, often, to clarify ends or engineer means) and morally or technically unable to bring about a humanistic revolution in education.

To speculate on the future curriculum worker is to attempt to reconcile those forces that have been shaping the field with a thrust that embodies the direction one would hope could dominate the field. These two concerns—to clarify the curriculum worker's past and to put forth a framework for changing his work—have dominated the writing of this chapter.

### THESIS: WHAT HAS BEEN AND LIKELY WILL BE

The substance of the argument can be stated quite simply and briefly. First, the curriculum field has been marked by a progressive bureaucratization, and the curriculum worker has been bureaucratized much as have the functionaries in other social institutions throughout the complex societies of the world. He has, in other words, increasingly become a servant of a system, largely impersonal in nature, which serves primarily to teach children the technological culture and to fit them into the economic and status systems of the society. Although this institutional system is (politically) organized as many relatively small school districts, schooling throughout the United States and much of the rest of the world is actually so similar that we have essentially one large national system that increasingly looks like one large international system as the eclectic world culture becomes more dominant and the technologies of education become more widespread and homogeneous. It is not entirely outlandish to compare the giant education bureaucracy with the postal system, except that instead of taking mail from one place to another, it receives people when they are children and delivers them when they are young adults into the adult economic family and the social and political systems. As in the case of the postal system, things are delivered much as they are mailed. In education it is the characteristics of the children and their parents that account for most of the character of the delivered product.[1]

The technologies (technology is used in the broadest sense to include scientific theories, the lore of practitioners, educational methods, and educational engineering: the available tools of the trade) of curriculum development, instructional materials development, supervision, and teacher training, the four domains of the curriculum worker, have all reflected the progressive bureaucratization of education. Each of these four has had its own characteristic bureaucratic flavor.

(1) Curriculum development, despite a paradoxical concentration at the theoretical level on personal and democratic processes,[2] has been concerned with the planning and management of instruc-

1. For an interesting review of the evidence about what variables account for academic achievement, see Edmund W. Gordon, "Introduction to Education for Socially Disadvantaged Children," *Review of Educational Research* 40 (1970): 1-12.

2. We believe this is because many of the writers in the curriculum field have been strongly influenced by the orientation toward personalism and social reform which characterized the Progressive movement. See Lawrence A. Cremin, *The Transformation of the School* (New York: Alfred Knopf, 1961).

tional systems and has increasingly turned toward the development and evaluation of a system implementable on a national or international scale.[3]

(2) Instructional materials development has been concerned with the improvement of devices designed to implement particular kinds of curricula and to do so efficiently and economically. Efficiency usually is best served by wide implementation of standardized materials and these have, indeed, dominated the educational scene. (The textbook, primarily, has been the form, but newer ones are becoming established.)[4]

(3) The functions of the curriculum supervisor have become regulatory in every bureaucratic sense, and, in most school districts, supervisors and teachers are separated from each other by a wide gulf of function. In many cases they keep a distance that tends to perpetuate the bureaucratic nature of their relationships and to minimize spontaneous, creative encounters between them. (Another paradox, since most supervision theory also stresses democratic procedures and enhances the uniqueness of individual teachers.)[5]

(4) Teacher training, operated chiefly by curriculum specialists, has leaned most heavily on student teaching, which is essentially an apprenticeship mode, designed to move the young teacher into the organizational patterns of the existing educational system and into the roles of functionaries in that system.

Present forces appear to be increasing and sophisticating the bureaucratic flavor. Content is gradually becoming more academically sophisticated, and instructional systems are now being developed which should be far more efficient both from the point of view of the school district, which wishes instruction to have a higher output, and in terms of the individual learner, whose characteristics the instructional systems will accommodate more efficiently than would a teacher in a class. Cost accounting procedures

3. See John I. Goodlad, *School Curriculum Reform in the United States* (New York: Fund for the Advancement of Education, 1964) for an account of the development of "national" curriculum projects.

4. Analyses of the standardization of textbooks are fairly common. For an analysis in one curriculum area, see C. Benjamin Cox and Byron Massialas, eds., *Social Studies in the United States* (New York: Harcourt, Brace & World, 1967).

5. This stress in the literature of supervision can be traced again to the heritage of the Progressive movement.

are being introduced into education, not only with respect to economic factors but also in connection with the assessment of alternative educational procedures.[6] Increasingly, commercial firms are now working on instructional materials development, evaluation systems, and cost accounting procedures. PERT procedures and PP&B (Planning, Programming, and Budgeting) procedures are being borrowed from the military-industrial complex and brought into the educational arena at an accelerating rate.[7]

In short, we are moving rapidly toward an industrial model of education, which is probably more efficient but even more bureaucratic in character than the inefficient "folk school" model it is replacing. Much of the public applauds the change. Even the recent humanistically oriented critics of schooling—Leonard,[8] Kohl,[9] Coles,[10] Kozol,[11] and others—while they have not been without effect, have been responded to in many quarters with the assertion that the ills they point to can be cured by making the system more efficient rather than by changing it in any fundamental way.

### THESIS: A HUMANISTIC ALTERNATIVE

What we would rather see come to pass can be best apprehended from an anthropological stance toward the role of education in a culture. A human culture can be described as an elaborate set of problem solutions.[12] Some of these solutions are addressed to physical problems and it was toward these solutions that our eco-

6. Jack Wiseman, "Cost-Benefit Analysis in Education," in Melvin R. Levin and Alan Shank, *Educational Investment in an Urban Society: Costs, Benefits and Public Policy* (New York: Teachers College Press, 1970).

7. Werner Z. Hirsch, "Education in the Program Budget," Levin and Shank (footnote 6); Melvin R. Levin, "Yardsticks for Government," in Levin and Shank (footnote 6); Desmond L. Cook, *Program Evaluation and Review Technique Applications in Education* (Washington: U.S. Department of Health, Education, and Welfare, 1966).

8. George B. Leonard, *Education and Ecstasy* (New York: Dell Publishing Co., 1968).

9. Herbert Kohl, *Thirty-six Children* (New York: New American Library, 1967).

10. Robert Coles, *Children of Crisis: A Study of Courage and Fear* (Boston: Little, Brown & Co., 1967).

11. Jonathan Kozol, *Death at an Early Age* (Boston: Houghton Mifflin Co., 1967).

12. This is a common anthropological definition. See Ina Corinne Brown, *Understanding Other Cultures* (Englewood Cliffs, N.J.: Prentice-Hall, 1962).

nomic and technological systems were originally developed. Other problems consist of meeting emotional needs, and some aspects of families and some modes of interpersonal interaction help to solve these for us. For each of us the culture largely defines the way we see problems and solutions and also enables us to share reality with other humans. That is, those of us who share the same culture tend to see things in similar ways and to respond similarly to other human beings, although there is of course a wide individual variation within any cultural pattern.[13]

A culture is never complete. It is in continuous need of regeneration and reorganization. Within every culture there are certain problems that have never been defined adequately and certain others for which there are no solutions, even though there are definitions. Within complex cultures such as ours there is at all times a multitude of problems begging for solution. Formal education systems have a potentially dynamic social role as a direct result of the incomplete and imperfect nature of the existing culture—the existing solutions to problems.

This opportunity exists, obviously, because education is a major agent in the transmission of culture. It fulfills the exceedingly important functions (shared with other socializing agencies) of giving us humaneness and transmitting to us a technology on which we can stand as we face the problems of human existence. Our present bureaucratic educational institution bids well to become increasingly effective at transmitting the general-purpose skills of the culture (especially reading and mathematics) and this is a role I would not want to undersell under any circumstances. (We are certainly not *against* absorbing the existing culture, although we do not believe it is perfect.) *However, the great dynamic challenge of the future is to develop, in addition to more highly efficient structures for education, entirely new modes of education designed to help people create new solutions to problems and to define problems that were not perceived before at all. Equally important, in a time when culture is growing ever stronger and more powerful and society is more urbanized and alienated, is to produce humanistic*

13. Leslie White's *A Science of Culture: A Study of Man and Civilization* (New York: Farrar, Straus, 1949) presents the extreme technocratic view, but in so doing clearly defines the dimensions of dependence each of us has with respect to his culture.

*modes of education which can help people make contact with each other in new and stronger ways and can help individuals create lives which are unique, uniquely fulfilling and socially productive, even transcendentally cooperative.* The increase of efficiency in the present kinds of education is not likely to bring about these changes, and it is due to this that we find tension between our expectations of what will come about and what we would like to see happen. We are afraid that the curriculum worker will become more effective in accomplishing an important and essential task (transmitting our existing technical culture) while neglecting a task of even greater urgency—helping people create a more humanistic experience (which is partly a technical task also, but of a very different kind).

To deal with the implications of this issue in a positive way, the remainder of this paper is structured into three sections. One section presents a historical synopsis of the factors which have led toward the progressive bureaucratization of the institution and the curriculum worker within it. In the second section, we will develop a platform for changing the roles of the curriculum worker. Finally, we will consider a framework for generating new types of educational institutions—a framework that curriculum workers can use to bring about different modes of education and correspondingly different roles for themselves.

### THE CURRICULUM FIELD: A BIASED HISTORY

The curriculum worker is a member of a large cadre of persons who deal with educational planning, the training and supervision of educational personnel, and the development of educational materials. The collectivity of these persons, their expertness, and their activity constitute the curriculum "field." As indicated earlier, curriculum workers engage in four kinds of activity: they plan educational programs, develop systems of instructional materials, train teachers, and supervise them. As any other worker, the curriculum specialist is greatly affected by the condition of his field, and curriculum specialists in all four spheres of activity are influenced by the same general field.

The curriculum field is still relatively undefined. Curriculum planners have no agreed upon set of concepts or modes which are known and used by all hands. There is no lack of "prescriptive" curriculum theories—that is to say, ideas about what school programs *ought* to be. Nor is there any lack of curricula.[14] On the contrary, there are a great many curriculum plans and a huge quantity of instructional materials built around those plans. School districts, publishers, research and development centers, and others create curriculum plans and/or materials, train teachers, and build evaluation systems. This mass of activity is conducted by people who use a great variety of procedures. Most curriculum creators use intuitive procedures while some use highly self-conscious "systems" procedures. They also vary in the implementation devices and strategies they use and they rely on a variety of tools. Some rely on curriculum guides as their chief vehicle, others use instructional materials, and still others use teacher training to carry on their business. Curriculum builders also differ in their view about freedom and control in curriculum matters. Some would create master man-machine systems in which rational decision-making procedures are administered by technocrats, teacher-technicians, or professional managers.[15] Others would give classroom teachers the central decision-making roles.[16] Still others would provide students with the central curriculum-making role.[17] A few curriculum specialists envision variations on all these, depending on what goals are to be sought.

The curriculum field has no overarching "metasystem," known to all or most of its practitioners, which enables comparisons of and choices between all the alternative approaches which are taken. This is not to say that there are no knowledgeable people who are acquainted with the alternatives. On the whole, however, curriculum planners "do their own thing." For instance, systems planners build and test instructional systems while child-centered edu-

14. For an authoritative definition of "curriculum," see Ralph W. Tyler, *Basic Principles of Curriculum and Instruction* (Chicago: University of Chicago Press, 1951).

15. Robert J. Seidel and Felix F. Kopstein, *A System Approach to Development and Maintenance of Optimal Learning Conditions* (Washington: Human Resources Research Office, George Washington University, 1967); Robert E. Herriott and Benjamin J. Hodgkins, *Sociocultural Context and the American School: An Open-Systems Analysis of Educational Opportunity*, OEG-2-6-062972-2095 (Washington: U.S. Office of Education, 1969).

16. Ole Sands, *Planning and Organizing for Teaching*, Project on the Instructional Program of the Public Schools (Washington: National Education Association, 1963).

17. The general view of A. S. Neill, *Summerhill* (New York: Hart Publishing Co., 1960).

cators develop reflective teaching procedures and group dynamics experts refine sensitivity training procedures. Generally the representatives of different persuasions do not talk to each other on a regular basis about the nature of the field.

*The thesis of this chapter is that curriculum specialists of all types do have one thing in common: they have been co-opted into the service of a bureaucratic, monolithic, largely dehumanized educational system and unless they change their orientations radically they will be unable to work for humanistic ends.*

The essential arguments of the chapter are devoted to the above thesis and to ways out of the dilemma of the field. First, we will deal with the circumstances that lead to the co-option of the curriculum planner by an antihumanistic bureaucratic form. Then, platforms for positive action will be presented and defended.

## Part I: The Dynamics of Difficulty: The Dilemma of the Curriculum Field

The difficulties in the curriculum field can be described in terms of three complex and interrelated factors which, by separating humanistic ideas from curricular practice, have made each appear irrelevant to the other. (Humanistic ideas are here defined as sharing an orientation toward helping people discover and actualize themselves as individuals and explore the creative possibilities in interaction with others. They view man as the end. Their polar opposite is *technical* education, in which man masters technologies and, hence, treats himself as a means. It is assumed that *both* technical and humanistic education are essential for full development of individual and society.)

The factors which have separated humanistic ideas from curricular practice will be described in terms of three theses, each of which describes one of the factors.

### Negative Thesis Number One

*By focusing on a certain kind of educational institution (the school) and by focusing on functionaries (teachers) whose roles have developed within the constraints of that institution, the curriculum field has forced itself to operate within parameters so restrictive that it has been unable to develop strong, validated theory and it has been impotent to improve education.*

Systematically, even *relevantly,* we (the curriculum workers) have missed the opportunity to improve education by addressing ourselves to it on its own terms.

Whether it is because we have yielded to the pressure of the practitioner or simply because we have been, as the French say, "boiled in the same soup" with them, we have tried to discuss education in an assumptive world something like the following:

First, that the kind of education with which we will concern ourselves takes place in places called schools. For many years, in fact, the definition of a curriculum has been "all the experiences which the youngster has within the influence of the school." By using that definition we have tried to say, of course, that it is not only the formal happenings of the school that are important, and that our domain includes the informal happenings as well. But most of us, as we have spoken about education, have been dreaming about a place pretty much like the schools we are familiar with, formal and informal aspects both included.

What we have evidently forgotten is that the school as an institution and the teacher role as we know it came into being a long time ago probably because it seemed logical at the time. As mass education came into being, the home tutorial system in which a tutor worked with the members of a family was simply extended, so that the "tutor" was teamed with more students, and, hence, became a "teacher" with a "class." In this country this teacher was, a century ago, very likely qualified by being the oldest unmarried girl in the community and she taught all subjects to all students. Hence, she would be helping beginning readers while assisting older students who were reading for college. The male teachers of the day were, for the most part, fringers in the society, and schoolmasters were far from respected members of the community except in rare cases.

Thus, the school began with modest personnel in impossibly difficult roles. Teacher of many subjects to children of many ages and talents, the key figure was also expected to be a strict disciplinarian. The New England schools, which influenced the rest of the nation, were dominated by Puritan theology, which held that the child was inferior to the adult by God's law and that he was damned forever unless he learned obedience and virtue. A harsh physical discipline prevailed and in addition to his other impossible burdens, the teacher was the moral guardian of the children.

As the numbers of children increased, classes were added and grades made their appearance. The graded school, with self-contained classrooms at the elementary level and subject specialists at the college preparatory level, became the form of the school as an institution.

Second, the curriculum field assumed that it was the teacher in this school who should have the initiative in matters of curriculum and instruction. Curriculum guides should suggest but not control.[18] The community should be involved in all matters affecting their children. Cooperative planning should insure the inclusion of the student. The local educational authority, the neighborhood school, the child's teacher, and the child himself were the center of power. The job of the curriculum specialist was to facilitate decision-making by these individuals. The field was to set before them the alternatives and the implications of the alternatives. The teacher was to be responsible and accountable, but he was thought to be the professional in charge. To violate his freedom would be a violation of professional ethics. This assumption neatly boxed the curriculum field inside the limitations of the average teacher. If he did not know mathematics, or did not want to teach it, the field was stuck firmly on the horns of a dilemma, for had it not defined the teacher as the center of power? If he would not or could not teach inductively, the field was in the position of having argued that this was a world of free choice. He should create his own style and if that style did not include induction, or an idea orientation, or any other desirable element, no doubt it provided its own compensation for his students. The teacher-student relationship had become sacred.

Third, the curriculum field not only assumed the school, with all its limitations and problems, but it made unwarranted assumptions about that school and the teachers. It was assumed that the social system of the school was democratic, and that the teacher wanted the responsibility for final curricular decisions. Thus, the curriculum field was not only forced to live at the technical level

18. C. W. Boardman and others, *Democratic Supervision in Secondary Schools,* rev. ed. (Boston: Houghton Mifflin Co., 1961).

of the local school (which prevented it from recommending any-thing requiring a high level of technical capacity or a fundamental knowledge), but in this third assumption it operated on false premises of a different order. For the fact was, the average schools simply had not very often operated in a style even remotely ap-proaching democracy, and most teachers did not want the respon-sibility which was thrust upon them.[19] (Not infrequently, curric-ulum theorists have railed against the textbook, told the teacher he was free, only to find him busily selecting *another* text.)[20]

Fourth, the curriculum field assumed the more or less perpetual existence of the then present curriculum areas—the ones in the practice of the schools. From time to time new ones were invented in order to pull the teachers towards different types of behavior. For example, the social studies and the language arts were in-vented to promote greater integration of subject matter and a more lively, problem-solving approach to instruction.

Probably the most effective curriculum workers specialized in curriculum areas because as long as one worked inside a curriculum area he could affect the school if he were able to affect the instruc-tional materials that went into it. Thus, as the content of textbooks was changed, the new textbooks slowly taught the teachers and slowly pulled them toward new methods. If textbooks changed too quickly, teachers had trouble with the material and rejected the innovation, but so long as curriculum specialists followed a policy of gradualism they could actually make some minor changes. Thus it is that the most prominent members of the curriculum field (and by far the richest) engage in the production of instructional ma-terials.[21] Unfortunately, as the curriculum field became tied to the curriculum areas, more was lost than gained in terms of flexibility, for as specific curriculum areas have lost validity we have not been able to replace them. Thus, although most schools pay little atten-

19. See James Hoetker and William P. Ahlbrand, Jr., "The Persistence of the Recitation," *American Educational Research Journal* 6 (1969): 145-68.

20. See C. Benjamin Cox and Byron Massialas, "The Inquiry Potential of the Social Studies," in Cox and Massialas, eds., *Social Studies in the United States,* p. 7.

21. The example of the reading field is representative. See Allen H. Barton and David E. Welder, "Research and Practice in the Teaching of Reading: A Progress Report" in Matthew B. Miles, ed., *Innovations in Education* (New York: Teachers College Press, 1964) for a penetrating analysis of the social psychology of the leadership within that curriculum area.

tion to the creative and performing arts, education for greater interpersonal sensitivity, philosophy, international concerns, and so
forth, and although major efforts have been devoted to increasing
attention to these areas, relatively little has been accomplished. The
existing curriculum areas absorb most of the efforts within the
schools, and innovation requires either the development of a new
area or the change of an existing one. Dramatic arts is an example
of a study which has not been implemented on a wide scale by
either means. It has been unable to compete with literature for a
significant portion of the English area or to become established
solidly in its own right.

## PARALYZING EFFECTS OF THE
### ASSUMPTIVE WORLD OF CURRICULUM

By far the most paralyzing effect of the assumptive world in
which the curriculum specialist lived was that it tended to filter
out all ideas which might have improved education but which fit
awkwardly into the school pattern. Because the curriculum developer assumed the school and assumed the teacher, he tended to
confine himself to recommendations that were in the teacher's terms
or in the school's terms. As a result, most of the prescriptive curriculum theory (and most of the descriptive curriculum efforts, in
fact) was in terms of what teachers did or should do, did not, or
should not do. Hence we had the arguments about whether learning should be child-centered, subject-centered, society-centered, and
so on. (The current advocacy of "inquiry" as a teaching method is
a revival of a prescription for problem-centered education.) Similarly, the studies of teaching, from Anderson and Brewer through
Withall and Lewis, Flanders, and Medley and Mitzel,[22] tended to
be in terms of whether instruction was "dominative," that is,
teacher-centered, or "integrative," that is, learner-centered—terms
that could be argued in relation to what teachers "should" do or
"might" do.[23] What has passed for curriculum theory, whether
prescriptive or descriptive, has usually been advice to the teacher
or specifications for instructional materials. Most of the literature

22. N. L. Gage, ed., *Handbook of Research on Teaching* (Chicago: Rand
McNally & Co., 1963).

23. John I. Goodlad, *School Curriculum and the Individual* (New York:
Blaisdell Publishing Co., 1966). See Chapter 7, "Curriculum Decisions," for distinction between alternative modes of decision-making.

in the field has related to specific proposals for implementation of favored views of learning but always to be implemented by a teacher and within a school. Hence, "Negative Thesis Number One" suggests that the curriculum field has not developed properly because it has thought in terms of a school and a teacher. The field has assumed, for the most part, both the institutional requirements of schools as we know them and the job demands and limitations of teachers as we know *them*.[24]

There is a sad paradox in this story. For most of this century the most active curriculum planners worked in an assumptive world which gave great prominence to a humanistic democracy. After Dewey,[25] curriculum workers assumed that the school and the classroom operated as a democracy in which teacher and children worked together to apply the scientific method to the betterment of society.[26] This practicing democracy would attend carefully to the needs of its members and to preparation for the active citizenship necessary for the development of a more humane and responsible society. That such a humanistic platform should be co-opted by bureaucratic functionaries is both paradox and tragedy.

## Negative Thesis Number Two

*The primary character of the school and the most valid descriptors of the activity of teachers reflect a progressive bureaucratization of the organization of the school.*

As hosts of social theoreticians have pointed out, with a special nod to Weber,[27] Western society has been marked by a progressive bureaucratization of most of its social institutions. Particularly, this is evident in the routinization of behavior within the organzation, a general apathy toward the acceptance of responsibility, an inability to respond to human needs, and a sense that the "system" is all-powerful and individualization or personalization is impossible within it.

24. Ibid.
25. John Dewey, *Democracy and Education* (New York: Macmillan Co., 1916).
26. Ibid.
27. Max Weber, *The Theory of Social and Economic Organization,* trans. A. M. Henderson and Talcott Parsons (New York: Free Press, 1968).

As organizations become bureaucratic, it becomes very difficult to make changes, *except* by imposing them through systematic modification of routine operations performed by many individuals —a bureaucratic method through which bureaucracy co-opts the innovator.

The schools have not been equipped to make changes even in this manner (probably only the most progressive industries or the most authoritarian governments are so equipped) and they became bureaucratic, therefore, and bureaucracy produced obsolescence. For the bureaucratization tended to freeze the operation of the school around behaviors which had been created for former generations, and which, while they *might* have had applicability to those generations, promised less and less as time went on. (It is easy to see why forward-looking educators frequently occupy themselves trying to make the "system" more "progressive," that is, *able* to change through efficient administrative action.)

Bureaucratization has brought the schools into a serious conflict with most of the prescriptive curriculum theories. (Prescriptive theory describes what *should* be done, while descriptive theory describes what will probably happen if certain conditions obtain.) Nearly all prescriptive theorists have advocated that the learner understand what he is trying to learn, that he share in the making of at least some of the rules of his education, and that the teacher be sensitive and personal in his dealings with the student. These are exactly the opposite of bureaucratic behavior. The bureaucrat becomes insensitive, puts the organization ahead of the individual, and sees authority as external to the participants in the situation.

This has resulted in a curious phenomenon—that of the curriculum specialist advocating personalized educational procedures, while the bureaucratic staff replies in impersonal terms which are not comparable to those used by curriculum workers. On the one hand, the specialist asks things like, "Why don't you organize the students into a democracy and help the democracy identify important social problems and educate itself by trying to learn about those problems and do something about them?" The teacher replies, "How would I ever manage that kind of circus? It's all I can do to manage the kids when I keep them working at their seats." Or, in the same vein, the specialist says, "Teach the kids to read through experience stories or by helping them select the books they will read." And the teacher replies, "How am I going to get these kids through the fundamentals if I waste a lot of time helping them make up stories?" And so it goes. On the one hand, we find the curriculum establishment preaching induction, child-centeredness, and problem-solving, and on the other side we find the practitioner facing the practical problems of his days and wondering why the curricularist is not more practical. The curriculum worker replies, "But I *am* practical. You *can* teach personally and inductively."

Differences are usually resolved in favor of the practitioner. A good case in point is teacher education where there is a blinding unanimity that the "most valuable component of the program is student teaching."[28] It is not surprising that unanimity occurs with respect to this. The school favors it because it inducts the new teacher into the bureaucracy. He learns to manage children, cope with supply problems, and contribute to order. The colleges like it because it is cheap to administer and because it passes the burden of teaching clinical skills directly to the schools, relieving the colleges of preparing really effective programs. The future teachers like it because it prepares them to cope with the forces that are most real in their world—the bureaucracy and children.

That student teaching socializes the student teacher to bureaucratic behavior should not be disputed casually. My associates and I have conducted four developmental studies of the teaching styles of student teachers. All have included the following findings: student teachers reward children verbally much less by the end of student teaching than at the beginning (only one-half as much, in fact); they come to ask fewer questions and fewer open questions proportionally (about 20 percent less); and they plan cooperatively with children about half as often by the time student teaching is over as they did when it began.[29]

28. For the unique contribution of student teaching, see Florence B. Stratemeyer and Margaret Lindsey, *Working with Student Teachers* (New York: Teachers College Press, 1958), p. 50.

29. Clark Brown, "The Relationship of Initial Teaching Styles and Selected Variables in Student Teaching," Ed.D. dissertation, Teachers College, Columbia University, 1967; Marvin Seperson, "A Study of the Influence of Teaching Style of Cooperating Teachers on the Teaching Style of Student Teachers," Ed.D. dissertation, Teachers College, Columbia University, 1970.

Thus, in teacher education, we find the mechanism for perpetuating the bureaucracy. However, many forward-looking teacher-educators hope that a way can be found to debureaucratize the system or at least humanize it at the point of teacher training.[30]

## Negative Thesis Number Three

*The school reflects the status system operating in the society as a whole. This alienates both young people and minority groups from education, although the reasons differ.*

George Counts, in his famous essay, has a marvelous passage which embodies his conviction that the curriculum leaders of the Progressive education movement have been unable to free themselves from the unthinking acting out of status values, especially the upper-middle-class version. His quote is particularly relevant to humanistic educators, for the now much maligned Progressive educators represented the first massive humanistic movement in American education. The fate of Progressive education should be a powerful warning to contemporary humanists in education.

The weakness of Progressive Education thus lies in the fact that it has elaborated no theory of social welfare, unless it be that of anarchy or extreme individualism. In this, of course, it is but reflecting the viewpoint of the members of the liberal-minded upper middle class who send their children to the Progressive schools—persons who are fairly well-off, who have abandoned the faiths of their fathers, who assume an agnostic attitude towards all important questions, who pride themselves on their open-mindedness and tolerance, who favor in a mild sort of way fairly liberal programs of social reconstruction, who are full of good will and humane sentiment, who have vague aspirations for world peace and human brotherhood, who can be counted upon to respond moderately to any appeal made in the name of charity, who are genuinely distressed at the sight of *unwonted* forms of cruelty, misery, and suffering, and who perhaps serve to soften somewhat the bitter clashes of those real forces that govern the world; but who, in spite of all their good qualities, have no deep and abiding loyalties, possess no convictions for which they would sacrifice overmuch, would find it hard to live without their customary material comforts, are rather insensitive to the accepted forms of social injustice, are content to play the role of interested spectator in the drama of human history, refuse to see reality in its harsher and more disagreeable forms, rarely move outside the pleasant circles of the class to which they belong, and in the day of severe trial will follow the lead

30. Stratemeyer and Lindsey, *Working with Student Teachers*.

of the most powerful and respectable forces in society and at the same time find good reasons for so doing. These people have shown themselves entirely incapable of dealing with any of the great crises of our time—war, prosperity, or depression. At bottom they are romantic sentimentalists, but with a sharp eye on the main chance. That they can be trusted to write our education theories and shape our educational programs is highly improbable.

Among the members of this class the number of children is small, the income relatively high, and economic functions of the home greatly reduced. For these reasons an inordinate emphasis on the child and child interests is entirely welcome to them. They wish to guard their offspring from too strenuous endeavor and from coming into too intimate contact with the grimmer aspects of industrial society. They wish their sons and daughters to succeed according to standards of their class and to be a credit to their parents. At heart feeling themselves members of a superior human strain, they do not want their children to mix too freely with the children of the poor or of the less fortunate races. Nor do they want them to accept radical social doctrines, espouse unpopular causes, or lose themselves in quest of any Holy Grail. According to their views education should deal with life, but with life at a distance or in a highly diluted form. They would generally maintain that life should be kept at arm's length if it should not be handled with a poker.

If Progressive Education is to be genuinely progressive it must emancipate itself from the influence of this class, face squarely and courageously every social issue, come to grips with life in all of its stark reality, establish an organic relation with the community, develop a realistic and comprehensive theory or welfare, fashion a compelling and challenging vision of human destiny, and become less frightened than it is today at the bogies of *imposition* and *indoctrination*. In a word, Progressive Education cannot place its trust in a child-centered school.[31]

We agree with Counts that the reform movements of the century have been compatible with the middle class he describes, if not, in fact, initiated entirely by them. The main thrusts of school improvement have been toward one or another of three middle-class value orientations. One has been toward the bland child-centeredness Counts characterized above. Another has been toward the values of the academic community (as with the recent "academic reform movement").[32] A third has been in the form of a compensatory education aimed at reducing class differences by co-opting the child

31. George Counts, *Dare the Schools Build a New Social Order?* (New York: John Day & Co., 1932), pp. 7-10.

32. Goodlad, *Curriculum Reform.*

toward upward mobility (as in the Bloom-Davis-Hess approach).[33]

There is, however, a much more dramatic way that the school has been co-opted by the status system. It has been most dramatically expressed by Edgar Z. Friedenberg in *Coming of Age in America*.[34]

Friedenberg argues that an open society, that is, one in which the status hierarchy can be penetrated by an upwardly mobile individual, and a society which also is technological, one in which status derives partly from technical achievement and capacity, places enormous pressure on youth. If they are to rise in status (or to maintain the status of their parents), they must become technically proficient. As they drive themselves toward technical proficiency, they find that they are using themselves as instrumentalities. They are seeking their education, not for greater growth alone but for the instrumental value it will have, and they are spending their youth, not on the development of their individualization and humanistic potential, but on homogenizing themselves in a technical way so that they can benefit from the possibilities of upward mobility. Furthermore, they are locked early into a competitive system which pits them against their peers and makes their studies an instrument not of cooperation but of relative success potential. By permitting itself to be locked into the vocational preparation business, the school has come to be almost completely dominated by the status system. Its academic studies have been turned almost entirely into instrumental rather than intrinsic currency. Its practical studies have become a second track for the nonmobile.

The effect of the status orientation of the school has been to alienate many large groups from it. It has alienated the school from the intellectual, who recoils from the idea that the curricula at each level are organized to prepare the student for the level that is to come, rather than for idea development on its own terms. The consequences of poor preparation at one level carry such a heavy economic penalty by shutting the doors at the high levels that the academically unswift are alienated (if not destroyed) in the

33. Benjamin S. Bloom, Allison Davis, and Robert Hess, *Compensatory Education for Cultural Deprivation* (Chicago: Department of Education, University of Chicago, 1964).

34. Edgar Z. Friedenberg, *Coming of Age in America* (New York: Vantage Books, 1963).

process. Since academic ability and social class are positively related, another effect has been to destroy the confidence of lower-class members in the very scholastic system that seemingly has proffered escape from the bottom of the opportunity barrel, but has actually denied them escape because it was locked into the opportunity system.

The curriculum field specifically has been co-opted by the status system in a number of ways. First, it has learned to speak the language of sequence, prerequisite, and mastery. Curriculum guides can hardly be written in such liberal terms that they do not seem to imply that the studies listed for the younger children are essentials for preparation for the work to be given the older children. (The status ladder becomes an academic ladder!) Separate curriculum areas for vocations, for commercial training for girls, and for college preparation have appeared and are rationalized by the field. Evaluation has become a high art, and the curriculum field abounds in ways that evaluation can be used within curriculum frameworks to reinforce and extend status differences.[35] The languages of curriculum are those of academic status-seeking (consider the phrases, "modes of inquiry," "structure of the discipline," "behavioral evidence").

For the curriculum field it is probably even more devastating that the status implications of progress in schooling have created such enormous pressure that it is very difficult to bring about any kind of curriculum change unless the public is satisfied that it will not affect the status probabilities for its children. If we try to change a mathematics curriculum in one suburb, for example, the parents will be afraid that the change will not be reflected in Educational Testing Services activities and, thus, that their children may be disadvantaged compared with those students from another suburb whose curriculum might be admittedly less relevant to the students and the times, but might be more relevant to the examinations on which the gateways to status so heavily depend. The curriculum theorist frequently responds to this problem by stating that specific

35. See James Coleman, *Equality of Educational Opportunity* (Washington: U.S. Office of Education, 1966). The evidence, however, should not be used as an indication that the measurement arts should not be practiced—measurement has become remarkably scientific. What is vulnerable is the uses of measurement, as when states restrict certain institutions of higher education to students of a certain achievement level, thus effectively closing those schools to lower-status students.

preparation for examinations does not affect the results very much, so parents and teachers should not worry about the effects of change. But no parent is likely to listen for long, and small wonder: if one believed that education did not affect performance on the examinations, it would be only a short step to accepting the proposition that education really does not matter very much in *any* way.

What about Negative Thesis Number Three—that the school has become locked into the caste system and thus has alienated the black community? The curriculum field was victimized by a number of kinds of understandable blindness in this case. When the specialist advocated the small neighborhood school, he was trying to personalize education—he did not intend to cooperate with de facto segregation. And yet he did so cooperate by such advocacy. When he wrote the social studies textbooks that ignored the plight of the black[36] and pretended that racial prejudice was on the way out as *enlightenment* progressed, he did not mean to alienate anyone. Yet he wrote those books and, if he was a professor, he recommended that they be purchased and taught courses on how to use them. If he was a curriculum director, he served on committees that adopted them. If he was a teacher, he more than likely used them. And now everybody knows what was done. It likely will be a number of years before many black people forgive the curriculum specialist for having cooperated in what they regard (and who can blame them) as a racist conspiracy.

Now, I think that no group would be more justifiably resentful of being called racist than the curriculum field members, among whom are some extremely "liberal" people. But the fact is that they *have* cooperated, tacitly at least, in what is now generally regarded as a racist activity, with the effect that it is going to be exceedingly difficult for them to regain credence in the black community. Also, this mistrust makes it difficult for the curriculum community to assist in the development of the community school districts in black areas or to make acceptable recommendations about the form that compensatory education should take. For one example, it is clear now that many of the black communities resist any form of compensatory education. They have come to believe that a different

36. James P. Shaver, "The Evaluation of Textbooks: A Curious Responsibility," *School Review* 74 (1966): 323-31.

education from that of the whites will prevent them from achieving within society. In other words, the view of many blacks is that they have been given a form of "compensatory education" all along, but a form which has kept them down rather than one which has helped them. Because of the general deterioration of ghetto schools and their education programs, they are able to bring some powerful rational arguments to the support of this position. We curriculum specialists, "liberal" almost to a man, are in a very bad position, and this includes both blacks and whites among us.

### THE IMPORT OF THE NEGATIVE THESES

The three general complexes of factors mentioned in the negative theses have interacted and it is worthwhile that we consider them together, for they have had a combined effect much greater than if they had been independent of each other. To begin with, by restricting most of its considerations to the existing type of school and the existing types of teacher roles, the curriculum field has greatly restricted its possibilities. Learning theories and educational ideas which did not fit into the current school or which did not seem feasible in terms of its teachers have tended to be neglected, if not actually rejected. In other words, nearly the entire curriculum field has operated under a self-imposed system for limiting the range of imagination it could express. This has been compounded by the increasing bureaucratization of the school in that many of the recommendations by curriculum specialists have, because the theorist was attempting to gear himself to the "real world of the school," become bureaucratic in nature. *In its very attempts to be relevant, the curriculum field has been co-opted by the very bureaucratic forces it opposes.* Since the bureaucracy of the schools has become directed along technical routes within the economic and status system, Negative Thesis One times Negative Thesis Two times Negative Thesis Three equals a proposition something like this: that the social status aspect of the society has co-opted schools which in turn have co-opted curriculum approaches. The effect has been to undermine the confidence of young people and minority groups in the professional educator and also to channel many of the recommendations of the curriculum specialist so that they have had effects almost opposite to those which were originally intended. By not developing sources or criticism independent of school-relatedness, we have been unable to put brakes on this process.

Many of the leaders of the curriculum field have seen all these things happening and have struggled against them. The concern of the curriculum field has been turned in general toward a more child-centered education (a more nonbureaucratic focus), which makes good sense as an antidote to the impersonal education in practice. The child-centered philosophy, however, did not easily mesh with academic reform. As a consequence, the highly energetic academic reform movement of the 1950s and early 1960s[37] took a great measure of influence away from the curriculum field as we usually think of it. The academic curriculum-makers were often people who were not curriculum specialists, nor in many cases had they been curriculum practitioners. In effect, a new curriculum field grew up alongside the old one. It was dominated by people who approached curriculum in an intuitive, matter-of-fact way with an emphasis on engineering procedures. They tended to examine the nature of the discipline, to develop particular ways of structuring that discipline for students, and to proceed immediately into the creation of materials, because they felt that through materials they could influence instruction more quickly and efficiently than in any other way. They were ruthless about publicizing their products and effective in creating inducements that brought teachers to their workshops. Presently they dominate the production of instructional materials in most of the academic fields and they continue to operate largely without reference to the "old" curriculum field, but tend to communicate directly with the schools through their own channels (chiefly those of materials procurement and in-service education) rather than through the organizations of professional curriculum workers.

While it has brought new energy and material into education, the academic reform movement has at the same time played directly into the hands of the status system. It has created curricula *very* appropriate for the talented from the middle class (in the sense of preparing them for later academic success) but almost totally alienating for others, at least on the surface. The curriculum specialist, awed by the products of the academic reform movement but

37. Goodlad, *Curriculum Reform.*

rejected by its leaders, has stood by helplessly or has been co-opted into disseminating its products.

To compound the problem for the curriculum field, the most vocal complainers about education have recommended the same remedies which the curriculum field found ineffective. Holt, Kozol, Kohl, Coles, Hentoff,[38] and others have made their way, in violet if not purple prose, to the center of the current stage, reiterating child-centered philosophies created years before by mainstream curriculum specialists (but generally not mentioning their predecessors!)[39]

*The silver lining.* We hope that no one regards what we have written thus far as pessimistic. *We* view it as positive. We *have* to recognize the problems in order to rebuild a curriculum-planning field that can effectively serve humanistic ends. For the field is in disrepair. It has lost much of its influence and much of its visible leadership. The field is without a distinctive technology and teachers and others are aware of this fact. *But what curriculum workers do have is a broad interest in schooling as a whole. Whether curriculum directors or researchers, they are bound together by this interest in schooling, and by the belief that it is possible to develop a reasoned body of knowledge about how to go about improving education, and a desire to use education to improve the quality of life. To rebuild the field and revitalize its humanism will require a vigorous program of action that avoids the bureaucratic linearity of schooling and creates a responsive institution devoted to the revitalization of the culture.*

## Part II: Positive Proposition for the Improvement of the Field

Let us turn now to the task of creating a different sort of future for the curriculum worker than history would lead us to expect and consider a set of propositions by which a different type of field might be developed. These propositions are intended to constitute the basis on which a technology of curriculum could be developed —one which would enable curriculum workers to set out the spe-

38. John Holt, *How Children Fail* (New York: Pitman Publishing Corp., 1964) ; Kozol, *Death at an Early Age;* Kohl, *Thirty-six Children;* Coles, *Children of Crises;* Nat Hentoff, *Our Children Are Dying* (New York: Viking Press, 1966).

39. *New York Times Annual Education Review,* January 12, 1970, pp. 48-84.

cifications for responsive, humanistic types of educations and non-bureaucratic institutions which could sustain and revitalize them *and* which would also enable curriculum workers to create these types of education and institutions.

## Positive Proposition Number One

*The curriculum field should develop a set of working, engineering theories about the improvement of education. We need some generic engineering theories that can embrace many different types of education missions and many different kinds of strategies for reaching them. In addition, we need sets of subtheories, which deal with particular assumptive worlds, particular media, and are addressed to particular types of educational problems.*

These working theories need to be institutionless in the sense that they do not assume that any particular type of institution and teacher will characterize the settings in which education will take place.

Because we have worked so long within the confines of the school as an institution and of the teacher role as usually defined, this task will not be easy, for most existing curriculum theory and subtheories are straightjacketed by the existing structure of the school and the ubiquitous teacher role. What we need to erect are sets of engineering propositions which can be used to bring about a wide variety of educational environments, including the institutional forms which can nurture them. To build these propositions we can draw upon some general tools and some specific ones.

### GENERAL TOOLS FOR CURRICULUM WORKERS

Some general program-planning tools can be applied to the development of engineering propositions. For instance, "systems"-planning procedures can be turned to this end if they are used to generate alternative goals and means rather than to identify the most economical path to given ends. A promising example of systems generation of alternatives is in the United States Office of Education Teacher Education Project. In that project, ten institutions were funded to develop (independently) the specifications for conceptual models of elementary-teacher education programs. Each of the ten teams applied roughly the same steps to planning (development of performance models, development of component specifications, analysis of support system needs, specification of management systems, and so on). The result was a variety of alternative conceptions of teachers, teacher education programs, and implementation plans that open up rather than restrict the possibilities of program planning in teacher education. This experience is encouraging in that it illustrates that systems procedures, the curriculum field's most powerful program-planning tool, can be used to generate more options. This application of systematic planning needs serious exploration,[40] for the curriculum field has long normed on a few curriculum alternatives rather than generating wide ranges of solidly rooted, testable possibilities.

### SPECIFIC TOOLS

In addition to the use of general tools like systems planning, specific theories and paradigms from the behavioral and social sciences can be drawn upon for the development of engineering theories which are useful for particular purposes. Some of these theories can be applied to particular educational problems. For example, Hunt has developed paradigms for applying psychological principles to the problem of developing procedures for personalizing instruction with resulting "differential training models" which can be used to prescribe optimal learning environments when a number of student characteristics are considered simultaneously.[41] Other work should lay the basis for general technological development. An example of such is Joyce and Joyce's[42] development and use of information support systems for elementary school children.

### VERY SPECIFIC TOOLS

Some of the engineering models can be built for achieving particular educational missions with specific teaching strategies. To consider the possibilities, let us look at several classes of educational

40. Joel L. Burden and Kaliopee Lanzillotti, *A Reader's Guide to the Comprehensive Models for Preparing Elementary Teachers* (Washington: ERIC Clearinghouse on Teacher Education, December 1969); Bruce R. Joyce, "Variations on a Systems Theme," *Interchange* (in press for fall, 1970).

41. David E. Hunt, "A Conceptual Level Matching Model for Coordinating Learner Characteristics with Educational Approaches," *Interchange* 1 (June 1970).

42. Bruce R. Joyce and Elizabeth Joyce, "Creating Information Systems for Children," *Interchange* 1 (June 1970).

missions and some of the strategies which are available and provide hypothetical and testable structures for achieving them.

*The mission of an educational program can be defined in terms of the domains through which it (the program) enters into the life of the student. Since education is an attempt to enter one's life and change it, the product of education can always be seen in terms of a developed capacity to respond to reality in new ways. The primary task in selecting an educational mission is to identify the domains through which the program will enter the life of the learner in order to change his responses to living in the world.*

The possible domains of missions[43] can be divided into three categories, with the caution that they overlap somewhat: (a) we can attempt to improve the capacity of the learner through direct intervention in the personal domain (as through a direct attempt to develop his creativity, or to influence his capacities for self-initiative and self-direction); (b) we can attempt to enter the social domain, then change him at a point where he is in interaction with his fellowman (as when we attempt to teach him social or economic skills); or (c) we can attempt to reach him through an academic domain, by teaching him academic skills and ways of dealing intellectually with complexity (as when we attempt to teach him the social sciences). Although these domains are not mutually exclusive (personal creativity, for example, may be an avenue to improve interpersonal and academic performance), we can use these three categories, the personal, the social, and the academic, to sort out some of the possible functions of education. For each mission we can attempt to design engineering principles for building programs to achieve them. For example, Rogers,[44] Maslow,[45] and others have developed approaches for achieving missions in the personal domain. The National Training Laboratory,[46] among others, has worked out principles to apply to the interper-

43. This description of educational missions has been amplified in Bruce R. Joyce, *Alternative Models for Elementary Education* (Waltham, Mass.: Blaisdell Publishing Co., 1969).

44. Carl Rogers, *Client-Centered Therapy* (Boston: Houghton-Mifflin Co., 1951).

45. Abraham Maslow, *Toward a Psychology of Being* (Princeton: D. Van Nostrand & Co., 1962).

46. Leland R. Bradford, Jack Gibb, and Kenneth Benne, eds., *T-Group Theory and Laboratory Method* (New York: John Wiley & Sons, 1964).

sonal domain. Psychologists Ausubel,[47] Piaget,[48] and others have developed theoretical structures from which engineering propositions in the academic domain can be developed, and developers like Schwab,[49] and Taba,[50] and Suchman[51] have developed engineering propositions with which academic missions can be approached.

The types of educational missions which can be imagined are numerous indeed, as are the possible means which might be used to achieve them. Some means are probably applicable to more than one mission and some missions would require a combination of means. Basic tasks of the curriculum workers are the clarification of missions, the identification of means which are potentially relevant to them, and the conduct of research to develop an empirically verified matrix. Such an array will be complex, because nearly all means will produce a range of effects which will vary by student and many other factors. Nearly every set of means will turn out to produce differential effects on students and thus will require a differential model a la Hunt's, which can guide its application.[52]

The result of this work should be an array of developed curriculum theories which can be applied to educational problems. Figure 1 displays the possible results of such an enterprise.

47. David Ausubel, *The Psychology of Meaningful Verbal Learning* (New York: Grune & Stratton, 1963).

48. For curriculum strategies built on Piaget's work, see: Edmund Sullivan, "Piaget and the School Curriculum: A Critical Appraisal," Bulletin #2 of the Ontario Institute for Studies in Education, 1967; Irving Siegel, "The Piagetian System and the World of Education," in David Elkind and John Flavell, eds., *Studies in Cognitive Development* (New York: Oxford University Press, 1969); Hanne Sonquist, Constance Kamii, and Louise Derman, "A Piaget-Derived Preschool Curriculum" to be published in I. J. Athey and D. O. Rubadeau, eds., *Educational Implications of Piaget's Theory: A Book of Readings* (Waltham, Mass.: Blaisdell Publishing Co., in press).

49. Joseph Schwab, ed., *The Biology Teacher's Handbook* (New York: John Wiley & Sons, 1965).

50. Hilda Taba, *Teaching Strategies and Cognitive Functioning in Elementary School Children,* Cooperative Research Project No. 2404 (San Francisco: San Francisco State College, 1961).

51. J. Richard Suchman, *The Elementary School Training Program in Scientific Inquiry,* Report of U.S. Office Education Project Title VIII Project No. 216 (Urbana: University of Illinois, 1962).

52. Hunt's work as it has become more generic has provided us with a structure for generating differential models. See Hunt, "Conceptual Level Matching Model."

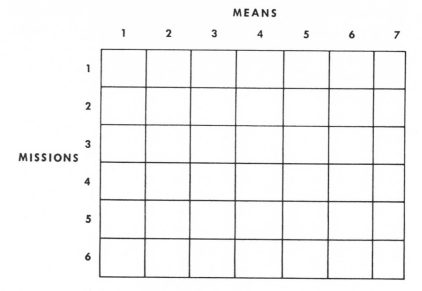

Fig. 1. Missions-means matrix

## GROUPS OF APPROACHES

It is possible to group the theoreticians on the basis of their shared points of departure and conceptions of the nature of human beings and of what constitutes human development. At least four groupings based on orientations of approaches seem warranted, and others will no doubt emerge when and if an array of well-developed engineering theories emerge.

(1) One of these groups can be referred to as "personalists" and includes theoreticians and practitioners who focus primarily on the individual's construction of his own reality. Thus they focus on the development of the individual or on some particular characteristics which affect his personality or his general ways of relating to the world. Therapists, especially, tend to share a concern for the distinctive ways each person constructs his world—they see human nature in terms of individual persons.

(2) The second family consists of educational theorists and practitioners who focus on the processes by which groups and societies negotiate rules and construct social reality. Some of these individuals see education as a process of improving the society.

Many of them have suggested an ideal model for society and procedures for creating an education which can help to bring that model into existence. Others who emphasize social behavior concentrate on interpersonal relations and the dynamics of improving them. The approaches to education in either case have distinctly social character.

(3) A third category consists of educational theoreticians and practitioners who are concerned with affecting the information processing system of the student. It includes those who have developed educational procedures designed to increase general thinking capacity (as the capacity to think abstractly or to think inductively). It also includes those whose focus is on ways of teaching students to process information about specific aspects of life. For example, many educational theorists believe that a major mission of education is to develop approaches to the teaching of the academic disciplines so that the student learns to process information in the ways that the academic scholar processes it and thus achieves the intellectual power of scholarship.

(4) A fourth group focuses on the processes by which human behavior is externally shaped and reinforced. The dominant theorist in this area is B. F. Skinner, and his major efforts have been devoted to understanding the shaping of human behavior and how education can be built on an understanding of processes.

It is to these four groups that curriculum workers can turn for ideas about educational means. On the following table there appears a list of some educational theorists and approaches from each of the four categories, grouped according to the domains of mission for which they appear most readily applicable.

The very partial list of approaches (Table 1) is presented simply to provide concrete illustrations of the really formidable array of ideas about how to educate people which can be drawn on by the curriculum worker in order to develop the engineering propositions that should constitute his technology. Many of the ideas have already been well developed into implementable teaching strategies. Others are relatively undeveloped. In general, the road to engineering propositions begins with a theory (or idea which is not yet a theory), is carried into specification as an educational environment or teaching strategy (or we might begin with a strategy or

TABLE 1

A List of Educational Approaches,
Grouped by Orientation and Domain of Mission

| Approach | Major Theorist | Orientation (Person, Social Interaction, Information Processing, or Behavior Modification) | Missions for Which Applicable |
|---|---|---|---|
| 1) Non-directive | Carl Rogers[a] | Person | Development into "fully functioning" individual (however, broad applicability is suggested, for personal development includes all aspects of growth). |
| 2) Awareness training | Schutz,[b] Perls[c] | Person | Increasing personal capacity. Much emphasis on interpersonal contact as well as personal development. |
| 3) Group investigation | Dewey,[d] Thelen[e] | Social interaction | Social relations are permanent, but personal development and academic rigor are included. |
| 4) Reflective thinking and social inquiry | Hullfish and Smith[f] | Social interaction | Improvement of democratic process is central, with more effective thinking the primary route. |
| 5) Inductive reasoning | Taba,[g] Suchman[h] and others | Information processing | Primarily designed to teach academic reasoning, but used for social and personal goals as well. |
| 6) Logical reasoning | Extrapolations from Piaget[i] | Information processing | Programs designed to increase thinking, but also are applied to moral development and other areas (see Kohlberg[j] for example). |
| 7) Psychoanalytic | See Tyler[k] and others; also, A.S. Neill[l] | Person | Personal emotional development is primary and would take precedence. |

TABLE 1 (cont'd)

| Approach | Major Theorist | Orientation | Missions for Which Applicable |
|---|---|---|---|
| 8) Creative reasoning | Torrance,[m] Getzels and Jackson[n] | Person | Personal development of creativity in problem-solving has priority, but creative problem-solving in social and academic domains is also emphasized. |
| 9) Academic modes | Much of the curriculum reform movement[o] (see especially Schwab[p] and Bruner[q] for rationales) | Information processing | Designed to teach the research system of the disciplines, but also expected to have effect in other domains (e.g., sociological methods may be taught in order to increase social understanding and problem-solving). |
| 10) Programmed instruction | Skinner[r] | Behavior modification and theory | General applicability —a domain-free approach. |
| 11) Conceptual systems matching model | D. E. Hunt[s] | Person | An approach designed to increase personal complexity and flexibility. |

a. Rogers, *Client-Centered Therapy.*
b. William Schutz, *Joy: Expanding Human Awareness* (New York: Grove Press, 1967).
c. Fritz Perls, *Gestalt Therapy: Excitement and Growth in Human Personality* (New York: Dell Publishing Co., 1965).
d. Dewey, *Democracy and Education.*
e. Herbert A. Thelen, *Education and the Human Quest* (New York: Harper & Bros., 1960).
f. H. Gordon Hullfish and Phillip Smith, *Reflective Thinking: The Method of Education* (New York: Dodd, Mead & Co., 1961).
g. Taba, *Teaching Strategies.*
h. Suchman, *Elementary School Training Program.*
i. Sullivan, "Piaget and the Curriculum"; Siegel, "Piagetian System."
j. Lawrence Kohlberg, "Moral Education in the Schools," *School Review* 74 (1966): 1-30.
k. Louise Tyler, "A Case History: Formulation of Objectives from a Psychoanalytic Framework." *Instructional Objectives* AERA Monograph No. 3 (Washington: National Education Association, 1969).
l. Neill, *Summerhill.*
m. E. Paul Torrance, *Guiding Creative Behavior* (Englewood Cliffs, N.J.: Prentice-Hall, 1962).
n. Jacob W. Getzels and Philip W. Jackson, *Creativity and Intelligence: Explorations with Gifted Students* (New York: John Wiley & Sons, 1962).
o. Goodlad, *Curriculum Reform.*
p. Schwab, *Biology Teacher's Handbook.*
q. Jerome S. Bruner, *The Process of Education* (Cambridge: Harvard University Press, 1960).
r. B. F. Skinner, *Verbal Behavior* (New York: Appleton-Century-Crofts, 1957).
s. Hunt, "Conceptual Level Matching Model."

activity), and is then ready for the development of engineering propositions.

The curriculum worker might, for example, begin with an idea about how mental development can be stimulated, work that idea into a specification of the kinds of environment (including teaching behaviors) that could be created to test the idea, and then proceed to develop propositions about how to bring that environment into existence.

### DESIGNING CURRICULUMS

One might build a curriculum around a single strategy or environment, or around a combination of them. Single-model curriculums are fairly common, but more complex approaches are also used and probably should be used more than they are. The Contra Costa County, California, social studies curriculum designed by Hilda Taba[53] used inductive teaching strategies as the models for most of the curriculum activities. Unit of instruction were constructed around the inductive paradigm, and specific lessons within the units were built on the inductive teaching models as well. Through the collection of data and its analysis, it was assumed that many facts would be learned and that, at the same time, inductive skills would be taught. In addition, the community of students working together in induction would develop the interpersonal skills appropriate for a democratic society and for vigorous scholarly analysis.

Quite a number of educational programs using behavior modification strategies have been designed. A very good example of these is the Individually Prescribed Instruction curriculums developed at the Research and Development Center at the University of Pittsburgh, which uses a variety of approaches but is characterized by liberal use of programmed instruction.[54]

Comprehensive systems-planning using behavior-modification strategies has recently been applied to the development of the teacher education curriculum. Michigan State University, for example, developed curricula, each of which is accompanied by an

53. Taba, *Teaching Strategies.*

54. Individually Prescribed Instruction, Learning Research and Development Center, University of Pittsburgh, Pittsburgh, Pa.

instructional module of a particular kind. All of these have been summarized and are stored in a computer retrieval system.[55]

This system is joined to a general management system which operates very much like the IPI system. Each student is tested and a developmental profile is created for him, on the basis of which he is placed on certain developmental paths within the curriculum. As he proceeds through the curriculum, further evaluation is made, on the basis of which he again works through segments of the program or moves into its higher levels. Gradually, he builds up the sets of behaviors that make up the expected competencies of the teacher as specified in the program.

Models drawn from the disciplines have been used in recent years to structure quite a number of curriculums. Such a model was used to structure the Biological Sciences Study Committee curriculum and similar models have been used to structure curriculums in such diverse areas as social psychology for elementary school children, anthropology for secondary school students, and in many other academic areas.[56]

"Group investigation" has been used to structure a good many curriculums. Especially, theoreticians have recommended that courses in social studies be structured around cooperative inquiry because of its promise to provide practice in democratic life, and this promises the development of social skills, societal knowledge, and democratic values more or less simultaneously. John U. Michaelis, whose book *Social Studies for Children in a Democracy*[57] is by far the most widely used methods textbook in the social studies for the elementary school, advocates a democratic process method as the central strategy in the social studies. He recommends that the teacher organize the students into a miniature democracy and that this democracy inquire into the society, attacking and probing those problems which puzzle the children, who thus acquire (a) knowledge about the society, (b) problem-solving skills, (c)

55. G. Wesley Sowards, project manager, *Behavioral Science: Elementary Teacher Education Program,* Michigan State University, ED-027-205, 6, 7 (Washington: U.S. Office of Education, 1968).

56. Goodlad, *Curriculum Reform.*

57. John U. Michaelis, *Social Studies for Children in a Democracy: Recent Trends and Developments,* 3d ed. (Englewood Cliffs, N.J.: Prentice-Hall, 1963).

democratic process skills, and (d) commitment to democracy, more or less simultaneously.

Curriculum workers need to develop clarity about the entire array of alternatives which are available and to codify knowledge about what is needed to make these alternatives operable. The creation of multistrategy curriculums which provide different avenues for differing teachers needs to be comfortably within the engineering capacity of the curriculum worker.

Curriculum design is not sufficient, however. A curriculum comes alive only when it is embodied in an institution, and the ability to create institutions should be a major competence of our future curriculum workers.

## Positive Proposition Number Two

*We need to develop generic and specific institutional development theories and engineering techniques for creating institutions.*

Given the specifications for an educational environment, our field needs to be able to speak to the creation of institutional forms which embody that environment. Thus we need techniques for developing and evaluating environments in terms of their presumed functions. As part of this, we need to learn how to train people who can build "partial institutions" around particular educational missions and means. Generally speaking, curriculum theory has been addressed to an institution which is responsible for nearly all the education of a child. It is possible to build much smaller institutions having much more limited functions, and we shall refer to these as "partial" institutions.

In other words, we need sets of studies about how human institutions work and how they can be created and modified and evaluated. Where our culture does not provide us with general information from which to work, we must produce it for ourselves. To do this we need stronger linkage to the theoretical and engineering work of scholars in the behavioral sciences. Such studies as the Smiths' investigation of the effects of school-building design,[58] Hunt's analysis of the training environment created in Upward

58. Louis Smith and Ruth P. Smith, *Social Psychological Aspects of School Building Design*, Cooperative Research Report No. S-223 (Washington, D.C.: U.S. Office of Education, 1967).

Bound programs,[59] Sullivan's analysis[60] of developmental psychological theories and their implications for education, and the sets of engineering studies by people such as Walter Borg at the Far West Laboratory at Berkeley[61] are exemplars of the kinds of things we need to link to if we are going to move ourselves in the direction of acquiring a sufficient set of empirically based theories about the creation of educational environments and educational institutions.

*The purpose of the curriculum field is to develop general knowledge about how to bring educational missions and means together in the real world. It is the creation of particular kinds of educational reality that is our business. These realities demand the ability to specify missions, to specify the means that will accomplish those missions, and to specify the engineering necessary to create the material, the social systems, and the instructional systems that will actuate them. By freeing ourselves from the school and from the traditional teacher role, we shall be able to consider a vastly greater array of alternatives than has hitherto been the case. Similarly, by conducting experimental studies in the creation of specific kinds of institutional environments, we shall be able to free ourselves from dependence on an environment created more or less by chance for us and one which is practically impossible to change.*

We need to develop laboratories in institutional development. We have the need for an institutional laboratory in which we can study the nature of the school as an institution and the nature of institutional creation and in which we can learn to do the kind of training mentioned in Positive Proposition Number Two. If we do not learn how to create institutional forms (and it should be asserted now that we do not at present know how to do this), we will be tied to the existing schools and the existing teachers, and we will suffer, we think quite properly, stigmatization of young people, social reformers, the blacks, and thoughtful Americans in

59. David E. Hunt and Robert H. Hardt, "The Role of Conceptual Level and Program Structure in Summer Upward Bound Programs," (Paper presented at the meeting of the Eastern Psychological Association, Boston, 1967).

60. Edmund Sullivan, "Developmental and Contemporaneous Differences and Their Role in Curriculum Decision-Making and Teacher Training," in *Teacher Education: Prespectives for Reformation,* Bruce R. Joyce and Marsha Weil, eds. To be published by Prentice-Hall.

61. Walter R. Borg, "The Minicourse as a Vehicle for Changing Teacher Behavior, the Research Evidence," ED-029-809 (Washington: U.S. Office of Education, 1969).

general. Our laboratory need not be a place, but rather a coalition which explores the creation of various kinds of institutional forms. Some of these forms should be highly technical in character, others should be very untechnical but be characterized by species of human relations that are rarely seen. We should learn how to create institutions that look like Esalen and institutions that resemble an airline-pilot training laboratory. We should learn how to create an educational form around an idea, a theory, a piece of hardware, the possibility for a social relation, a social problem, and talent trying to develop. We need, in other words, to learn how to embody a good range of educational missions and means in the institutional clothing needed to make them useful and acceptable. Our laboratory will have many concrete manifestations. It will live in television studios, homes, and data storage and retrieval systems, in retreat centers in the mountains, and in whatever other kinds of places that are necessary to breathe life into the institutional forms that we need to study and to create.

*We need to develop (within this laboratory) linkages with the work of educators representing a very wide range of the educational spectrum.* Room has to be made for Rogerians, Skinnerians, technocrats, sensitivity trainers, and others. They do not have to work with each other all the time or talk to each other all the time, but we must have linkages with them. (It would be better if they could work under our umbrella.) Some will be creating indigenous community schools, some will be trying to reduce alienation, some will be eager to get children together with electronic devices. They will be a motley, even outlandish, crew. And around their work will arise a vast array of activities which in turn will engender many specific engineering theories about how to create educational environments. Our laboratory workers will systematically help specify missions and means, will try various institutional forms to embody them, and will develop ways of criticizing missions, means, and forms as well as ways of creating them.

There is as yet no science of institutions which can be transferred to the field of education—curriculum workers will have to develop institutional forms and engineering theories simultaneously. There are beginning to be, however, some very broad analytical stances and studies on which we can draw in order to begin.

1. Several studies of the social systems of institutions have been shaped to provide cues about the construction of the social aspects of institutions. For example, John and Elaine Cumming's *Ego and Milieu*[62] provides a framework for the development of therapeutic environments. Although their work originated in another field, it has clear applicability to education, for it provides a framework for organizing the social system of an institution so that it will have a productive effect.

2. A number of theories provide specification for social environments which have theoretically predicted effects on development. For example, we have already mentioned several times that Hunt and his colleagues have developed a theory which postulates personality development. His research includes a major study of the interaction between institutional environments and the educational effects of Upward Bound programs.[63] His work (and that of several others) builds on earlier studies by scholars such as Pace[64] and Coleman[65] and brings us closer to operational principles for *approaching* the *development* of humanistic institutions.

3. "Systems" design is developing at a rapid rate and is being applied to education almost as fast as it develops. The activities of the Southwest Regional Laboratory are illustrative.[66]

4. A variety of new institutions have developed during the last few years. Such widely different institutions as the Esalen Institute at Big Sur,[67] the so-called Parkway school in Philadelphia,[68]

62. John and Elaine Cumming, *Ego and Milieu: Theory and Practice of Environmental Therapy* (New York: Atherton Press, 1962).

63. Hunt, "Conceptual Level Matching Model."

64. Robert Pace and G. G. Stern, "An Approach to the Measurement of Psychological Characteristics of College Environments," *Journal of Educational Psychology* 49 (1958): 269-77.

65. James S. Coleman, *The Adolescent Society: The Social Life of Teenagers and Its Impact on Education* (New York: Free Press of Glencoe, 1961).

66. "The SWRL Tutorial Program: A Progress Report," Southwest Regional Laboratory, ED-031-451 (Washington: U.S. Office of Education, 1969); Seidel and Kopstein, *Systems Approach*.

67. George Brown, *Humanistic Education,* Report to the Ford Foundation on the Esalen Project, A Pilot to Explore Ways to Adapt Approaches in the Affective Domain in the School Curriculum, 1968.

68. William K. Stevens, "Students Flock to Philadelphia 'School Without Walls'," *New York Times,* January 23, 1970, p. 49.

the Nova school in Florida,[69] Harlem Prep in New York,[70] and the street academies and other informal organizations deserve careful study for what we can learn about the creation of new institutional forms of education.

5. Contemporary technologies provide the opportunity to create more facilitating environments. A wide range of support systems can be put together to make an institutional milieu in which individuals, both teachers and learners, have much more control over their activities.[71]

### Positive Proposition Number Three

*In order to progress, we need to face George Counts's propositions about whether the schools dare change the social order.*

We need to change his question somewhat, however. The question, Dare the schools change the social order? was bound to be answered in the negative. Societies have created the schools and have locked them into the socialization systems and into the status system. Socializing agencies are all dominated by the conservative forces in the existing culture.

But if we change Counts's question to ask, Can education change the society; can institutional forms be created which will educate people in such a way that it will free them from their culture yet enable them to capitalize on its merits? the proposition would appear to be more acceptable to the society. In time, no doubt, such new institutional forms will be co-opted by the culture and turned entirely into its general flow. For a short while, however, new institutions can flare briefly, can create a new and positive reality for students, and can bring benefit and progress to their culture. The curriculum worker who turns his attention entirely to education within the schools has as his upper limit the possibility of making the society a little more efficient, but he will not make it anything that it is not. The children will be more, when they leave school, of what they were when they came to it.

69. Sherwood D. Kohn, "Nova: Nova High School, Fort Lauderdale, Florida," in *Profile of Significant Schools: Three High Schools Revisited: Andrews, McPherson and Nova* (New York: Educational Facilities Laboratory, 1967).

70. "Getting It Together: The Young Blacks," *Time,* April 6, 1970, pp. 46-47.

71. Bruce R. Joyce, *The Teacher and His Staff: Man, Media and Machines* (Washington: National Education Association, 1967).

The curriculum worker, however, who considers the creation of entirely new institutions is singing a different song. He can create institutions than can do new things with people and help them develop a more humane culture. It is there that we have our challenge.

*Out of this activity—this attempt to develop new institutions— a dialogue on the Countsian question will be renewed.* We will be attempting to build the technology by which we will create new educations. In so doing we will develop the technology for having, even if only for a brief moment, the possibility of improving the course of human society. We will be able, in sum, to create places for schooling which are not restricted by the same sets of factors that are restricting the present ones. As we develop that capacity, we can ask the Countsian question with a new optimism and we can create a continuous dialogue on the nature of a good and creative life and on how to help young persons recreate their lives and society.

In order to bring all this about, we need a new base of operations. The kinds of schools and universities we now have are designed primarily for graduate training, transmitting existing knowledge, and (largely on an individual basis) attempting to create new knowledge. They are woefully inadequate for institutional experimentation. The curriculum worker needs, instead, to have a network of operations in various parts of the nation, where teams work on various aspects of the enterprise of creating a new technology of curriculum. This network will be bound together by rapid communication about what they are doing and by a continuous dialogue over its implications. Teams in various parts of the country can tackle different types of jobs. The most difficult task will be to stimulate the development of the teams, to nurture their work, and to provide a forum for dialogue, a clearinghouse for theory and engineering developments, and a place for work on generic questions. Inevitably, if we are able to learn anything about the actual creation of more effective educational forms, groups will begin to band together and share counsel and accept challenge and to do something not only about schooling but about the human condition in general. Very different kinds of "schools" will result from this activity—partial institutions using a wide variety of instructional modes and ways of furthering individual development.

These schools will not assume a single kind of organizational structure, a single type of teacher role, or a single kind of education. Rather, they will be a coalition of institutions, each serving students in a particular kind of way.

Eventually, students will create their own school by selecting from a wide offering of planned educational programs. These programs will be built around a variety of approaches to learning and they will be adapted to a variety of learning styles. To see how this might work, let us look at several modes of education—curricular modes, we shall call them—and see how they might be brought together in a student's life.

THREE CURRICULUM MODES

One kind of curriculum mode that we will learn to engineer can be called the *individualized self-teaching mode*. It is characterized by being made up of preplanned materials, largely automated, utilizing self-instruction by individuals or groups for whom instructional activities have been prescribed, also by an automatic assessment system that feeds back progress reports to the learner. The self-teaching mode will present to the student a large array of self-administering courses or programs in many areas. He will put together much of his education by selecting from this bank of alternatives.

A second curricular mode centers around individual counseling to help the learner structure his own educational goals and activities. The learner might be led to encounter some kinds of preselected problem situations, but learning is seen as personal and continuity as psychological. We can call this the tutorial mode.

A third curricular mode involves group inquiry. Groups analyze problems, try out ideas from the disciplines, and explore social values. The scholarly endeavor of the group and its interpersonal processes are included as subjects for study. The disciplines are learned by practicing them. Democratic process is valued. Feedback is collective and emergent. Content may be partly preselected and partly produced by active inquiry and dialogue on the nature of society.

Each of these curricular modes can be adapted to perform a unique and important function in education. Blended, they can offer a common general education, create conditions for the development of personal talent, and provide the humanizing effects of cooperative inquiry into critical issues. Let us examine them individually and then see how they can be used together.

*The individualized self-teaching mode.* We are more certain of some educational objectives than others. The individualized self-teaching mode is appropriate in areas of curriculum in which:

(1) *We have relatively stable agreement about cognitive or skill objectives.* That is, we are relatively sure that we want to accomplish those objectives and will want to accomplish them for some time to come. A good example is skill in the four fundamental arithmetical operations, integers and rational numbers. For the next few years it seems safe to say that we will want all possible children having ability to do so to develop reasonable proficiency in this area. Reading skills is another area in which we are sure that in the foreseeable future all possible learners should be brought to a high level of competence. It will not be necessary to decide annually that arithmetic operations or reading skills will be taught. We can stabilize these and certain other areas for a long period so far as general objectives are concerned.

(2) *We can construct adequate self-instructional devices for the vast majority of students.* "Self-instructional" should be broadly defined here. One can learn many things by reading about them. Books are self-instructional devices. *Programmed instruction* should be included. Units using films, tapes, and other media have been developed. Computerized games can teach many things. Simulation techniques will expand self-instructional possibilities greatly.

(3) *We can develop automated feedback systems for keeping the learners and responsible adults informed of progress.* Programmed instruction has an advantage here because of the precision with which objectives are specified and ordered and the easy amenability of the process to "embedded" tests. However, precise automated evaluation is possible in nearly any instance in which objectives are clear and self-instruction is possible.

(4) *The area can be learned as well alone as in a group.* Many aspects of social dancing might be acquired in response to films

and computer-controlled instructions, but much of the appeal would be gone. On a more serious side, controversial issues, drama, and the improvement of social and sociointellectual skills require group activity for a good bit (rarely all) of the instruction. Learning map skills, on the other hand, does not *require* group interaction or very much didactic presentation by a teacher.

(5) *Pacing of instruction is important.* For example, in any curricular mode many arithmetic and reading skills are achieved at enormously different rates. In fact, teachers working alone and with traditional materials and normal pupil-teacher ratios have been unable to achieve adequate individualization of instruction in most skill areas.

With respect to the social atmosphere in this mode, the norms would stress independence and industriousness. Students would need to learn to judge their own progress and "reward themselves" for it. An air of calm support and mutual help would be important, as well as openness about progress. Teachers would function as facilitators and trouble-shooters.

To summarize, where we have curricular objectives that are very stable but are achieved effectively by self-instruction that can be monitored by automated feedback systems, we can apply systematic planning principles to create instructional programs. *Such programs would not work for all students,* and effective diagnosis would result in placing some children with tutors, some with remedial specialists, and others with teachers in groups, but the programs could work effectively for many. Subprofessional technicians could be trained to work with the children and the feedback scrutinized constantly by a specialist who would sound the alarm for students for whom the program was not working.

Because of the negative reaction of so many educators to automation, we must stress again that the individualized self-teaching curriculum need not be a deadly array of sequenced "programs." It can be a rich multimedia program, using diversely film, games, books, programs, and other devices. Also, it would not be appropriate for all parts of any curricular area. For example, while much science instruction might be automated, instruction requiring a cooperative attack on original problems could not be accomplished by such means.

The self-teaching mode would be under constant revision as objectives changed and technology improved. At any given time it would represent a bank of programs which students could dip into to construct part of their education. (High schools, for example, might offer an array of short courses in each curriculum area. By selecting a combination in a subject, a student could create his own larger program in required and elective areas.)

*The tutorial mode: the idiosyncratic curriculum.* The creation of tutorial modes challenges the curriculum worker in different ways. Mark Hopkins and the log have long symbolized a delightful and wise teacher and the idea of having one's personal teacher. We are always trying to find ways of giving students personal attention, whether by individualizing reading programs, providing guidance counselors, or offering the opportunity to learn the French horn. The ratio of pupils to teacher has been against us, however, and so has the idea that the "curriculum" must be "covered."

The cybernetic curriculum mode puts books and machines to work, freeing manpower for the development of curricula devoted not to the individualization of common learnings but to the development of personal talents and interests. The idiosyncratic curriculum is appropriate for those ends which:

( 1 ) Are defined by the learner in his personal quest for understanding and self-development.

( 2 ) For which personal counseling is needed to assure definition and availability of any special resources and to provide advice which the learner needs.

( 3 ) While they might be achieved in group activity, they are accomplished socially only through interest groups in the generic sense of the term. In other words, where personal interests are congruent enough, group inquiry serves idiosyncrasy.

An idiosyncratic curriculum might be achieved by assigning students to a kind of tutor whom we could describe as an academic counselor who meets with each student regularly and helps him define personal educational goals and the means for achieving them. In some cases he might serve as a more traditional tutor. In other cases he might help the student to locate a teacher, resource person, community resource, or whatever would help. If a student were studying justice, the counselor might help him find a court where he could watch cases. If the child were interested in the French horn, the counselor would help arrange for a teacher.

The counselor would help the child develop a program of wide personal reading (we do not want him stopping with what we provide in the cybernetic curriculum). Also, the counselor would help him get together with others of similar interests.

Our academic counselor could have overall charge of insuring that the child's life in school is a good one and that he receives help with out-of-school problems. If he shows talent or creativity, the counselor would see that it receives nourishment. If things are not going well for the child in the cybernetic or group inquiry portions of the educational program, the counselor would be able to intervene drastically if necessary.

We might envision some teachers whose sole function would be that of academic counselor, each with an assigned quota of students. Available to them would be subject specialists of many kinds. Developing the functions of the academic counselor for the six- and seven-year-old should provide some interesting research, since relatively few people have tried this sort of relationship with the younger child. It should be evident that such a mode would emphasize rewards for initiative and exploration. Seeking, probing, questioning would be highly valued. The technical support systems would need to be responsive to the demands of a great many students seeking a great many ends.

The curriculum worker will have to face an enormous variety of tasks in order to depict and engineer tutorial modes. The possible tutorial roles, possible support systems, alternative ways of bringing students together with tutors and resources provide a dizzying matrix of important engineering questions to be addressed.

The personal discovery curriculum belongs to the student. It can exist because of energy saved by the cybernetic curriculum. Both of these modes emphasize the learner as the individual. That is not all he is, however, so we need another curricular mode.

*The group inquiry curricular mode.* The inquiring group was at the core of the Progressive movement's approach to education. The group of students, with their teachers, would learn democratic skills and scientific method simultaneously while they explored their world and developed a commitment to the ideals of democracy. Until the academic curriculum projects began in the 1950s the chief thrust for social reform was provided by the legatees of the Progressives. An overwhelming proportion of curriculum supervisors in the schools of today were influenced by this tradition.

The Achilles heel of Progressive education was always its dependence on teachers with extraordinary skills. Given the supply of talent available to education, the demands made were simply too great for the average teacher. He could not know enough and handle groups well enough to cope with the range of educational objectives.

However, group inquiry as a mode is extremely useful when:

(1) Group skills and interdependence are to be acquired. The democratic way must be learned *in situ*.

(2) The learner should test himself against the ideas of others. Controversial issues and contemporary social movements, for example, need the interplay of diverse reactions to events. Many kinds of thinking can be learned if we have to balance our ideas against those of others.

(3) Group dynamics is an important learning agent. The power of the reference group, for example, can accomplish many things. The intellectual and social climate of the school is a consequence of the group process. Students can teach each other a good deal about social life. Drama, debate, and the like are social and dependent on social feedback as well. Interaction games require groups.

(4) Mixing individual differences is advantageous. A homogeneous group, studying its society, would probably develop much less vigor and heat than a heterogeneous one.

As in the case of the other model, the curriculum worker has to face a large number of tasks in order to engineer the setting for academic inquiry. Teaching strategies have to be developed, studied, modified. The kinds of teachers who can employ them need to be identified. Academic inquiries in the various disciplines need to be compared and contrasted and ways of combining or separating them have to be clarified. Alternative technical support systems can be studied. The creation of each mode requires the use of systematic planning techniques and a range of instructional technologies.

## A Spinning of Dreams

As if the task of creating and studying curriculum modes were not enough, the curriculum worker needs to develop plans for constructing well-balanced educational programs which can be orchestrated to serve a wide variety of students.

To illustrate this task, let us construct a design for a school (remembering that "school" means "pattern of education," not a specific building) in which the basic organization of the school consists of four teams of teachers and clusters of support systems built around each of the three curricular modes. One team will use the cybernetic mode, one the tutorial mode, and two will employ group inquiry.

( 1 ) In the first case, let us build a self-instructional mode, using cybernetic principles and consisting of self-instructional units of many kinds which give the learner the option of developing himself in a number of areas. First of all, in terms of reading skills, then in terms of arithmetic, and then in terms of world history, let us build a chronological course within this mode. Let us also make available courses in several foreign languages, in art history, music history, and literature. The teaching team will need to learn how to build alternative routes for students who are unable to teach themselves by this mode. They will need to be experts in diagnosis and in the training of aides who will do much of the work in these areas. The support systems clearly will have to be massive self-instructional systems employing many media—television, tape, programmed instruction, conventional books, workbooks, language laboratories, activities packets that instruct people on projects to be carried out, and many other things.

( 2 ) Second, let us build a tutorial mode of the kind that we described earlier. The team which will administer this mode will be skilled in training people to counsel with children and to facilitate their personal inquiry. Each youngster will need to contact his tutor several times a week and the tutors will need to call in consultants as the students develop interests in problem areas which are beyond their particular competencies. The support systems for this mode will need to include an enormous library and to utilize many media—television, tape, contact films, motion-picture films, filmstrips, slides. Books of many sorts will need to be developed and arrangements made to enable the students to reach out beyond the walls of the school for instruction and information.

(3) Let us also include a scientific inquiry system. In this mode, skilled group leaders will lead groups of children in inquiring into significant problems and in so doing will teach them the modes of inquiry and structures of academic disciplines. Each child should be engaged in several groups during each year. The support systems for this layer need to include the products of the academic reform movement, the systems for teaching the disciplines to the children. Since many of these teachers will be expert in their disciplines, more important, probably, are laboratory facilities, excellent libraries, and aides who can construct materials when they are needed and help the youngsters get needed data and ideas. In this mode, each group will identify problems and attack them in a relatively leisurely manner. Scientific inquiry should not be hurried, for it is in the dialogue and the debate that the structures of the disciplines become clear and the modes of inquiry become explicated.

(4) The fourth layer of this school will be devoted to a dialogue on the nature of the society and on the future courses that it should take. In this mode, again, skilled group leaders will help groups of children identify and study serious social problems. Also, television programs will bring to the youngsters, on a weekly basis, information and analysis about contemporary events. At the present writing, activities in such a mode would deal with the problems of the cities, the problems of poverty, the problems of building an international community, and the like. The teachers need to be skilled in group inquiry and to be backed up by support systems and materials which include not only magnificent library facilities of the kind described for the preceding layer, but also by people who can help construct materials when they are needed. The learning of some aspects of this layer can be accomplished through the mass media, as indicated before. Television programs can bring to the students of an entire city information and opinion about certain events, and this should be done regularly. Other activities should be performed at the group level where clusters of youngsters attack and try to solve problems that seem worthwhile to them.

THE BALANCE IN A MULTIPLE-MODE EDUCATION

In such a school teachers would work in teams. As a result, the student would not be exposed to the personality and opinions of one person at a time, but would be a constant participant in a dialogue about what to do next and how to do it. If one teacher could not help him learn the skill he needs, then he could turn to others. If one teacher had strong opinions about some segment of academic inquiry, or about society, then that teacher's opinions could be balanced by those of the other members of the team. Furthermore, such a school would balance the possibilities in the life of the learner. He would not be dominated by skills nor by the dialogue on society. He would have opportunity to participate in all of these. Also, because each teacher would not be responsible for all kinds of learnings, it would be possible for them to become experts and teach each other the skills needed to operate in their particular mode.

In today's schools too many teachers perform too many functions, and students are clustered together in such a way that enormous effort has to be expended to treat them as individuals. In the multimode school, some activities would be organized for individualization and others for group inquiry, and there need be no conflict between the two. Furthermore, the mass media, instead of being argued about as an alternative for the classroom teacher, could be utilized to perform its natural function.

The political organization of such a school should provide places for students to share in steering committees that operate the support systems, create materials, and shape the ways that students select curriculum alternatives. For example, the library should be operated by a faculty, student, and teacher-aide committttee that would keep in continuous touch with the needs of the students and the faculty, and with the demands that are made on the staff. All the other support systems, too, should have steering committees of this kind so that the governance of the daily life of the school is a "cooperation" among all the members of the community.

## Summary

The task of the curriculum worker is to engineer a wide variety of approaches to education and to generate alternative institutional forms in which they can be embodied. The result should be to in-crease on a continual basis the options which are available to the population and the flexibility with which they can be made avail-able. By developing more options, making more and more kinds of education commonplace, and giving students the power to educate themselves in increasingly humane ways, the curriculum worker will be making his contribution in the search for an in-creasingly humanistic education. He will be helping people to clarify alternative educational missions or purposes and to select from among them; he will develop alternative curricular strategies for achieving those missions; and he will develop the means of institutionalizing a very wide range of missions and means in an increasing variety of institutional forms.

Hence, the curriculum worker will have an array of technologies which he can bring to bear on educational problems so that the society and students will have a wider range of options. Presently, schools present very limited alternatives to children and these alter-natives are focused to help them toward technical proficiency. The wider range will enable students to create much of their own educa-tion and a large proportion of the remainder to be devoted to a dialogue on the humanization of their society.

Thus, the curriculum worker can become a full participant in the basic contemporary task of revitalizing the humanistic possibilities in the society. In the past he has let himself be controlled by the bureaucratic nature of the educational institution. In his hoped-for future, he will lead the society to the discovery of humanistic institutions in which bureaucratic routine is anathema and self-discovery and cooperative action are de rigueur.

# Index

357

# INFORMATION CONCERNING THE NATIONAL SOCIETY
## FOR THE STUDY OF EDUCATION

1. PURPOSE. The purpose of the National Society is to promote the investigation and discussion of educational questions. To this end it holds an annual meeting and publishes a series of yearbooks.

2. ELIGIBILITY TO MEMBERSHIP. Any person who is interested in receiving its publications may become a member by sending to the Secretary-Treasurer information concerning name, title, and address, and a check for $8.00 (see Item 5), except that graduate students, on the recommendation of a faculty member, may become members by paying $6.00 for the first year of their membership. Dues for all subsequent years are the same as for other members (see Item 4).

Membership is not transferable; it is limited to individuals, and may not be held by libraries, schools, or other institutions, either directly or indirectly.

3. PERIOD OF MEMBERSHIP. Applicants for membership may not date their entrance back of the current calendar year, and all memberships terminate automatically on December 31, unless the dues for the ensuing year are paid as indicated in Item 6.

4. DUTIES AND PRIVILEGES OF MEMBERS. Members pay dues of $7.00 annually, receive a cloth-bound copy of each publication, are entitled to vote, to participate in discussion, and (under certain conditions) to hold office. The names of members are printed in the yearbooks.

Persons who are sixty years of age or above may become life members on payment of fee based on average life-expectancy of their age group. For information, apply to the Secretary-Treasurer.

5. ENTRANCE FEE. New members are required the first year to pay, in addition to the dues, an entrance fee of one dollar.

6. PAYMENT OF DUES. Statements of dues are rendered in October for the following calendar year. Any member so notified whose dues remain unpaid on January 1 thereby loses his membership and can be reinstated only by paying a reinstatement fee of fifty cents.

School warrants and vouchers from institutions must be accompanied by definite information concerning the name and address of the person for whom membership fee is being paid. Statements of dues are rendered on our own form only. The Secretary's office cannot undertake to fill out special invoice forms of any sort or to affix notary's affidavit to statements or receipts.

Cancelled checks serve as receipts. Members desiring an additional receipt must enclose a stamped and addressed envelope therefor.

7. DISTRIBUTION OF YEARBOOKS TO MEMBERS. The yearbooks, ready prior to each February meeting, will be mailed from the office of the distributor only to members whose dues for that year have been paid. Members who desire yearbooks prior to the current year must purchase them directly from the distributors (see Item 8).

8. COMMERCIAL SALES. The distribution of all yearbooks prior to the current year, and also of those of the current year not regularly mailed to members in exchange for their dues, is in the hands of the distributor, not of the Secretary. For such commercial sales, communicate directly with the University of Chicago Press, Chicago, Illinois 60637, which will gladly send a price list covering all the publications of this Society. This list is also printed in the yearbook.

9. YEARBOOKS. The yearbooks are issued about one month before the February meeting. They comprise from 600 to 800 pages annually. Unusual effort has been made to make them, on the one hand, of immediate practical value, and, on the other hand, representative of sound scholarship and scientific investigation.

10. MEETINGS. The annual meeting, at which the yearbooks are discussed, is held in February at the same time and place as the meeting of the American Association of School Administrators. Members will be notified of other meetings.

Applications for membership will be handled promptly at any time on receipt of name and address, together with check for $8.00 (or $7.50 for reinstatement). Applications entitle the new members to the yearbook slated for discussion during the calendar year the application is made.

5835 Kimbark Avenue
Chicago, Illinois 60637

HERMAN G. RICHEY, *Secretary-Treasurer*

i

# PUBLICATIONS OF THE NATIONAL SOCIETY FOR THE STUDY OF EDUCATION

NOTICE: Many of the early yearbooks of this series are now out of print. In the following list, those titles to which an asterisk is prefixed are not available for purchase.

POSTPAID
PRICE

*Distributed by*

THE UNIVERSITY OF CHICAGO PRESS, CHICAGO, ILLINOIS 60637
1971